# CANADIAN BUSINESS WRITING

## >> A STRUCTURAL APPROACH

# CANADIAN BUSINESS WRITING

## >> A STRUCTURAL APPROACH

*second edition*

**NATHAN M. GREENFIELD**
Algonquin College

**STEPHEN B. GOBAN**
Centre for Excellence in Communication, Ottawa

THOMSON

NELSON

Australia    Canada    Mexico    Singapore    Spain    United Kingdom    United States

THOMSON
NELSON

Canadian Business Writing: A Structural Approach
Second Edition

by Nathan M. Greenfield and Stephen B. Goban

**Associate Vice President, Editorial Director:**
Evelyn Veitch

**Publisher:**
Joanna Cotton

**Marketing Manager:**
Sandra Green

**Senior Developmental Editor:**
Rebecca Rea

**Developmental Editor:**
Sandy Matos

**Permissions Coordinator:**
Paula Joiner

**Copy Editor/Proofreader:**
Cathy Witlox

**Indexer:**
Edwin Durbin

**Senior Production Coordinator:**
Hedy Sellers

**Design Director:**
Ken Phipps

**Interior Design:**
Tammy Gay

**Cover Design:**
Liz Harasymczuk

**Cover Image:**
ColorBlind Images/Blend Images/Getty Images

**Compositor:**
Tammy Gay

**Printer:**
Webcom

Library and Archives Canada Cataloguing in Publication

Greenfield, Nathan M., 1958—

Canadian business writing : a structural approach / Nathan M. Greenfield, Stephen B. Goban. — 2nd ed.

Includes index.
ISBN 0-17-640705-7

1. Business writing—Textbooks. 2. English language—Business English—Textbooks. I. Goban, Stephen B. II. Title.

HF5718.3.G74 2006   808'.06665
C2005-907783-2

# Dedication

This book is dedicated to Micheline R. Dube, whose love and support brighten the world.

*Thank You*

I would be remiss if I did not thank two dear colleagues: Margery West, who has not only encouraged me in my writing career but also informed me that Thomson Nelson (formerly Harcourt) was looking for a new type of textbook; and Glenn Clarke, with whom I argued much about teaching writing and who, I trust, would have said to me with his sly smile, "I'm not reading anything you wrote." *Requiescat in pace.*

—————————————————————————————— NATHAN M. GREENFIELD

This book is dedicated to my father, the late F. H. A. Goban, and my mother, Anne Goban, who valued the word.

*Thank You*

As any writer knows, encouragement is a precious thing when trying to find the phrase that seems always to elude. My thanks, therefore, to Bonnie, Chantal, and Stéphane Goban for all that they bring.

—————————————————————————————— STEPHEN B. GOBAN

# Instructor Preface

With apologies to Oscar Wilde, we would like to observe that a second edition is "the triumph of experience over hope." And, for this experience, we would like to thank our students, the students of our reviewers, and, of course, the professors (and our editors) who have provided us with helpful suggestions for this second edition of *Canadian Business Writing: A Structural Approach*.

Our book differs from most other writing textbooks. This book deals with more routine forms of business writing that graduates of business programs are likely to encounter on the job: accident reports, short proposals, newsletters, grant applications, progress reports, cover letters, and Web content. We focus on these forms because our experience—teaching at the college and university levels and as professional business communicators—and our research tell us that the vast majority of recent graduates do not write 20-page analytical sales reports or 25-page market surveys. No doubt, the ability to do such analysis is an important foundation for later career success. However, teaching the skills needed to undertake properly these types of reports belongs to classes other than business writing—especially now, since in many programs, business writing is limited to a single 15- or 16-week course.

More important, the pedagogy at the heart of *Canadian Business Writing: A Structural Approach* differs from that of other popular textbooks, many of which accept the precepts of what has come to be called "progressive, child-centred education." Dating back a century to John Dewey and his followers, progressive educationists have believed that writing is an act of self-discovery, that the content of writing must be generated from within. This thesis declares, in fact, that teachers must give up their role as "sage on the stage" and embrace the idea of being a "guide on the side." (Some of the more extreme adherents to this theory go so far as to argue that assigning of grades is impossible because form, grammar, and content are also supposed to be personally, rather than conventionally, true.)

In business writing textbooks, the most obvious signs of this pedagogy are the ubiquitous chapters on brainstorming and idea mapping. Both techniques seek to help students learn to generate ideas, discover linkages, realize patterns, and rule out the extraneous. Our experience tells us, however, that—especially with untrained writers—both activities are less than efficient.

The problem is not just that students and other untrained writers often feel adrift facing a blank page that must end up filled with words, circles, and arrows. Rather, the problem is that brainstorming and idea mapping leave too much to untrained writers who, more often than not, are unable to generate ideas on their own. It is not that they do not know where or how to find information about, for example, the difficulties with their office's telephone system, what features coworkers would find useful, and their organization's equipment budget. Even when untrained writers have the information, brainstorming or idea mapping is not a reliable way of making sure all of it gets recorded and structured in such a way as to guide the writing of the memo that describes the situation and suggests changes.

What happens if on a busy day in a noisy office an idea does not spring fully formed like Minerva into a writer's head? What happens if when jotting down an idea, the writer phrases it so badly that it simply is not clear by the time he or she goes back and begins to connect the dots on the map? And, perhaps most importantly, why should we assume that students and newly minted graduates always know how to generate ideas and then organize them on their own? Our experience and, we assume, that of most writers and writing teachers, is that organizing ideas is a complex task that requires a great deal of practice as well as rather detailed knowledge of organizational patterns, rhetorical forms, and clear structural thinking.

*Canadian Business Writing: A Structural Approach* is, then, built on a different, more traditional, pedagogy, which we have found to be more effective, both for teaching and, most importantly, for helping students. Broadly put, our method is Socratic, which is to say it employs a question-and-answer strategy that is designed to lead students to the desired outcome: a well-organized business letter, memo, or report that meets the requirements of the reader. The questions are divided into two groups:

- Purpose Questions (PQs) that are common to all forms of business writing;
- Focus Questions (FQs) that are specific to each type of business document.

Together, these questions help students recall and organize the information they need so that it can be used to write a document that is useful to its reader (as opposed to being an expression of the author's personal feelings). In other words, this book does not shy away from being *directive*.

A writer facing all of the distractions of a busy workplace will, we believe, find our structured method more efficient than a brainstorming session. Such a session requires that, in the face of other pressures, the writer find the time to allow ideas to appear and for patterns to emerge. Our method, by contrast, provides students and other untrained writers with sets of questions that must be answered and patterns that move writers along toward conventional organization.

Our distance from neo-Deweyite pedagogy also explains our emphasis on summary writing. We admit that summary writing is not particularly exciting to teach or do. However, we believe it is important—and not just because many memos or reports require that information be summarized, paraphrased, or quoted. Rather, we use the practice of writing summaries to teach students how good writing works (and sounds to the trained writer).

Students are often baffled by terms like *clear, concise, logical, ordered,* and *consistent*. English professors and business communication specialists know what they mean. They have this knowledge because they have undergone long apprenticeships—as university essay writers and writers whose work is submitted to editors. In addition, most English professors and business communicators read a tremendous amount, which supplies them with schemes, models, and rhetorical strategies. Generally speaking, business students have no equivalent training. We believe that mastering the practice of writing a summary will go a long way toward helping students and other untrained writers develop, to use another term that baffles students, "an inner editorial eye."

The act of reading critically (that is, reading for logic, structure, argument, and evidence)—the first part of writing a summary—teaches students that good writing contains within it an armature or frame that is surprisingly simple. All too often, however, students cannot fashion this frame because they are unfamiliar with its shape. Strip away the second and third examples or the reasons an author presents and the rhetorical flourishes, and you will find that an article on the wild gyrations in currency markets has a simple structure. Boil down a five-page president's report to the board of directors, and you will find that it is divided into three sections, each of which makes one or two clear points that are supported by logically arranged evidence. Reading and summarizing such documents is an interactive process that, because the ideas must be unpacked and then cast in one's own words, teaches students how good writing is organized and structured.

To sharpen students' reading (a necessary skill to be a good writer since editing is critical reading), we include questions with each summary exercise. The questions reinforce the idea that writers must always be concerned with their readers by asking, "Who is the intended audience?" and "What is this text about?" Further, the questions guide students to a more critical understanding of a text by asking them to distinguish between the author's voice and that of someone being quoted or paraphrased, and by asking them to examine the arguments or statistics that support the text.

We have divided business writing into two types of writing—internal and external. With the exceptions of chapters one and two, each chapter begins with a **Preliminary Exercise** in which students are asked to summarize an article or business document that relates to the topic being covered in that chapter. For example, in the chapter on the instructional memo, students summarize the part of an article on the Gimli Glider that explains how both the refuellers and the flight crew erred in their calculations about the amount of fuel the airliner had onboard.

Following the Preliminary Exercise is a brief **Introduction** that explains the business purpose of the particular form being discussed and highlights significant questions writers of that form must face. After the Introduction is an **Editing Practice** exercise, which presents students with examples of a "good" and a "poor" memo or report and a series of questions that draws attention to specific problems in the "poor" memo. The aim of this exercise is to have students get the "feel" of what good writing looks and sounds like.

The central part of each chapter is entitled **The Process of Writing....** It begins with a methodological introduction that

- defines the writing form vis-à-vis the world of work;
- underscores that business documents are not expressions of personal opinion but presentations of reasoned, professional judgments;
- points out special technical problems, such as the use of tense in a job completion report;
- provides a structural plan for the writing form being considered.

The second part of The Process of Writing is a narrative that illustrates how to use the Purpose Questions (PQs) and Focus Questions (FQs) that apply to the writing form. The narrative shows writers how to

- use the questions to identify the reader;
- use the questions to organize their thoughts and the evidence;
- use their answers to draft a Purpose Statement and (in some cases) part of the memo or report;
- use their answers to the PQs and FQs to identify logical and organizational errors in their work.

The Process of Writing section ends with an annotated well-written memo or report. This section also contains **Writing Tips** that highlight special technical problems (e.g., avoiding the passive voice) that often stymie students.

The last two sections of chapters two through thirteen include two different sets of exercises. The first, **Editing Practice**, which is designed so that students can practise their theoretical knowledge of the form, asks them to edit (using the questions provided) sample memos. The second, **Writing Assignments**, which is designed so that students can practise their practical writing skills, asks students to write a series of memos or reports. In the chapter on cover letters and résumés, for example, students are asked to write cover letters using information we provide as well as their own cover letters and résumés.

Our method of teaching business writing is the fruit of much trial and error over more than 35 years of teaching at the college and university levels, and working in the public, private, and nonprofit sectors. We know that users of this book will bring their special touch to the classroom. Our hope is that our text helps you teach your students what we have tried to teach ours: that if students learn to think clearly about their audiences and possess a scheme that orders their thoughts, they can learn to write clear, concise, and informative messages that will enhance their reputation in the company or organization for which they work.

Thomson Nelson would like to thank those who reviewed *Canadian Business Writing: A Structural Approach*, Second Edition, for their insightful comments:

- Chris Legebow, St. Clair College
- Dr. Patricia A. Post, University of New Brunswick
- Rhonda Sandberg, George Brown College
- Trevor Tucker, University of Ottawa

# Student Preface

Had we written this book 35 years ago, it would probably be titled, simply, *Business Writing*. The world of global communications networks based upon the linking of computers and telecommunications—the wired world—existed in science fiction only. The telephone, electric typewriter, and telex machine were the main communications technologies on which organizations relied. Indeed, the photocopier and fax, as we know them, were years away from being found in every office.

We would not, of course, have given any instructions about how to format an e-mail memo. Nor would we have warned against changing fonts too often, for even after IBM's electric typewriter became standard office equipment (which allowed typists to change typeface by changing the print ball), changing fonts was a time-consuming, messy business. Likewise, though we would have written a chapter on how to use graphs and charts, we would have warned that since they were time-consuming to produce and expensive to reproduce, great care would have to be taken in the decision to include one or the other.

But that was then and this is now. Today, almost everyone has a personal computer with word processing capabilities that would have stunned the members of the typing pool. We send e-mail messages so often that we have almost forgotten what life was like before e-mail existed. We surf the Web for information and post our thoughts online. Type for a few moments and click the mouse a few times and messages are created, spelling and grammar are checked, paragraphs are deleted or merged, highlighted, illustrated, formatted—and then sent either to the next office or to the other side of the world in an instant. Writing has never been easier. Or has it?

The famous quip that "writing is 10 percent inspiration and 90 percent perspiration" applies to business writing as well. In this context, however, "inspiration" is less a gift from a poetic muse than it is an understanding of how your organization works, the place your message has in it, and the research you have conducted. In other words, despite the fact that technology allows us to effortlessly move paragraph nine so that it is now paragraph six (and vice versa) business writing is hard work and must be distinguished from good word processing.

Even though we can call up templates for letters, forms, reports, and other documents, good business writing starts where it has always started—with clear analytical thinking. Good business writers must resist the temptation to, as Clifford Stole, a writer and self-confessed computer junkie, put it "write first, think second."

Though almost all of us write using computers, these devices cannot begin to answer the questions that are central to good writing. Have you ever seen a program that can tell you who your audience is? Or one that knows what the audience's expectations are? Can any programmer write the computer code that would allow the machine to answer the question "Where should I begin?" Grammar checkers can tell you if you have misused words, but they cannot tell you the proper order in which to present your ideas. And, of course, no computer can tell you if what you wrote (and may just have e-mailed to your supervisor) is what you really meant.

You are probably familiar with two ways of dealing with this problem: brainstorming and idea mapping. However, business writers, who are deluged with information, time pressures, meetings, and performance goals, cannot take the time to brainstorm and map their thoughts. Accordingly, this textbook opts for a different approach. We believe that the best way for business writers to organize their thoughts is to begin by answering a series of carefully structured, rigorous questions that we have divided into two groups: Purpose Questions (PQs) and Focus Questions (FQs).

The following PQs remain the same whatever type of document you are writing:

- What is my goal?
- Who is going to read this memo or report?
- What does my reader already know about the topic/issue?

The FQs change depending on the type of document you are writing. For an accident report, for example, we have you answer questions such as the following:

- Where did the accident occur?
- At what time did the accident occur?
- What part of my body was injured (e.g., left leg, right knee)?
- What is and who made the official diagnosis?

These questions are designed to help you organize your thoughts. Answering them ensures that you (1) know to whom you are writing and what your reader knows about the issue or topic; (2) have the information that your readers need to know; (3) structure your memo, report, or letter in a logical format; and (4) have a tool to help you edit your work.

Editing your work requires that you be able to read it critically. In other words, you must be a good reader but not just *any* kind of reader. You have to stand in the shoes of the person to whom you are sending the memo, report, or letter. You have to take on the role of the person reading it in a business setting.

Reading for business differs from reading for pleasure. Business readers read to acquire information. More often than not, they are reading in busy offices that are full of distractions, including pressures on their own time. You, not they, are the one responsible for making sure your document makes sense. The shorter and clearer it is, the better the chance it will make the impact you want.

To help you hone your reading skills, you will be required to write a number of summaries. We recognize that summary writing is "a drag," as one of our students pointed out recently. But it is an important skill because if you can write a good summary, then you can be sure that your reading skills are good—and you rely on those skills when you edit. Knowing how to write a summary means you know how to pay attention to the words and structure of a letter, memo, report, or article. Thus, it means you know how to identify the logical structure of what you are reading.

The heart of this book are the narratives that appear under the heading "The Process of Writing ..." in chapters two through thirteen. These narratives show you how business writers use the PQs and FQs to determine whom they are writing to; what the purpose of the letter or memo is; what information should be included; and how they should structure the memo or letter to best present the information. As well, we show how to use the PQs and FQs to guide a rereading of the first drafts of the memos and letters.

To help you gain practical experience in writing and editing, we also include in every chapter several Editing Practices and Writing Assignments. Finally, you will find in Appendix I a guide to using spell- and grammar-checking programs.

# Brief Table of Contents

# Table of Contents

# C H A P T E R  • 1 •

# Business Writers, Business Readers

## LEARNING OBJECTIVES

In this chapter, you will learn

- how to ensure that a business message has a clear purpose that responds to your reader's expectations and needs;

- how to use Purpose and Focus Questions to write business messages that meet your reader's needs;

- how to use Purpose and Focus Questions to organize and structure your writing;

- what the parts, organization, and structure of a business message are;

- what the limitations of spell- and grammar-checking programs are;

- how to use the plain language approach to business writing;

- how to use visual cues and format to help your reader grasp your message;

- what the difference is between business and academic writing.

## Box 1.3 NAMING DOCUMENTS SO THEY CAN BE RETRIEVED

Computer-generated documents are saved in files on either the writer's hard drive or the company's network. Unless you are careful when you name a document, you can easily end up with numerous documents named "Proposal." To avoid this problem, name the first version of the document "Storage Room Lighting Proposal 1." Name the final version "Storage Room Lighting Proposal Final."

## Writing Tip—Subject Line Format

To ensure that your subject line is clearly visible on-screen and on a printed copy, capitalize and underline each word.

Compare the following:

Subject: Proposal to purchase three computers

Subject: Proposal To Purchase Three Computers

### Introduction

The introductory paragraph is the most important paragraph and not only because first impressions count. In a busy office, oftentimes it is the only part of the report that is read. It is the one your readers use to decide whether to read further or to ignore your message.

The introductory paragraph must be short and to the point, but it must also make the context and message clear to the reader. One well-constructed sentence often will do. A memo that proposes summer hours for the company could begin

I am proposing that for the summer we change the hours of operation from 9:00 a.m. to 5:30 p.m. to 8:30 a.m. to 4:00 p.m.

At other times, one sentence will not suffice. The introductory paragraph of a job progress report tells whether the project is on schedule, whether there have been any problems, what the expected completion date is, and whether the project is on, over, or under budget.

### Body

The length of the body of a business message is determined by what it must communicate. Obviously a general announcement memo indicating when and where the office Christmas party is going to be held need not be more than a few sentences.

**Box 1.4** INTRODUCTIONS CONTAIN THE ANSWERS TO
THE PQS AND FQS

## Writing Tip

Every introductory paragraph answers both the PQs and the FQs that apply to
the type of memo, letter, or report you are writing.

> The installation of the new computer network and database will be delayed due to
> unforeseen difficulties encountered with the delivery of components and time lost
> due to dealing with network problems. The expected completion date is June 25,
> 2005, two weeks later than originally scheduled. The project is $5,000 over budget.

The answers to the PQs and FQs for the above paragraph are as follows:

## Purpose Questions

1. What is my goal?
   To explain that there have been delays and what the new schedule is.
2. Who is going to read this memo?
   My manager, Millicent Fenwicki.
3. What does Ms. Fenwicki already know about this issue?
   She knows that there have been delays, is concerned about feasibility of new deadline,
   wants to know about the budget.

## Focus Questions

1. Is the project on schedule?
   No.
2. Was the delay foreseeable?
   No.
3. What caused the delay?
   Delivery problems/network problems.
4. What is the new expected completion date?
   June 25, 2005.
5. Is the project on/over/under budget?
   Over.

The body of the progress report referred to earlier could have eight or more paragraphs,
including the following:

1. Introduction
2. Background (project history)
3. Explanation of original plan of work

4. Original schedule
5. Progress until delays
6. Explanation of delays
    a) time lost due to late delivery of equipment
    b) time lost due to network problems
7. Explanation of why the new completion date is feasible
8. Revised schedule
9. Project analysis
10. Financial analysis
11. Conclusion

## Paragraphing Business Writing

Paragraphs in business writing differ from those used in other types of writing. As a quick check of your local paper will show, newspaper stories often treat each sentence as a separate paragraph. Essay writers pride themselves and are praised by their readers for constructing long, well-written paragraphs that develop complex ideas in subtle ways. Consider the following published example:

> For as long as Edmontonians can remember, the biggies (important politicians and sports figures) were elsewhere. Though they had contributed many fine hockey players to the game, they could only hear about their feats on radio or later see them on television. Hockey was their game, damn it, their national sport, but New York, Chicago, Detroit, and Boston were in the NHL long before the league's governors adjudged Edmonton not so much worthy as profitable. But in 1984, Canada's hockey shrines were either in decline, as was then the case in Montreal, or in total disrepute, as in Toronto. In those glory days, if easterners wanted to see the best player in the game more than twice a season, if they wanted to catch a dynasty in the making, why, then, they had to pack their fat coats and fur-lined boots and head for Edmonton, home of the Stanley Cup Champions, and the Great Gretzky himself.
>
> —Mordecai Richler, "Gretzky in Eighty-Four"

Business writers write paragraphs that are somewhere in the middle. A series of one-sentence paragraphs would not only be difficult to read but, more importantly, would leave the impression that your thoughts are not fully developed. A memo filled with paragraphs as long and as intricate as Mordecai Richler's would be difficult for a busy person in an organization to follow and quickly understand.

Every paragraph should explain one and only one idea. To ensure this, business writers should begin each paragraph with a clear topic sentence, the sentence that announces what the paragraph is about. Every sentence that follows either supports or amplifies the claim or point made in the topic sentence. English teachers call this unity, coherence, and development.

The sentences that follow the topic sentence "My training in Bow Valley College's dental hygiene program has equipped me to work in a pediatric practice such as yours" develop or support the claim.

> My training in Bow Valley College's dental hygiene program has equipped me to work in a pediatric practice such as yours. My field placement, for which I received a mark of A, was with Dr. R. L. Green, a pediatric dentist. For my public health class, I prepared a presentation on oral hygiene that I delivered at a local primary school. As well, for my psychology class, I prepared and delivered a 40-minute presentation on cognitive development and hand/eye coordination of 10-year-old children.

## Box 1.5 DIFFERENCES BETWEEN ACADEMIC AND BUSINESS WRITING

| Business Writing | Academic (Student) Writing |
| --- | --- |
| Focuses on business problem | Focuses on interesting issue |
| Proposes an action or idea; sells or responds to complaint; written to show solution | Written to highlight critical thought processes and/or research skills |
| Written for coworkers and/or managers | Written for professors |
| Can affect business plans/functions | Cannot affect business plans/functions |
| Can have economic effect | Cannot have economic effect |
| Can have legal implications | Cannot have legal implications |
| Foregrounds findings (limits background information to minimum) | Shows how all background information fits into conclusions |
| Normally written in inverted pyramid style | Conclusions normally held till end |
| Follows memo, report, or business letter format | Follows essay format |
| Premium put on short sentences | Premium put on using longer sentences to explain complex ideas |
| Uses short paragraphs | Uses longer paragraphs to explain complex ideas |

## DOUBLE-CHECK AFTER SPELL-CHECKING AND GRAMMAR-CHECKING

Nothing makes a business writer look more unprofessional than spelling or grammatical errors, which is why you probably already use spell- and grammar-checking programs. But spell-checking programs can be too accepting. Look at what our spell- and grammar-checking programs accepted in this sentence: *It wood be foolish two rely on spell-checking programs to much.* It accepted "wood," "two," and "to" because they were correctly spelled words; though, to be fair, the grammar checker flagged "to much" as being worth a second look. The spell checker, which is the helping program most often used, did not know that "w-o-o-d" is a substance and not a verb and that "t-w-o" is a number and not the first word in the English infinitive. Nor did it realize that "t-o" is a preposition and not an adjective. And then, of course, there are the words "there," "their," and "they're," whose incorrect usage is not identified by a spell checker.

Grammar-checking programs, by contrast, tend to be quite rigid. If you set your grammar checker to the highest level, it will likely reject quotations, especially if they originated in speech (which tends to be less formal than Standard Written English). And sometimes grammar-checking programs miss errors.

As useful as these programs are, treat them as you would any other rule of thumb. Use them, but remember that ultimately you are responsible for your writing, which means that you must still proofread your work. Even when writing an e-mail memo, it is wise to print a copy because proofing on-screen is extremely difficult. Appendix I contains a guide to using spell- and grammar-checking programs.

## WRITE IN PLAIN LANGUAGE

The plain-language approach to business and government writing is based upon making documents as easy as possible for the audience to read.[1] According to plain language writing consultant William H. Dubay (http://www.impact-information.com), "Plain-language revision of 200 forms used by Alberta Agriculture, Food, and Rural Development saves the department a total of $3.4 million Cdn. per year."

Plain language

- uses simple words and phrases;
- avoids the use of the passive form of verbs;
- avoids clichés;
- uses visual cues (such as the bullets in this list) to help the reader through a text;
- keeps sentences short.

---

[1] The federal government (and most provincial and local governments) has adopted a plain-language policy. The Communication Policy of the Government of Canada (2004) states: "To ensure clarity and consistency of information, plain language and proper grammar must be used in all communication with the public. This principle also applies to internal communications, as well as to information prepared for Parliament or any other official body, whether delivered in writing or in speech."

The website of the Plain Language Association International lists numerous examples of unclear writing that have been rewritten in clear prose. Compare the following:

**From an insurance company form letter:**

We have recently implemented an enhancement to our computer system that will enable us to provide better service to our valued customers. This has resulted in a slight delay in the processing of your renewal. The difference you will notice is in the payment schedule. Your annual policy premium has been divided over 11 (eleven) months, and as a result your monthly payment will have increased due to the reduced number of monthly installments.

**Rewritten in plainer language:**

We are a little late in sending your renewal documents because we have made a change in our computer system in order to provide better service. Your annual premium will now be divided over 11 months instead of 12, so the monthly payment will increase slightly.

Courtesy of the Plain Language Association International.

## Box 1.6 PLAIN WRITING DURING THE SECOND WORLD WAR

During the Second World War, the following air-raid instructions, written by an unnamed Washington bureaucrat, came across the desk of U.S. President Franklin D. Roosevelt:

Such preparations shall be made as will completely obscure all Federal buildings and non-Federal buildings occupied by the Federal Government during an air raid for any period of time from visibility by reason of internal or external illumination. Such obscuration may be obtained either by blackout construction or by termination of the illumination.

The president, who prided himself on his ability to write, uncapped his fountain pen and wrote the following:

Tell them that in buildings where they have to keep the work going to put something over the windows; and, in buildings where they can let the work stop for a while, turn out the lights.

### Short Words

Untrained writers (especially those who have easy access to a thesaurus through their word processing programs) often make the mistake of thinking that if they use many polysyllabic words (e.g., disembarkation), they will impress their readers. Is it really more impressive to read "perpetuate" than "continue," or "conflagration" than "fire"? If you have any doubts about the effectiveness of shorter words, think of Winston Churchill's famous June 4, 1940, speech to the British House of Commons:

> We shall fight on the seas and oceans ... we shall defend our island ... we shall fight on the beaches, we shall fight on the landing grounds, we shall fight in the fields and in the streets, we shall fight in the hills; we shall never surrender.

Would this speech, which rallied the British people to stand against Nazi Germany after the fall of France, have been as effective had he said the following:

> Our native population will engage in battle with the foreign foe when he disembarks on our beaches intending harm ... our native population will never consider to lay down its arms in dishonourable, weak-kneed defeat?

## Clichés

Another way to undermine your reader's confidence in your ability to express yourself is by using clichés. English professors define clichés as overworked analogies, such as "there's no free lunch" or "sticky wicket." For our purposes, we can expand the definition to include all overworked expressions. Inexperienced writers often believe that phrases such as "you are hereby advised" make their writing sound impressive. In fact, when used outside of its traditional legal context, "you are hereby advised" sounds trite; it also signals to your reader that you are ignorant of its proper usage. Clichéd expressions are often longer than the word or phrase that should be used: "in the foreseeable future" can be replaced by "in the future" or, if a definite time is known, "next month."

| **Avoid** | **Use** |
|---|---|
| according to plan | on schedule |
| along the lines of | like |
| as a matter of fact | in fact |
| attached hereto | attached (or enclosed) |
| at this point in time | now |
| by means of | by |
| conspicuous by its absence | absent |
| due to the fact that | because |
| escalate | increase |
| in/with reference to | regarding |
| in the final analysis | finally |
| in the foreseeable future | in the future (or a specific time) |

| | |
|---|---|
| in the long run | long term |
| last but not least | finally |
| par for the course | normal |
| please feel free to call | call |
| proactive | active |
| pursuant to your request | as you requested |
| save face | protect the company's image |
| the bottom line | main point (or decision) |
| we are pleased to advise you | this is to advise you |
| you are hereby advised | you are advised |

## PASSIVE VOICE

Your readers want to have confidence in you. One of the quickest ways to undermine their confidence is to write in "bureaucratese." The sentence "The decision was taken to delay the construction of the new high school" is grammatically correct, but it is written in the "passive voice,"[2] leaving the reader guessing at who made this decision. The school board? The board's chair? The Ministry of Education?

The sentence "Sales quotas were shown to be unrealistically high" is grammatically correct; however, it fails to answer the question "Who is saying this?" Did you find that the quotas were unreasonably high after you had undertaken a rigorous analysis? Did other employees reach the same conclusion?

Who's doing the thinking in this sentence: "The conference was considered to be not worth the time or expense"?

### Box 1.7   USING THE PASSIVE VOICE APPROPRIATELY

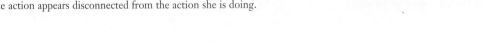

## Writing Tip

There are a few instances when it is appropriate to use the passive voice.

- If you do not and cannot know the name of the chief actor in the sentence:
  The orders could not be processed on schedule because our computer system was hacked.
- When reporting technical information in which the doer is unimportant or understood:
  The computers were tested and found to be working properly.
- When it is tradition to use it in an introduction: The audit was performed by KPMG, Canada.

---

[2] Unlike sentences written in the "active voice," where a clear "actor" is doing an action—e.g., Janice kicked the ball—sentences written in the passive voice communicate that the person (or thing) doing the action is receiving the action expressed by the verb. Thus, in the passive sentence "The ball was kicked by Janice," the person doing the action appears disconnected from the action she is doing.

Most managers know that if you are writing in the passive voice ("The decision was taken" as opposed to "The committee decided," which contains an identifiable subject that performed the action), you are either unsure of your statement or you don't want to take responsibility for it.

Passive sentences can be fixed by recasting them so that the verb does not use some form of "to be." When you change "were found" to "found" or "was considered" to "considered," you will have to add a clear active subject. The above examples become

> My analysis showed that sales quotas were unrealistically high.

> Allison Walker, John Ferry, and Mia Misrahi found that the conference was not worth the time or expense.

## TONE AND STYLE

The tone of a letter or any piece of writing is the impression the reader forms from your choice of words. Depending on how well they know the reader and the subject of the letter, business writers strive for either a semiformal or informal (conversational) tone. A formal tone is normally used when writing to people senior in status to you within or outside your organization or when writing about very important or significant matters: e.g., a complaint with serious consequences, a major order, or legal matters. The PQs and FQs process will help you choose the right tone for a letter by identifying the goal you wish to achieve, the reader's expectations, and the importance of the content.

The topic of the following paragraphs is the same but the tone and style—and the likely effect upon the reader—are quite different.

### Formal Tone

> I have today received your letter of May 12, 2006, in reference to the matter of the claim for replacement of damaged goods, submitted by Enright Ltd. on April 3 last. I would note that it is not this company's policy to settle such claims until a full and complete investigation has been conducted and the results considered by the appropriate staff. I can assure you that once these steps are taken, we will be pleased to inform you of such action as may be able to be taken with regard to the claim submitted.

### Semiformal Tone

> Thank you for your May 12, 2006, letter concerning your company's April 3, 2006, claim for replacement of damaged goods. We are currently dealing with your claim, and I will let you know the outcome as soon as possible.

*Informal Tone*

> Thanks for your May 12 letter about the damaged goods claim
> from April. As you know, these things can take a little while, but
> I'll be back to you just as soon as possible.

## FORMAT IS IMPORTANT

The way a text looks—the amount of space between paragraphs, the use of headings and subheadings, the bolding of titles—can help or hinder readers. These visual cues are an important part of readability—how easy it is for a reader to grasp and understand the messages and information being presented.

While business readers do not expect every memo or letter to be formatted by a desktop publisher, they do expect memos and letters to be formatted for ease of reading. If you doubt that the layout of a page matters to a reader, think of how you would react to a memo that contained a one-page paragraph explaining how to drive to the airport. Long, dense paragraphs slow down reading and prevent readers from assimilating information in a logical order.

Given the amount of information they have to deal with, business people rely more and more on the visual organization of the writing they receive to quickly guide them to its important points. This means that

1. subject lines should be underlined or put in **boldface** type;
2. headings and subheadings should be **bolded**;
3. paragraphs should be no longer than 10 lines or, as a rule of thumb, five sentences;
4. bullets should be used to break up text and quickly make individual points;
5. *italic* text should be used for emphasis;
6. plenty of space should be left between paragraphs and sections.

Your goal is to ensure that the appearance of your message does not confuse the reader but indeed makes it clearer. In his memo to Nadia Kazlovski (see Figure 1.2), David Smith uses a range of visual cues to help her quickly grasp his main points.

FIGURE 1.2

FORMAT OF A MEMORANDUM

**EDUCATION OPERATIONS SUPPORT & MANAGEMENT INC.**

Memorandum

TO:        Nadia Kazlovski, President

FROM:    David Smith, Marketing

DATE:     May 9, 2006

SUBJECT:  Testimonials Gathered For The New Sales Brochure

Introduction
The Testimonial Collection working group has finished collecting testimonials
and has developed criteria on how to use them in our new sales brochure
and materials. We have collected 22 school- and non–school-based testimonials from across the country.

Gaps in Coverage
There are gaps in our coverage. So far there are no

- Quebec Anglophone schools;
- French-language schools from provinces other than Quebec and Ontario;
- schools from New Brunswick, PEI, Nova Scotia, Yukon, Nunavut;
- non-school customers apart from one in Alberta.

Criteria for Using Testimonials in the Sales Brochure
The production committee developed the following criteria for using testimonials:

- reflect as many parts of the country as possible;
- balance English- and French-language representation;
- show school and non-school customers;
- illustrate the various aspects of our service package.

*David Smith*

David Smith

FIGURE 1.3

NON–READER-FRIENDLY MEMORANDUM

# MIC Maltimax International Corporation

MEMORANDUM

TO:        Internal Communications Committee Members

FROM:      Wendy Muir, Director, Corporate Communications

DATE:      21 November 2006

SUBJECT:   Internal Communications Study

As you will recall, it was agreed at the meeting of the Internal Communications Committee on March 13, 2006, that a full study should be undertaken to determine both the current situation with regard to employee morale and communications activities with a view to identifying and recommending a new internal communications strategy. The committee felt strongly that, while there was no doubt that much effort was being made, the results appeared to be less than what had been expected when senior management instructed it in April 2005 to find approaches to improve communication within the company. Much has taken place in the last year but I think that the work that was done between April 2005 and March 2006 was valuable and did produce some results, particularly at the plant level. However, the labour difficulties we encountered in the latter part of 2005 made for a difficult situation for undertaking any new internal communications initiatives as well as making it a challenge to keep lines of communication open.

The study was undertaken by Jawal & Associates, a firm of consultants that specializes in internal communications in large organizations. The contract for the study was approved in early April 2006 and work began in early May. Jawal assigned a highly experienced team to the project and developed a research strategy in conjunction with the Corporate Communications Division.

A sample of employees was interviewed—some 750 people—using a questionnaire sent through the internal mail system. In addition, a series of 10 focus groups with employees was held across the country in our different locations. Focus groups were divided by type and level of employees to ensure that people could speak freely and to ensure proper coverage of the work force. Finally, people were encouraged through the company's

*continued*

newsletter and intranet and by managers at their own regular meetings with their staff. Finally, Jawal used a benchmarking approach to determine our situation in relation to other organizations. The company took a confidential "best practices" study it had done of a number of firms of roughly comparable size and compared what it found in our case with these companies' practices to arrive at an evaluation. We are, it turns out, about 75 percent of where we should be to be an excellent organization for internal communications.

The study found in particular that we had serious difficulties in terms of employee perceptions of the company's willingness to communicate openly and the commitment of management, especially senior management, to communicate with staff. It also found that the labour troubles of last year were less important than we had expected, that different parts of the company and different locations across Canada showed considerable variations in trust of company information, and that the technical staff were the most skeptical of management and any management-originated communication. There were no significant differences among staff by gender, language, or age. The study made a series of recommendations that we will need to deal with as quickly as possible so that we can report to senior management on the next steps to be taken. In this light, I would ask that each of you in your respective areas please ensure that for the next meeting you bring details of the initiatives you are taking, those you intend to take, those that have been proposed by your staff or by colleagues, those items that have not worked in the past, and any other ideas.

This study, I believe, has already been and will continue to be an excellent learning opportunity for the more junior members of the committee. They can use it to expand their knowledge of internal communication; understand how to organize and execute an internal communications study; become aware of the type of report that should be expected and its level of expense; and become familiar with the steps necessary to implement the recommendations of such a study. This is a complex matter but it is vital for the organization. The study can be written up and used as a case study for training new managers and for briefing and orienting new members of the committee in future.

*Wendy Muir*

READER-FRIENDLY MEMORANDUM

# MIC Maltimax International Corporation

MEMORANDUM

TO:      Internal Communications Committee Members

FROM:    Wendy Muir, Director, Corporate Communications

DATE:    21 November 2006

*Informative subject line.*

SUBJECT: Internal Communications Study Final Report

*Heading bolded.*

## Background

As you will recall, it was agreed at the meeting of the *Internal Communications Committee* on March 13, 2006, that a full study should be undertaken to

*Clear presentation of study purpose.*

1. determine the current situation with regard to employee morale and communications activities; and
2. recommend a new internal communications strategy.

*White space.*

The Committee felt strongly that, while there was no doubt that much effort was being made, the results appeared to be less than what had been expected when senior management instructed it in April 2005 to find approaches to improve communication within the company.

*First paragraph broken into three smaller paragraphs.*

Much has taken place in the last year but I think that the work that was done between April 2005 and March 2006 was valuable and did produce some results, particularly at the plant level. However, the labour difficulties we encountered in the latter part of 2005 made for a difficult situation for undertaking any new internal communications initiatives as well as making it a challenge to keep lines of communication open.

*White space.*

*Heading bolded.*

## Research Contractor

The study was undertaken by *Jawal & Associates*, a firm of consultants that specializes in internal communications in large organizations. The contract for the study was approved in early April 2006 and work began in early May. *Jawal* assigned a highly experienced team to the project and developed a research strategy in conjunction with the Corporate Communications Division.

*continued*

Heading bolded.

## Research Process

### Employee Interviews

A sample of employees was interviewed—some 750 people—using a question-naire sent through the internal mail system.

Subheading italicized.

### Employee Focus Groups

In addition, a series of 10 focus groups with employees was held across the country in our different locations. Focus groups were divided by type and level of employees to ensure that people could speak freely and to ensure proper coverage of the work force.

White space.

### Manager Feedback

People were encouraged through the company's newsletter and intranet and by managers at their own regular meetings with their staff.

Third paragraph broken into smaller paragraphs.

### Benchmarking

Finally, *Jawal* used a benchmarking approach to determine our situation in relation to other organizations. The company took a confidential "best prac-tices" study it had done of a number of firms of roughly comparable size and compared what it found in our case with these companies' practices to arrive at an evaluation.

We are, it turns out, about 75 percent of where we should be to be an excel-lent organization for internal communications.

Heading bolded.

White space.

## Study Findings

- We had serious difficulties in terms of employee perceptions of the com-pany's willingness to communicate openly and the commitment of man-agement, especially senior management, to communicate with staff.
- The labour troubles of last year were less important than we had expected.
- Different parts of the company and different locations across Canada showed considerable variations in level of trust in company information.
- Technical staff were the most skeptical of management and any manage-ment-originated communication.
- There were no significant differences among staff by gender, language, or age.

Use of bullets.

Fourth paragraph broken into smaller paragraphs.

Heading bolded.

White space.

## Recommendations

The study made a series of recommendations that revolve around developing a new, integrated internal communications strategy. These are laid out in *Jawal & Associates'* report (attached). We will need to deal with these as quickly as possible so that we can report to senior management on the next steps to be taken.

*continued*

In this light, I would ask that each of you in your respective areas please ensure that for the next meeting you bring details of the initiatives you are taking, those you intend to take, those that have been proposed by your staff or by colleagues, those items that have not worked in the past, and any other ideas.

White space.

Heading bolded.

**Learning and Development Opportunity**

This study, I believe, has already been and will continue to be an excellent learning opportunity for the more junior members of the committee. They can use it to

Use of bullets.

- expand their knowledge of internal communication;
- understand how to organize and execute an internal communications study;
- become aware of the type of report that should be expected;
- understand the level of expense that can be expected;
- become familiar with the steps necessary to implement the recommendations of the study.

This is a complex matter but it is vital for the organization. The study can be written up and used as a case study for training new managers and for briefing and orienting new members of the committee in future.

Final paragraph broken into two smaller paragraphs.

Att: *Jawal & Associates'* Report

*Wendy Muir*

---

## E-MAIL MESSAGES

Despite the immediacy of e-mail messages and the habits many have picked up in chat rooms, a writer of well-written e-mail messages should follow the same rules outlined above. In his "Why Euromail Is Better,"[3] Eric Weiner, a correspondent for National Public Radio in the United States, points out that for North Americans, e-mail has replaced the telephone. For Europeans, by contrast, it has replaced letter writing. Accordingly, North American e-mail suffers from "brain dump"—the "unloading of the content of the cerebral cortex onto the screen and hitting the send button." His point is that conversational English is as out of place in a business e-mail as it is in a seven-page proposal.[4] The same holds true, of course, for the use of emoticons.

---

[3] "Why Euromail Is Better" is the summary assignment for chapter 10 (page 249).

[4] Conversational English can, however, be used in a short message asking Jozef if he wants to go to lunch with you.

The empty "white space" of regular business paper might be dark green or blue on-screen, but it is just as important to be aware of the empty space as when preparing a printed memo. Indeed, it is probably more important, given that reading a screen is itself a somewhat unnatural act. Computer screens are normally about 18 inches (45 cm) away from the computer user; when we read a paper or book, the printed surface is normally 12 inches (30 cm) away. Furthermore, computer screens are in front of us while paper and books are normally below us—the position they were in when we were taught to read as children. Add to this the fact that the average screen displays significantly less text than a written page, with the resulting need to interrupt the act of reading to scroll down, and you can see that great care should be taken in formatting on-screen messages.

We have adapted to the difficulties of on-screen reading by getting used to scanning or skimming. Accordingly, it is important to structure properly any memos that are going to be read on-screen. Compare the two screens in Figure 1.5.

## FIGURE 1.5

### SAMPLE E-MAIL SCREENS

**E-mail screen A**

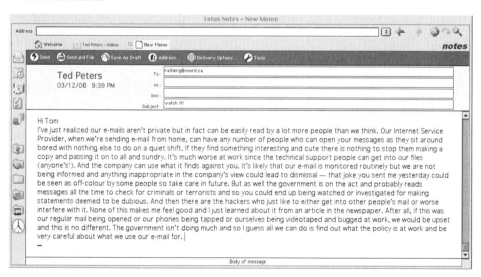

*continued*

**E-mail screen B**

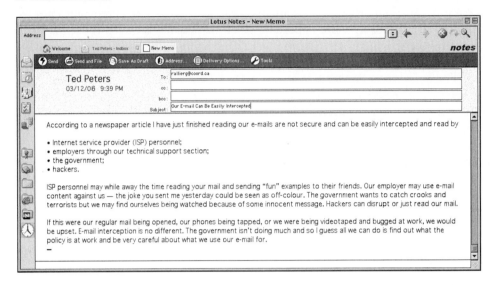

Lotus Notes - New Memo

Address

Welcome | Ted Peters - Indbox | New Memo

*notes*

Send | Send and File | Save As Draft | Address... | Delivery Options... | Tools

Ted Peters
03/12/06  9:39 PM

To: rallierg@coord.ca
cc:
bcc:
Subject: Our E-mail Can Be Easily Intercepted

According to a newspaper article I have just finished reading our e-mails are not secure and can be easily intercepted and read by

- Internet service provider (ISP) personnel;
- employers through our technical support section;
- the government;
- hackers.

ISP personnel may while away the time reading your mail and sending "fun" examples to their friends. Our employer may use e-mail content against us — the joke you sent me yesterday could be seen as off-colour. The government wants to catch crooks and terrorists but we may find ourselves being watched because of some innocent message. Hackers can disrupt or just read our mail.

If this were our regular mail being opened, our phones being tapped, or we were being videotaped and bugged at work, we would be upset. E-mail interception is no different. The government isn't doing much and so I guess all we can do is find out what the policy is at work and be very careful about what we use our e-mail for.

## Box 1.8   ATTACHMENTS

The small size of the windows of many e-mail programs makes anything longer than a one-screen e-mail cumbersome to read. As a result, longer memos and reports are generally sent as attachments. When sending an attachment, use the same subject line for the e-mail that you use for the memo or report. Also, be sure to tell your reader what the attachment contains.

Subject Line:     Report On Industrial Cleaners Convention, 2005

Body:     John:

     Attached is my report on the 2005 Industrial Cleaners Convention.*

*If you are sending the report outside of your organization, remember to indicate what program will open the attachment: "Attached in WordPerfect is my...."

# Types of Business Writing

Business writing has one of two purposes: to inform or to persuade.

Accident reports, instructional memos, trip/conference reports, replacement letters, and newsletters are informative. Proposal memos, grant applications, analytical and refusal letters, and even cover letters and résumés are persuasive.

Our point is not, we hasten to underline, that a proposal is simply the expression of personal opinions or feelings. Quite the contrary, persuasive writing is filled with factual information. The manager who asks for an analytical proposal on which photocopier is best suited to the office is not interested in your personal opinion. He or she is asking for and expects a *reasoned comparison* of various makes and models of photocopiers and a ranking of them against the office's needs (which you have also identified).

Each type of writing requires that you—the writer—see your reader differently. This is so even if, as is often the case, you generally write for your immediate supervisor. You can see how your reader changes by considering the following scenarios:

- At 10:00 a.m. on a Monday morning, Alice James, your manager at Thompson Marketing (which employs 30 people), reads your *suggestion memo*, in which you outline what, after checking with your coworkers, you believe to be the problems with the firm's telephone system.
- Two weeks later, she reads your *analytical proposal*, which, after comparing several different telephone systems, recommends one of them.
- Four weeks later, she reads your *accident report*, which explains how you were injured while the new telephone system was being installed.

Each of these memos presents Ms. James with information she did not know before she read it. Among other things, the suggestion memo informs her that internal conference-calling would be a useful feature to have. The analytical proposal informs her about each system's features, the cost of these systems, and which one of these (in your reasoned judgment) would best fulfill Thompson Marketing's needs. The accident report tells her how you fell, dislocating your right shoulder, and how long you will be away from the office.

The difference between these three business messages is their contexts. Ms. James is likely aware that there have been problems with the telephone system but may not know exactly the nature and scope of these problems or what employees consider should be done. Once she receives this information, she has you write the analytical proposal so that she will not have to pore over the brochures and spend time with salespeople. While she may not know exactly what features and benefits are available from the various telephone systems on the market, Ms. James knows that there are basic features and that different models offer different extras and benefits. Most importantly, her request for the proposal and the fact that she sets the phone equipment budget within which you must work mean that she understands the context of your writing.

By contrast, the accident memo gives Ms. James information about something she did not request. True, by the time she receives the accident memo, she probably already knows about your accident, and, of course, she knows the layout of the office. Nevertheless, she lacks important information. There are no company policies on how to have accidents. She was not there to see you stepping into the coil of telephone cable that caught your leg, making you fall to the right. In effect, then, when Ms. James reads this memo she is a different reader than when she read your suggestion memo and your analytical proposal on telephone systems.

# Summary

Business writing is professional writing, which means it must be based on your reasoned judgment and not your personal opinion. As well, because everything you write—from short memos to longer analytical proposals and Web documents—is in a professional context, your writing must be free from usage, grammatical, spelling, and formatting errors. Although other organizational patterns exist for paragraphs, for ease of reading in a busy office, each paragraph should begin with a clear topic sentence.

Professional writing is oriented toward the needs of the reader. The Purpose and Focus Questions help orient you toward your reader by asking you to

- define your reader;
- understand what your reader knows about the issue about which you are writing;
- establish your goal;
- clarify other issues, such as the steps that an instructional memo must discuss.

Business writers should write in plain language, avoid the passive voice and clichés, omit needless words, and use "white space" and subheadings to help their readers.

# Discussion Questions

1. How do readers of business writing differ from readers of fiction?
2. How can you use the PQs and the FQs to tailor your message to your reader's knowledge and to help you meet your reader's needs?
3. What is the purpose of a purpose statement and how should you write it?
4. How should you write a subject line?
5. How should paragraphs in business writing be structured?
6. What is the role of the introductory paragraph?
7. How should you structure the body of the memo or report?
8. Why should each paragraph begin with a topic sentence?
9. What are some of the limitations of spell- and grammar-checking programs?
10. Why should you use short words?
11. Why should you avoid the passive voice?
12. What words can you use instead of clichés?
13. How can you use visual cues to help your reader grasp your printed/e-mail messages?
14. What does it mean to say that memos and reports are based on facts and reasoned judgment and not on personal opinion?

# Writing Assignments

## Assignment 1.1

Fix the following passive sentences:

(Note how in each case, there is no "actor" doing the action.)

1. The failure of the elevator mechanism was due to the fact that it had not been inspected according to the provincially mandated schedule.
2. The decision was taken to reduce the pension contributions.
3. The cigarette was not put out before it was tossed in the garbage can full of paper.
4. Your address has been corrected by the new computer system.
5. The cooling system was found by the expert to be leaking.
6. Every effort is being taken to avoid layoffs.
7. The computer has been found to be unable to run that program.
8. The streets around the school have been blocked off.
9. The election was carried out under supervision.

## Assignment 1.2

Rewrite the following paragraphs into plain language. You can find the answers at http://www.plainlanguagenetwork.org/Samples/#business.

**1. From an insurance application form:**

If you fail to comply with your duty of disclosure, and we would not have entered into the contract on any terms if the failure had not occurred, we may void the contract within three years of entering into it. If your non-disclosure is fraudulent, we may void the contract at any time. Where we are entitled to void a contract of life insurance we may, within three years of entering into it, elect not to void it but to reduce the sum that you have been insured for in accordance with a formula that takes into account the premium that would have been payable if you had disclosed all relevant matters to us.

**2. From a travel agent:**

METHOD OF PAYMENT: All quotes are for cash or certified cheque only. A personal or company cheque will take 10 working days to clear. Documents cannot be released until we are in receipt of cleared funds. Payment within 7 days of departure may incur courier charges.

*(Hint: A clear version of this message is longer than the original.)*

**3. From instructions for an electronic toll system:**

Make sure that the account holder's name on the account is the same as the name of the customer to whose account the transaction should be attributed.

Samples courtesy of the Plain Language Association International.

# Web References

### Owl Online Writing Lab: Revision in Business Writing

 http://owl.english.purdue.edu/handouts/pw/p_revisebus.html

This site is maintained by Purdue University and contains a useful discussion of editing and revision.

### The Editorial Eye Index

 http://www.eeicommunications.com/eye/eyeindex.html

This site is maintained by EEI Press, the publisher of *The Editorial Eye*, and contains links to many articles about the peculiarities of English, business writing, writing e-mails, and writing for the Web.

### Humboldt University—Buried Under Words?

 http://www.humboldt.edu/~gbn2/wordyhlp.htm

This site is maintained by Humboldt State University and contains useful exercises that teach writers how to reduce wordiness.

### Cliché Finder

 http://www.westegg.com/cliche/

This site is privately maintained; it includes a cliché finder, which allows you to key in a phrase and see if it is a cliché.

### Impact Information: Plain Language Services

 http://www.impact-information.com

This site is maintained by William H. Dubay, a communications consultant, and contains interesting information on the costs of poorly written business documents.

### Plain Language Association International

 http://www.plainlanguagenetwork.org

This site is maintained by the Plain Language Association International and contains many examples of poorly written (and rewritten) business, scientific, and legal prose. It also contains a useful links page.

# CHAPTER • 2 •

# Summary Writing for Business

## LEARNING OBJECTIVES

In this chapter, you will learn

- why summary writing is a key business communication skill;

- what the differences are between summarizing, paraphrasing, and quoting;

- how to analyze a piece of writing to extract its essential points;

- how to write a descriptive summary in paragraph and bullet point forms;

- how to write an evaluative summary.

# Introduction

Information drives business organizations. It is the basis for making decisions about which presentation software package to purchase, Internet service provider to contract, or product to bring to the market. Decisions like these involve money, people, time, and equipment. Usually there is too much information rather than too little, and decision makers rarely have time to read and review everything concerning a particular problem. Therefore, they need the essential elements presented in a logical and easy-to-understand form that helps them quickly grasp the issues at hand—they need a summary.

Summarizing has never been more important. Thanks to information and telecommunications technology, we have the capacity to develop, transmit, and process more information than ever before. The amount of information, as well as the speed of its transmission, is constantly increasing, leading in turn to a speeding-up of business transactions. There is less time and greater pressure to make decisions, but more information available for making them.

Perhaps the most immediate benefit of summary writing is that it teaches you how complex thoughts are organized. Clear, concise writing contains within it a structure that is surprisingly simple. Remove the second and third examples or reasons an author presents, and you will find that a five-page article on writing clear e-mail messages has a simple structure, most probably related to the standard five-paragraph essay taught in high school.

The first step to summarizing is to recognize the structure, or arrangement of parts, of the piece of writing (e.g., a report or a speech by the chief executive officer) you are summarizing. You are looking for the type, number, and arrangement of its sections or divisions and how they are related. This allows you to understand the organization and the main points of the piece and to get to the essentials. Developing skill in analyzing structure will help you look at any text and quickly grasp its main points and determine whether it is logical and easily understandable.

Mastering the summary is key to becoming an effective business communicator. In business and other organizations, the emphasis is on presenting the essential information relevant to an issue or situation. You must be brief yet not omit any important details.

This chapter teaches you the importance of summarizing for organizations and individuals, the six-step process for writing summaries, the paragraph and bullet point formats for summaries, and the difference between descriptive and evaluative summaries. You will also learn how the Purpose and Focus Questions can be used in writing summaries, when to boil down information by using quotations and paraphrases, and when these techniques are appropriate.

# The Process of Writing a Summary

When you take what someone else has written and reduce it to a concise, accurate, faithful version of the original, you are summarizing. A summary

1. provides the sum of the significant points;
2. contains nothing new;
3. has a clear structure, which usually reflects that of the original piece;
4. is independent of the original writing and can stand on its own;
5. the reader can get all the essential information in the original document without having to refer to it.

The length of a summary will vary depending on the length of the original and its style—for example, how dense it is, how closely packed the information it provides is. Length will also vary with the reader's needs. Contrary to what you might expect, the more senior the decision makers in the organizations, the shorter the documents are that are given to them. As a rule of thumb, a summary should be about 15 percent of the original text, but it is better to have a longer accurate summary than a shorter inaccurate one.

## Box 2.1    PLAGIARISM VERSUS SUMMARIZING

Plagiarism is passing off someone else's ideas or writing as your own; that is, not acknowledging the source of the information you are presenting. This is not summarizing. If you use someone else's words or their ideas, you must tell readers that you have done so and where they can find the original material—the source of the information—you have used. A summary must allow the reader to go back to the original if wanted and so always gives details of *what* is being summarized. If you don't do this, you risk being accused of plagiarism, which in college is normally treated as a very serious offence, one that could lead to expulsion. The business world also considers plagiarism to be unacceptable for various reasons: it is deceitful and takes credit from others and, if it occurs within an organization, may affect relations between employees or between employees and the organization; it can publicly embarrass an organization that uses information believed to be original but later is publicly revealed not to be; it may lead to decision-making based on a mistaken or incomplete understanding of a situation.

## SIX STEPS FOR WRITING A SUMMARY

You can use the following six-step process to write a summary.

### Step 1: Read the material carefully for understanding
- What is it about?*
- Who is the intended reader?*
- What does my reader know about the topic?*
- Are there any specialized terms and jargon?**

---

* These are the three Purpose Questions discussed in Chapter One.

** These are the Focus Questions for this form of writing.

- Can these terms be simplified for a summary?**
- What is the tone of the text—personal, impersonal, friendly, formal, bureaucratic?**

### Step 2: Read the material again and note the main ideas
- Read the material slowly.
- Identify the main ideas put forward in each part.
- Be sure you understand *all* words, phrases, and numbers/statistics.
- Note each main idea in a word or phrase in the margin.
- Circle the key words, terms, phrases, and ideas and link these with arrows.
- Look for any further information that could make the text easier for you to understand (e.g., another article that refers to the article you are summarizing).

### Step 3: Lay out the structure
- Take each word or phrase relating to a main idea and write it down in the order it is presented.

### Step 4: Write out sentences
- Write a concise, simple sentence for each main idea.

### Step 5: Write a first draft
- Combine the sentences into a first draft using the structure in Step 3.
- Check that the draft reproduces the basic structure and logical flow of the original.
- Check that the draft reflects the essential content of the original.

### Step 6: Revise, revise, revise
- Look at the original again, compare it to your draft, and revise as necessary.
- Review the draft for ease of reading—does it flow? Are there any awkward phrases or sentences?
- Check the draft for grammar, spelling, punctuation, and usage errors—don't assume that a spell checker or a grammar checker will catch every mistake.

## Box 2.2    SUMMARIZING THE SAME INFORMATION FOR DIFFERENT NEEDS

The increased speed of business and the amount of information to be dealt with are only part of the story. The ability to summarize is crucial for your success. More and more, employees are asked to take information prepared for one purpose and rearrange it to meet a different need. You may have to take three previous memos or a six-page report on sick leave, for example, and prepare a one-page summary for your boss, who will be giving a presentation on the topic. You may be required to take a long market survey report and give a marketing team a concise, main-points-only version. Or perhaps you are the administrative assistant for a committee or a work team and have to prepare the record of what was discussed and resolved. All of these tasks require summarizing skills.

## SOME POINTS ON STYLE

*Subject Line*

The subject line of the summary, whether sent in a memo format or in an e-mail, must identify the author, title, and source. The subject line is underlined and the first letter of each word is capitalized. If you were summarizing "The boss on the sidelines: How auditors, directors, and lawyers are asserting their power" (the cover story of *Business Week*'s April 15, 2005, issue), your subject line would read

> **Subject:** Summary of "The Boss On The Sidelines: How Auditors ... Are Asserting Their Power (*Business Week*, April 15, 2005)

*Opening*

There are various ways to begin summaries but two main patterns are to state the thesis or to give the purpose.

- The thesis (main point, argument, thrust, finding, recommendation, etc.) of (give title) by (give author) is that (state the main idea). For example:

  > The thrust of Moving into the Twenty-First Century, the company's new marketing plan developed by the marketing and sales division, is to concentrate on penetrating the youth market through aggressive, youth-relevant promotional campaigns.

- The purpose of (give title) by (give author) is to (state the author's intention). For example:

  > The aim of *The Need to Invest in Technology and Innovation* by Merrick Waters and Barbara North is to put forward the case for tax policies that will increase technological development.

*Conclusion*

Summaries normally do not have formal conclusions. You can signal that the summary is ending by using transitional phrases such as "in conclusion," "the final section of this article," "finally," or "the author's last point is that."

*Tense*

In business communication, you would normally use the present tense for directness and simplicity when summarizing. For example:

> The author stresses that the normal profit level is inadequate and a significant improvement is needed.

> The president's report for the first quarter highlights the strong earnings shown by the company.

In cases where you are, for example, summarizing a speech or a presentation that your company's president made a week ago, you would use the past tense where appropriate to indicate that the words summarized were spoken at an event that has taken place. However, you would summarize the content of the speech using the present tense. For example:

> In a speech at the annual sales meeting in Toronto last week, the president said that he expects to see strong growth throughout the year as well as a further increase in share price.

> The minister told the association's board of directors that he sees no possibility of changing the legislation in the near future.

## QUOTATIONS AND PARAPHRASES

Apart from summarizing, there are two other standard methods of boiling down information: quotations and paraphrases.

### Quotations

When you directly repeat someone else's words, you are quoting that person. A quotation may be from a text, an interview, or any other source and can vary in length from a word to several paragraphs. Quotes help make and/or support a point and, most importantly, add credibility to your text. Writers must always give the source of a quote. If the quote is less than four lines long, it is integrated directly into the text and surrounded by quotation marks. If it is five lines or longer, it is indented from both right and left margins with no quotation marks and is single spaced.

If, like Alistair Crowley (see Figure 2.1), you were writing a memo to other staff members about following proper company purchasing procedures after a meeting between the purchasing director, divisional managers, and financial officers, you might include a short quotation to underline a point. Or you might choose to quote the purchasing director more extensively if you considered this necessary.

When you are using quotes, it is important to integrate them smoothly into the text and to be careful not to quote out of context—that is, quoting in a way that gives a false impression of what the person actually said.

Business communication is designed to transmit only the information required for a task to be undertaken, a decision to be made, or a customer to be served. In this context, quotes should be used sparingly and kept short. It may be tempting to quote at length the company president's recent pronouncement on the need for increased productivity, but it is probably more useful to readers for you to paraphrase or give a brief quote and refer them to the company intranet or Internet site for the full statement.

## FIGURE 2.1

### Using Quotations

**Acme Medical Supplies Ltd.**

Memorandum

TO:      All Staff

FROM:    A. Crowley, Corporate Services Division

DATE:    July 23, 2006

SUBJECT: Compliance With Company Purchasing Procedures

*Introduction.*

We wish to draw to the attention of staff that use of the company purchasing procedures is required for any purchase of any item of any amount. These procedures are contained in the company's policies and procedures manual, available in print or on the intranet (http://www.acmemed.com/internal/procedures).

*Body paragraph using a short quotation.*

The situation concerning purchasing was reviewed at a recent meeting between purchasing director Charles Hewitt, divisional managers, and financial officers. Mr. Hewitt noted during the meeting that "current purchasing of small items by staff is unsatisfactory" and emphasized the need for procedures to be rigorously followed. Divisional managers and financial officers will be ensuring that all staff are familiar with the purchasing procedures, particularly with regard to items under $500.

The situation concerning purchasing was reviewed at a recent meeting between purchasing director Charles Hewitt, divisional managers, and financial officers. Mr. Hewitt said:

*Body paragraph using a long quotation.*

> The current purchasing of small items by staff is unsatisfactory and the present situation cannot continue. The company has standard purchase order forms for use by all staff for small items and these must be used in order for us to keep track of our expenditures and which departments have made purchases.

*Conclusion.*

Finance officers will be ensuring that staff are familiar with purchasing procedures, particularly with regard to small items (under $500).

*A. Crowley*

**Box 2.3** ACKNOWLEDGING THE SOURCE OF QUOTATIONS AND PARAPHRASES

## Writing Tip
## Quotations

State directly and accurately where the quoted words came from, whatever the source. This can be done in different ways:

- The minister said during his May 7, 2006, speech to the industry association's annual meeting in Ottawa that "Canada's prosperity depends upon keeping pace with our major trading competitors."
- According to an article by Bogdan Bershoviz in the July 7, 2000, issue of the *Journal of Forms Management*, "75 percent of business forms are poorly designed and lead to significant unnecessary costs as well as frustrated clients."
- It is generally agreed by the experts that "improving risk management systems requires a complete study of the organization's formal and informal procedures and processes" (Frederica D. Jones. "Approaches to Risk Management Improvement." *Journal of Risk Assessment and Management,* August 1998).

## Paraphrases

State in the text of the paraphrase itself the source of the information. For example:

- In her June 25, 2007, memo to staff on new standardized accounting procedures, Ms. Williams stated that all parts of the company would be converted to the upgraded system over the next few months although existing systems would continue to be used in the meantime.
- David Johnson, in his article in the February 1999 issue of *Personnel Progress,* points out the need to review and revise approaches to sick leave policies and procedures, given the increasing costs to companies.

Appendix II provides more detail on acknowledging and referencing sources of information.

*Paraphrases*

When you take what someone else has said or written and put it in your own words, you are paraphrasing. A paraphrase is your version of the original. Paraphrase when you can transmit the information more succinctly than if you quoted the original. You should always indicate and acknowledge the source in the text when you have paraphrased (see Box 2.1 on plagiarism) but, unlike a quotation, paraphrased material is not set off from the text by quotation marks or indents.

## FIGURE 2.2

Using Paraphrases Effectively

### Acme Medical Supplies Ltd.

Memorandum

TO:        All Staff

FROM:    A. Crowley, Corporate Services Division

DATE:     July 23, 2002

SUBJECT:  Compliance With Company Purchasing Procedures

We wish to draw to the attention of staff that use of the company pur-          Introduction.
chasing procedures is required for any purchase of any item of any amount.
These procedures are contained in the company's policies and procedures
manual, available in print or on the intranet
(www.acmemed.com/internal/procedures).

The situation concerning purchasing was reviewed at a recent meeting          Body paragraph
between purchasing director Charles Hewitt, divisional managers, and finan-    with paraphrase of
cial officers. Mr. Hewitt noted that the current situation was unsatisfactory  Mr. Hewitt's words.
and could not continue. Staff could not just order items but must use the
standard purchase order forms so that expenditures and purchasing departments could be tracked.

Divisional managers and financial officers will be ensuring that all staff are   Conclusion.
familiar with the purchasing procedures, particularly with regard to items
under $500.

*A. Crowley*

---

   You might decide to paraphrase the purchasing director rather than quote him at length.
Thus, in the version of Mr. Crowley's memo in Figure 2.2, the second paragraph no longer
uses Mr. Hewitt's own words but still gives an account of what he said at the meeting.
   Note that the verb tense used in the paraphrase is different than that used in the direct quotation. In the quotation, the present tense is used—Mr. Hewitt's words as spoken are reproduced. In the paraphrase, Mr. Hewitt's words from a past moment are indirectly reported.

# Descriptive Summary

## PARAGRAPH FORM SUMMARY

In scanning the media, a regular part of her job, Brianna Smith, a marketing officer at the Centre for Excellence in Communications (CEC), came across an article (see Figure 2.3) commenting on electronic books that she knew would be of interest to her supervisor, Gilles Tardiff, the CEC marketing manager. She was aware that Mr. Tardiff did not have time to read everything that crossed his desk and insisted that a summary accompany any articles, reports, or memos longer than two pages sent to him. Mr. Tardiff would expect her to be able to tell him the article's main points as concisely as possible.

To prepare the summary, Ms. Smith went through the following process. First, she read the article to get an initial understanding of its contents. Then she went through the article again, this time more slowly. As she did so, Ms. Smith identified the main idea in each part and noted it in a word or phrase in the margin. She also circled key words, terms, phrases, and ideas and linked these together with arrows to see how they were related. This would be used to check that in her finished summary she had not omitted something important.

When she had a good view of the important ideas of the article and their sequence, Ms. Smith turned to her computer and, using her word processing program, briefly entered each idea on a separate line. By creating this list, she had set out the basic structure and organization of the significant points in the original text. Next, she wrote a sentence setting out each idea contained in the original article. She worked with these sentences to produce a summary text that combined the sentences in a coherent and appropriate structure with a logical flow of ideas faithfully representing the original material. She checked the text again and revised it until she was satisfied with her one-page summary. Then she put it into her memo format macro, printed it out, attached the article, and put the summary (see Figure 2.4) on Mr. Tardiff's desk.

## BULLET POINT FORM SUMMARY

Brianna Smith chose to use a paragraph format for her summary. Increasingly, however, a bullet point form summary is used in organizations as a way of forcing a focus on paring down to the essentials, cutting the amount of text, and making it easier visually for the reader. Bullets may be combined with headings to help the reader "see" and absorb the information as quickly as possible. A bullet point format does not change the process of summarizing or the need to present the essential ideas of the original material accurately, coherently, and logically.

Conrad Volpone, a human resources specialist at ProCasting Ltd., a large engineering company, prefers the bullet point format for summaries and memos. Mr. Volpone has read an article on literacy skills (see Figure 2.5) that he believes could be of interest as part of a possible personnel skills upgrading program for the company and decides to send it with a

FIGURE 2.3

## E-BOOKS PERFECT FOR MANUALS, TEXTBOOKS, NICHE AUTHORS

### Universal e-book standard now under development

1 The grief and upheaval inflicted on the music recording companies by the Internet should teach valuable lessons to the book publishing industry. In the music world, artists are fighting with their labels, lawsuits are being scattered like confetti, consumers are confused, and music fans by the millions are allegedly breaking the law. It didn't have to be this way.

2 The music industry could have shown leadership and actively pursued the new opportunities afforded by the Net, rather than sullenly insisting the industry was in no need of reform.

3 On the book front, the arrival of so-called e-books could enhance the appeal and utility of the written word. Writers needn't suffer from rampant pirating of their work and consumers could enjoy a wider selection of affordable content.

4 Compared to the music industry, book publishing offers greater opportunity for innovation and creativity because the products are more varied. While a CD is a CD, books range from 50¢ diet guides proffered at supermarket checkout counters to glossy five-kilo coffee table art publications costing more than $100.

5 While the paperback thriller has many years of life left because of its low cost and convenience, some industry segments, such as school textbooks, cry out for reform.

6 Knowledge is expanding at an ever-increasing pace, yet school boards are tempted to defer buying new textbooks as an easy way to save tax dollars.

7 But if students were issued inexpensive e-book reading devices, their textbooks could be updated annually at minimal cost. For some courses it could even make sense to update the e-books daily with newspaper and magazine articles.

8 The same benefits apply for technicians repairing machinery such as aircraft or automobiles. Rather than manuals thousands of pages thick, one e-book device could contain all the info and be much easier to use.

9 Until now, e-book reading devices have been relatively expensive and bulky, but this is quickly changing. The technology is getting cheaper and better, making the devices clearly more cost-effective in many applications than their pulp and paper counterparts.

10 Devices that weren't originally designed for e-book purposes are also now being modified to provide the service. Last week, Microsoft spearheaded the unveiling of a new line of small portable computers designed to compete head on with popular personal digital assistants such as the Palm. Called Pocket PCs, the devices use new software to produce screen images of text approaching the quality of text printed on paper.

11 Microsoft is busily lining up as many content providers as possible in order to spur sales of the new gadgets. The software giant will also make available a specially designed small-screen version of its on-line magazine Slate. According to Slate's editor, a common complaint from Slate readers is that they didn't like being forced to sit at a computer in order to read the magazine. Now they won't have to.

12 Fortunately for all stakeholders in the publishing industry, including consumers, software companies such as Microsoft and Adobe are now working together to implement a universal e-book standard.

*continued*

Authors and publishers can format their material to this common denominator, knowing it will function properly on all the competing e-book devices coming to market. Consumers burnt by previous standards wars, such as the beta versus VHS battle, can buy new e-book devices with confidence. 13

The increasing appeal of reading information on electronic screens enables new revenue models for traditional book publishers. Rather than selling constantly revised versions of medical textbooks, for example, publishers are experimenting with doctors buying annual subscriptions to electronic versions with updates available on-line. Encyclopaedia Britannica abandoned selling its costly product door-to-door completely, opting instead to make the English world's greatest compendium of knowledge available on the Net without charge, funded completely by advertising and commercial tie-ins. 14

The ability to transmit a book's contents anywhere in the world via the Internet opens new markets for niche authors previously ignored by traditional publishing houses. As one e-author recently noted in an on-line discussion group, if an e-book "is well-written, be it fiction or non-fiction, there's a market for it. It may not be a big enough market for the huge financial investment of a print publisher, but an e-publisher can make it available to every person in that market in the world, who's on-line." 15

Publishers will continue to perform their valuable editing and quality-control function. And while it is theoretically possible for writers to sell directly to consumers, it won't happen on a large scale. Retailers will continue the key role of aggregating the available titles to make browsing and selection more convenient to consumers. 16

Done properly, e-books should prove to be a win-win for everyone involved. 17

Source: Tapscott, Don. "E-books Perfect for Manuals, Textbooks, Niche Authors." *Financial Post* 12 May 2000.

summary to Erica Bruce, Director of Human Resources. Mr. Volpone knows that Ms. Bruce is overloaded by all the material that she receives. It is important to give her the essential points in an easily readable format.

Mr. Volpone goes through the same process as Brianna Smith but ends up with a series of bullet points rather than a summary in complete paragraphs. However, he combines Step 4, Write out sentences, and Step 5, Write a first draft, to produce his summary, although he is still careful to check and revise his text before printing a final version. He sends the memorandum (see Figure 2.6) and the article by internal mail to Ms. Bruce.

**FIGURE 2.4**

SUMMARY OF AN ARTICLE

 *Centre for Excellence in Communications (CEC)*

Memorandum

TO:        Gilles Tardiff, Marketing Manager

FROM:    Brianna Smith, Marketing Officer

DATE:    May 27, 2006

SUBJECT:    Summary Of Article "E-books Perfect For Manuals, Textbooks,
                 Niche Authors" by Don Tapscott, Financial Post, May 12, 2000

I am attaching a copy of the above article by Don Tapscott in view of CEC
discussions on possible electronic distribution of books and manuals.

According to Tapscott, book publishers should learn from the Internet's dis-
ruptive effects on the music recording industry, which, rather than pursuing
the new opportunities offered by the Internet, ignored them. E-books could
bring benefits to writers and increase the written word's appeal and, unlike
the music industry, book publishing has more opportunity for innovation and
creativity because its products are more varied.

*Tapscott's main
ideas 1–4.*

While book industry segments like paperback thrillers have many years of
life, given low cost and convenience, others, like school textbooks, need revision. Providing inexpensive e-book readers to students would, Tapscott
argues, allow for cheap, annual—or for some courses, daily—updating to
match the increasing rate of knowledge growth and avoid school board
temptations to economize by deferring textbook purchases. Likewise, e-books
could replace thick paper-based maintenance manuals for repairing
machinery.

*Tapscott's
supporting ideas
5–8.*

E-book reading technology is getting cheaper and better, making the devices
more cost-effective than traditional paper materials for many applications.
Moreover, other devices are being modified to provide for reading e-books.
Microsoft has introduced the Pocket PC line, small personal computers that
produce screen text at near printed-paper quality, to compete against the
Palm and other personal digital assistants. To encourage sales, Microsoft is

*Tapscott's
supporting ideas
9–11.*

*continued*

Tapscott's
supporting ideas
12–13.

lining up content providers and, responding to subscriber complaints about reading from a computer screen, making available a small-screen version of *Slate*, its online magazine.

Companies such as Microsoft and Adobe are working on a universal e-book standard, ensuring that authors and publishers can produce material that can be used on any type of e-book device and allowing consumers to buy any of the competing e-book devices coming to market without worrying about different standards.

Tapscott's
supporting ideas
14–15.

The growing popularity of reading information on electronic screens means new revenue models for publishers to experiment with, such as annual subscriptions to online updates of medical texts for doctors or, in the case of the Encyclopaedia Britannica, free access via an Internet site funded by advertising and commercial tie-ins. And, Tapscott believes, since it can transmit a book's content anywhere, the Internet opens new markets for niche authors ignored by traditional publishers because of the costs involved in addressing small markets.

Tapscott's
concluding points
16–17.

Publishers will continue to ensure quality control and retailers will continue to group available titles for consumer convenience in browsing and selection. Direct selling by writers is possible but unlikely on a large scale. For Tapscott, e-books should be good for everyone involved.

*Brianne Smith*

---

## FIGURE 2.5

## LITERACY SKILLS PAY IN CASH

Workers with high literacy skills earn a lot more than those without—thousands of dollars more a year and more than half a million dollars over a lifetime. But higher literacy skills among employees also add to the employers' bottom line.

Those are among the conclusions in a Conference Board of Canada report which explores the economic benefits of improving literacy skills in the workplace from the perspective of both employers and employees.

The study is based on a recent survey of employers and information from a 1994 international survey of adult literacy skills. It divides literacy skills into the ability to understand and use prose, documents, and numbers in printed material.

*continued*

Volpone's memo's
first bullet.

"No matter how much capital investment occurs, without adequate literacy training and education, employers and their employees will remain unable to maximize the potential of that investment," says Brenda Lafleur, co-author of the study.

Volpone's memo's
second bullet.

"Companies offer literacy skills training to their employees because enhanced reading, writing and numeracy skills will ultimately contribute to a strong bottom line through time savings, increased output, lower costs and improvements in the quality of work," she says. "And these direct benefits are just the tip of the iceberg."

Volpone's memo's
third bullet.

Other benefits, according to the study, were the unleashing of the potential of employees, improved labour–management relations, and the moving of management and workers toward common corporate goals.

Volpone's memo's
fourth bullet.

The study found that a male with higher literacy skills makes an extra $585 000 over his lifetime and a female $683 000. Those with higher skills are also less likely to suffer unemployment and experience shorter durations of joblessness.

Volpone's memo's
fifth bullet.

In 1994, the average male with high "document" literacy skills earned $43 495; one with low skills $24 029. For females the difference was $27 424 versus $13 964.

Note Volpone's
summary of wage
differences in his
bullet point.

The board says the study also provides "concrete evidence" of the benefits of literacy to employers in the increased ability of workers to handle on-the-job training, improved quality of work, reduced time per task, increased production, fewer work errors, better health and safety records, reduced waste, increased customer satisfaction, reduced absenteeism, and increased profitability.

Yet, it adds that the "message has not yet reached many Canadian workplaces."

Volpone's memo's
sixth bullet.

"Many employers do not yet recognize that a decision to invest in literacy will have a positive overall impact on their organization and their bottom line," it says, adding that the findings of the study should be a "call to action" to help encourage employees to improve their literacy skills.

At the same time, many employees are unaware that improving their literacy skills will improve their chance of success in their jobs.

As a result, there is not enough literacy skills training, development, and application in the workplace, it says.

---

Source: Beauchesne, Eric. "Literacy Skills Pay in Cash." *Cape Breton Morning Post* 7 May 1997. Reprinted by permission of Southam News.

FIGURE 2.6

## BULLET POINT FORM SUMMARY

### ProCasting Ltd.

## MEMORANDUM

TO: Erica Bruce, Director of Human Resources

FROM: Conrad Volpone, Recruitment Specialist

DATE: September 5, 2006

SUBJECT: Summary Of Article "Literacy Skills Pay In Cash," By Eric
Beauchesne, *Cape Breton Morning Post,* May 7, 1997

The attached article could be useful for recruitment purposes. It states:

- A Conference Board of Canada report says that the potential of capital investment can't be maximized without adequate employee literacy training and education.
- Companies offer training because enhanced reading, writing, and numeracy skills ultimately contribute to a strong bottom line.
- Direct benefits of training are time savings, increased output, lowered costs, and improved work quality.
- Indirect benefits include unleashing employee potential, improving labour relations, and moving labour and management toward common corporate goals.
- Higher literacy translates into less likelihood and/or duration of unemployment and an extra $585,000 (men) and $683,000 (women) in earnings over a lifetime; equally, 1994 wage gaps between workers with high and low literacy skills were approximately $20,000 (males) and $13,000 (females).
- Many employers don't recognize, and many employees are unaware of, the benefits of literacy training, with the result that there's not enough of it in the workplace.

Volpone begins his summary with a brief one-sentence introduction telling Erica Bruce why she is getting the summary and the article.

# Evaluative Summary

The evaluative summary differs from the descriptive summary. In addition to summarizing the content of the original material, the evaluative summary draws the reader's attention to important questions that should be considered when judging the appropriateness and correctness of the information in the original. Such questions may point out the lack of sources for quotations or statements, or that a source for a fact or statement is not necessarily reliable, or that the authority for a statement is a website whose owners are either difficult to identify or are strongly in favour of a particular viewpoint on an issue.

It is often difficult to be sure of the reliability and accuracy of information put out in the public domain. This is especially true in a world where the Internet allows virtually anyone or any organization to create and instantly distribute information about any chosen topic. The basic approach, especially with the time pressures of the workplace, is to carefully check the source of the information you are concerned about. Which organization or individual is making the statement or putting out the information? Is it a credible source? What is its reputation? Does it have a point of view? Is the information complete?

Evaluating statistics in an article, report, or other text does not require an advanced course in calculus or the ability to "regress to the mean." Rather, evaluating statistics can be done by asking a series of questions about the numbers being presented and their use. Broadly speaking, the questions involve accuracy, source, appropriate linkage to context, and the particular statistic used, this last being the most complicated.

## ACCURACY

Accuracy relates to whether the statistics or numbers given in the material being summarized are faithful to the source from which they were taken. For example, an article reports that the unemployment rate overall has dropped by 1.5 percent for skilled workers in Canada since 1999 according to Statistics Canada. The first question is whether this is the figure put out by Statistics Canada. Often writers round up or down and thus 1.5 percent could be, in fact, 1.52 percent or 1.48 percent. This may not seem a great difference but could, in terms of the actual number of people unemployed, mean a difference of many thousands. Furthermore, giving the percentage without providing the raw numbers the percentage represents of the total population in question—in this case the number of skilled workers in Canada—makes it difficult to fully understand the reality of the situation. If your company's business were to consist of training and placing workers, this type of information would likely be important to you.

## SOURCE

The source of a statistic is important for a reader in assessing its credibility. Statistics Canada has a worldwide reputation for the accuracy and integrity of the statistics it produces. An article using numbers attributed to Statistics Canada immediately has a greater level of credibility than an article on the same topic using statistics from a less reliable source.

A frequent problem, however, is when statistics are taken from a reliable source but wrongly applied to a situation or problem. For example, there may not be data available on Canadians' use of a dangerous substance, so the writer of a report or article may use American data, divide it by a factor of 10 to allow for population differences, and then extrapolate to the Canadian situation. The difficulty is that the situations in the two countries are different (environmental laws, size and characteristics of the industrial and household markets, etc.), and the reality portrayed by the American figures is not the Canadian reality.

## LINKAGE TO CONTEXT

The third issue related to use of statistics in written material is that of linkage to context; that is, the common problem of a text's narrative or argument not being properly related to the statistics it presents. Frequently, writers will take a figure and describe it inaccurately. For example, the 29 percent of voters shown in the opinion poll chart in a newspaper article as "undecided" is written about as "almost a third of voters." A third, however, is 33 percent, and the difference between 29 percent and 33 percent is 4 points out of 100 (29–33/100) and 4 points out of 29 is in fact a leap of 13.79 percent! The impression has been given in the narrative that 33 percent of voters are undecided but the reality is somewhat different.

## USING STATISTICS

The type of statistic used can make a great difference in the message delivered by an article, report, or proposal. Benjamin Disraeli, who served as prime minister of Great Britain in 1868 and from 1874 to 1880, understated the issue when he declared that "there are three kinds of lies. Lies. Damnable lies. And statistics." Although statistics (which appear most often in the form of "an average") purport to represent reality, there is no assurance that they do so or that they are not being purposely misused. Part of the problem is that there are three kinds of mathematical units that can rightly be called "average" and none of them may actually represent what we think of as "average" (i.e., generally common or regularly occurring). Because of this confusion, it is easy to select those statistics that best represent the case you want to put forward.

### The Arithmetic Mean

The "mean" is the most common form of average to which people refer. For example, if you told your friend that the average grade on the business law midterm examination was 65, she would assume that you arrived at this by adding up all the grades and then dividing them by the total number of students who took the exam. Similarly, if you reported that your company's stock had risen by an average of $7.55 over the past five years, most listeners would assume you arrived at this figure by adding the growth for each year and then dividing that figure by five.

For most purposes, the "mean" is about as close to "the normal" as you can get. However, even though it is mathematically unassailable, the "mean" may not actually reflect reality. If, to take a sports example, you heard on the radio that a Toronto Blue Jays player had batted .300 over the course of the Jays' most recent home stand, you might believe that he had hit safely in three of every 10 at bats. However, assuming 20 at bats in the home stand, mathematically, he could have hit .500 over the first 10 at bats and .100 over the second 10.

## Box 2.4   THE ARITHMETIC MEAN

|  | .300<br>(at 3 of every 10) | .300<br>(.500 in first 10 and .100 in second 10) |
| --- | --- | --- |
| First 10 | 3 divided by 10 = .300 | 5 divided by 10 = .500 |
| Second 10 | 3 divided by 10 = .300 | 1 divided by 10 = .100 |
| Total | 6 divided by 20 = .300 | 6 divided by 20 = .300 |

The average "batting average" of .300 does not, in fact, tell you anything about how he hit in either of the 10 at-bat segments of the home stand or how he will hit in the game you are going to see tonight at the Rogers Centre.

The same might well be true of the average age of the 25 people in your class, which might work out to 22 years, 3 months. This was the arithmetic average for one of our classes last fall, but no one in the class was 22 years, 3 months old. The mean may not, then, actually represent any single part of the reality of the population being discussed.

### The Median

As its name suggests, the "median" is the middle of a series. Thus, if your grades were 85, 75, 70, 65, and 63, your "median average" would be 70. This would be true even if the assignments were not weighted equally; that is, if the first was 10 percent of your final grade and the last was 25 percent of your final grade. Medians can, thus, often be used to "hide" information or to "massage" it so that it proves the writer's point of view, even when it would appear to misrepresent the facts as normally understood—especially when writers do not signal that they are using "median averages."

### The Mode

Unlike mean averages, which, as we just saw, may not even represent a single item in a series, "modal averages" definitely represent items in a series. A modal average is the number that occurs most frequently in a series. If, for example, the series represented the number of people employed at local computer stores—21, 21, 22, 32, 33, 34, 40, 60, and 61—the modal average would be 21. On the other hand, if the numbers were 20, 21, 22, 33, 33, 40, 60, and 61, the modal average would be 33, about one-third higher than the modal average of 21 (despite the fact that the arithmetic average, 36, remains the same).

The difference between the various averages means that writers can pick the one that will best support the point they want to make. Suppose, for example, you were asked by the chair of your college's General Arts and Science (GAS) program (the one students enter if they do not already know in which program they want to concentrate) to help her argue that the college should increase daycare funding for students in the program. Obviously, this case would be strengthened if you could show that the average student was likely to be of an age at which he or she would have young children. Which of the following "averages" would you use:

- mean: 21 years, 3 months;
- median: 25 years, 2 months;
- mode: 18 years, 7 months?

No doubt you would use the median, even though only one person in the 250-student program was 25 years, 2 months old. If, on the other hand, you wanted to argue that more resources should be devoted to helping GAS students plan for their future, you would probably choose the mode, because administrators understand that the younger the students, the more support they tend to need.

## Box 2.5   BASIC QUESTIONS FOR REVIEWING A SUMMARY

### Writing Tip

You can use the following basic questions to help review any summary to see if there are errors or if it can be improved in some way. These basic questions will probably lead to others as you review your text:

1. Does the summary accurately and fully present the essential points, messages, and information in the article? If not, what is left out or not properly presented?
2. Is the structure of the summary logical and easy to follow?
3. Is the text clear and easy to read?
4. Are there grammatical, punctuation, spelling, or usage errors?
5. Are the style and tone professional and appropriate?
6. Are any issues of information accuracy or reliability identified?

# Editing Practice One

Henrietta Lopez is a co-op course student in business at Lakeside College working for a term with OX4 Inc. Her supervisor, Mary Onewing, the marketing manager, asked her to prepare a summary of an article from *The Globe and Mail* on workplace health and safety to be sent to the executive vice president, Rupert Afdidi, for possible use in a speech he was writing. Read the article in Figure 2.7 and Ms. Lopez's summary in Figure 2.8 and then consider the questions on page 56.

## FIGURE 2.7

### VIOLENCE, REPETITIVE STRAIN INJURY AMONG MODERN WORKING WORLD'S DANGERS

**Economic, demographic changes create new set of health and safety hazards for today's workers**

Think about workplace hazards and you'll likely conjure images of being maimed by a machine or poisoned by chemicals.

But the threats to health and safety are often more subtle and more varied in today's fast-changing, high-pressured workplaces.

The growing problem of workplace violence, for instance, has been highlighted by last year's shooting death of four employees by a coworker at an Ottawa bus depot and the more recent killings of two Toronto-area taxi drivers.

Workplace violence is one of many trends and concerns the Workplace Safety and Insurance Board is trying to address, in the light of economic, social, and demographic changes that are transforming people's work experiences.

Bryan Evans, a senior policy adviser with the WSIB, says such changes have created a new set of problems for today's workers and the system overseeing occupational health and safety.

Earlier in the 20th century, when the workers' compensation system evolved, the typical workplace was an industrial setting where the most common health and safety risks were associated with physical labour, machinery, and exposure to hazardous materials.

With the growth of technology and a service economy, many of today's workers are more likely to suffer from repetitive strain injuries caused by working too long on computer keyboards than to get maimed by machines.

And the greatest dangers to many workers arise in settings where they may encounter anger, rage, or random violence.

Incidents like the Ottawa tragedy are just the tip of the iceberg, says Dave Carter, coordinator for area managers for the Municipal Health and Safety Association, who is trying to do something about the frictions endemic in many workplaces.

*continued*

Mr. Carter and other members of WSIB-funded health and safety associations are working on the creation of a video that will help workers identify and address the kind of problems that lead to workplace violence.

"We want to deal with the subtle violence that can lead to the big stuff so that we can address problems while they are still manageable, before they escalate into something more extreme," he says.

Statistics are hard to come by, since incidents of workplace violence often go unreported and those that are reported have not been tracked in any formal way. But employee assistance firms and unions, particularly those representing health-care workers and teachers, have voiced concerns about rising rates of violence and abuse.

For example, airlines in Canada reported 120 incidents involving air rage—abusive behaviour by flying passengers—last year and, internationally, the airline industry reports a 400 percent rise in such incidents since 1995.

A recent survey of nurses in Britain found that nearly half had been physically assaulted by patients and 72 percent said they felt vulnerable at work, while only a third felt they were at risk off duty. Four out of five survey participants interviewed by the publication *Nursing Times* said that they believe their workplace is more dangerous now than ever before in their careers.

The U.S.-based National Institute of Occupational Safety and Health (NIOSH) reports that one million U.S. workers are assaulted in the workplace every year, most occurring in service settings such as hospitals, nursing homes, and social-service agencies.

What can be done to make workers safer? The inquest into the OC Transpo shooting recommended that companies adopt a zero-tolerance policy toward workplace violence and intimidation. The NIOSH has also called for zero-tolerance policies.

Evidence at the OC Transpo inquest showed that the perpetrator had previously complained about being harassed in the workplace over his stuttering. Mr. Carter says this is the kind of low-level abuse his video is addressing.

"People often treat other people miserably in the workplace and this kind of subtle violence needs to be addressed before it leads to something bigger," he says.

The video will encourage people to identify violent behaviour in the workplace and create a culture where abuse is unacceptable and everyone is treated with respect.

Violence is just one of several key trends the WSIB is monitoring. Mr. Evans says there are also various issues resulting from the aging of the baby-boom generation.

He notes that older workers have a culture of workplace safety and years of experience that help them judge which practices are safe, and which are not. As they retire in large numbers, they will be replaced by younger workers who have neither the culture nor experience. The WSIB is responding to this challenge by mounting campaigns directed at younger workers.

Another problem associated with an aging workforce is that it is often difficult to determine whether an ailment is related to working conditions, long-term exposure to workplace hazards, or problems that have nothing to do with the job.

There are also major health and safety issues associated with a shift in the workforce from long-term, full-time employment to part-time, self-employed or contract work.

*continued*

When workers are juggling different part-time jobs or changing jobs several times a year, it may be difficult to determine, for compensation purposes, which job was responsible for a chronic work-related injury, such as carpal tunnel syndrome. Furthermore, the compensation paid by one employer may not be enough to make up for the lost income of a person who was working on several different jobs but is now incapacitated.

The shift to a service economy in which small business is a major employer also means many workers no longer come under workers' compensation programs and sometimes they may not even realize that they are not covered, according to independent labour market economist John O'Grady.

Mr. Evans says that the lines between workplace health and community health may need to be redrawn, so that more emphasis is placed on enhancing the health of the population as a whole.

He adds that planning needs to address emerging trends. "We have to think long term."

Source: "Violence, Repetitive Strain Injury among Modern Working World's Dangers." *The Globe and Mail* 12 May 2000: W4. Reprinted by permission of the Workplace Safety and Insurance Board.

## FIGURE 2.8

### EDITING PRACTICE ONE: SUMMARY OF A NEWSPAPER ARTICLE
**A poorly written summary**

# OX4Inc.

Memorandum

TO:      Mary

FROM:    Henrietta

DATE:    May 12, 2006

SUBJECT:  Article On Workplace Safety For Mr. Afdidi

Here is the summary of the article you asked me to do.

There's a lot of violence taking place in the workplace. This is really a lot to do with health and safety of people and last year Ottawa workers were shot and taxi drivers in Toronto as well. This trend is being looked at by the Workplace Safety and Insurance Board (WSIB) since there are major changes affecting people at work creating problems.

In the early 20th century when workers compensation started the major risks were from physical work and machinery and hazardous materials. Nowadays its injuries like repetitive strain from keyboards and the big risk is for many

*continued*

workers workplace violence. Dave Carter of the Municipal Health and Safety Association is trying to do something about it by making a video. They want to show people how to deal with the small things before they escalate into something extreme.

Its hard to get statistics on workplace violence but things seem to be getting worse according to unions and employee assistance firms. Canadian airlines reported 120 air rage incidents last year and internationally there's been a 400 percent increase since 1995. In Britain half of nurses have been assaulted and 72 percent said they were vulnerable at work. The survey showed four out of five nurses believe there workplace is more dangerous now than ever before. In the United States more than one million workers are assaulted in the workplace annually.

Some argue for zero tolerance policies for workplace violence and harassment. The inquest into the Ottawa bus company shootings showed the killer had complained about harassment about stuttering. Dave Carter's video is about stopping this type of harassment before it leads to violence and creating respect in the workplace.

Brian Evans of the WSIB says violence is one of several trends being monitored and there are problems from aging baby boomers. They have a safety culture and experience but now large numbers are retiring and younger workers have neither so the WSIB is mounting campaigns toward them. Another problem is that its hard to tell if aging workers ailments are from working conditions, long exposure to workplace hazards or other problems unrelated to work. And, there are problems with the change to more part timers, self-employed, and contract workers because when people are juggling jobs or changing jobs often its hard to determine which job has caused a work-related injury for compensation purposes. And one employer's compensation could be inadequate for someone previously working at different jobs but who's incapacitated. Finally, with a shift to a service economy and small business as a big employer many people aren't covered for workers compensation and many don't realize.

Brian Evans says that workplace and community health must change to enhance the health of the population as a whole. Planning must be for emerging needs and be long term.

*Henrietta*

## QUESTIONS TO CONSIDER

1. Is Ms. Lopez's subject line appropriate?
2. Does Ms. Lopez's first paragraph properly reflect the article's main point and thrust; namely, that workplace health and safety concerns are changing as economic, social, and demographic changes transform the workplace, the nature of work, and how people experience work?
3. Does the summary as a whole properly capture the article's content?
4. Is the summary accurate with regard to the statistics presented in the article? For example, Ms. Lopez writes that "The survey showed four of five nurses believe there workplace is more dangerous now than ever before." Does the article actually say this?
5. Would a reader know the source of the figures to which she refers?
6. Apart from use of numbers, are there instances where Ms. Lopez has either wrongly stated something or left out information required by a reader to get a full picture of the original article? How, for instance, does "Brian Evans" spell his name?
7. Are there grammatical, spelling, punctuation, or usage errors? Is there confusion between "their" and "there"? Or "its" and "it's"? Are there any unclear sentences?
8. Is there any new information in the summary; for example, an opinion?

# Editing Practice Two

Daniel Osbourne has recently joined WOW Inc., an event marketing and sponsorship company, as an events coordinator. He has been asked by his boss, Harry Helman, to draft a summary of the article in Figure 2.9 on the annual meeting of the American Association of Advertising Agencies. Read Mr. Osbourne's summary in Figure 2.10 and then consider the questions on page 59.

**FIGURE 2.9**

## AGENCIES SEEK POSITION IN NEW ECONOMY

How does the advertising industry position itself as a major player, both exciting and essential, in a digital economy?

Top ad executives are in Bermuda this week for the annual meeting of the American Association of Advertising Agencies (AAAA) to address ways to broaden the industry's role to something more than being simply the makers of 30-second TV spots.

Among the topics on their agenda are a new business model for ad agencies, how to push the creative edge, and how to attract and hold top talent against the lure of the dot-coms.

All the discussion takes place against the backdrop of major industry consolidation: The proposed takeover of Young & Rubicam Inc. by British holding company WPP Group PLC to create the world's largest advertising company moved closer to reality with the agreement in principle reached May 10.

The deal, when completed, would put one more global ad network, another public-relations firm, and another media-buying agency under the WPP umbrella, which already includes ad agencies Ogilvy & Mather Worldwide and J. Walter Thompson.

For many ad executives, the combination also underscores why the industry has an image as a commodity provider instead of as a powerful partner in the corporate boardroom.

Jonathan Bond, co-chairman of the independent agency Kirshenbaum Bond & Partners, said consolidation is being driven by financial efficiencies instead of a push for greater creativity.

Like many of his peers, Mr. Bond asserts that the agencies must evolve into broad-based creative organizations that develop ideas across all media, including television, print, and the Internet, to drive a client's success.

Echoes Ogilvy & Mather Worldwide chairwoman and chief executive officer Shelly Lazarus, who is outgoing chairwoman of the advertising trade group: "Our role has become much more fundamental and essential to commerce."

She says the role of the ad agencies had been overshadowed over the years, but that has begun to change as companies, especially Internet start-ups, realize the value of creating an image or brand that differentiates itself.

The unexpected boom in business last year from dot-coms and demand from traditional advertisers have taxed the industry.

The new chairman of the AAAA, Phil Dusenberry, says he plans to make creativity a renewed priority for ad agencies. Now flush with clients, the industry should feel free to push the creative edge with inspiring work, he says, but that hasn't happened across the board.

**FIGURE 2.10**

## EDITING PRACTICE TWO: SUMMARY OF A NEWSPAPER ARTICLE

**A poorly written summary**

MEMORANDUM

TO:       Harry Helman

FROM:     Daniel Osbourne

DATE:     April 17, 2002

SUBJECT:  "Agencies Retool for New Economy," Article on American
          Association of Advertising Agencies Annual Meeting, *The Globe
          and Mail,* May 10, 2000

The American Association of Advertising Agencies (AAAA) annual meeting is looking at how to broaden its role beyond TV commercials, Discussion will be on a new business model for agencies, how to push the creative edge and attracting and keeping talent from going to the dot-coms.

Industry consolidation is going on with Young & Rubicam being taken over by WPP Group PLC, which is British. This will be the worlds largest advertising company, which already includes agencies Ogilvy & Mather Worldwide and J. Walter Thompson. Many think this emphasizes why advertising is seen as a commodity provider and not a boardroom partner. Agency co-chairman Jonathan Bond said consolidation stems from financial efficiencies rather than for more creativity and believes agencies must be broad based developing ideas across all media including the Internet for clients.

Shelley Lazarus, Ogilvy & Mather Worldwide's CEO, chair of the AAAA, says advertising's role is more fundamental and essential to commerce. Agencies role is changing as companies and Internet start-ups especially realize the value of creating an image or brand. Last year business boomed from dot-coms and traditional advertisers and strained the industry. New AAAA chair Phil Dusenbury plans to make creativity a renewed priority since with many clients the industry should feel ready do inspiring work—but this hasn't happened all over.

## QUESTIONS TO CONSIDER

1. Is Mr. Osbourne's opening paragraph accurate? Does it capture the main idea of the article?
2. Is it the AAAA that wants to broaden its role or the advertising industry? Is discussion to be limited to the topics mentioned by Mr. Osbourne or are these among the items on the agenda?
3. Who is Jonathan Bond?
4. What is Shelly Lazarus's role in the AAAA?
5. Are all Mr. Osbourne's sentences grammatical and well structured?
6. Whose "role is changing as companies and Internet start-ups especially realize the value of creating an image or brand"? Is this sentence grammatical? Structured for clarity?
7. Are there any punctuation or spelling errors? Will the merged Young & Rubicam and WPP Group PLC agency be the "worlds" or the "world's" largest advertising company?

# Editing Practice Three

Arthur Larwood is an intern at Delta Community Development Works (DCDW), a Delta, British Columbia, not-for-profit organization that works to help people find employment and provides various other community services. He read the following article in the *Financial Post* on his way to work and determined that a summary would be useful for his manager, Jack Elliot, to have for a management meeting later in the morning. Since time is pressing and Mr. Elliot dislikes long memos, Mr. Larwood decides to use a bullet form approach. Read the article in Figure 2.11 and Mr. Larwood's summary in Figure 2.12 and then consider the questions on page 61.

## CANADIAN AUTOPARTS TOYOTA EXPANDS IN DELTA, B.C., WITH $39M INVESTMENT

DELTA, B.C. (CP) – Canadian Autoparts Toyota Inc., which makes aluminum wheels for Japanese automaker Toyota Motor Corp., is expanding its operations in British Columbia with a $39 million investment.

The CAPTIN expansion will increase wheel capacity at the Delta site almost 17 per cent to 1.68 million units annually starting July 2007, the company said. Cumulative investment in the firm will reach $232.2 million. The 19,000-square-metre plant produces 22 wheel models for Toyota's vehicles and employs about 230 people, a number that will increase to 260.

Earlier Thursday, the Japanese automaker announced its widely anticipated move to build a new Toyota plant in Woodstock, Ont., creating 1,300 jobs in 2008.

"The expansion of CAPTIN's presence in B.C. is a vote of confidence in its employees and in B.C.'s strong economy," B.C. Premier Gordon Campbell said in a release.

"For 22 years, CAPTIN has made a significant contribution to our province and we look forward to their continued success here as we build B.C.'s strong ties with the Asia-Pacific to attract similar investment across the province."

The firm was incorporated in 1983 by Toyota Motor and was the first Canadian manufacturing investment by a Japanese automaker.

"This investment demonstrates the national nature of the automotive industry and the benefits the whole country can reap when it thrives," federal Minister of Industry David Emerson said in a release.

"We are proud that this world-class company is investing further in British Columbia."

Toyota has five vehicle manufacturing plants and six power train and component plants in North America. Its North American–produced vehicles include the Avalon, Camry, Corolla, Matrix, Sienna, Solara, Sequoia, Tacoma, Tundra and the Lexus RX330.

Source: "Canadian Autoparts Toyota Expands in Delta, B.C., with $39M Investment," Canadian Press dispatch in the *Financial Post* Online Edition 1 July 2005.

**FIGURE 2.12**

## Editing Practice Three: Summary of a Newspaper Article

### A poorly written summary

Memorandum

TO:        Jack Elliot, Manager, Community Programming

FROM:    Arthur Larwood, Intern

DATE:     4 July 2007

SUBJECT:  Article on Delta Toyota Plant

I thought a summary of this article might be useful for the management meting.

- Canadian Autoparts Toyota Inc. (CAPTIN) is expanding its Delta operations by $39 million.
- This will increase Delta's wheel-making capacity by 17% to 1.68 million units
- Total investment will be $232.2 million.
- There will be 30 new jobs for a total of 260.
- This is after Toyota's expansion of its Ontario plant to another 1,300 jobs in 2008.
- Premier Campbell says it's "a vote of confidence."
- Toyota has five vehicle, and six component, plants in North America.

### QUESTIONS TO CONSIDER

1. Is the subject line appropriate?
2. Is the summary as a whole complete and accurate in relation to the article's content?
3. Does the summary indicate that the Delta plant is specialized in wheel-making?
4. Is it clear what the total investment figure refers to (i.e., the new investment only or the investment that the company will have made in the plant with the new investment)?
5. Is the sentence about Toyota's Ontario plant clear? How many jobs has the Ontario plant now—1,300?
6. Does the summary capture the meaning of Premier Campbell's remarks and what he is referring to?
7. Are there any grammatical, spelling, punctuation, or usage errors?

# Summary

Information is the basis for decision-making in business organizations. However, there is so much information available that it must be summarized to enable decisions to be made quickly and efficiently. Summarizing is taking what someone else has written and reducing it to a concise, accurate, faithful version of the original. A summary may be descriptive (it sets out the content of the original) or evaluative (it also deals with whether the information in the original is accurate, reliable, or appropriately presented). There is a six-step process for writing a summary:

1. Read the material carefully for understanding.
2. Read the material again and note the main ideas.
3. Lay out the structure by taking each word or phrase relating to a main idea and writing it down in the order presented.
4. Write out sentences setting out each main idea.
5. Write a first draft.
6. Revise the draft several times until you are satisfied.

Generally, a summary should be about 15 percent the size of the original text and written in either paragraph or bullet point form.

Quotations and paraphrases are two other standard methods of summarizing information. Quoting is directly repeating someone else's words. A quotation can be from any type of source and can vary in length. Using a quote helps support a point and adds credibility to the text. Paraphrasing is taking what someone else has said or written and putting it in your own words. Using a paraphrase allows for transmitting information more succinctly than quoting the original directly.

# Discussion Questions

1. What is the importance of summary writing in business communication?
2. What are the differences between quotations, paraphrases, and summaries?
3. What are the six steps of the summary writing process?
4. What is the difference between paragraph and bullet point form summaries?
5. What is the difference between descriptive and evaluative summaries?
6. What are the types of errors that editing your summaries can correct?

# Writing Assignments

## Assignment 2.1

You are a traffic analyst at the Great Information Highway Navigation Company Inc. Write a paragraph form summary of the article in Figure 2.13 and transmit it in memo format to Arthur Littlehampton, Manager of Traffic Analysis.

### FIGURE 2.13

## WILL THE YOUNGER GENERATION KEEP ON TRUCKING?

In an era when high technology and high education seem to be the hallmarks of jobs in a modern economy, you might not guess that the single most common occupation among men is truck driver.

They are people you probably see, without really noticing, every time you leave home. Take a closer look. In their work life, they are very different from the rest of us.

Compared with the average Canadian worker, they are older, less educated, and manage to earn a good living only by working punishing hours. As they head toward retirement age, some experts wonder whether younger generations will be willing to step into their seats behind the wheel.

Irwin Bess of Statistics Canada has profiled truckers in the latest issue of the agency's *Perspectives* magazine and his sketch, based on data from a variety of sources, serves up a fascinating insight into how truckers work and live.

Trucking is not just an important industry—two thirds of all Canadian trade with the United States moves by road—but a growing one. While the whole economy grew by an average of 2 percent a year from 1990 to 1998, trucking expanded at a pace of 5 percent annually. Airlines and railways saw their business grow by only 1 percent a year, while marine shipping dropped 1 percent annually.

Such growth generated more demand for truck drivers. By 1998, about 231,000 people, 1.6 percent of the entire labour force, were at the wheels of commercial transport trucks. In this decade, their numbers have grown 13 percent, compared with a 9 percent gain for all jobs.

In fact, in the 1996 census, truck drivers rank No. 1 out of all occupations for men.

A little more than half work for what is called the "for hire" segment of trucking, meaning the main business of the company is trucking. The rest work in private trucking for companies whose main business is not trucking, but use trucks (and drivers) to deliver the goods they sell.

Truckers are not your average worker, as Mr. Bess's research makes clear.

Overwhelmingly, this is men's work. In 1998, men accounted for about 54 percent of all workers but 97 percent of truck drivers.

They are about three years older than the average. Almost 13 percent of truck drivers are 55 or older, compared with 10 percent of the entire work force. An additional 55 percent are 35 to 54, compared with a little more than 50 percent of all workers.

They have less formal education than the work force as a whole. Only 27 percent of truck drivers have more than a high school education, compared with 52 percent of all workers.

*continued*

Truckers work longer hours than the rest of us. Salaried drivers who worked for a trucking company put in an average of about 50 hours a week in 1998, while self-employed drivers worked more than 52 hours. That compares with a little more than 36 hours for all employees. About one fifth of salaried truckers worked 60 hours or more each week, compared with only 2 percent of workers in other industries.

The habit of long hours is especially noticeable among for hire drivers, who spend more time on the road than private truckers, for two reasons. They are more likely to work for companies engaged in long-distance trucking rather than cross-town deliveries, and they are more likely to make trips to and from the United States. Almost one third work 60 hours a week or more, compared with only one tenth of the drivers working for private carriers.

There is plenty to do besides drive. Truckers often load and unload their vehicles at each end of the journey; those heading south have to clear customs as they cross the border; and many, especially the self-employed, have their own small business to administer in addition to driving.

They can make a decent living, but only because of those long hours. In 1998, the average earnings of a fulltime truck driver came to $673 a week, just above the $666 average for all fulltime employees. But on an hourly basis, a for hire driver made only $13.94 an hour, almost 7 percent less than a machine operator or assembler in a manufacturing plant.

Their work affects their home lives as well. Among couples in other occupations, almost 80 percent had a spouse doing paid work outside the home; among truckers, the figure was 42 percent. Mr. Bess figures this pattern "could explain drivers' willingness to take on longer routes or work weeks as a way of supporting their families, or perhaps it reflects the challenges of reconciling a trucker's schedule with the demands of a dual earner household."

But the hours they work and the irregularity of those hours doubtlessly takes a toll on family life. About 70 percent of all workers have regular daytime schedules, but only 40 percent of salaried, for hire truckers do. Long haul drivers especially "may not see their families for days or, in some cases, for several weeks" at a stretch. Driver alertness and overall driving performance may also suffer, according to some federal studies.

And then there is the future. Older drivers are approaching retirement age, but fewer Canadians are choosing to work the kind of grinding hours that truckers put in. Over time, Canada's trucking industry may have a tough time finding people to fill the gap.

Source: Little, Bruce. "Will the Younger Generation Keep on Trucking?" *The Globe and Mail* 1 October 2000. Reprinted with permission of *The Globe and Mail*.

## Assignment 2.2

You are a trainee at the municipal recreation department. The article in Figure 2.14 was circulated by parents in your city opposed to a new municipal bylaw on children's playgrounds. Your boss, Mahalawalla Farmi, has asked you to summarize it in bullet point form for him to send to the city manager, Marise Jonkas. Although you may disagree or agree with Mr. Byfield's views, you remind yourself that your task is only to summarize them.

FIGURE 2.14

## What Children Need Even More than Safety Is a Little Self-Selected Danger

For the longest time we considered adding another news department to the magazine (in addition to Ottawa, Law, Crime, and Calamity, etc.). It would be called "If It Saves Even One Life …" and would include all those tedious causes normally justified by, "If it saves even one life surely it's worth it." Whenever I hear this monstrous sentence there arises within me a terrifying sense of being smothered.

I got this same feeling of strangulation when I read about a decision to pull the playground equipment out of Tipton Park, a perfectly unremarkable patch of grass in the pleasantly lived-in district of Queen Alexandra in south Edmonton. Some officious city bureaucracy had already yanked out the tall slide, and was preparing to remove everything else when a civic-spirited neighbour intervened. Since then the community league has been negotiating with the city to replace what they have with "CSA-approved" material. More plastic and rubber. Less dare-devil height. More safety. Less fun.

Some neighbourhood mothers are quite upset, and if I lived in Queen Alexandra I suspect I would be too. It's not just that the old equipment is familiar and quite safe enough. And it's not just that its replacement will pointlessly cost the community league money. No, what really rankles is the fusspot intrusion of people who are becoming increasingly known, hyperbolically, as safety nazis.

Imagine you are with other families at someone's backyard barbecue when a young child rides past and isn't wearing one of the new mushroom-cap helmets. A civilized person, if he noticed it at all, would give it no more thought, knowing that the odds of the child being really hurt are, to say the least, remote. A less civilized person might cluck his or her tongue and make a remark. Well, no harm done. But not a safety nazi. A safety nazi will loudly denounce the recklessness of parents who let children ride helmetless. A safety nazi of the harder variety will demand that there be a law and an immediate investigation by social services. And (unfortunately) nobody will quietly tell this horrible person that she is a sociopathic busybody.

In the case of Tipton Park, the safety nazis confiscated the sixteen-foot slide because a child might fall off it. They want it replaced with some sort of large sculpture. When the mothers pointed out that children will more often fall off a large nondescript sculpture than a slide, the experts suggested the sculpture be designed to be non-climbable. As if. The merry-go-round is another menace. It's "psychologically damaging," said the experts, because big kids catch the little kids on it and spin them mercilessly. After much negotiation, it was agreed the merry-go-round could stay, provided it was "stationary"—a merry-go-nowhere, as it were. The monkey bars were deficient because children falling from the upper bars might hurt themselves on the lower ones. There were problems with the swings, and other problems with the teeter-totters.

I can see from all of this how terribly neglected I was as a child. When I grew up in Winnipeg, the local teeter-totters were a set of slivery planks set on a fulcrum about four feet off the ground: heaven help you when your partner wickedly jumped off, leaving you to plummet about seven feet. The swings were on rusty chains that gave each of us about a hundred blood blisters, and the sheet-steel slides sent you at 60 miles an hour onto hard dirt packed with bottlecaps. As for the merry-go-round, it spun around inside a deep deposit of vomit, which had permeated the soil over several generations. It was a wonderful, terrifying place.

*continued*

My earliest memories of outdoor play in West Kildonan are ones of utter freedom. It was the 1950s, and there were mobs of kids—almost every house had several, and nobody seemed to care what we did or where we went. Some mothers actually locked their children outside for half a day at a time. We would prowl around construction sites, snitch crab apples from backyards, play what we called "guns" up and down whole blocks, root around in the trash along the back lanes, climb in Sullivans' maple until the old man chased us off, play hockey in the street and bumper-slide when cars came by, and clamber about on the huge steel storm sewer outflow into the Red River. I'm always puzzled when I hear people my age talk about how stifling childhood was in the 1950s. They must have grown up in a weird neighbourhood.

There were no fatalities among anyone I knew, though we had the usual tally of broken collarbones, chipped teeth, stitches, and black eyes. A few kids got in trouble with the police, and some went pretty wild. And yes, every so often there was a tragedy somewhere. But as the Tipton Park moms point out, all these things still happen anyway. So why screw up the playground?

Source: Byfield, Link. "What Children Need Even More than Safety Is a Little Self-Selected Danger." *Alberta Report* 19 June 1998.

## Assignment 2.3

You are a communications specialist with ReddiGrow Ltd., a biotechnology company specializing in developing new crop varieties. Prepare a summary of the article in Figure 2.15 for your boss, Charles Martin, Director of Marketing Communications.

### FIGURE 2.15

## PSST. GMOS ARE SCARY. PASS IT ON.

Europeans have been running scared for more than a year and a half from food tainted by genetic modification. Now, the fear appears to have crossed the ocean blue. Recent news reports have said a majority of Canadians is concerned about the safety of genetically modified (GM) food: "Consumers reject GM foods" (*The Ottawa Citizen,* Apr. 1) and "Canadians distrust the technology" (CBC Radio News, Apr. 3).

But are Canadians really so troubled? How do the media know Canadians are concerned? The polling firm Environics conducted a telephone survey for the Council of Canadians, an activist organization, arguing that three-quarters of Canadians worry about the safety of GM foods, based on a national extrapolation from this poll. As Jennifer Story of the Council put it, "People are talking about this, and they know more about it now."

One cannot easily substantiate Ms. Story's assertions, however, because there are problems with the Environics poll. The Council of Canadians carefully highlights the sample size (902 Canadians), the time period (Dec. 22 to Jan. 16) and the margin of error (+/- 3.3 percent) in the survey. The clincher, unreported in the media, was that the questions about GM food safety were only asked of respondents "somewhat or very familiar with" GM foods.

So how many Canadians are actually concerned about GM foods? Since the Council has yet to establish how many people were contacted in order to screen out this sample, nor the overall response rate, we have no clue. It could be that the 902 people were the most knowledgeable sub-set of a much larger

*continued*

sample. But it could also be that only a small number of the 902 were asked the detailed questions. With certainty, we know that 75 percent of the people Environics was able to contact who felt they knew about GM foods were concerned about them. But that is all we know.

Although public opinion surveying is a science, both methods and results can be manipulated to service certain ends. Given the overriding tendency of the media to turn the GM food issue into a scare story, perhaps all this poll indicates is that those who are learning about GM foods are not really getting the whole picture. Foods are being genetically modified for relatively sensible reasons, like to reduce pesticide usage or to prevent blindness by adding vitamin A to rice (a staple food in Asia). The esteemed National Academy of Science in the U.S. affirmed April 5 that there is no scientific evidence of harm from GM foods to either the environment or human health.

It did, however, note some potential reasons for concern. And concern, as opposed to fear, calls for appropriate oversight and evaluation of both negative and positive potentialities.

In a world of general public ignorance of true science, reporting claims of how many Canadians are frightened becomes a self-fulfilling prophecy—it has the effect of convincing others that they should also be frightened. It creates a peculiar echo chamber, where the public gets scared because they are informed that they are supposed to be scared. Fear by false peer pressure cannot substitute for science and fact. If such fear supplants good judgment, Canada and the rest of the world may well be deprived of the vast benefits genetically modified crops have to offer.

---

Source: Fienberg, Howard. "Psst. GMOs Are Scary. Pass It On." *National Post* 13 April 2000. Reprinted by permission of the author.

## Assignment 2.4

You are a member of a team developing an e-mail use policy for your company. You have decided to summarize the article in Figure 2.16 for use in a presentation to the team at its next meeting.

### FIGURE 2.16

## USER BEWARE: E-MAIL NOT AS PRIVATE AS YOU THINK

The next time you go through your e-mail routine—trashing the junk, answering the important stuff and forwarding the ones you want to share—stop and think about this for a moment. Your "personal" e-mail can be read by a lot more people than you think, and if you're not careful what you write, it could be used against you.

Most of us go about our e-mail business assuming that any correspondence is a private matter between the sender and receiver.

Someone sends you a cute little animation file via e-mail, you have a little chuckle, and send it off to some friends for their amusement.

Or you send an e-mail to a coworker or friend and carelessly describe your spouse or your boss as a "tyrant"—just as you might in a casual one-on-one conversation.

*continued*

No real harm done, you assume; it's not like anyone else is seeing this stuff, right?

Well, think again. The truth is, in most cases e-mail is anything but private.

If you're using an e-mail system at home, it's quite likely that any number of people working at your Internet service provider can easily open your mail files as they sit on the provider's computer.

It's dead simple for them to have a read and, if it's interesting enough, perhaps pass on a copy to a buddy. No doubt this can be an amusing pastime for the provider's lonely technical support guy who's waiting for the phone to ring while manning the help desk at 2 a.m.

If you're using the e-mail system at work, the situation is even worse. Not only can your employer's technical support people get into your e-mail files (as well as the boss's), but your employer actually has the right to do so, and to use it against you.

In fact, many companies are happily taking advantage of this, and routinely sniffing through their employees' e-mail. (In a number of cases, employees have been sacked after the employer discovered they were sending or receiving x-rated material via the company e-mail.)

As if all this controlled invasion of privacy wasn't bad enough, unprotected e-mail files can also be easily intercepted and hacked by all kinds of bad guys, as well as government snoops, as the messages travel through cyberspace between destinations.

In the United States, the National Security Agency reportedly does just that, with ongoing wide-scale scans of e-mail messages in search of certain key words that crooks or terrorists might use.

The same lack of privacy and security that applies to e-mail also applies to your Internet browsing. Logs of what Web sites you visit and what files you download are just as accessible as your e-mail.

Even if you have nothing to hide from the law, your spouse or your boss, you should feel a bit uneasy about having so many people having access to your words, your thoughts, and your deeds by tapping into your e-mail. Shades of Big Brother, indeed!

When you think about it, it's really not that much different from having your paper mail opened and read by someone at the post office, or having your phone tapped by the government, or having a camera filming your every move at the office, or having your employer bugging the tables in the staff cafeteria.

You'd probably raise quite a fuss if any of that happened, even if you had absolutely nothing to hide. Maybe it's time you thought about e-mail privacy in the same way.

Of course, unless you were the subject of a criminal investigation, the government or your employer would probably never even think of tapping your phone or bugging the water cooler. But for some strange reason, e-mail sniffing is widely accepted, and quite lawful.

How did this happen? Well, for the most part, there was nothing sinister or planned about it—it just happened. When e-mail systems were first set up, most technical and administrative people thought about functionality, but few gave much, if any, thought to privacy. The system was open to snooping by default.

Remember, too, that e-mail for the masses is still relatively new, and still evolving. Like most new technologies, e-mail has been adopted by people and companies without the administrators and users fully understanding how it will be used or, for that matter, misused. Systems are installed on company networks, staffers are told they've got their own e-mail, icons to launch the e-mail program suddenly appear on their desktops, and a sheet of basic instructions is handed out.

But there is no corporate policy, and no warning to users about privacy, or lack thereof.

And because governments take forever to get a handle on new technologies, there are still no laws covering e-mail usage, at least not in Canada. Nor, despite what you may think, is the right to privacy guaranteed in the *Charter of Rights and Freedoms*.

*continued*

You shouldn't expect governments and businesses to do much to change the situation, either, because both are only too happy to have the ability and the right to monitor your e-mail messages.

In the final analysis, though, the company that snoops on its employees and sniffs through their e-mail will eventually get burned. Sure, the employer may nab someone who's doing something he or she shouldn't be, but the downside is that staffers don't feel trusted and are nervous about what they write.

The smart company will respect its workers' rights and give them the privacy and trust that most of them deserve.

As far as legislation goes, the federal government has promised that data protection legislation for the private sector will be introduced before the turn of the century, but what the legislation will cover is unknown.

Clearly, if the situation is going to change, it's up to individuals, and groups who represent individuals, to speak up for the right to e-mail privacy.

If this is starting to bother you and you're concerned about e-mail privacy, here are some of the options you have in dealing with this:

- First and foremost, be very careful what you write. (Unless you know otherwise, assume that whatever you write is being read, and act accordingly.)
- Ask your service provider about its e-mail privacy policy: How secure is the e-mail server? How many of the ISP's staffers have access to the e-mail files? What policies (if any) are in place to keep them out of your e-mail? What's their policy if the police ask for access to the files? If the answers are unsatisfactory, you may want to bounce the same questions off other providers and choose the one that gives you the answers you want to hear.
- Review the e-mail policy at your workplace, if there is one. If the policy allows your company's tech support people, or your boss, to read your e-mail, you may want to challenge that policy.
- Explore whether you can have encryption built into your e-mail systems at home and at work. Encryption is a system for scrambling data so it can only be unscrambled and read by the person or persons for whom the data is intended. There are a number of encryption/decryption programs available, including some that are free, that can run in conjunction with your existing e-mail program. Of course, the recipient of your scrambled e-mail needs a compatible piece of software to unscramble the message on that end, but it's usually not difficult to set up. If you're looking for such a program, you may want to start with the popular and reliable PGP (Pretty Good Privacy), available via http://www.mcafeesecurity.com/us/about/partners/oem/mcafee_encryption.asp.
- Finally, you may want to send a letter (maybe even an e-mail) to your member of parliament, the prime minister, or justice minister, letting them know how you feel about the issue.

Source: Diener, Seymour. "User Beware: E-Mail Not as Private as You Think." *The Ottawa Citizen* 3 June 1998.

# Web References

### Writers' Workshop—Writing Summaries

http://www.english.uiuc.edu/cws/wworkshop/writer_resources/writing_tips/summaries.htm

This site is maintained by the University of Illinois at Urbana-Champaign and contains a short discussion of the need for and ways to produce summaries.

### The University of Victoria Writer's Guide

http://web.uvic.ca/wguide

This site is maintained by the University of Victoria and contains a detailed discussion about how to write summaries as well as useful grammar, spelling, usage, and logic guides.

### Avoiding Plagiarism

These sites at the University of Alberta and the University of Toronto offer excellent information explaining what plagiarism is, its consequences, and how to recognize and avoid it.

http://www.library.ualberta.ca/guides/plagiarism

http://www.utoronto.ca/writing/plagsep.html

http://www.ecf.utoronto.ca/%7Ewriting/handbook-plagiarism.html

# PART 2

## Internal Writing

# CHAPTER · 3 ·

# Accident and Incident Reports

## LEARNING OBJECTIVES

In this chapter, you will learn

- what the purposes of and the differences between accident and incident reports are;

- how to write accident and incident reports that are factual, objective, complete, relevant, and non-speculative;

- what the structure and content of accident and incident reports are;

- how to use Purpose and Focus Questions to organize, develop, and write accident and incident reports that meet your reader's needs and level of knowledge.

# PRELIMINARY *exercise*

You are the media relations officer for the Youth Services Bureau (YSB), a nongovernmental agency charged with helping troubled and street youth. At last week's staff meeting, the program director asked for ideas for programs that would attract the attention of the YSB's clients, many of whom seemed uninterested in the existing programs. After reading the Canadian Press article in Figure 3.1, you decide to suggest at the next staff meeting that YSB explore setting up an "on-the-job safety program" (many of its clients end up working as casual workers in factories and on construction sites). Although you will bring the article to the meeting, you decide to write a summary that will be attached to the meeting's agenda so that your colleagues will be familiar with the background of your suggestion.

## FIGURE 3.1

### YOUNG WORKERS MOST AT RISK FOR INJURY ON THE JOB, EXPERTS SAY

No one knows exactly what tripped the gear of the 10-tonne agricultural sprayer that lurched from its trailer to crush James MacMillan as he tried to unload the machine just two months ago. MacMillan, 24, an ambitious, well-liked agriculture student at the University of Guelph, was only a few weeks into a summer job at the Waterloo–Oxford Co-operative in Lynden, Ont., when he was killed by the sprayer. It was a death not unlike the many preventable accidents that are maiming and killing an alarming number of young workers across Canada.

On the country's factory floors and construction sites, 61,620 workers between the ages of 15 and 24 were injured and 57 killed on the job in 1998. Last year, 15 young workers lost their lives on Ontario job sites. Another nine were killed in the forests and factories of British Columbia.

"Young people are extremely vulnerable," said Maureen Shaw, president of the Industrial Accident Prevention Association. "Young people see themselves as invincible. They don't really think at that stage of their life about their longevity. They tend not to ask questions because they're scared to and they want to please their boss. If they ask questions or refuse to do something unsafe, they'll lose their job."

In the booming economy of the past few years, small companies without the financial resources or sophistication to provide health and safety training are hiring as never before and, with unemployment rates tumbling, they're turning to students to fill those jobs. At the same time, tuition rates are soaring and students who once travelled during the summer are now being forced to work to cover the rising cost of postsecondary education.

Already this year, several young workers have been killed and injured on the job in Ontario alone. A week ago, Matthew Crichton, 19, died of severe head injuries after becoming entangled in machinery while doing maintenance work at a wood-treatment plant in Shelburne, Ont., northwest of Toronto. In May, a 22-year-old man died on a construction site north of the city after being run over by an excavator.

*continued*

A 23-year-old man was crushed to death at the end of February when his clothes were caught in a piece of machinery at a metal-working plant in Smiths Falls, Ont. While Ontario's Ministry of Labour is still investigating MacMillan's accident, it immediately slapped six orders against the co-op for breaches of the province's occupational health and safety legislation.

Some provinces are coming to grips with the staggering numbers of young people being injured on the job. The new high-school curriculum in Ontario requires instruction about health and safety issues in various subjects. The workers' compensation boards in Ontario and British Columbia are both in the middle of splashy advertising campaigns to raise awareness about injuries and deaths among young workers. And Ontario's Labour Ministry has just opened an office dedicated to the workplace safety of young employees.

In Ontario courts, companies found in violation of health and safety laws are being fined an average of $51,869, more than double the fines charged four years ago. Last month, an Ontario judge sentenced a bakery owner in Oakville to a three-week jail term in the death of 18-year-old David Ellis, whose head was crushed while extracting cookie batter from a mixer last year.

The case, experts say, is a turning point in the battle to make the public aware of the dozens of young workers who die each year.

---

Source: Canadian Press Newswire 10 July 2000. *The Canadian Press.*

## QUESTIONS TO CONSIDER

Before summarizing the article, answer the following questions:

1. What is the article about?
2. Who is the article about?
3. Who is the intended reader?
4. How many workers were killed in industrial accidents?
5. How many young workers were killed in industrial accidents?
6. Is it necessary to quote Maureen Shaw's words directly?
7. How many "main points" does this article contain?
8. Is it necessary to list which province is doing what to educate young people about industrial safety?

# Introduction

This chapter deals with accident and incident reports. Accident reports detail injuries to people; incident reports detail damages to equipment or property.* These reports are, unfortunately, a necessary part of business writing, for in Canada there are tens of thousands of work-related accidents or accidents involving the public on business premises every year.

---

\* Although many employers have preprinted accident/incident report forms with checklists, small employers normally do not have such forms; every such form we have seen contains a section where the accident must be narrated. This chapter does not cover reporting motor vehicle accidents, because that is a species of police writing.

Even if an insurance claim is not being filed, most organizations require that accidents and incidents be reported to ensure that a record exists so that if you later claim disability due to an injury suffered at work, the facts are "on record."

Some accidents, like the Westray mining disaster of 1992 in which 26 miners died as a result of an explosion in the Plymouth, Nova Scotia, mine, are, of course, much too large to be the subject of a short report. After five years of work, the public inquiry that investigated that tragedy issued a report in several volumes on the condition of the mine prior to the explosion, the sequence of events that occurred, and the underlying causes of the disaster. Many if not most workplace accidents, however, are small enough in scope (slipping and falling at the office, colliding with the parking lot fence, being knocked on the head or shoulders by something that fell off the top of a bookcase) to be dealt with in a short memo.

An accident memo is a factual narrative that details how a person was injured, while an incident memo is one that tells of damage to equipment. These types of reports include only firsthand information, the kind that can "stand up in court." You'll find that Purpose and Focus Questions help in defining your readers and their knowledge of the place where the accident occurred, as well as in describing the event so that it is understandable to someone who did not witness it. In accident and incident reports, details, such as which side of the table you were walking around when you fell and which side of your head hit the floor, are important.

This chapter does not deal with completing insurance documents that are required by the organization's insurer.

# Editing Practice One

Stephanie Zowisky is a steam ironer at Modern Dry Cleaning. Using her accident memo (Figure 3.2) and the Questions to Consider on page 78, as guides, examine Muriel McDonald's accident memo in Figure 3.3. McDonald was injured during renovations to the offices of Big Burgers Inc., a chain of 100 fast-food restaurants in Eastern Canada.

**FIGURE 3.2**

ACCIDENT REPORT

 **Modern Dry Cleaning**

Memorandum

TO:      Julius Salerno, Foreman

FROM:    Stephanie Zowisky, Steam Ironer

DATE:    April 5, 2007

SUBJECT:   <u>Report Of An Accident In Which I Was Injured On April 4, 2007</u>

My left arm was burned on April 4, 2007, in an accident that occurred in the ironing room. I was taken to Eastland Hospital, where my arm was bandaged. I will not be able to iron for at least two weeks. I will be able to work the cash.

The accident occurred at approximately 1:25 p.m. while I was using the steam ironer. I was standing in front of the ironer when the shirt I was ironing fell off the platen.

I bent down toward my right to pick up the shirt. When I stood up, my left arm touched the top of the steam ironer, which I had forgotten to lift all the way up. As the top of the steam ironer burned my left arm from my elbow to near my wrist, I called for help.

William O'Connor, the shift manager, immediately came to my aid. He took me to the office and applied ice to the burn, which had begun to blister. After wrapping my left arm with gauze, he drove me to Eastland Hospital.

According to Dr. Alberta West, I have a third-degree burn. I will be on antibiotics for two weeks. My arm must be kept bandaged.

Dr. West said that I may return to work as long as I do not have to lift my left arm or do heavy work. Accordingly, I will not be able to use the steam ironer. I will, however, be able to work the cash.

*Stephanie Zowisky*

Stephanie Zowisky

**FIGURE 3.3**

## EDITING PRACTICE ONE: ACCIDENT MEMO

**A poorly written accident memo**

 **BIG BURGERS INC.**

Memorandum

TO:          David Lynx

FROM:     Muriel McDonald, Receptionist

DATE:       May 12, 2007

SUBJECT:  My Accident

As you already know, I was injured during the renovations to the reception area last Tuesday. My arm and shoulder were hurt and I won't be able to work for a few weeks.

The problem began when the telephone guys were stringing wires. Some of the wires were on the floor and when I got up to go to the bathroom, I stepped into some wire that was pulled by the guy in the next room. The wire caught my foot.

I tried to steady myself by pulling my foot but I couldn't. I began to fall and then I smashed to the floor. My shoulder hit the side of the reception desk which gave it a big bruise. I landed on my hand which I was sure broke my wrist. The telephone guys were really sorry I got hurt.

David ran to get ice for me and told Diane to put down what she was doing so she could take me to the hospital. I have a badly bruised shoulder and sprained hand. They said it would take about three weeks before I will be able to come back to work.

*Muriel McDonald*

Muriel McDonald

1. Is the subject line clear?
2. Does the memo relate a clear narrative?
3. Does the memo tell exactly when the accident occurred?
4. Does the memo indicate exactly where the injuries are?
5. Is the "David" referred to in the last paragraph David Lynx?
6. What does the pronoun "it" in the third sentence of the third paragraph ("My shoulder hit ...) refer to?
7. Is there any subjective language?
8. Does Ms. McDonald have firsthand information of all the events she relates in the memo?
9. In which direction did Ms. McDonald fall?
10. Who are David and Diane? Are they the "they" in the last paragraph?
11. What or who is the authority for Ms. McDonald's statement that she has a sprained wrist? Who told her? Should that person's name, presumably a doctor's, be mentioned?
12. Is it necessary to tell either her manager or the insurance company that the "telephone guys were real sorry"?
13. Is the memo free of grammatical, punctuation, spelling, and usage errors?

# The Process of Writing an Accident or Incident Report

Accident reports and incident reports are informative, factual narratives. Their purpose is not to tell how scared you were when you saw the delivery truck hit the loading dock or how much it hurt when you slipped, fell, and landed on your right hip. Nor is their purpose to propose changes to procedures or office structures that would prevent further accidents; this is the job of a subsequent proposal memo. The purpose of an accident or incident report is to

1. tell who or what was involved in the accident or incident;
2. explain whether a person was injured or any equipment damaged;
3. set the scene of where the accident/incident occurred;
4. provide a (factual) narrative of the accident/incident;
5. summarize the effects of the accident/incident (e.g., the time needed to recover from the accident or the cost of repairs to the truck).

Readers are interested only in statements that can be verified—the type of statements that would "stand up in court."

Accident and incident reports usually have financial and legal implications. Muriel McDonald will, for example, be on sick leave for three weeks. She will have to be replaced, and her case might end up at either Big Burgers' insurance company or workers' compensation. Likewise, a report that details how a printer was damaged while moving it to a new location would have to be filed with your company's insurer for your company to collect on its policy. Accordingly, claims adjusters, human resources personnel, indeed, even your manager, need to have "just the facts."

## ACCIDENT REPORTS ARE NOT FOR YOUR MANAGER ONLY

Accident reports are often read by persons outside of the organization, a fact that places special demands on the writer. If the only person to read your report was your manager, you would be able to rely on his or her knowledge of the layout of the office in which you slipped and sprained your back. The sentence "I fell while walking from my office to the main boardroom" would not, however, mean much to an insurance adjuster who has never been in your office. Just as a car accident report must indicate where the car was and in what direction it was going, accident and incident reports must include enough of the "setting" of the incident to ensure the subsequent description of events makes sense.

It might seem obvious, but a report that tells how you were injured when you tripped over a briefcase that was left on the right side of your desk must indicate that the briefcase was left on the right side of your desk *and* that you were walking around that side of the desk.

## THE "FACTS" OF AN ACCIDENT OR INCIDENT REPORT

Accident and incident reports narrate events that occurred over time (albeit a short period of time) and describe the accident or incident and any relevant subsequent events. The "facts" of interest include

- the location of the accident;
- a description of what happened from the moment before the event began until it ended;
- a time span that includes the aftermath.

Accident and incident reports must also explain the effects of the accident. Is the victim's left or right leg broken and how long will that person be off work and/or what equipment was damaged and how long will it be out of service?

Accident and incident reports must not contain subjective language. You might have been "frightened out of your wits" when you saw the truck heading for the loading dock, but your emotional state is unimportant in this context. You may have felt like she "smashed to the floor," but to a reader who is used to playing hockey, her fall might not be considered a "smash." The fact is that she *fell*.

Just as the report's facts do not include the writer's feelings about what happened, they do not include surmised information, however logical it might be. In the accident described in Figure 3.3, McDonald is probably right that the wire she stepped into "was pulled by the guy in the next room." But—and this is important—she could not know it as a "fact" that would be accepted in court, were her case to end up there. However, had this report been written by a witness who was walking down the hall and saw the wire McDonald was stepping into being pulled, that person could have said this because he or she would have had firsthand knowledge of it.

**Box 3.1** SUBJECTIVE WORDS AND PHRASES

## Writing Tip

Here are some subjective words and phrases to avoid:

- bled all over
- careened
- crashed
- crumpled to the floor
- dropped like a stone
- fell with a thud
- hurt like hell
- screamed
- smashed
- swelled like a ball
- swore
- yelled
- yelped

## BASIC STRUCTURE OF AN ACCIDENT OR INCIDENT REPORT

An accident or incident report is structured as follows:

- Introduction: summarizes the report (i.e., Who was injured? When? Where? What will happen to the injured person now?).
- Background: sets the stage for the event, explaining the layout of the location in which the accident or incident occurred and the events leading up to it.*
- Events: narrates the sequence of events that comprise the accident or incident.*
- Outcome: explains the ongoing ramifications of the accident or incident (e.g., expectations for recovery and time off from or restrictions at work, period machinery will be out of service, or need for replacement).

*The Background and Events sections must be in separate paragraphs.

## AN ACCIDENT REPORT WRITTEN BY THE INJURED PERSON

The accident report in Figure 3.4 was written by Paul Sarbanes, a trainer at Training Solutions, an information technology company, after he tripped and fell, breaking his right leg, while giving a training session in one of Training Solutions' classrooms.

## Purpose Questions

Before turning on his computer, Mr. Sarbanes wrote down and answered the three Purpose Questions (PQs) he had learned in college:

1. What is my goal?
   Explain how I broke my leg.
2. Who is going to read this accident report?
   Mr. Sullivan, my manager.
3. What does my reader already know about the topic/issue?
   He already knows I broke it tripping over the power cord to the computer projector.

## Focus Questions

Mr. Sarbanes turned next to the Focus Questions (FQs) for accident reports, which was available on Training Solutions' intranet:

1. Who is the victim of the accident?
2. Where did the accident occur?
3. At what time did it occur?
4. Where was the victim? What was the victim doing immediately before the accident?
5. What equipment did the accident involve?
6. Can the accident be broken down into discrete units?
7. What part of the body was injured? Condition?
8. Did the victim lose consciousness?
9. Was the victim able to move? If not, was the reason clearly visible?
10. Did the victim bleed?
11. Did anyone come to the victim's aid?
12. If the victim was seen by a health professional, how did the victim get to the hospital or clinic?
13. What is and who made the official diagnosis?
14. If the victim is an employee, how will the injury affect work? Will it require time off?
15. Will there be medical follow-up?

Satisfied with his answers to the questions in these two lists, Mr. Sarbanes wrote a first draft of the introductory and background paragraphs.

> I broke my ankle when I tripped and fell at 11:45 on 17 October 2006 while teaching. Since I will be in a cast for the next three weeks, I will not be able to teach, but I will be able to work in the office.
>
> My ankle was broken on Tuesday when I was in my classroom after I tripped over the cord of the projector that I was using to teach PowerPoint presentations. I tried to avoid it but didn't

and fell, smashing my leg first against a desk and then smashing to the floor, twisting it. I knew immediately that it was broken, and the student that helped me agreed.

Mr. Sarbanes stopped after these paragraphs to check his work against the PQs and FQs. *No need to tell Mr. Sullivan anything else about where the accident took place*, he thought. *He already knows about it and he knows where I teach*. But then, he remembered this accident report would be filed along with the workers' compensation report that he was going to write later that day, and whoever read that report would not know which room was his. *Better put in the room number*, he thought.

Then he noticed that nowhere in the first two paragraphs did he say which leg had been broken. When he found that he hadn't even put it in his answers to the FQs, he thought, *Better go back to square one*. He then produced the following revised list of FQs:

1. Who is the victim of the accident?
   Me, Paul Sarbanes.
2. Where did the accident occur?
   Room 231, the IT classroom.
3. At what time did it occur?
   11:45 a.m.
4. Where was the victim? What was the victim doing immediately before the accident?
   Stepping past the computer projector to answer a student's question.
5. What equipment did the accident involve?
   Power cord of computer projector.
6. Can the accident be broken down into discrete units?
   Tripped on cord and fell.
7. What part of the body was injured? Condition?
   Right leg. Could not move.
8. Did the victim lose consciousness?
   No.
9. Was the victim able to move? If not, was the reason clearly visible?
   The victim could not move right leg.
10. Did the victim bleed?
    No.
11. Did anyone come to the victim's aid?
    Mary Thomas, an RPN and student in class.
12. If the victim was seen by a health professional, how did the victim get to the hospital or clinic?
    Ms. Thomas drove me to Central Hospital.
13. What is and who made the official diagnosis?
    Broken leg. Dr. James.
14. If the victim is an employee, how will the injury affect work? Will it require time off?
    Can work, but can't teach.

15. Will there be medical follow-up?

  Cast will come off in three weeks.

## Purpose Statement

After looking at his answers to the PQs and FQs, Mr. Sarbanes turned to writing his purpose statement. "My purpose is to explain to Mr. Sullivan and anyone else who reads this memo for insurance reasons how I broke my right leg in an accident that occurred in Room 231."

Using this purpose statement and his revised list of answers to the PQs and FQs, Mr. Sarbanes wrote the memo in Figure 3.4.

As indicated through the explanatory notations in the margins of the memo, Paul Sarbanes did more than simply turn the answers to the PQs and FQs into sentences. He continually asked himself the following questions:

- Is this memo clear?
- Is there some further background that would help my reader understand the point being made?

## FIGURE 3.4

## ACCIDENT REPORT

**TRAINING SOLUTIONS** ——————————
*Helping you keep up with rapidly changing skills* ⌐

TO:        James Sullivan, Director of Computer Training

FROM:    Paul Sarbanes, Computer Trainer

DATE:     October 18, 2006

SUBJECT:  <u>Report Of An Accident In Which I Was Injured On October 17, 2006</u>

My right leg was broken on October 17, 2006, in an accident that occurred in training room 231. I was taken to Central Hospital, where my right leg was put in a cast. I will not be able to teach for three weeks but will be able to work in the office.

Sarbanes indicates
- who was injured;
- where the injury occurred;
- what the injury was;
- what the outcome will be.

The accident occurred at approximately 11:45 a.m. while I was teaching PowerPoint presentations. I was standing on the right side of the PowerPoint projector, which was in the middle of the room pointed toward the screen, when a student close to the door asked for my help.

Sarbanes begins the background with the time and a clear description of where he was just before the event happened.
*Note how this information appears in its own paragraph.*

*continued*

Sarbanes describes the event here. *Note the care with which directions and distances are indicated.*

As I walked around the back of the PowerPoint projector, my right leg became entangled in the power cord plugged into the outlet in the front of the class. I lost my balance and fell toward my right, further twisting my right leg. I landed on my right knee.

Immediately after I fell, Mary Thomas, one of my students, went to get some ice from the cafeteria. By the time she came back, five minutes later, my knee had become very swollen and I could barely put any weight on my right leg. Ms. Thomas helped me out of the room and took me to Central Hospital.

Sarbanes gives both the diagnosis and the authority for it.

According to Dr. L. James, the X-rays showed that my right leg had been broken. He found no damage to my knee other than a bruise.

I will be in a full leg cast for the next three weeks. Dr. James said that as long as I do not have to stand for long periods, I may return to work.

Sarbanes explains the ramifications of the accident for his employer: i.e., that he will not be able to teach but can work in the office.

*Paul Sarbanes*

Paul Sarbanes

Sarbanes is careful to include who Ms. Thomas is.

Sarbanes indicates the time it took for Ms. Thomas to return with the ice in order to tell how long it took for his knee to swell.

Sarbanes makes sure to record that he could not put much weight on his right leg.

Sarbanes tells how he was taken to Central Hospital.

## REPORTING ON AN ACCIDENT YOU WITNESSED

If someone who is not an employee is injured on your organization's premises, that person does not write the accident report. Typically, the report is written by the employee who witnessed the accident or, if no one witnessed it, by the employee who "finds" the injured person.

When writing this kind of accident report, be sure to indicate the source of your information. If you saw Mr. Littlefoot slip on the newly waxed floor in front of the video camera showcase, then you can write, "I saw Mr. Littlefoot's left foot slip out from under him on the newly waxed floor in front of the video camera showcase." If, on the other hand, you did not see him turn, step, and fall but, rather, heard him yell and fall, you cannot attribute the fall to the "newly waxed floor." In this case, you would write, "I heard Mr. Littlefoot yell and fall, and when I turned back toward the video camera showcase, I saw him lying on his left side grasping his left ankle." The third possible source of information is Mr. Littlefoot himself. If you decide to include in your report his explanation of what happened (which, of course, you must if he is found injured), you should make clear that it is he who is speaking (see example in Box 3.2).

## Box 3.2 EXPLAINING WHAT HAPPENED

| Poor | Better |
|---|---|
| Mr. Littlefoot was standing in front of the video camera showcase and did not notice that the floor was slippery because it had just been waxed. He fell to the floor, landing on his left arm, which immediately began throbbing and could not be moved. | According to Mr. Littlefoot, whom I found lying on his left side grasping his left ankle, he was standing in front of the video camera showcase and had not noticed that the floor was slippery. He said he slipped and fell when he stepped back from the showcase to walk to the poster display to his left. His ankle was swollen, and he said it was throbbing and he could not move it without severe pain. |

## AN INCIDENT REPORT INVOLVING DAMAGE TO EQUIPMENT

An incident report that details how equipment was damaged should indicate if the equipment can be repaired. Note that in Ms. Kurokachi's incident report (see Figure 3.5), she indicates the make and serial number of the damaged piece of equipment.

# Editing Practice Two

The accident report in Figure 3.6 was written by Laura Hitchen, a dental hygienist at A1 Dental Appointments, who was working on James Mallory's teeth when he was injured in an accident. Using the Questions to Consider on page 88, edit Ms. Hitchen's report.

## FIGURE 3.5

INCIDENT REPORT

### A Small Video Company
Filming, so others see your ideas

Memorandum

TO:      Eleanor Washington, President

FROM:    Kumi Kurokachi, Photographer

DATE:    June 5, 2007

SUBJECT: Incident That Damaged Sony Video Camera (#25148L)

*Kurokachi indicates what was damaged, where the incident took place, and the state of the equipment.*

On June 4, 2007, the Sony camera (#25148L) I was using was damaged beyond repair during the filming of the Music Universe commercial outside of the Music Haven Building (241 Laurier Avenue).

The incident occurred at approximately 12:30 p.m. I had positioned the camera on its tripod facing the Music Haven Building. Before calling for the sound check, I left the camera to perform one last light check with my hand-held light meter at the filming site.

*Kurokachi begins the background with the time and a clear description of where she was and where the equipment was just before the event happened.*

*Kurokachi describes the event here. Note the care with which directions and distances are indicated.*

A moment after I walked to the Music Haven window, a distance of 10 metres, one of the dogs that was to be in the commercial broke loose from its handler, David Marshall. The dog ran from the portable kennel, situated 10 metres to the west of where the camera was set up, and straight for the camera. The dog jumped, apparently to play with the shoulder strap, knocking the camera over.

The camera landed on the right side of the lens, bending the barrel and cracking the lens. The tripod was scratched but is otherwise undamaged.

*Kurokachi details how the event ended and the damage to each item.*

*Kurokachi explains both how she finished the filming assignment and the ramifications of the accident for her employer: i.e., that according to Mr. Gibson, the camera cannot be repaired.*

After filming the commercial with the spare camera, I took the damaged camera to Gibson's Camera Repair. Mr. Gibson said that it could not be repaired.

Equipment involved:
1 Sony digital camera, damaged beyond repair
1 tripod, scratched, but otherwise undamaged

*Kurokachi lists the equipment and gives a quick summary of its status.*

Kumi Kurokachi

FIGURE 3.6

## EDITING PRACTICE TWO: ACCIDENT REPORT

**A poorly written accident report**

A1 Dental Appointments _____

Memorandum

TO:        Mary Titelbaum, DDS

FROM:    Laura Hitchen, RDH

DATE:     April 9, 2007

SUBJECT:  Accident Involving James Mallory

James Mallory, a 10-year-old boy, hurt himself when he fell out of the examination chair and landed on his right shoulder.

The accident occurred at around 10:50 a.m. I had just finished cleaning James Mallory's teeth and had reached for a mirror on the instrument tray. After seeing that the mirror was scratched, I stood up and went to the drawer to get another one.

As I turned back to the examination chair, I heard James Mallory yell and saw him tumble out of the right side of the chair and smash to the ground with a great thump and in extreme pain. I rushed to him in a flash, and asked him if he could move his arm. He said he could but that it hurt. I called for the receptionist to get some ice and his mother, who was in the waiting room, and put it on Mallory's shoulder.

The pain went away in a few minutes. Mallory fell because he had been trying to look under the examination chair and lost his balance. He tipped over the armrest and smashed to the ground.

Mallory's mother took him to the clinic downstairs and phoned up to say that he had only a bruise.

The rest of his checkup appointment was rescheduled for next Tuesday at 3:00 p.m.

*Laura Hitchen*

Laura Hitchen

_____

## QUESTIONS TO CONSIDER

1. Is the subject line adequate?
2. Does the memo make clear where/when the accident occurred?
3. Does Ms. Hitchen use appropriate business language?
4. Does Ms. Hitchen have firsthand knowledge of how the accident occurred?
5. Does the memo contain any subjective language?
6. Is the phrase "in a few minutes" in paragraph four appropriate for an accident report?
7. Is the memo free of grammatical, punctuation, spelling, and usage errors?

# Editing Practice Three

The accident report in Figure 3.7 was written by David Smith, a maintenance worker in an office building who injured himself in a fall from a ladder while repairing a light fixture in the reception area of the Canadian Optical Fibre Association. Using the Questions to Consider on page 89, edit Mr. Smith's report.

**FIGURE 3.7**

EDITING PRACTICE THREE: ACCIDENT REPORT

**A poorly written accident report**

the **Collins Building**
Regina, Saskatchewan

Memorandum

TO:        Tom Dewitt, Manager, Building Services

FROM:    David Smith, Maintenance

DATE:     January 3, 2007

SUBJECT: My Accident

I was injured when I fell off the ladder I was standing on while fixing light fixture. I was taken to Mercy Hospital where I was diagnosed with a dislocated right shoulder. I will be unable to work for 3 weeks

The accident occurred at approximately 11:45 while I was repairing the wall light fixture above the corporate logo behind the reception desk of CCCTA, suite 1011.

I was standing on the middle rung of an aluminum ladder positioned in front of the logo. In order to remove the light fixture, I had to reach about three-quarters of a metre to my right. As I did this, the ladder began to sway. I tried to balance it by quickly throwing my weight to the left. The ladder then shoved off to the left and I fell to the right.

I landed extremely heavily on my right shoulder. I screamed very loudly in pain. I tried to get up but could not until Dawn McInnes, the secretary at CCCTA came to help me.

She drove me to St. Mary's Hospital where we were told that my shoulder was dislocated and that I will not be able to return to work for about three weeks.

David Smith

## QUESTIONS TO CONSIDER

1. Are the From and Subject lines correct?
2. Would this memo be clearer if Mr. Smith had included a diagram?
3. Does the memo include any subjective language?
4. Should the memo have indicated what happened to the ladder?
5. Can you tell from the memo what time the accident occurred?
6. What or who is the authority for the diagnosis? What error has Mr. Smith made that hampers the credibility of his report?
7. What is the authority for the time off work?
8. Is the memo free of grammatical, punctuation, spelling, and usage errors?

# Editing Practice Four

The accident report in Figure 3.8, which reports on Nicolas Marin's accident, was written by Anne-Marie Dubois, Assistant Greenhouse Director for Green Thumb Flower Nurseries, a company that supplies bedding plants and other gardening materials to stores across the Maritimes. Using the Questions to Consider on page 91, edit Ms. Dubois's report.

## FIGURE 3.8

EDITING PRACTICE FOUR: ACCIDENT REPORT

**A poorly written accident report**

Memorandum

TO:        David LaPierre, President

FROM:    Anne-Marie Dubois

DATE:     June 17, 2006

SUBJECT: Accident involving Nicolas Marin

On June 17 Nicolas Marin was injured in the greenhouse. I took him to Moncton General Hospital. He cut and bruised his head and right shoulder. He will be out of work for a week.

Nicolas's accident occurred right after the morning coffee break.

I found him on the floor next to the table with the pink roses when I came back from my coffee break. He was lying on the floor rubbing the side of his bloody head.

He fell when he came back from his coffee break. He had been walking down the aisle. He did not see that the hose that runs across the aisle—but is supposed to be in the floor holder—had somehow twisted its way out of the floor holder and was therefore looping up. He stepped into the loop and fell forward. Because he stepped into the loop with his right foot, he fell toward his right and hit his head on the table before falling forward and landing hard on his shoulder.

When I found him his face was covered in a blood and his shoulder hurt like hell.

I immediately ran to the First Aid station and got some cotton and gauze to clean Nick's head. He had trouble getting up because he had had a small concussion.

On the way to my car, we got some ice to place on his head.

I then took Nick to the hospital where he was seen by a nurse and Dr. Boudreau.

Instead of stitching Nick's cut, the Doctor used a new glue to close the wound. He tested him and said Nick had a slight concussion.

Nick will be out of work for a week.

---

## QUESTIONS TO CONSIDER

1. In the introduction, does Ms. Dubois indicate clearly which of Mr. Marin's shoulders was injured and which side of his head was cut?
2. Should Ms. Dubois use the phrase "rubbing the side of his bloody head"?
3. What is Ms. Dubois's authority for her narrative of the accident in paragraph four? (Hint: Did she see Mr. Marin fall?)
4. Is Ms. Dubois correct to state in paragraph six, "He had trouble getting up because he had had a small concussion"?
5. Should Ms. Dubois refer to the accident victim as Nick?
6. Should Ms. Dubois have placed the words "hurt like hell" in paragraph seven within quotation marks?
7. Should Ms. Dubois have written "Instead of stitching Nick's cut, the Doctor used a new glue to close the wound" in paragraph nine?
8. Who is Ms. Dubois?

# Summary

Accident reports narrate the events that led to the injury of a person and the outcome of the injury; incident reports narrate the events that led to the damage to equipment and whether or not the damage can be repaired. An event in which a person was injured and equipment damaged is usually reported in a single accident report.

While both reports are normally written to your manager, both have a secondary audience, such as your employer's insurance company and/or workers' compensation. Although your manager may know the layout of the office in which you were injured, it is unlikely that an insurance agent will. Accordingly, you must provide detailed information about where the accident occurred.

Both accident and incident reports are legal documents that contain "just the facts," meaning their writers must avoid using subjective language and must limit themselves to information of which they have firsthand knowledge.

An accident report must indicate where and how the injury occurred, what kind of first aid (if any) was administered, if (and how) the injured person was taken to a doctor or hospital, what the diagnosis and prognosis for recovery are, and who has performed the diagnosis and prognosis.

# Discussion Questions

1. Why are accident and incident reports written?
2. Why must accident and incident reports "stick to the facts"?
3. Should you use subjective language in an accident or incident report?
4. What is the structure of an accident or incident report?
5. How do you divide up the parts of the incident or accident?
6. Why is it important to remember that your reader may not know the setting in which the accident or incident occurred?
7. What is discussed in the part of an accident or incident report that deals with the aftermath?

# Writing Assignments

## Assignment 3.1

Assume the role of David Babad, coach of a municipal peewee hockey team. During a game, one of your players hit a slap shot that shattered the glass to the right of the visitors' net. No one was injured, but, of course, the game had to be suspended and rescheduled. Write the incident report to Katherine Bradbury, Facilities Manager.

## Assignment 3.2

Assume the role of Sandy Crosby, a computer technician with Install Computers. You were sent to install a new network hub at the head office of Pets Must Eat Too, which has stores across Canada. Installing the network hub required you to replace the optical cable that came out of the wall behind a table. As you were moving the table, you cut three fingers of your right hand on a jagged piece of aluminum that protruded from the metal frame of the table. Write an accident report to your manager, Ahmed Nanni.

## Assignment 3.3

Assume the role of Sergio Verdi, a gym teacher at Central High School. During a gym class, while you were demonstrating how to throw a free-throw shot in basketball, your back was turned to the other end of the court, where a game was being played. You heard a scream from a student. When you turned, you saw two students on the floor: one facedown and the other on his back clutching his right leg. You ran to the student who was facedown and found that, while dazed, he was otherwise unhurt. Then you checked on the other student, who could not put any weight on his leg, which had begun to swell.

Since you did not see the accident, you must interview the students involved and several other witnesses in order to write the accident report. Remember to tell the school's principal, Andrew Markham, what medical treatment was given to the students.

## Assignment 3.4

Assume the role of Benjamin Mercredi, a foreman at a large warehouse, who saw a stack of boxed tables fall over. No one was injured, but three tables were broken in the fall. Write the incident report to Zachary Klimt, the company's comptroller.

## Assignment 3.5

Write the incident or accident report for an incident or accident you have witnessed.

# Web References

## Report Writing Procedures

http://www.bcsra.com/topics/rep_wertz1112.html

This site is maintained by the British Columbia Soccer Referees Association and contains a useful article on the importance of and tips on writing accident reports.

# CHAPTER · 4 ·

# Instructional Memos

## LEARNING OBJECTIVES

In this chapter, you will learn

- why it is important to write clear instructions in business and in other organizations;

- what the structure and components of an instructional memo are;

- how to use Purpose and Focus Questions to organize, develop, and write an instructional memo that meets your reader's needs, level of knowledge, and experience;

- how to use different formats for an instructional memo;

- how to use visual aids to support an instructional memo.

# PRELIMINARY *exercise*

You are on a college field placement at Technological Safety Inc., an engineering firm that specializes in industrial safety. You have been assigned to work with the marketing department on a project to redesign the company's sales materials. Ann Bagley, the marketing director, has decided that the marketing kit should include a summary of the famous Gimli Glider episode. She hands you the article from *Soaring Magazine*, found in Figure 4.1. You read it and decide that while the second half of the article—how the pilots saved the plane—is interesting, it would not fit with the part of the brochure you are working on (which details the consequences of poor safety procedures). You mention this to Ms. Bagley, who thanks you for bringing this to her attention and then asks you to write a summary of the first part of the article.

## FIGURE 4.1

### THE GIMLI GLIDER

If a Boeing 767 runs out of fuel at 41,000 feet, what do you have? Answer: A 132-ton glider with a sink rate of over 2,000 fpm (feet per minute) and marginally enough hydraulic pressure to control the ailerons, elevator, and rudder. Put veteran pilots Bob Pearson and cool-as-a-cucumber Maurice Quintal in the cockpit and you've got the unbelievable but true story of Air Canada Flight 143, known ever since as the Gimli Glider.

Flight 143's problems began on the ground in Montreal. A computer known as the "Fuel Quantity Information System Processor" (FQIS) manages the entire 767 fuel loading process. The FQIS controls all of the fuel pumps and drives all the 767's fuel gauges. Little is left for the crew and refuellers to do but hook up the hoses and dial in the desired fuel load. But the FQIS was not working properly on Flight 143, later discovered to be due to a poorly soldered sensor.

A one-in-a-million sequence of mistakes by Air Canada technicians investigating the problem managed to defeat the redundancy built into the system. This left Aircraft #604 without working fuel gauges.

In order to make their flight from Montreal to Ottawa, and on to Edmonton, Flight 143's maintenance crew resorted to calculating the 767's fuel load using a procedure known as "dripping" the tanks. "Dripping" might be compared to calculating the amount of oil in a car based on the dipstick reading. Among other things, the specific gravity of jet fuel is needed to make the proper drip calculations.

The flight crew had never been trained how to perform the drip calculations. To be safe, they re-ran the numbers three times to be absolutely, positively sure the refuellers hadn't made any mistakes, each time using 1.77 pounds/litre as the specific gravity factor. This factor was written on the refuellers' slip and was used on all of the other planes in Air Canada's fleet. The factor the refuellers and the crew should have used on the brand new, all-metric 767 was .8 kg/litre of kerosene.

*continued*

After a brief hop, Flight 143 landed in Ottawa. To be completely safe, Pearson insisted on having the 767 re-dripped. The refuellers reported the plane as having 11,430 litres of fuel contained in the two wing tanks. Pearson and Quintal, again using the same incorrect factor used in Montreal, calculated they had 20,400 kilos of fuel on board. In fact, they left for Ottawa with only 9,144 kilos, roughly half what would be needed to reach Edmonton.

Lacking "real" fuel gauges, Quintal and Pearson manually keyed 20,400 into the 767's flight management computer. The flight management computer kept rough track of the amount of fuel remaining by subtracting the amount of fuel burned from the amount (they believed) they had started with. Their fate was now sealed.

According to Pearson, the crew and passengers had just finished dinner when the first warning light came on. Flight 143 was outbound over Red Lake, Ontario, at 41,000 feet and 469 knots at the time. The 767's "Engine Indicator and Crew Alerting System" (EICAS) beeped four times in quick succession, alerting them to a fuel pressure problem. "At that point," Pearson says, "we believed we had a failed fuel pump in the left wing, and switched it off. We also considered the possibility we were having some kind of a computer problem. Our flight management computer showed more than adequate fuel remaining for the duration of the flight. We'd made fuel checks at two waypoints and had no other indications of a fuel shortage." When a second fuel pressure warning light came on, Pearson felt it was too much of a coincidence and made a decision to divert to Winnipeg. Flight 143 requested an emergency clearance and began a gradual descent to 28,000. Says Pearson, "Circumstances then began to build fairly rapidly." The other left wing pressure gauge lit up, and the 767's left engine quickly flamed out. The crew next tried crossfeeding the tanks.

Pearson and Quintal immediately began making preparations for a one-engine landing. Then another fuel light lit up. Two minutes later, just as preparations were being completed, the EICAS issued a sharp bong—indicating the complete and total loss of both engines. Says Quintal, "It's a sound that Bob and I had never heard before. It's not in the simulator." After the "bong," things got quiet. Real quiet. Starved of fuel, both Pratt & Whitney engines had flamed out. Pearson's response, recorded on the cockpit voice recorder was "Oh ****."

At 1:21 GMT, the forty-million dollar, state-of-the-art Boeing 767 had become a 132-ton glider. The AU, designed to supply electrical and pneumatic power under emergency conditions, was no help because it ran off the same fuel tanks as the engines. Approaching 28,000 feet, the 767's "glass cockpit" went dark. Pilot Bob Pearson was left with a radio and standby instruments, noticeably lacking a vertical speed indicator—the glider pilot's instrument of choice. Hydraulic pressure was falling fast and the plane's controls were quickly becoming inoperative. But the engineers at Boeing had foreseen even this most unlikely of scenarios and provided one last failsafe—the RAT.

The RAT is the Ram Air Turbine, a propeller-driven hydraulic pump tucked under the belly of the 767. The RAT can supply just enough hydraulic pressure to move the control surfaces and enable a dead-stick landing. The loss of both engines caused the RAT to automatically drop into the airstream and begin supplying hydraulic pressure....

Source: Nelson, Wade H. "The Gimli Glider." *Soaring Magazine.* © Copyright WHN 1997. All rights reserved. Reprinted with permission from the author, Wade H. Nelson.

## QUESTIONS TO CONSIDER

Before summarizing the article, answer the following questions:

1. What is the article about?
2. Who is the article about?
3. Who is the intended reader?
4. What is the meaning of specialized terms such as "dripping"? Does it have to be included in the summary? Can specialized terms be simplified for the summary?
5. What are the major divisions of the text? Does every one merit inclusion in the summary?
6. Are there any direct quotes that need to be paraphrased?
7. Is it important for your reader to know that Captain Pearson and Copilot Quintal had neither heard of nor trained in the simulator for such an occurrence?
8. Is there any additional information you should include in your summary to help your reader understand the point of the news story?

# Introduction

This chapter deals with writing instructional memos or memos that give directions, sometimes called process memos. The subject of an instructional memo can vary from explaining how to complete the health insurance form that enrolls you in your company's plan to more technical topics such as how to use the photocopier to print double-sided reduced copies that are collated and stapled. A convention manager who writes directions on how to drive from the local airport to the convention site is also writing an instructional memo.

Everybody has heard of instructions that make no sense. The instruction to put "Tab A" into "Slot B," when no such slot can be found, is almost a cliché. The frustration generated by the instructions that accompany gas barbecues is a staple of comedy routines.

Although difficult to determine precisely, the annual cost to Canadian businesses of poor instructions (both in terms of malfunctioning equipment and time lost) is in the hundreds of millions of dollars. One badly explained programming sequence can bring down an entire network. Phones, which were once relatively easy to use, now come with instructional manuals that are thick and frequently poorly written.

Problems arise when the writer of the instructions fails to think through the process from the point-of-view of the reader/doer who is going to be following the steps. Authors of instructional memos often forget that their readers have little or no actual experience with the process in question. To write an effective instructional memo requires that from the start the author understand and take into account the intended reader's knowledge and experience (or lack thereof).

This chapter teaches you how to write a list form and a paragraph form instructional memo. You will learn how to use Purpose and Focus Questions to define your reader and the reader's knowledge of the process, as well as how to divide the process into steps that can be followed. You will learn why it is necessary to tell your reader what actions the device will perform on its own (e.g., a screen popping up) and when it is important to give your reader additional background information. As well, you will learn when to use visual aids to help orient your reader.

# Editing Practice One

David Bond is an IT technician at Western Canada College. Using his instructional memo (Figure 4.2) and the Questions to Consider on page 100 as guides, examine Nan's instructional memo in Figure 4.3. Nan is the Technical Support Coordinator at Ifoserve Inc.

## FIGURE 4.2

INSTRUCTIONAL MEMO

WESTERN CANADA COLLEGE

Memorandum

TO:      Employees of WCC

FROM:    David Bond, IT Technician

DATE:    June 13, 2007

SUBJECT: Accessing E-Mail Through The Internet

Starting Wednesday, July 6, all employees will be able to access their corporate e-mail accounts via the Internet. This memo explains how to access your e-mail.

Unless you delete your e-mail, e-mails read on the Net will automatically download to your office computer the next time it logs into your office e-mail; all e-mails sent via the Web interface will download to your office computer the next time it logs into your office e-mail.

You will use the same access name and PIN that you use on your office computer.

1. Go to WCC.ca.
2. Click on Mail, the icon on the upper right-hand corner of the college's home page.
3. The e-mail access screen will open.

*continued*

4. Enter your e-mail and PIN in the appropriate fields.
5. A screen named "Security Code" will open.
6. Enter the last three digits of your PIN and the first two letters of your last name.
7. The e-mail screen will open.
8. Click on the "Download" button on the upper left-hand corner of the screen.
9. The in-box will open.
10. You may now click on your e-mails to read them.

Contact me at ext. 6066 if you have any problems.

David Bond

---

**FIGURE 4.3**

EDITING PRACTICE ONE: INSTRUCTIONAL MEMO

**A poorly written instructional memo**

# IFOSERVE Inc.

Memorandum

TO:        Everybody

FROM:      Nan

DATE:      April 7

SUBJECT:   Updating the brand new Membership Database

As you know the Membership Database has been a pain for a long time. I'm writing to tell you that it's been fixed and now it's much easier to put information into it.

To input information all you have to do is

1. Log-in to the Membership Database, click on the icon that says Database.
2. Then click on the field that says Update.
3. A new window will pop up.

*continued*

4. In that window you can put the information you want.
5. The information should be saved by clicking on "Save" with your mouse.
6. Since the Database recognizes only whole words, don't use any abbreviations (Rd., etc.).

If you are updating the dues a member paid or how much we invoiced them, click on dues or invoice in the window instead of the address window after you click on Update in step 2.

# *Nan*

Nan

---

## QUESTIONS TO CONSIDER

1. Is this memo written in a professional tone?
2. Is the subject line effective?
3. Does the memo include information that is redundant for people who work with computers every day?
4. Does the memo include a contact number for further guidance?
5. Do the items follow in logical order?
6. Is the memo free from grammatical, punctuation, spelling, and usage errors?

# The Process of Writing an Instructional Memo

When you write an instructional memo, you should think of yourself as a teacher and of your reader as a student who is as unfamiliar with the task as you were when you learned how to multiply or how to type.

Teachers do two things to lead students to understanding. Firstly, they divide the process of learning into small steps, beginning with the information their students already know or skills they already possess. For example, grade-three teachers begin their explanation of multiplication by building on their students' ability to count by twos and fives. Similarly, in today's workplace, people do not need to be told what a mouse is, how to "click" on a link, or why insurance forms need to be signed. What they need to be told is what steps to follow to accomplish a specific task.

Secondly, teachers warn students about pitfalls. Your teachers did not have you memorize the "I before E except after C" rhyme because it is great poetry but because it warns of a common spelling fault. Instructional memos must include warnings about what not to do or what should be double-checked. The instructional materials used by the technicians responsible for the NASA Mars Climate Orbiter that crashed into Mars on September 23, 1999, did not warn them to be sure that everyone involved in the mission was using the same measurements. In the United States, both imperial (miles) and metric (kilometers) systems are used. The result was the fiery destruction of the Orbiter as it entered orbit at 57 km above the planet instead of the intended safe orbit of 140 km.

An instructional memo must be coherent; that is, it must deal with only one process, though that process can have several parts. A memo that explains how to use the new photocopier is coherent because it deals with one process. A memo that tries to explain both how to retrieve voice mail and how to deal with customer complaints on the phone is not coherent, even though both activities involve the phone.

## BASIC STRUCTURE OF THE INSTRUCTIONAL MEMO

The instructional memo consists of the following three parts:

- Introduction: explains what needs to be done and the reason for it.
- Steps: details the steps that must be followed (usually in a numbered list); when necessary, the description of a step should be accompanied by relevant background or other contextual information.
- Contact: indicates the name and phone number of the person in charge of the equipment or procedure that is being written about.

## A SAMPLE LIST FORM INSTRUCTIONAL MEMO

The memo in Figure 4.4 was written after Dawn Labelle, the account clerk at Media Relations, Inc., realized that the postage meter would have to be filled while she was on vacation so that a large mailing planned for June 5 could go ahead. Until last year, the postage meter was filled at the post office, so all she would have had to do was leave a cheque and a note telling her replacement to take the meter to the post office a day before the mailing. Now the meter is filled by Postage By Phone, a system similar to banking by phone.

Ms. Labelle reached for the Postage By Phone instructions manual and then stopped, remembering that the instructions for filling the postage meter were not in it. They had been given to her during the in-house training session.

### Purpose Questions

*I'd better write my replacement a memo saying how to use Postage By Phone*, she thought as she took out a piece of paper on which to start organizing her thoughts. Ms. Labelle began by asking herself the Purpose Questions (PQs) used to organize memos:

1. What is my goal?
2. Who is going to read this memo?
3. What does my reader already know about the topic/issue?

She answered the first question by writing, "My goal is to fill the postage meter," which made sense until she answered the second question: "My temporary replacement, Bill Baines."

*My goal can't be to fill the postage meter if it's going to be Bill Baines doing it*, she thought as she erased what she had written. After thinking for a moment, she wrote: "My goal is to explain to Bill Baines how to fill the postage meter."

Ms. Labelle now turned to the third question. She did not know Bill Baines. However, she knew that Jiffy Replacements would not send someone unfamiliar with the usual office equipment and systems—photocopiers, fax machines, computers, e-mail, voice mail, and postage meters. She would not have to explain how to follow phone prompts. What Mr. Baines would not know, of course, was what buttons to press on the meter and how to use the information he would get from Postage By Phone.

## Focus Questions

Once she had her goal and audience clearly in mind, Ms. Labelle asked herself the Focus Questions (FQs) for instructional memos:

- What steps must be followed to complete this process?
- Do any steps require additional background information?

She listed the following steps:

1. Go to the postage meter.
2. Press button "View/change reset info."
3. Press "Print account information."
4. Call the number on the report.
5. Enter 555616.
6. Follow the phone prompts.
7. Press "Enter reset number" (on the machine).
8. Enter the number given by the recording.
9. Confirm amount in postage meter.

Ms. Labelle reviewed the list, smiled to herself, and decided to omit telling Mr. Baines to go to the machine. She was less amused, however, when she realized that while this list was an accurate description of what she did, she had forgotten to list the effects of her actions and the steps performed by the postage machine or the electronic attendant at Postage By Phone, such as the issuing of a code number that refilled the meter. Between steps three and four, she inserted, "Postage machine prints report" and "Use the phone number printed on the report (step 3)." She read the list again and made a few other changes.

Her revised list of steps read:

1. Press button "View/change reset info."
2. Press "Print account information."
3. *Postage machine prints report.*
4. Call Postage By Phone using the *phone number printed on the report (step 3)*.
5. Enter 555616.

6. Follow the phone prompts to indicate that you want to charge the postage meter.
7. Press "Enter reset number" (on the machine).
8. Enter the number given by the recording.
9. Check to confirm amount in postage meter.
10. Examine reports to confirm postage in meter after filling.

## Purpose Statement

With these answers in mind, Ms. Labelle wrote the following purpose statement: "My purpose is to explain to Bill Baines what steps must be followed to fill the postage meter."

## Writing the First Paragraphs

Ms. Labelle turned next to writing the introductory paragraph of the memo in Figure 4.4. Knowing that memos are brief and to the point, she wrote a one-sentence introduction: "The following steps explain how to charge the postage meter." She thought for a moment and realized that, while there was nothing wrong with the sentence, it did not provide Baines, her reader, with background information. *Baines will probably notice that the postage meter is not empty and might think that because it is not empty, it is not necessary to fill it; but he doesn't know about the big mailing to go out on Tuesday. Better tell him that,* she thought.

Accordingly, Ms. Labelle deleted her first sentence and then wrote, "In order for the mailing scheduled for June 5 to go ahead (1000 pieces @ $.97/piece), the postage meter will have to be charged. This memo explains the steps you must follow to charge the meter, which is charged through the services of Postage By Phone."

As indicated by the explanatory inserts, Ms. Labelle did more than just turn the steps on the list into sentences. After each step she asked herself several questions:

- Is this clear?
- Is there some background that would help Bill Baines understand this step?
- Is there a visual aid that will help make things clear for him?

## How to Use Visual Aids

Instructional memos often include illustrations to help orient the reader. As with all visual aids, you must ask yourself, "Does this visual aid *reduce* my reader's confusion and/or help my reader's understanding?" The copy of the report printed by the postage machine that Ms. Labelle attached to her memo to Mr. Baines would be difficult to understand had she not highlighted the sections where Mr. Baines would find the information he needs, such as how much postage is in the postage meter.

Ms. Labelle considered including photocopies of the screens referred to in steps 2 and 3. However, she decided against it, because she assumed that Mr. Baines would be familiar with similar keypads (where each key's function changes as indicated by arrows on the screen).

FIGURE 4.4

LIST FORM INSTRUCTIONAL MEMO

## Media Relations, Inc.
MEMORANDUM

TO:     Bill Baines, Replacement Clerk

FROM:   Dawn Labelle, Account Clerk

DATE:   May 28, 2007

SUBJECT: Filling Up The Postage Meter For Mailing On June 5, 2007

In order for the mailing scheduled for July 5 to go ahead (1000 pieces @ $.97/piece), the postage meter will have to be charged. This memo explains the steps you must follow to charge the meter, which is charged through the services of Postage By Phone.

> Although not part of the process Baines must follow, Labelle includes this information because it sets a context for him.

1. Record the amount of postage registering in the upper right-hand corner of the display screen on the postage meter.
2. Press the button that points to the line on the screen that says "View/change reset information."
3. A new screen will come up.
4. Press the button that points to "Print account information."
5. The meter will then print a report (see Attachment A).
6. Call the phone number printed on the report (1-800-368-5112); be ready to record the reset code number Postage By Phone will issue at the end of this call.

> Labelle includes this information to prepare Baines for Step 8.

7. The phone prompts will ask you to key in:
   a) Media Relations' account number: 555616;
   b) the meter's number: 78945952;
   c) the reset request code indicated on the report you printed; see Attachment A to locate the reset request code;
   d) the amount of money ($1,500) to be deposited into the postage meter (the mailing will cost $970; Media Relations' policy is to maintain at least $500 in the meter at all times).

> Labelle tells Baines this so he will know not to alter the amount of money to be programmed into the meter.

8. Record the reset number issued by Postage By Phone.
9. Press the button that points to "Screen" two times.
10. Press the button that points to "Enter reset number."
11. Key in the reset code issued by Postage By Phone.
12. Repeat steps 2, 3, and 4.

> Labelle adds these steps when she realizes that Baines would not know how to double-check the settings.

13. Compare the amount of postage indicated on the first and second reports. The second should be $1,500 more than the first. If it is not, alert Isham Taylor.

*continued*

14. File the two reports in the Postage By Phone file in the top drawer of the filing cabinet marked Administration.

Contact Isham Taylor at ext. 5845 if you have any difficulties.

*Dawn Labelle*

Dawn Labelle

---

**Attachment A:**

```
METER RESET INFORMATION
Media Relations, Inc.
454 Albert Street
Ottawa, ON
```

| Configuration Item | Value |
|---|---|
| Ascending Register | 978947.897 |
| Descending Register | 21343.980 |
| Control Sum | 8843994.980 |
| Piece Count | 108974 |
| Postage By Phone Phone Number | 1-800-368-5112 |
| PBP Reset Request Code | 007 |
| PBP Centre Balance Request Code | 898 |
| PBP Centre Account Number | 89898454 |
| Meter Serial Number | 78945952 |
| Access | 11858674 |
| Reset | $2,000.00 |

Labelle highlights important information for Baines.

---

## PARAGRAPH FORM INSTRUCTIONAL MEMO

Instructions are normally written as numbered lists. If you have to supply a great deal of background or ancillary information, however, it is usually better to write the memo in paragraph form. You should always start by preparing a list as Ms. Labelle did.

### A Sample Instructional Memo

The memo in Figure 4.5 was written by Lee Tan, the events coordinator for the Centre for Excellence in Communications, to David Kowalchuk, President of Polling International, Inc., who is scheduled to drive to CEC after flying into Ottawa from Calgary.

After answering the Purpose and Focus Questions, Ms. Tan wrote the following purpose statement: "My purpose is to explain to Mr. David Kowalchuk how to drive from Ottawa International Airport to CEC." However, Ms. Tan could reasonably assume that, unlike Ms. Labelle's audience, Mr. Kowalchuk is not familiar with either the route from the airport to CEC or the landmarks he would pass. Therefore, she knew she would have to write in paragraph form so that she could provide background information as necessary.

### Time and Sequence in the Sample Instructional Memo

Because Lee Tan's memo gives driving directions, she signals the transitions and sequence by the words *turn, continue,* and *when you can see....* Obviously, such transitions do not apply to most office procedures, which tend to be more concerned with time than movement through space. Accordingly, paragraph form instructional memos usually signal transitions via words such as *before, after, next, then, first, second, third,* and *finally.* If your paragraph contains more than two such transitions, it loses coherence and becomes confusing for your reader (who, you must always remember, is not familiar with the process you are describing). You can fix this by dividing a larger paragraph into smaller coherent paragraphs as shown in Box 4.1. Note how the shorter paragraphs allow the writer to include more background information without overloading the reader.

---

## FIGURE 4.5

### PARAGRAPH FORM INSTRUCTIONAL MEMO

 *Centre for Excellence in Communications (CEC)*

Memorandum

TO:      David Kowalchuk, President, Polling International, Inc.

FROM:   Lee Tan, Events Coordinator (CEC)

DATE:    May 18, 2007

SUBJECT: Directions From Ottawa International Airport To CEC

Tan tells Kowalchuk this so that he knows she sent him the most up-to-date information available to her.

Travelling time between Ottawa International Airport and the Centre for Excellence in Communications at 456 Preston Street West is normally 45 minutes. Construction at the airport and major roadwork in the city may increase travelling time by as much as 20 minutes. To ensure the directions below are still current, I checked them with both the airport and the City of Ottawa Roads Department.

*continued*

After picking up your rental car from Cheap but Good Rentals, exit from Gate 2 and turn right onto Service Road; you will be going west. Continue for approximately 1 km, at which point Service Road enters the toll booth plaza of the Day Parking Lot.

Stay on your right and drive through the Auto-Pay kiosk; your rental car is equipped with an automatic counter. You will now be on Airport Parkway.

Continue on Airport Parkway for 15 km, passing the exits for Hunt Club and Walkley Roads. Exit at Riverside Drive.

The Riverside Drive exit can be confusing. As indicated on the attached diagram, the Riverside Drive exit merges with Data Road (the exit from the office building off to your right), which then divides. Stay to the right and then make your first right so that you are going downhill toward your right. (If you go straight, you will enter the merge lane for the Bronson Avenue Bridge.)

Continue down Riverside Drive to Bank Street. Before arriving at Bank Street, Riverside Drive passes several ball fields and the Billings Bridge Shopping Centre. When you see the Billings Bridge Shopping Centre on your right, move into the left lane, which becomes the turning lane onto Bank Street.

Turn left onto Bank Street; you will be heading north. Continue for 10 km, until you reach Preston Street. Bank Street passes over the Rideau Canal, passes Landsdown Football Stadium and goes under the Queensway (Ottawa's main expressway) before you reach Preston Street, which is four traffic lights after the Queensway underpass.

Turn right onto Preston Street; you will be heading east. The Centre for Excellence in Communications, which will be on your right, is one block farther, at 456 Preston Street West.

Parking is available in the lot across the street.

If you have any difficulties, you can reach me on my cell phone: (613) 566-1234.

*Lee Tan*

Lee Tan

---

Tan includes the direction so that Kowalchuk will be able to orient himself to exits that may indicate north, south, east, or west.

Tan tells Kowalchuk that the road becomes the toll plaza so that he does not think his directions have missed a step.

Tan warns Kowalchuk here.

Tan refers Kowalchuk to the enclosed map to help him understand how the road merges.

Tan provides Kowalchuk with her cell phone number so that she can be reached no matter where she is while he is driving.

## Box 4.1 NARRATING EVENTS OVER TIME

### Writing Tip

The following paragraphs come from a memo that explains how to use three-part cheque-printing forms.

**Poor**

Once the cheques have been printed, separate them. Then attach each one to the correct invoice with a paper clip and send to the VP for signature. When the cheques are returned with signature, remove the pink and yellow copies. Then, attach the signed cheque to the part of the invoice to be returned. After you have mailed the cheque and the invoice, staple the yellow copy of the cheque to the other part of the invoice and file it alphabetically by vendor name in the vendor file. Finally, file the pink copy by cheque number in ascending order in the cheque copy file.

**Better**

After the cheques have been printed, separate them. Attach each cheque to the correct invoice and send them to the vice president for signature.

When the signed cheques have been returned, separate the pink and yellow copies. Attach the signed cheque to the part of the invoice to be returned and mail them.

The pink and yellow copies form part of Davis Engineering's permanent record. Staple the yellow copy to the remaining part of the invoice and file alphabetically in the vendor file. File the pink copy in ascending order in the cheque copy file.

# Editing Practice Two

The memo in Figure 4.6 was written by Steve Gibbons, the manager of We Are Parts, Inc., a nationwide chain of appliance parts stores. Using the Questions to Consider below, edit Mr. Gibbons's memo.

### QUESTIONS TO CONSIDER

1. Is the subject line clear and correct?
2. Is the introductory paragraph as focused as possible?
3. Does Mr. Gibbons include information that is redundant for his audience?
4. Are all the instructions clear?
5. Does Mr. Gibbons always follow the conventions of list form instructional memos?
6. Is the use of capital letters in step 10 effective?
7. Would a visual aid have been useful?
8. Is the memo free of grammatical, punctuation, spelling, and usage errors?

**FIGURE 4.6**

## EDITING PRACTICE TWO: LIST FORM INSTRUCTIONAL MEMO

**A poorly written instructional memo**

# We Are Parts, Inc.

Memorandum

TO:        All Salesmen

FROM:    Steve

DATE:     Monday, May 21, 2007

SUBJECT:  The way to use the new database to find and order parts

As you know as of August 1, 2007, we will be switching over from the Blue binder Parts Order books to the computer system. Although you have had training in using the computer system, I'm writing this short memo to remind you how to use the system.

1. Turn your terminal on by flicking the switch on the right-hand side of it.
2. Use the keyboard to type in your password.
3. You will then see a green screen with several options.
4. Move the mouse so it is over the blue square that says Appliance Parts. Click on the button on the left side of the mouse.
5. Locate the type of appliance on the list and click on it two times.
6. Next, you should see a screen with the type of appliance on top, a box with a blinking line, and a list of appliance numbers underneath.
7. You can either type the model number in the box with the blinking line or you can find the model number on the list and then click twice. If you typed in the number, you have to hit enter.
8. Use the mouse to move the arrow over the part of the appliance that the part you have been given by the customer comes from. Then click on it.
9. The screen will then split. The left hand will be a list of parts, prices, and availability. The right will show an exploded view of the part of the appliance.
10. To order a part, put the arrow over it and click, THIS TIME USING THE RIGHT MOUSE BUTTON.
11. You will then see a screen that looks like the order forms we have been using. Simply fill it out as you would have previously.
12. If you have to order more than one part, you must click on More Than One Order at the bottom of the right-hand side of the screen of the left-hand side of the screen that showed the parts, prices, and availability.

If I can be of any assistance, call me at 7854

*Steve*

Steve

# Editing Practice Three

The memo in Figure 4.7 was written by Mary Hodgins, Assistant to the President of Davis Marketing, Inc., which has recently entered into a strategic alliance with Products Development, Inc., a product development and venture capital firm. Using the Questions to Consider on page 113, edit Ms. Hodgins's memo.

## FIGURE 4.7

### EDITING PRACTICE THREE: PARAGRAPH FORM INSTRUCTIONAL MEMO

**A poorly written instructional memo**

## Davis Marketing, Inc.

Memorandum

TO:     All Managers

FROM:   Mary Hodgins, Assistant to the President

DATE:   28 April 2007

SUBJECT:  Procedures to follow for meetings (Agendas and Minutes)

Our recent strategic alliance with Products Development, Inc. has resulted in the need to formalize some of our procedures that up to now have been informal. I have been asked to ensure that all managers who call chair joint committees or working groups follow the same procedures for setting agendas, holding meetings, and reporting on them.

The agenda for your meetings should be set a week before the meeting is to be held. Two weeks before the date of the scheduled meeting, you should e-mail all of the participants to see if they have any items.

As you can see from the attached sample agenda, meetings are divided into two parts: Action Items and Discussion Items. Participants should indicate to you under which heading any issue they bring up should go.

Meetings should end at the time indicated on the announced agenda. Any items not covered by the announced end of the meeting must be carried over until the next meeting. It is possible for the committee to vote itself extra time for discussions.

*continued*

The Meeting Minutes are now to be reported by the secretary following the format shown in Attachment B. The secretary is named on the Agenda, see Attachment A. Make sure that the secretary knows that the minutes must record who is responsible for any actions that are to be taken. This is done in the format indicated in Attachment B.

Meeting Minutes can be sent to all participants for their comments before being finalized and submitted to the divisional director.

Mary

---

Attachment A: Sample Agenda

To: Members, Strategic Alliance Review Committee (SARC)

The regular monthly meeting of the SARC will be held in the small board-room of Products Development, Inc. at 11 a.m. on Friday, 11 May 2007. Following is the agenda:

**Action Items:**
- Completion of marketing strategic plan (S. Greene, Davis Marketing)
- Definition of shared cost arrangements (L. Banderas, Products Development, V. Callan, Davis Marketing)
- Linkage of intranets (M. Lemon, Davis Marketing)

**Discussion Items:**
- Feasibility of joint training (J. Piero, Davis Marketing)
- Opportunity for Internet-based marketing (S. Greene, Davis Marketing)
- Sales commission structures (A. Alvarez, Consultant, Alvarez Financial)
- Social activities (N. Brandon, Products Development)

Secretary: J. Kay
Manager's Signature

---

Name:
Title:
Date:

---

*continued*

**Strategic Alliance Review Committee**
(Davis Marketing, Inc. and Products Development, Inc.)

**Minutes of Meeting**
Friday, 11 May 2007, 11 a.m.

Present:
L. Banderas (Products Development)
N. Brandon (Products Development)
V. Callan (Davis Marketing)
V. Duer (Products Development)
S. Greene (Davis Marketing)
M. Lemon (Davis Marketing)
J. Piero (Davis Marketing)
T. Marchant (Products Development)
R. Littlefoot (Davis Marketing)
M. Said (Products Development)
O. Tadkov (Computing Solutions), invited guest

Regrets:
J. Tompson (Products Development)

**Minutes**
Action Items

1. **Report of study of computer software compatibility**

   The SARC approved the report of Computing Solutions (O. Tadkov), which determined that with minimal alterations the computer systems of Davis Marketing and Products

   R. Littlefoot

   M. Said

   Development can be made compatible.

2. **Establishment of expenditure authority of joint projects**

   The SARC began implementation of the directive on joint expenditure authority signed by the joint financial officer.
   Expenditures of over $5,000.00 will

   S. Greene

   *continued*

require signatures of financial officers
of both Davis Marketing, Inc. and
Products Development, Inc.

**Discussion Items:**

1.  Report on the technical implications    J. Piero
    of establishing a joint website.         V. Duer

2.  Procedures to be used to ensure that    L. Banderas
    staff of both companies are kept
    up-to-date on projects being undertaken
    by the strategic alliance.

3.  Proposed agenda for staff retreat.      M. Lemon

Signature of Secretary

J. Kay

---

## QUESTIONS TO CONSIDER

1. Is the subject line clear?
2. Does the introduction clearly state what the memo is about?
3. Is the meaning of a term such as "Action Items" clear?
4. Does the memo make clear which attachment is which?
5. Is the memo free of grammatical, punctuation, spelling, and usage errors?

# Editing Practice Four

The instructional memo in Figure 4.8 was written by Donna Bartholomew, Assistant to the Vice President (Internal) of the Canadian Public Employees' Association. The memo explains new elections procedures that the association's stewards are to follow. Using the Questions to Consider on page 115, edit Ms. Bartholomew's instructional memo.

**FIGURE 4.8**

## Editing Practice Four: Paragraph Form Instructional Memo

### A poorly written instructional memo

Memorandum

TO:        Chief Stewards

FROM:    Donna Bartholomew, Assistant to the Vice President (Internal)

DATE:     7 March 2007

SUBJECT:  <u>New Elections Procedures that Must Be Followed</u>

As you know, beginning with the elections that are to be held for officers taking office in September, you must follow the new elections procedures that are designed to ensure that the elections we hold are easier to run and run more smoothly. The procedures explained here are those that you must follow.

Begin the elections by e-mailing your members informing them that elections are going to be held one month after you send the e-mail. Include in the e-mail the nomination form as an attachment. Tell your members that they must send back the nomination form within one week.

Once you have received the nomination forms, e-mail your members with a list of nominees and the date for the General Meeting at which each nominee will present his or her platform to the membership. This meeting must be held at least one week before the election.

Under the new rules there are two ways your members can vote. The first is at the old style vote box stations that you have to set up on election day. The second is online. To vote online, your members will have to sign on to their CPEAforMe account and then click on Local Elections 2007; we will have put an electronic election form on the secure part of the site for your members to use (to ensure this, make sure you send the nominations list to us as soon as you can after you draw up the list).

*continued*

Because there are two ways to vote, there will be two sets of tabulating votes. The first—from the vote boxes—will proceed as it has in the past. In other words, you will, in the presence of three scrutineers, count the ballots. Once you have completed the counting, sign on to the CPEAforMe site and click on the Scrutineers section. You will see the online tabulation.

Add the two sets of numbers together and you will have your election results. Enter those results in the "Results" field and our office will certify the winners.

---

## QUESTIONS TO CONSIDER

1. Is the subject line clear?
2. Is the introduction clear and concise?
3. Is the first sentence of the second paragraph, "Begin the elections by e-mailing your members informing them that elections are going to be held one month after you send the e-mail," clear?
4. Should paragraph four be divided into two?
5. Is it proper for Ms. Bartholomew to use the phrase "old style vote box stations"?
6. Is the instruction to the stewards that they must forward the nominees' names to Ms. Bartholomew's office (so the online voting can be arranged) in the correct paragraph?
7. Are there other wordy and unclear paragraphs?
8. Is the memo free of grammatical, spelling, punctuation, and usage errors?

# Summary

Instructional memos are routine business documents that are used to explain everything from how to fill in an insurance form to how to drive from a particular hotel to a conference centre.

When you write an instructional memo, you take on the role of a teacher and your readers become your students. They do not know what you already know. Accordingly, you must divide the process into discrete units and, when necessary, provide background information and/or reasons. When writing instructions for computer devices, be sure to include all actions (such as a screen popping up) that will occur; if there is usually a time delay, include that information as well.

Instructions are usually written in list form; however, directions are often written in short paragraphs when background information is needed. Visual aids are included when necessary (e.g., computer screen information).

# Discussion Questions

1. Why are clear instructions important to an organization?
2. What is the process of writing an instructional memo?
3. How do you use the PQs and FQs to tailor your instructional message to your reader?
4. How do you use the PQs and FQs to ensure that your message meets your reader's needs?
5. How do you divide a process into its component parts?
6. How can editing improve an instructional memo?

# Writing Assignments

## Assignment 4.1

You are the office manager for Grovel, Benjamin and Laff, a legal firm with 75 lawyers, legal secretaries, and other staff. Next Monday, the new phone system will be in use. Although the plans were for everyone to have training, many of the lawyers, especially the senior partners, were too busy to attend the sessions. Nor have most of them come to you to receive their new Personal Identification Numbers (PINs). In order to avoid a disaster on Monday morning, you have decided to prepare a memo addressed to each staff member informing each of his or her PIN, how to access voice mail, and how to record greetings. Write the instructional memo in list form.

## Assignment 4.2

You are the events coordinator for WOW, Inc., a company specializing in off-site strategic planning sessions that has been retained by a large accounting firm to plan a weekend session at a secluded country resort 100 km from your city. You have reserved all the hotel and conference rooms, arranged for breakfast, lunch, dinner, and between-session refreshments, as well as for the evening entertainment.

All that remains is to make sure that the 45 participants arrive on time, which should not be a problem since each participant was given a map in the retreat kit. To be on the safe side, however, you call the Ministry of Transportation to check that the route indicated on the map provided by the resort will not be disrupted by roadwork. You discover that the roads indicated on the map will, in fact, be closed for resurfacing; the ministry suggests an alternative route and answers your questions about landmarks on the secondary roads.

After hanging up the phone, you turn to composing the memo, explaining how to get from WOW's downtown office to the resort. Since, for part of the time, the staff will not be on the primary roads, you must include landmarks that will assure nervous drivers that they have not gotten lost in the country. Include a map with your paragraph form instructional memo.

## Assignment 4.3

Donald Davies, President of Effective Media Relations (EMR), has seen his company grow from 15 to 140 employees over the past two years. Now, he, his two vice presidents, and four directors routinely authorize contracts for goods and services such as printing, translating, and design. Nguyen Tran, EMR's accountant, has just left a meeting with Mr. Davies in which he agreed that with so many people letting contracts, the old reporting system was breaking down. In order to ensure that Mr. Tran would be able to manage the budget and properly code and process incoming invoices, Mr. Davies agreed that all contracts over $1,000.00 be processed through Mr. Tran's office and that all contracts provide Mr. Tran with the information he needs to do his job. Mr. Davies instructed Mr. Tran to establish the new procedures and send out the memo explaining them under his own signature.

Take the role of Mr. Tran and write a memo in which you explain the reason for instituting the new procedure, the date the new procedure comes into effect, and the kind of information you require to process new contracts. The information you need includes:

1. type of goods or services;
2. term of contract;
3. compensation/cost;
4. termination date;
5. other special terms (e.g., will EMR be providing facilities and equipment?).

As well, the memo must make clear that all new contracts must be initialled by you.

## Assignment 4.4

You are the new network manager for Milton Plumbing Supply and Repair Service, which employees 50 plumbers. Next week, the new inventory supply program will be in place. Although the plumbers and salespersons have had a half-day training session on the new system, you have been asked to write a memo instructing them on how to access the program, search for items, make special requests, and submit online orders (each plumber's truck is now equipped with a wireless link to the company's website). Include visual aids with your memo.

## Assignment 4.5

You are working in your school's student services department. The school has recently installed a new computer system that will allow students to check their grades online. Write an instructional e-mail to the students telling them how to check their grades online.

# Web References

### Writing a Procedure That the Reader Can Follow

 http://www.mapnp.org/library/writing/procproc.htm

This site is maintained by the Free Management Library in Minneapolis and contains an excellent step-by-step guide to writing instructions.

### Online Technical Writing: Instructions

 http://www.io.com/~hcexres/tcm1603/acchtml/instrux.html

This site is maintained by Austin Community College and contains useful information about how to write instructions.

# CHAPTER • 5 •

# Convention and Training Reports

## LEARNING OBJECTIVES

In this chapter, you will learn

- what the purposes of convention and training reports are and their importance to organizations and managers;

- how to distinguish the components and structure of convention and training reports;

- how to write convention and training reports that relate the facts objectively and present the writer's professional judgment about the usefulness of the convention or training session concerned;

- how to use Purpose and Focus Questions to organize, develop, and write convention and training reports that meet your reader's needs and level of knowledge.

# PRELIMINARY *exercise*

As a researcher for the Canadian Labour Conference (CLC), your work includes updating the files on proposed construction projects (which, of course, will generate jobs for the CLC's members). In addition to clipping articles, you must summarize the most important ones and e-mail these to other interested CLC staff. Your automatic Internet search program has found the article in Figure 5.1 from *Business First of Buffalo*, published in Buffalo, New York, which you must now summarize.

## FIGURE 5.1

### ONTARIO MAKES PITCH FOR CONVENTION CENTER

Niagara Falls, Ontario, is making a push to be ground zero for the convention market. Niagara Falls leaders, including Mayor Wayne Thomson and Tony Zappitelli, owner of the Sheraton Fallsview hotel, are leading an effort to construct a 125,000-square-foot convention center.

"Call me optimistic, but I'd like to see it open within the next three or four years," Thomson said. Despite its popularity as a tourist destination, Niagara Falls has never capitalized on the fast growing convention business. Conventions are considered key economic development generators for most communities. "Niagara Falls, Ontario, is not on any meeting planner's radar screen because we don't have the facility," Zappitelli said. "As a hotel operator, I know we need more than just the leisure market to fill our rooms. We need conventions and trade shows."

Those plans in Niagara Falls are creating a new sense of urgency for Buffalo leaders who are pushing for a 125,000-square-foot downtown convention center. The Buffalo project, which has strong public and private sector support, remains mired in the political process. "Hopefully, Niagara Falls' plans will move our project along more swiftly," said Richard Geiger, Greater Buffalo Convention & Visitors Bureau president. "Niagara Falls, to me, is an example of what we should be doing here. In a way, it's like having oil nearby and not drilling for it. Niagara Falls is a huge resource and we're not taking advantage of it."

At the same time, if both Niagara Falls, Ontario, and Buffalo build convention centers, it may spell further trouble for the financially ailing and troubled Niagara Falls, New York, Convention Center. The 26-year-old facility has about 90,000 square feet of space. A Niagara Falls, Ontario, convention center, coupled with that city's $500 million permanent casino project, would cement its position as the region's tourism capital and further hurt any development plans for Niagara Falls, New York. "It could make it competitively tougher in the outside marketplace," said Roger Trevino, executive vice president of Niagara Falls Redevelopment Corporation, a group that is attempting a massive urban renewal project. "But we do have a brand name and that name is Niagara Falls."

*continued*

"It doesn't make the job of selling Niagara Falls (to convention planners) any easier," added Jacek Wysocki, co-chairman of the Coalition for Downtown Development, a private sector–led group that's supporting the new Buffalo convention center. "On the positive side, a Niagara Falls, Ontario, center could generate enough generic interest in the region that both their facility and Buffalo's would have enough business."

Plans for a Niagara Falls, Ontario, convention center have been discussed periodically but never have left the preliminary stages. This time, however, plans have strong support from the Ontario city's private sector, including many people who are willing to ante up some of the seed money to build the facility. The center is taking on a new sense of purpose given the popularity of Casino Niagara, the city's rapid development pace, and plans for a new mega-casino/entertainment complex taking hold. Construction on the casino project is expected to start later this year. The project includes a 45,000-square-foot meeting hall. "Chances are as good now as they've ever been for a convention center," said Noel Buckley, general manager of the Niagara Falls, Ontario, Visitors Bureau. "That the private sector is taking the lead on this is a very positive sign."

Casino Niagara attracted 10.2 million people during its 1998–99 fiscal year. It had drawn 5.4 million people, for a daily average of 32,152 visitors, through the second quarter of its 1999–2000 fiscal year.

Niagara Falls, Ontario, attracts about 15 million visitors annually. In Canada, only Toronto and Vancouver have more hotel rooms than the 13,000 in Niagara Falls. Another 1,000 are planned for this year.

"There is agreement amongst most of the players that we need the center," Zappitelli said. "Unlike other communities, we can't sit back and wait for a convention center to be dropped in our laps. If it is going to happen, we're going to have to make it happen ourselves." Thomson, at the Feb. 27 Niagara Falls City Council meeting, revived an ad hoc convention center development committee. Zappitelli agreed to chair the committee with the mayor. The committee will meet for the first time March 8. While there is strong support for the Niagara Falls project, Zappitelli and Thomson agree there are more questions than answers at this point. Chief among the questions is the center's location, cost, and who is going to pay for the building. The proposed Buffalo convention center is carrying a price tag that's approaching $151 million.

Funding may be troublesome. While the Niagara Region's hotel operators may favour creating a bed tax to cover the center's development and debt service costs, Ontario lawmakers are reluctant to approve such a measure. In effect, the hotel operators would have to create a stealth-like fund to underwrite the project. Niagara Falls will be asking both the Ontario provincial and Canadian national governments to help with the project's development costs.

"There are all kinds of scenarios that must be discussed and reviewed, that's why I convened this committee," Thomson said. "The decision I made (on Feb. 27) was the first step in getting the process going." Thomson said the center would help the city's hotels during their slower winter periods. Many of the hotels have higher than average vacancy rates during the weekday periods of the first quarter.

"It's essential to have a convention center to get us through the January–February–March blahs," Thomson said. Zappitelli added a convention center is an almost essential economic development element for the city's hotel operators. "You can have all the beautiful hotel rooms you want, but if you don't have the people in there to fill them up on a 12-month basis, you're not getting the job done," Zappitelli said.

---

Source: Wright, Jeff. *Business First.* Copyright 2000 by AM CITY BUS TOURS INC. Reproduced with permission of AM CITY BUS TOURS INC. in the format Textbook via Copyright Clearance Center.

## QUESTIONS TO CONSIDER

Before summarizing the article, answer the following questions:

1. What is the article about?
2. Who is the article about?
3. Who is the intended reader?
4. Where is the convention centre to be built?
5. How many main points does the article discuss?
6. Is there a direct quote that should be used?
7. Were you to be writing an evaluative summary, does the fact that this is an American article matter to the data?

# Introduction

This chapter deals with convention and training reports. To remain competitive and efficient, organizations must ensure their employees are aware of the latest trends and developments in their industry and have the right skills, particularly as new technology is introduced into the workplace. Sending employees to conventions is an important means for companies and other organizations to make sure staff are up-to-date with what is going on in their industry or market. Developing an appropriately skilled work force involves providing training, whether on-the-job or from outside sources such as specialized firms or educational establishments.

However, the costs of sending employees to conventions or training courses can be considerable, and the worth of the event or session has to be evaluated. Most organizations require that managers and their employees agree on the reasons or objectives for attending a convention. Similarly, before being permitted to take a training course, the new skills or knowledge that the employee will obtain must be identified and accepted. In both instances, the important consideration is the benefit that the organization will gain from the employee's participation.

Reporting by employees on their attendance at a convention or course is, therefore, important since it allows managers to meet several needs. First, these reports confirm that indeed the people scheduled to attend a convention or take a training course actually did so. Second, the reports help managers assess whether what the employees gained was worth the cost. Third, managers are able to gather information relevant to the organization's business and progress. Without proper reports from the people who attended the convention or the training course, managers would have to rely on their memory of an office discussion or a conversation beside the water cooler.

This chapter teaches you how to write convention and training reports. You will learn that these reports are factual, analytical narratives that are designed to give your manager a clear idea of whether or not it was worth sending you to the convention or workshop. You will learn how to use the Purpose and Focus Questions to help ensure that your report

- reminds your manager of your intended goals;
- informs your manager about what you did at the convention or training session;
- states your reasoned judgment about what you did;
- details how any unexpected meetings you may have had could impact on future plans of the organization.

# Editing Practice One

Evelyn LaPierre is a marketing specialist with Dugais et Pelletier, a marketing firm in Quebec. Using her report (Figure 5.2) of the marketing convention she went to in Dallas, Texas, and the Questions to Consider on page 126 as guides, examine Sakin Paru's convention report in Figure 5.3. Paru is a salesperson for Halifax Cable; she went to the annual convention of the National Cabling Association.

CONVENTION REPORT

Dugais et Pelletier, Marketing

Memorandum

TO:      Jean-Guy Dugais, President

FROM:    Evelyn LaPierre

DATE:    Dec 15, 2006

SUBJECT: Report On The International Marketeers Convention (IMC), 2006

The International Marketeers Convention I attended December 5–6 in Dallas, Texas, was something of a disappointment. I accomplished 1 of my 3 goals: learning how the Martrex demographic analysis system works.

On the first day of the convention, Tuesday, I attended the session on International Copyright and the Internet. It was scheduled to be given by Allison Blair, a well-known international copyright lawyer, who became ill shortly before the convention. Her replacement, Alexandra Vlachuck, was quite knowledgeable about American law but did not speak much about the international aspects of copyrights.

*continued*

During Tuesday afternoon, I went to the trade show. My main goal was to try out the It's-So-Alive graphics program. I spent an hour at the company's computers. While the program's interfaces were easier to navigate than in the program we use, I did not find that the graphics were any more lively than the ones that we presently produce.

The full-day workshop put on by Martrex on the second day of the convention was extremely useful. The morning session was devoted to showing how to customize the program, which can then "slice and dice" market statistics. During the afternoon session, I was able to plug in some of our numbers. I have attached to this report the printout Martrex produced, which shows the amount of money females between 11 and 25 spend on hair care (products and services) in 25 different markets in Quebec and the Francophone parts of New Brunswick and Eastern Ontario.

I will be organizing an information session on Martrex in the near future.

Encls:      Program
           Sample Martrex Report

---

## FIGURE 5.3

### EDITING PRACTICE ONE: CONVENTION REPORT

**A poorly written convention report**

# Halifax Cable ————————————

Memorandum

TO:      Mary Yale

FROM:    Sakin Paru

DATE:    January 8, 2007

SUBJECT:  Toronto Convention 2006

The NCA Convention in Toronto that I attended was great. I learned lots and met lots of people who are facing the same difficulties we are in sales.

The convention was at the new part of the Toronto Convention Centre, which is really beautiful, and featured 100 technical exhibits and more importantly for me, several panel discussions dedicated to small cable operators.

*continued*

I was there for three days. On the first day, Monday, I attended three sessions. I have attached copies of handouts from each to this memo. You will be especially interested in the handouts from session II entitled "Small Cable Operators: How to Compete with Satellite Companies." The panel of this session included Philip Leland. He presented some very interesting ideas about how small cable operators can position themselves in markets like ours.

On Tuesday morning, I decided to go to the Technical Show. I brought back several technical documents for Joe. He had told me to be on the look out for blue boxes and I saw several different kinds. That afternoon, I attended a boring session entitled "Cabling the Community."

I think the most interesting thing that happened to me at the convention was the unplanned meeting I had with Tracy Roberts and Daniel Meintzer of Halifax Cable and Avalon Cable. We met at lunch on Wednesday, after a fascinating session on the Internet. We talked about lots of things, including the idea of a purchasing group that we have been talking about. Tracy was very keen on it and Daniel felt that it was probably a good idea. We agreed to meet here next week with you to discuss it further.

In sum, I think it was a good convention and that the connections we get to make and maintain make attending it worthwhile.

Encls. 3

---

## QUESTIONS TO CONSIDER

1. Is the subject line clear?
2. Is the first paragraph written in a professional style?
3. Does the paragraph that refers to Philip Leland (paragraph three) explain what his ideas were?
4. While the session Mr. Paru attended on Tuesday afternoon may have been "boring," is it appropriate to write this in a convention report?
5. Is the main idea of paragraph five clear?
6. Does the report make a case that Halifax Cable received value for money by sending Mr. Paru to the convention?
7. Would this memo be easier to understand if Mr. Paru used subheadings?
8. Is the memo free of grammatical, punctuation, spelling, and usage errors?

# The Process of Writing a Convention or Training Report

Sending employees to conventions and training courses costs organizations money: directly in the form of fees, travel, and hotel costs, and indirectly in the form of covering for the employees who are out of the office. Managers need to know that this investment—which on a North America–wide basis costs tens of billions of dollars annually—represents value for money.

To justify the expense of sending you from St. John's to an industry convention in Calgary, your manager requires a report that does more than provide a chronology of what sessions you attended and your impressions about the convention. In fact, your personal experiences (e.g., emotions) are generally not included in convention or training reports, unless you can argue, for example, that the computer system was so inadequate you became too frustrated to follow the instructions.

Convention and training reports are therefore factual, analytical, and normally in memo format. They pull together and present the facts of your experiences and include your professional judgments about the convention sessions you attended or training you received.

These reports should do the following:

- remind your manager what you set out to learn or accomplish—your objectives—or why you went to the convention or training course;
- indicate whether your objectives were met and if not, why not;
- detail any unexpected meetings or conversations that would be of interest to your manager and organization;
- show how what you did or learned at the convention or training course affects the organization.

## BASIC STRUCTURE OF A CONVENTION OR TRAINING REPORT

The convention or training report consists of the following parts:

- Introduction: summarizes the report (e.g., Where did you go? When did you go? Did you accomplish the objectives that your manager agreed to? What were the objectives? What topics will you be reporting on?).
- Details: indicates the sequence of convention sessions and activities and explains what was accomplished or learned; indicates whether the trip or course was worth your time and the company's expense.
- Implications: explains what will follow from what you learned or lists the contacts you made at the convention or training session.

## A SAMPLE CONVENTION REPORT

The analytical convention report in Figure 5.4 was written by Mary Pratt, the assistant materials manager for Industrial Cleaners, after she returned from the industry's two-day convention in Vancouver. Before beginning the report, she printed off a copy of the proposal memo that had been approved by her manager, Andrew Polis, Industrial Cleaners' materials manager. In it, she had listed the following three objectives:

- attend workshop on new environmental regulations;
- examine new equipment;
- find out how other companies are dealing with staff recruitment and retention problems.

Ms. Pratt went through the following process to prepare her analytical convention report.

### Purpose Questions

Ms. Pratt answered the Purpose Questions (PQs) she had learned in college:

1. What is my goal?
   To tell about the convention.
2. Who is going to read this memo?
   Andrew, my manager.
3. What does my reader already know about this topic/issue?
   He approved my going to the convention.

### Focus Questions

Ms. Pratt thought for a moment and then jotted down the Focus Questions (FQs) for analytical convention/training reports and her answers:

1. What objectives were established *before* you went on the trip?
   My objectives were to
   a) learn about new environmental regulations;
   b) examine new floor cleaning equipment;
   c) search for solutions to recruitment problems.
2. Were each of these objectives met? If not, why not?
   I learned about new environmental regulations and I examined new floor cleaning equipment, but I did not pick up any new ideas on staff recruitment and retention; other small companies have the same problem.
3. If so, what information/material/contacts/procedures did you acquire or learn?
   I learned that new environmental regulations will require that cleaners dispose of Solvex. I tried out two different floor cleaners: Super Jet and Scrub Clean, both produced by Cleaning Pro; the Scrub Clean has larger handles that will make it easier for our staff to use.
4. Did you learn anything unexpected that applies to any immediate corporate situations or plans?
   No.

5. Would a general information session in which you or a contact you made speaks to the office be worthwhile?
Yes, a session on the environmental law changes would be useful.
6. Was the convention/training worth the time and expense?
Yes, due to the information learned relating to environmental law.

## Purpose Statement

Ms. Pratt then drafted the following introductory paragraph:

> I have just come back from the Industrial Cleaners Convention in Vancouver. I accomplished most of what I set out to do. And, as is often the case at these things, I had conversations with other industry people that were useful.

Ms. Pratt paused, reread the paragraph, looked back at the proposal memo for attending the convention, and examined what she had jotted down for the PQs and FQs. She realized that this paragraph failed to properly introduce her analysis of the convention. *It doesn't say that I found the convention worthwhile or what I had hoped to accomplish*, she thought.

After deleting the paragraph, she wrote out the purpose statement that guided her while writing the rest of the report: "My purpose is to explain that I accomplished most of what I set out to do at the convention in Vancouver."

She then wrote the analytical convention report shown in Figure 5.4.

---

**FIGURE 5.4**

## ANALYTICAL CONVENTION REPORT

 Industrial Cleaners *A Little Cleaning Goes A Long Way*

Memorandum

TO:      Andrew Polis, Materials Manager

FROM:   Mary Pratt, Assistant Materials Manager

DATE:    November 10, 2006

SUBJECT:  Report On Industrial Cleaners Convention (ICC) 2006

The Industrial Cleaners Convention (a copy of the program is attached) I attended from 6 to 8 November in Vancouver was extremely useful. I accomplished two of my three goals: learning about new environmental regulations and examining new floor cleaning equipment.

Pratt presents her overall judgment in the summary.

Pratt reminds Polis of some of her goals.

*continued*

| Pratt details her activities on the first day of the convention. |

On the first day of the convention, Monday, I attended the session on environmental law given by T. L. Davis, Q.C. As you can see from the attached handouts, the Ministry of the Environment will soon be issuing regulations that ban the disposal of certain cleaning solutions (Solvex is the only one we use) through the sewage system. Under these regulations, companies will be required to save, store, and pay for the safe disposal of these cleaning solutions.

Pratt summarizes important environmental legislation and how it will impact the company.

Pratt explains her first impressions of the two floor cleaners she examined.

I spent most of the second day at the trade show examining floor cleaning equipment. I was able to try Super Jet and Scrub Clean, both manufactured by Cleaning Pro, the two models that we have been thinking would best replace our present floor cleaners/polishers.

Both are well designed with easy-to-use hoses and easily removed filler caps. The Super Jet is a bit more maneuverable. However, the Scrub Clean, which has oversized handles and hand controls, would, I think, go a long way toward solving the hand-fatigue problems that have recently come to our attention.

Pratt gives her professional judgment of the usefulness of one of the seminars Polis believed to be especially important.

Pratt explains what was covered in this session and why it was a disappointment.

The session on recruitment and retention of employees was disappointing. Neither the main speaker, Mary Tonge of Toronto Business Cleaners, nor the other participants presented any ideas we had not already considered.

I will arrange for a general information meeting in which I can inform the cleaners about the new rules regarding Solvex. As well, I will meet with Joe Montgomery from Machine Services, to discuss what I learned about the new floor polishers.

Pratt indicates what further action she will take following the convention.

Encls. 4

# Editing Practice Two

Patricia Grimes is the administrative assistant to Reginald Hnatyshan, a senior partner in the law firm of McMillan, Ryan, and Hnatyshan. After attending a one-day Microsoft Word training session, she filed a report (see Figure 5.5) with Claudine Bourassa, the firm's office manager. Using the Questions to Consider on page 131, edit Ms. Grimes's report.

FIGURE 5.5

## EDITING PRACTICE TWO: TRAINING SESSION REPORT

**A poorly written training session report**

---

### McMillan, Ryan, and Hnatyshan
B a r r i s t e r s  a n d  S o l i c i t o r s

────── MEMORANDUM ──────

TO:        Claudine Bourassa, Office Manager

FROM:    Patricia Grimes

DATE:     March 7, 2007

SUBJECT:  The terrible Word Training session I went to

The one-day Word training session that I went to on February 28, 2007, was a waste of time. Though I did learn a few good tips.

The session was put on by Computer Training Inc. at the downtown YMCA campus and lasted the whole day.

The morning session was supposed to be devoted to learning how to use Word to address things like envelopes, print in columns, make business cards. The problem was that most of the participants were barely familiar with regular word processing functions such as bulleting or changing margins. So the teacher had to spend lots of time going over things I already knew.

The afternoon session was a bit better. By then, the instructor had divided us into groups. The one I was in knew their way around Word and would have been able to learn how to format newsletters if we had been able to print them. The printers were not working well, so we could not see our work.

I was so angry at the end of the course that I went to Stollery and told him that I thought the course had been a complete disaster and informed him that I would tell you to request a refund. He told me that he would be willing to enroll someone from the office in another course free of charge.

---

### QUESTIONS TO CONSIDER
1. Is the subject line clear and correct?
2. Should Ms. Grimes indicate her position next to her name?

3. Does the introductory paragraph summarize the training session in a professional manner?
4. Is the tone professional and analytical?
5. Is the use of the word "problem" (in paragraph three) correct?
6. Is the memo free of grammatical, punctuation, spelling, and usage errors?

# Editing Practice Three

Dennis Norman is an accountant with Kowalski Furniture. After attending the annual convention for Chartered General Accountants, he wrote the report in Figure 5.6 for Jan Hardy, Kowalski Furniture's comptroller. Using the Questions to Consider on page 133, edit Mr. Norman's report.

---

**FIGURE 5.6**

EDITING PRACTICE THREE: CONVENTION REPORT

**A poorly written convention report**

KOWALSKI FURNITURE ◆ SIMCOE, ONTARIO
*Simcoe's Finest Furniture Store*

Memorandum

TO:      Jan Hardy

FROM:   Dennis Norman

DATE:    August 8, 2006

SUBJECT: Report on CGA Convention 2006

The CGA convention I attended in Ottawa from 17 to 19 July was an exceptionally worthwhile experience. The sessions that I planned to attend were well organized, well attended and taught me a great deal.

The meetings were at the Westin Hotel. Following the opening session, entitled "The Depth of Taxes," we were able to choose different smaller meetings. I went to the ones we had discussed. "New Rules for Remitting," which met on the afternoon of the first day, was fascinating. I had gone with the hope

*continued*

of learning about what happens if we are late in remitting taxes to the government. This topic was covered in detail. I found out lots of good information.

On the morning of the second day, I attended the session on technology. There I saw a demonstration of software that enables companies like ours to send the payroll directly to the bank. This will allow us to centralize payroll in the head office.

I will schedule a meeting with you to discuss this last issue.

---

## QUESTIONS TO CONSIDER

1. Are the To, From, and Subject lines correct?
2. Is it likely that Ms. Hardy will care that the sessions Mr. Norman attended were "well attended"?
3. Should Mr. Norman have found a different way of saying "I went to the ones we had discussed" in paragraph two?
4. Does the sentence "I found out lots of good information" tell Ms. Hardy enough?
5. Is the memo free of grammatical, punctuation, spelling, and usage errors?

# Editing Practice Four

Kaitlin Van De Hague is the assistant acquisitions director of Can-Books, a large Canadian publisher. She is reporting on the North American Book Fair that she attended in Vancouver in August 2006. Using the Questions to Consider on page 135, edit Ms. Van De Hague's report.

**FIGURE 5.7**

## EDITING PRACTICE FOUR: CONVENTION REPORT

**A poorly written convention report**

### CAN-BOOKS ❧ The Canadian Book Publisher

Memorandum

TO:        Livia Lipsett, Acquisitions Director

FROM:    Kaitlin Van De Hague

DATE:     August 23, 2006

SUBJECT:  Report On 2006 North American Book Fair

The 2005 North American Book Fair I attended from 15–18 August in Vancouver was a really great experience. I accomplished 3 of my 4 goals.

The convention was held in Vancouver's new Convention Centre, which meant that unlike last year's convention in Mississauga, there was a lot more room for exhibits. Also, the presenters and the exhibitors were able to have much better graphics.

On the first day of the convention, I went to the session put on by American Historical Publishers, Inc. As you know, it was entitled "World History Is Hot." The speaker from AHP showed us that the sales figures for world history titles have gone up way up over the past three years. Of course, one of the most popular writers is Simon Winchester. Another is John Keegan. The most important thing I learned at this session was that the marketing of history books has changed with the way writing history has changed.

During the afternoon of the first day, I went to the trade show. One of my goals was to see how other publishers are designing their displays and, if possible, make contact with a design company. We had agreed before I left that our publicity was "tired." We did not know how tired our displays and designs are. At the kiosk for Turning Planet Press, one of the largest publishers in Australia, I saw a display for a book on the history of Ayer's Rock, that not only had a film loop that showed aerial shots of the famous landmark, the display also had models of the rock. The best art design work was probably that of Virgo Design from Calgary. They designed a dust jacket for a university press book entitled *Alberta: Mountains, Rivers, Prairies*, that, as you can see from the attached brochure, is truly eye-catching. I am especially

*continued*

impressed with the way the lines of the mountains merge with the lines of the rivers to become at the bottom of the front of the book, waving fields of wheat.

The second day was less fruitful. During the morning session put on by Press/Presse Canadian, we heard some interesting information about how to market French authors in English Canada. According to Michel Levesque, "success comes from making sure that your readers know that the author is French and that because of that what he or she is writing about is going to be a bit exotic." He also gave sales figures that I have attached to this report.

I was very disappointed with the Insta-Book demonstration session I went to that afternoon. I had hoped to see the machine that does the printing and binding at work. Instead, we were shown a video of the machine. There were about 100 people there and there were only 20 or so copies of the books produced by the machine. I was sitting in the back and was not able to actually hold a copy. I took Insta-Book's publicity and have attached them to this report.

All in all, I am very pleased with the convention. I think we got our money's worth.

---

## QUESTIONS TO CONSIDER

1. Should Ms. Van De Hague have included her title with her name?
2. Did Ms. Van De Hague remind Lipsett of what her goals were?
3. Is the second paragraph written in a professional tone?
4. Simon Winchester is the author of several bestsellers including *The Professor and the Madman* and *Krakatoa*. John Keegan is a bestselling author of military history. Should Ms. Van De Hague have included in her discussion which of their books were referred to by the speaker?
5. Should she have presented some numbers?
6. Is the fourth sentence of the fourth paragraph, "We did not know how tired our displays and designs are," written in a professional tone?
7. Should Ms. Van De Hague have divided the fourth paragraph?
8. Is the report's final paragraph detailed enough?
9. Is the memo free of grammatical, punctuation, spelling, and usage errors?

# Summary

Convention and training reports are factual, analytical narratives. These reports have four main purposes:

- to remind your manager what you set out to learn or accomplish;
- to indicate whether these objectives were met and if not, why;
- to explain how what you did or learned at the convention or training session affects the organization;
- to detail any unexpected meetings you had or information you learned that would be of interest to your manager.

These reports must provide a reasonably detailed sketch of events; for example, which sessions were attended on each day of a convention. As well, they must provide a judgment as to the usefulness of each session. You are allowed to include personal observations in your report if such observations (e.g., the speaker's voice was difficult to hear or the speaker was uninspiring) are immediately relevant to your reasoned judgment about whether the organization received "value for money" by sending you to the session or convention.

# Discussion Questions

1. Why are convention and training reports written?
2. What is the primary question a convention or training report must answer?
3. Do convention and training reports present your opinions or your professional judgment?
4. Why should you avoid subjective words and phrases?
5. Why should you include information about unexpected meetings?

# Writing Assignments

## Assignment 5.1

You have just returned from a one-day training session in business writing. The first part dealt with writing for the Web; the second with using spell- and grammar-checking programs (see Appendix I for the kind of information you were hoping to learn). You found the theoretical information both interesting and useful. However, during the afternoon sessions, the computer network you were using began malfunctioning. Accordingly, you found it very difficult to apply what you were being taught. Write a training report in which you suggest to your manager that he or she lodge a complaint with Biz-Training, the company that put on the session.

## Assignment 5.2

You are the comptroller of your college's student society. You have just returned from the annual University and College Student Associations Conference held in Saskatoon on the weekend of June 10, 2006. Your memo report, which will be e-mailed to the members of the student society's board of directors, 10 of whom represent outlying campuses, will state that the conference was worthwhile. You accomplished two of the three objectives that the board had approved: (1) to learn about which kinds of websites attract students, and (2) to learn how to attract sponsors. You did not accomplish your third objective, to find other colleges with which to set up student exchanges. The person who gave the session on finding sponsors, Melvin Douglas, will be in your city in a few months. Propose that he give a session to the board.

## Assignment 5.3

David Johansson is the assistant to the vice president, Personnel, of a large software development firm. He has just returned from a much-promoted conference entitled "Equity in the New Economy: Ways to ensure that visible minorities, Aboriginal Canadians, and women will prosper in cyberspace." The sessions he was scheduled to attend at the four-day event in Toronto included (1) Representations of Minorities in Advertising and Other Visuals; (2) From the Trap Line to Online: Computers for Aboriginals; and (3) From Chat to Technology: How to help women use the Net. None of the sessions lived up to his expectations, though in a few he heard one or two interesting ideas. Write Mr. Johansson's convention report.

## Assignment 5.4

You are the bookkeeper for a 30-person company in Winnipeg. You have just returned from a two-day training session in using ACCPAC software given by Figuresplus Training Inc., a national firm with offices in Winnipeg and other major cities. The session was very useful. Write the training report.

# Web References

### Urbana 2000 Convention Report

http://www.urbana.org/u2000.report.cfm

This site shows the convention report for Urbana's year 2000 convention.

# CHAPTER • 6 •

# Suggestion Memos and Short Proposals

## LEARNING OBJECTIVES

In this chapter, you will learn

- what the differences are between suggestion and short proposal memos;

- how to understand a problem and use facts and reasoned judgment to present a solution to it in a suggestion or short proposal memo;

- what types of facts are used in suggestion and proposal memos;

- what the structure and components of a proposal memo are;

- how to use Purpose and Focus Questions to organize, develop, and write suggestion and proposal memos that meet your reader's needs and level of knowledge.

# PRELIMINARY *exercise*

You are the assistant to Tomaso Nkomo, the supervisor of Accounting Services, one of the several divisions of Thorne's Business Services, which provides project management, marketing, and strategic planning services to firms across Canada. You see an article in *CA Magazine* (see Figure 6.1) and decide to write a summary of it for Mr. Nkomo, who recently discussed with you the idea of proposing that Accounting Services explore business opportunities outside Canada.

## FIGURE 6.1

### PROPOSED GLOBAL BUSINESS DESIGNATION OPENS NEW OPPORTUNITIES FOR MEMBERS

The Canadian Institute of Chartered Accountants (CICA) and seven other leading accountancy institutes from around the world have formed a Global Task Force to explore the creation of a new global business professional designation. The proposed designation would enable professionals from a variety of disciplines to provide a broader range of globally relevant services to clients, customers, and employers by building on their ethical standards, traditional skills, and expertise.

"The new designation would provide its holders with international recognition and credibility as business professionals operating in the global marketplace," says outgoing CICA Chair, Guylaine Saucier, FCA. "We expect our Canadian business professionals will be able to maximize the strategic use of their collective knowledge assets to benefit an ever widening range of business users."

The global designation is intended to be an "umbrella" professional credential under which different traditional professions can operate in an integrated fashion based on global standards. It would complement the work of the International Federation of Accountants (IFA) and the International Accounting Standards Committee (IASC) as well as existing professional designations. Selected professions would become key practice areas within the more broadly defined designation, and professionals who achieved this new global designation would be expected to retain their existing credentials as well.

"The proposed new global designation would offer the CA profession a unique opportunity to expand—in fact, to globalize—the scope of our practice while retaining the valued attributes of our profession such as high professional and ethical standards," says incoming CICA Chair, Bob Lord, FCA. "Worldwide market research shows that leaders of the global marketplace are demanding a broader range of competencies and an expanding range of services from business advisers. The proposed new global designation would offer CAs a professional competitive edge, enhancing our members' capacity to practise across borders and create value for local, regional, national, and international clients and organizations of every kind and industry."

*continued*

"The creation of this new designation opens up exciting opportunities for members in both public practice and in industry," said CICA President Michael Rayner, FCA. "The designation will distinguish its holders as multidisciplinary business advisers and strategic thinkers; enhance their marketable skills, earning capacity, and employment prospects. It will also create global professional opportunities, enabling them to work and travel all over the world, and provide them with access to a professional association that offers products, services, representation, and networking opportunities on a global scale," CEOs of the other participating institutes agreed. "I am delighted that our institute is a member of the new Task Force," said John Collier, secretary general of the Institute of Chartered Accountants in England and Wales. "The Institute's membership already has a huge worldwide presence and we are ideally positioned to bring a real degree of expertise to the table."

According to Robin Hamilton Harding, FCA, former CFO of Bell Canada who has been appointed interim chief operating officer of the Task Force, discussions are underway with other professions and other accountancy institutes around the world to attract support for, and membership in, the new designation. The Task Force will also consider how diverse business professionals can best leverage their combined capabilities to meet the complex information and decision-making needs of the global economy.

AICPA President and CEO Barry Melancon adds: "The new global designation is an important strategic objective that positions the profession as a worldwide leader today, and will help sustain it as a very viable profession fifty years from now."

We'll be keeping members informed on an ongoing basis about this exciting new initiative, and seeking your input. We're building an interactive communications area in the Members Only section of the CICA Web site this fall, to hear from you and respond in a timely way. Meanwhile, please send us your questions and feedback to global@cica.ca. As well, you'll soon be getting a special report on the state of the profession and the global initiative.

---

Source: "Proposed Global Business Designation Opens New Opportunities for Members." *CA Magazine* 1 June 2000, Vol. 133, No. 5: 49–50.

## QUESTIONS TO CONSIDER

Before summarizing the article, answer the following questions:

1. What is the article about?
2. Who is the article about?
3. Who is the intended reader?
4. How many main points does the article contain?
5. Are there any direct quotes that must be maintained?
6. What is the rule to be followed when using either initials or acronyms?

# Introduction

Suggestion and short proposal memos from employees inform managers of ideas for doing something presently not being done by the organization or doing it differently. Both types of memos outline a solution to a problem.

There are two types of suggestion memos. The first addresses a relatively minor issue such as suggesting to a section manager that a reminder to keep the kitchen area clean be sent under the manager's signature. The second is often the first piece of paper in a continuum that, for example, begins with your memo drawing a manager's attention to the office lighting and suggesting that it be improved. If the manager agrees that this issue is worth the company's time, he or she will tell you to prepare a proposal that the lighting be changed. Then you will research the issue—determining if the lighting is in accord with recommended standards (lumens, wattage, glare, etc.), what the cost of changing the lighting will be, and what, if any, dislocations to the office will occur during the installation of the new lighting fixtures. You would then write a short proposal that analyzes the problem in detail and recommends changes that are needed and which lighting supplier you believe will best suit your organization's needs.

While researching a short proposal, you will, to stay with the above example, contact several contractors, but you will recommend one only. A longer analytical proposal analyzes alternatives, compares them, and presents them in a way that anticipates questions that might arise in your reader's mind about why you chose company A over B.

This chapter teaches you how to write suggestion and short proposal memos. You will learn that both present reasoned arguments—based on facts—for changes to a business practice, an organizational structure, or certain equipment, such as computers or phone systems. You will learn how to use the Purpose and Focus Questions to define your readers and their understanding of the problem and solution that you have identified. You will learn that short proposals present more analysis and detail than suggestion memos: they make clear what financial or other costs your employer could face if the problem is not fixed, what the actual cost of the change is, and how the proposed change will benefit the organization.

# Editing Practice One

Amy Stone is the ecumenical coordinator of the Canadian Ecumenical Council. Using her proposal memo (Figure 6.2) and the Questions to Consider on page 144 as guides, examine Patricia Groulx's proposal memo (Figure 6.3). Groulx is assistant to Angelo Mosconi, Office/Building Manager of InJect Forms, a plastics manufacturing company in Hamilton, Ontario, that occupies its own building, set back 200 metres from a major highway. The company has 200 employees, 45 of which work the 4:00 p.m. to 12:00 midnight production shift.

FIGURE 6.2

SHORT PROPOSAL MEMO

# Canadian Ecumenical Council

Memorandum

TO: Justin Bent, Vice President, Administration

FROM: Amy Stone, Ecumenical Coordinator

DATE: December 5, 2006

SUBJECT: Proposal To Contract With A World of Meals

I propose that we contract with A World of Meals for the catering of the council's formal meetings. A World of Meals will insure that the food and drinks supplied at the council's committees and annual general meetings will adhere to the religious dietary laws (kosher and hallal) of our members. A two-year contract would cost $16,380.

At present, the council and its departments arrange for catering for meetings on a case-by-case basis. Twice during the past year, the publishing department contracted with local caterers who, though they had verbally promised to provide kosher food, did not. Last January 10, the sandwich tray included ham and Swiss-cheese sandwiches, which greatly upset Rabbi David Wein, who had travelled to Ottawa from Moncton for the meeting. Planning of the Ecumenical Conference held last March was complicated by the fact that none of the caterers we have used in the past were able to provide hallal-certified meats (as required by the council's Muslim members).

A World of Meals guarantees that its meals are both kosher- and hallal-certified. As well, A World of Meals is able to provide low-salt and vegetarian meals as needed.

Over the past five years, the council has spent an average of $6,995 per year on catering. The cost of a two-year contract with A World of Meals is $16,380.* Given the fundamental beliefs of ecumenism, I consider that it is worth $1,195 a year to ensure that we comply with our members' religious dietary restrictions.

May I have your approval to contract with A World of Meals to cater the council's formal meetings?

*This $16,380 is for catering for 2007 and 2008:

*continued*

| Annual General Meeting | 250 | persons |
| Three Senior Managing Committee Meetings | 30 | (10 x 3) |
| Three Publication Council Meetings | 24 | (8 x 3) |
| Three Issues Meetings | 24 | (8 x 3) |
| Two Education Committee Meetings | 18 | (9 x 2) |
| One Faith Explanation Day | 200 | |
| Total Number of Meals: | 546 persons x 2 = 1,092 meals | |

## FIGURE 6.3

### EDITING PRACTICE ONE: SHORT PROPOSAL MEMO

**A poorly written short proposal memo**

 **InJect Forms** Shaping your tomorrows, today

Memorandum

TO:      Angelo Mosconi

FROM:   Patricia Groulx

DATE:    8/12/2006

SUBJECT:  Changing the lights in the parking lot

I think we should change the lights in the parking lot out back. Everybody thinks its very dark back there, especially in winter.

New lights will put an end to all the break-ins that people have been complaining about. They will also make people feel safer. Angie Dewitt from the evening shift told me she felt really unsafe walking to her car at the back of the parking lot.

After I contacted Nordic Construction that repaved the parking lot two years ago, I found out that they can install new lights in the centre of the parking lot for about $4,000. Doing this will be very worthwhile because it will make everybody feel safer.

May I go ahead and ask Nordic Construction for a formal quote?

## QUESTIONS TO CONSIDER

1. Does the subject line clearly indicate the nature of the memo?
2. Does the second sentence of the first paragraph present facts?
3. Is the meaning of "New lights" in the first sentence of the second paragraph clear?
4. Is the first sentence of the second paragraph verifiable?
5. In the second sentence of the second paragraph, what does "They" refer to?
6. Does Ms. Groulx's memo make a business case for the proposed installation of new lights?
7. Is it necessary to say in the first sentence of the third paragraph, "After I contacted Nordic Construction ..."?
8. Do you think Mr. Mosconi would be moved to act by this proposal?
9. Is the memo free of grammatical, punctuation, spelling, and usage errors?

# The Process of Writing Suggestion Memos and Short Proposals

Suggestion and short proposal memos are forms of persuasive writing. Although a suggestion memo may originate from an idea that you had, neither it nor the proposal memo should be rooted in your opinion or "feelings." Rather, both are products of your *reasoned judgment*—your professional point of view.

The difference is important, especially in a business environment. Opinions and "feelings" are perfectly valid (though, as English and Communications professors we like to insist that they are not interchangeable, the former being a thought and the latter an emotion). Both are, however, personal. That is, they are based on individual predilections and preferences.

It may be your opinion that *Titanic* is the best movie of all time or the Rolling Stones the greatest rock band. You may even be able to mount an argument, using facts such as box-office receipts, number of number-one hits, longevity, and so forth. However, at bottom, your argument is based on your personal preference, even your emotional attachment to the film or Mick Jagger's lyrics. Such is not the case at a staff meeting. There, if an idea is being discussed—whether to introduce a new product line, install a new phone system, or even stagger lunch breaks so the office is not emptied for an hour—and you are asked for your "opinion," your manager and coworkers are not interested in your emotions. They are interested in what you have to say about the issue as a professional. In this instance, the word "opinion" means reasoned judgment. And reasoned judgment means expertise backed up by professional knowledge, experience, and facts. If you have any doubt about the two, remember, at work you are not being paid for your feelings but for your professional views.

## THE DIFFERENCE BETWEEN A SUGGESTION AND A SHORT PROPOSAL MEMO

Both suggestion and short proposal memos identify a problem in the present that can be solved by someone taking some sort of specified action; that is, doing or changing something. The problem may involve procedures, equipment, or schedules, and both types of memos provide a solution that can be implemented in the near future. Generally speaking, however, suggestion memos originate with your idea, whereas proposal memos are assigned. In some cases, the responsibility for the identification of a problem and the writing of a proposal is part of the position you occupy in the organization.

## SUGGESTIONS ARE LESS FORMAL THAN PROPOSALS

Suggestions are both less formal and less researched than proposals (though, again, we want to emphasize that they are firmly rooted in facts and represent your professional point of view). A suggestion memo might, for instance, suggest that it is time to consider replacing the photocopier or that due to complaints about poor service from the company's health insurance provider, consideration should be given to transferring to another one. Such memos must present valid reasons, usually backed up with quick research; for example, a short summary of complaints and, in the case of the photocopier, a reminder of what happened last month when it failed. Your manager will, of course, likely be aware of much of this, so your job is to bring it together in a way that matters to the organization, which normally means how the issue you have identified causes problems for the organization (e.g., decreased efficiency, increased or unnecessary costs, needless stress on employees, etc.).

## PROPOSAL MEMOS REFLECT MORE RESEARCH THAN SUGGESTION MEMOS

Proposals pick up where suggestion memos leave off, or, to be more precise, after your suggestion has been accepted and you have spent time researching its implications. The longer analytical proposal normally presents an analysis of two or three options and then argues for the one that you believe is the best. The shorter proposal presents one course of action.

## SUGGESTIONS AND PROPOSALS MAKE THEIR CASE ON THE BASIS OF FACTS

You may remember from essay writing classes that writers who aim to convince people to agree with them and/or act on their recommendations utilize several strategies. If you were writing a persuasive essay urging that your college cut down on the waste generated from the cafeteria, you might appeal to your fellow students' pride at being part of the environmental movement. If you were writing a persuasive essay designed to generate support for a political candidate, you might appeal to your reader's self-interest in seeing taxes lowered. Generally speaking, such strategies are not appropriate to the writing of suggestions or proposals. (The statement in a suggestion memo that the installation of a new printer will make it easier to provide your manager with financial statements or the like may technically state both your self-interest and imply that your manager has an interest in the timely production of reports, but it is not "self-interest" in the way essay writers use the phrase.)

## THE TYPE OF FACTS USED IN SUGGESTION AND SHORT PROPOSAL MEMOS

A suggestion or short proposal memo makes a business case for a change. This case rests on three different sets of facts. The first set is your analysis of the present situation; for example, the staircase at the loading dock has become dangerously worn or the decision to open the store on Sundays using mainly part-time help has created a shortage of locker space. Note how your understanding of the present situation depends on facts that *come out of the past*.

The second set of facts is made up of the details of the proposed solution to the problem. If the problem is the space shortage in the library, and your proposed solution is to replace the journals section with CD-ROM or online access, your second set of facts would include how much space will be saved, where the CD-ROMs will be stored, and how far back in the journals' life electronic access allows users to go.

The third set of facts consists of the costs. Chief among these are the financial implications of a proposal; for example, the financial implications of your proposal to hire a part-time receptionist to work the 6:00 a.m. to 9:00 a.m. and the 5:00 p.m. to 8:00 p.m. (EST) shifts so that a "real live human" will answer calls coming from St. John's, Newfoundland, and Vancouver, British Columbia. However, other costs must also be considered. In the above example about the staircase, other costs could include the period of time the loading dock will be out of service because of the construction. A convincing proposal will show that the costs are exceeded by the benefits of what you are proposing.

## BASIC STRUCTURE OF A SHORT PROPOSAL MEMO

A short proposal memo is composed of the following parts:

1. Introduction: summarizes what the memo proposes and gives a quick sketch of reasons.
2. Background: explains the problem you have identified; explains what is wrong with the procedures and equipment that are presently in place; explains costs (financial and otherwise) that the organization will incur if nothing is changed.
3. Proposal: explains details of the proposed change; what should be done to remedy the situation or what should be purchased.
4. Cost: details financial and other costs (e.g., downtime of computers) that will be incurred as a result of undertaking the change.
5. Permission: asks for permission to go ahead with the proposed plan.

## A SAMPLE SHORT PROPOSAL MEMO

The short proposal memo in Figure 6.4 was written by Emily Madison, the accounting clerk for Jump Higher, Run Faster, a large sports clothing store. Several weeks ago she wrote a suggestion memo to Ian McMaster, the company's comptroller, suggesting that the company upgrade its accounting software from AccountPro DOS to AccountPro for Windows. A few days later Mr. McMaster told her that he agreed with her suggestion and asked her to write a short proposal that he could take to the budget committee.

After calling Jump Higher, Run Faster's software supplier to find out the cost of the upgrade (including installation and training), Ms. Madison clicked on her file for memos, opened the one for proposals, and saw the three Purpose Questions (PQs) that she used to organize her thoughts before writing memos and the Focus Questions (FQs) that apply to suggestions and proposals. She then went through the following process to prepare her short proposal memo.

## Purpose Questions

1. What is my goal?
   To propose we upgrade to AccountPro for Windows.
2. Who is going to read this proposal memo?
   Ian, the chief accountant.
3. What does my reader already know about the topic/issue?
   Not much.

## Focus Questions

She turned next to the Focus Questions:

1. What is the present situation?
   Using AccountPro for DOS.
2. What is wrong with the present situation?
   Often loses connection to server; formatting cumbersome.
3. If this situation continues into the future what problems may arise?
   Possible future loss of data; technical support will soon end.
4. How will these problems affect the organization or employees?
   Loss of financial data; accounting procedures take longer than they should.
5. What is the proposed solution?
   Upgrade to AccountPro for Windows.
6. How will this solution solve the problems identified in question two?
   Better connectivity; Windows-based formatting.
7. Are there other benefits to be gained?
   Easier move to Excel; easier and more exact importing of financial information; reduces chance of loss of data.
8. What is the financial cost of this solution?
   $4,000 (installation and training included).
9. Are there other costs, such as training or downtime?
   One day for installation; five days for training.

## Purpose Statement

After answering her PQs and FQs, Ms. Madison wrote the following purpose statement: "I want to tell Ian and any other person who is responsible for deciding about acquisitions of new computer equipment that in order to solve problems encountered by the accounting department and make preparing financial reports easier, we should upgrade our accounting software from AccountPro for DOS to AccountPro for Windows." She then drafted the opening paragraphs of her memo.

> I propose that we upgrade our accounting software from AccountPro for DOS to AccountPro for Windows. This upgrade will solve several problems currently faced by the accounting department, including frequent loss of connectivity to the server, and will ensure that we will be able to receive ongoing technical support from AccountPro. AccountPro for Windows will also facilitate accounting activities not now easily performed. The total cost of the upgrade is $4,000.

> AccountPro for DOS, the accounting program that we have used for the past 10 years, no longer meets our needs. Because it is a DOS program, it is not especially compatible with our server, which is Windows based. The accounting department must deal with disrupting crashes. Furthermore, formatting information for reports is a cumbersome process. In addition, according to our software provider, AccountPro will soon be phasing out technical support for AccountPro for DOS.

*Nothing technically wrong with this*, she thought after pausing and rereading her opening paragraphs. *Still, it just doesn't seem strong enough.* After another reading, she noticed several problems. *What does "facilitate accounting activities" mean? What kind of crash is not disrupting? Guess the committee will also wonder what I mean by saying that formatting information for reports is a cumbersome process*, she thought.

After asking herself these questions, she went back to her answers to the PQs and FQs and realized she had not included some important information that would have guided her. She changed her answer to the second PQ from "Ian" to "Ian and the Management Committee," and the third PQ from "not much" to "Ian, a great deal; other members of the committee, not much."

Then she turned to examine her answers to FQs two and four. She changed part of her answer to question two from "formatting cumbersome" to "does not allow for the production of the type of financial reports we currently use." She also changed part of her answer to question four from "accounting procedures take longer than they should" to "ongoing risk of loss of information because of crashes and time wasted formatting information as required."

Ms. Madison reread her purpose statement, PQs, and FQs, and then wrote the short proposal memo found in Figure 6.4.

As indicated on the explanatory inserts, Ms. Madison did more than simply turn the answers to the PQs and FQs into sentences. She kept asking herself the following questions:

- Is this clear?
- Is there some further background information that would help my reader understand the point being made?

**Box 6.1**   LETTER PROPOSALS

Unlike short proposals, which are internal documents, letter proposals are written for a company or organization separate from that for which the author works. Although letter proposals share certain characteristics with sales letters, generally speaking, letter proposals are not "prospecting documents." Advertising consultants do not send out hundreds of proposals, as, for example, a new paint store might. Rather, letter proposals are prepared after the advertising consultant has already met with the company or organization that is seeking advertising services—and thus after the consultant has had a chance to identify the company's needs and assess how his or her expertise fits those needs.

Figure 6.5 is a letter proposal written by Vincent Di Angelo, a communications consultant with DDT Communications Inc., to Arthur Snelgrove, Director of External Relations, Wood Users Association.

**FIGURE 6.4**

Sᴍᴀʟʟ Pʀᴏᴘᴏsᴀʟ Mᴇᴍᴏ

# *Jump Higher, Run Faster Sports Clothes*
*Where you can dress for sports success*

Memorandum

TO:        Ian McMaster, Comptroller

FROM:    Emily Madison, Accounting Clerk

DATE:     January 25, 2007

SUBJECT:  Proposal To Update Accounting Software From AccountPro For
          DOS To AccountPro For Windows

| | |
|---|---|
| Madison summarizes the key points of the proposal. | I propose that we upgrade our accounting software from AccountPro for DOS to AccountPro for Windows. This upgrade will solve several problems currently faced by the accounting department, including loss of data due to loss of connectivity to the server. The total cost of this upgrade is $4,000. |

Madison states the problem, then gives three different examples to support this claim.

AccountPro for DOS, the accounting program we have been using for the past 12 years, has become outdated.

1. Because it is a DOS program, it is not especially compatible with our server, which is Windows based. Accordingly, AccountPro is prone to crash, with the resulting loss of data.
2. Since the importation of financial data to Excel and the formatting of it for specialized financial reports is difficult in AccountPro for DOS, it is not an efficient system to use to create the type of financial reports that we instituted last January.
3. Our software provider has advised me that AccountPro will soon be discontinuing technical support for AccountPro for DOS.

Madison ends with the problem of ongoing support, because she knows that it will be the easiest for people untrained in financial matters to understand.

The upgrade to AccountPro for Windows will solve these problems. As well, since it is easier to work with, it will increase the efficiency of the accounting department.

Madison states the solution.

The total cost of this upgrade including installation and training will be $4,000—an amount that can be accommodated within this year's computer upgrade budget ($15,000, of which only $2,500 has been spent).

Madison shows that the upgrade will not "break the budget."

May I have your approval to contract with CompuSoft for the installation of AccountPro for Windows and for the training sessions?

FIGURE 6.5

## LETTER PROPOSAL

Arthur Snelgrove
Director, External Relations
Wood Users Association
Ottawa, ON  K3T Y5P
23 April 2006

Dear Mr. Snelgrove,

It was a pleasure to meet with you and your colleagues yesterday and to discuss your requirement for an outside review of the Wood Users Association's draft external-communications strategic plan to be completed within the next three weeks. Given our experience in strategic communications planning at DDT, both in writing and evaluating plans, and our knowledge of your industry, I am sure we can meet your requirement in a timely and efficient manner.

Based on our discussions, we propose, first, a review of the documentation used in the development of the strategic plan; second, interviews with you and your key colleagues to ensure we fully understand the context of the plan and its objectives; third, an analysis focused on assessing the

- realism and measurability of the strategy's objectives;
- realism and practicability of the implementation timeline;
- coherence between the proposed communications tools and activities;
- match between objectives and communications tools and activities;
- match between objectives and resources allocated;
- potential risks involved in implementing the strategy.

Once the analysis is done, we will provide you with a report on our assessment and recommendations for any modifications needed to the strategic plan and will meet with you to review the report.

Given your timetable, the work would be completed within 10 working days once it is agreed to. I would be the principal consultant, supported by my colleague Heather Reid, whom you met yesterday. The cost would be $10,000.00 plus GST, payable upon completion of the project.

I look forward to working with you and your colleagues.

Yours sincerely,

Vincent Di Angelo,
Senior Consultant

# Editing Practice Two

Jeff Hopewell is the assistant produce manager of Taking Care of Food, a large food chain in Southwestern Ontario. He wrote a proposal after a short discussion with Tarika Bassal, the store's manager (see Figure 6.6). Using the Questions to Consider on page 153, edit Mr. Hopewell's memo.

### FIGURE 6.6

EDITING PRACTICE TWO: SHORT PROPOSAL MEMO

A poorly written short proposal memo

## Taking Care of Food *Making your life more tasteful*

Memorandum

TO:       Tarika Bassal, Store Manager

FROM:     Jeff Hopewell, Assistant Produce Manager

DATE:     October 8, 2006

SUBJECT:  Proposal To Contract For Produce From Local Specialty Farms

I am proposing that we begin selling produce grown on local specialty farms.

At present most of our produce is supplied by two national produce companies National Produce, Inc. and From the Land. Seasonal items such as strawberries, blue berries, and pumpkins are supplied by local farmers. Customers have responded enthusiastically when asked if they like buying local produce and when asked if they support the idea of us supporting local producers.

I have checked with many local farmers and found that in addition to the seasonal items mentioned above, they are capable of supplying various varieties of corn, fresh peas, eggplants, specialty lettuces, and several other types of produce. Though the cost for things like corn and beans will be a bit higher for consumers than it is now, I am sure that they will be willing to pay it.

Adding local suppliers, like Major's Farm, fits well with the policy we adopted last year to further involve the store in the community. The decision to begin selling LeMoyne's breads was a good one, sales are strong and have not cut into other bread sales. In addition, as you probably already know, shoppers seem happy.

*continued*

My plan is to either place signs above the local produce or place it in portable kiosks in the centre area of the produce section with appropriate signage ... and perhaps a taste counter.

Of course, I will have to reduce the amount of produce we order from our regular suppliers. My estimate is that depending on the time of year and the specific product, locally supplied produce will account for 15 percent of total produce sold. Five points of the 15 percent will probably be new purchases, so I plan to reduce orders from our regular suppliers by a total of 10 percent.

## QUESTIONS TO CONSIDER

1. Does the first paragraph summarize the contents of the proposal?
2. Is it necessary to write both "two national produce companies" and their names?
3. Are statements such as "Customers have responded enthusiastically ..." clear?
4. Mr. Hopewell's statement that he is sure that customers will be willing to pay higher prices for locally grown produce might reflect what will happen. But he does not present any evidence to support this judgment. What kind of evidence would support this claim?
5. Is it appropriate to present two possible plans and other options as Mr. Hopewell does in paragraph five?
6. In paragraph six, is the use of the introductory "Of course" appropriate?
7. Could the logical organization of the memo be improved?
8. Is the memo free of grammatical, punctuation, spelling, and usage errors?

# Editing Practice Three

Famis Mohammad, Office Manager of Smith, Jason, Lacroix, and Juarez, a large engineering firm, wrote the proposal in Figure 6.8 after David Sawchuck, Vice President of Operations, agreed with her suggestion (see Figure 6.7) that the firm should contract with Pikitch Printing for all large print jobs. The Questions to Consider on page 156 refer to Figure 6.8.

## FIGURE 6.7

## SUGGESTION MEMO

SMITH, JASON, LACROIX, AND JUAREZ

Victoria, British Columbia
Structural Engineers

Memorandum

TO:        David Sawchuck, Vice President, Operations

FROM:    Famis Mohammad, Office Manager

DATE:      February 19, 2007

SUBJECT:   Suggestion: That Consideration Be Given To Contracting With A Single Company For All External Printing

We should consider contracting with a single company for our out-of-house printing jobs. Contracting with a single company should allow us to

•lower costs;
•ensure consistent quality.

Although the number and types of jobs have remained constant, over the past three years printing costs have risen from $24,000 to $35,000. Currently, each department is responsible for choosing the printer for its job; this makes it difficult to ensure consistent quality of presentation.

May I have your approval to investigate this suggestion further?

## FIGURE 6.8

EDITING PRACTICE THREE: SHORT PROPOSAL MEMO

**A poorly written short proposal memo**

SMITH, JASON, LACROIX, AND JUAREZ

Victoria, British Columbia
Structural Engineers

Memorandum

TO:       David Sawchuck

FROM:    Famis Mohammad

DATE:    March 5, 2007

SUBJECT:  Proposal To Contract With Pikitch Printing

I am proposing that we contract with Pikitch Printing for our larger and more complex printing jobs. The contract will cost $30,000 a year.

At present, when a large printing job or smaller one that requires high-quality colour graphics are to be produced, they are sent to various different printers around town. Each division of the company has its favourite printer—and in some divisions some engineers have their favourite printer.

This arrangement results in inconsistent printing quality and reflects badly on our company. Perhaps more importantly, it is expensive. Although the number, types of jobs, and copies needed has remained relatively constant for the past three years, the cost of this printing has risen from $24,000 to $35,000. My research, which involved calling several of the printing houses, indicates that the reason for the increase is that they are charging more for small specialized jobs.

Pikitch Printing, which already does the printing for the Home Design Division, has indicated that it is willing to contract for our larger and complex printing jobs for a cost of $30,000 a year (based on the average of the last three years).

In addition to costing less, contracting with Pikitch Printing has one other benefit. They have recently installed a new online system that will allow our formatters to e-mail many jobs directly to the printing shop. This will cut down on costs relating to the use of messengers.

May I have your approval to ask Pikitch Printing for a formal quote.

## QUESTIONS TO CONSIDER

1. Does the subject line clearly announce the subject of the proposal memo?
2. What does "they" in paragraph two refer to?
3. In paragraph three, what does Ms. Mohammad mean by "reflects badly on our company"?
4. Should Ms. Mohammad have included examples of jobs done by different print shops?
5. Is it an effective strategy for Ms. Mohammad to introduce her discussion of costs with the phrase "Perhaps more importantly"?
6. Could the sentence "My research, which involved calling several of the printing houses, indicates that the reason for the increase is that they are charging more for small specialized jobs" be stated more succinctly?
7. Mr. Sawchuck probably knows what Ms. Mohammad means by saying "based on the average of the last three years." What do you think it means?
8. Would this proposal have been easier to read if it had been formatted in bullet point form?
9. Is the memo free of grammatical, punctuation, spelling, and usage errors?

# Editing Practice Four

Esther Grabitts is a product specialist in a division of Markaid, a medium-sized company producing specialized novelties and other products to support clients' marketing campaigns. Ms. Grabitts decided to write a proposal (see Figure 6.9) to her unit's manager, David Doolittle, after becoming concerned about the amount of paper waste in her division. Using the Questions to Consider on page 157, edit Ms. Grabitts's proposal.

## FIGURE 6.9

EDITING PRACTICE FOUR: SHORT PROPOSAL MEMO

### Markaid Inc.
Making Markets Produce

Winnipeg • Toronto • Montreal • Halifax

TO:       David Doolittle, Division Manager

FROM:     Esther Grabitts, Product Specialist

DATE:     12 August 2006

SUBJECT:  Waste Paper Disposal and Recycling

I would like to propose we reuse and recycle our waste copier and other paper we generate in the office.

*continued*

As you know, we generate a lot of waste paper from our two copying machines, from printing out emails and generally in the course of our work. Right now, we may scribble on the back of the odd bit of scrap paper but most people just throw used paper in the wastepaper basket. The same goes for copies that are not needed or not properly copied.

This means we have a lot of wastepaper over the course of a week or a month and most of it is just thrown out. We could save the company money by ensuring that all paper is reused whenever possible and we could respect the ecology. This means, first, getting people to write on both sides of a sheet of paper, including used copier paper. It also means getting people to stop automatically printing out e-mail messages and to only do when really necessary. We should third set up a recycling bin for used paper that would be specifically sent for recycling.

From what I can observe, this would not require a great deal of action but rather making people aware of the need to reuse and recycle and to get a specific recycle bin for them to use. We would also have to arrange with the cleaning staff to get the paper sent for recycling.

Should I contact the cleaners and prepare a memo for you to send to the staff?

---

## QUESTIONS TO CONSIDER
1. Does the subject line clearly announce the subject of the proposal memo?
2. Is it clear what Ms. Grabitts means by "respect the ecology"?
3. Could the logical organization of the memo be improved and the structure changed?
4. Does Ms. Grabitts give any evidence of the amount of paper involved and over what time period (week/month/quarter)?
5. Does she provide any information on the cost savings that might be involved?
6. Does Ms. Grabitts indicate that she has checked whether it is practical for the cleaners to recycle paper or if it is done in the rest of the company?
7. Is the memo free of grammatical, punctuation, spelling, and usage errors?

# Summary

Suggestion and short proposal memos are persuasive documents that present your reasoned judgment for changing a process, equipment, or organizational structure presently being used by your employer. Both are based on facts, not personal opinions. The reason for change could be either that the process, equipment, or system is already insufficient to the organization's needs or soon will be.

Suggestions are less formal than short proposals and generally request permission to go ahead and further research an issue. Short proposals, by contrast, present a business case for a specific change. A short proposal includes an analysis of possible costs (financial and otherwise) if the change does not occur, the financial costs of implementing the change, and whether implementing it will result in any downtime. The writer of a proposal must remember that financial decisions are often made by a committee or executives senior to the manager to whom the proposal is addressed. Accordingly, the audience often includes people far removed from the problem or an immediate understanding of it. Thus, suggestions and proposals must include background information that might seem obvious to the writer but will be new to the more distant readers.

# Discussion Questions

1. What is the difference between a suggestion and a short proposal memo?
2. How many options does a short proposal identify?
3. Do suggestion memos require research?
4. Why do suggestion and short proposal memos deal with only one problem?
5. Why is it important to remember that suggestions and proposals rely on your reasoned judgment instead of your opinion?
6. What is the role of "facts" in a suggestion or proposal?
7. What are the different kinds of "costs" that a short proposal memo must detail?

# Writing Assignments

## Assignment 6.1

You are the office manager of a medium-sized manufacturing company in your home city. Write a suggestion memo to the vice president of administration in which you suggest changing office-cleaning companies. Be sure to include a statement about complaints you have received.

## Assignment 6.2

You are working in the marketing department of a medium-sized chain of video rental stores. Write a short proposal that the chain donate some of its old stock to local hospitals for their video libraries. Remember to include such information as how often such stock is rented and how a donation would dovetail with the company's upcoming advertising campaign.

## Assignment 6.3

You are a project manager for Davis Training, a 20-person firm that specializes in providing on-site communications and management training to small companies and organizations. Write a short proposal to Pauline Davis, the firm's owner, in which you argue that she should hire a full-time salesperson. Point out to her that now that the firm has grown, it is difficult for the three project managers to effectively run their projects and act as salespersons. Furthermore, point out to her that Davis Training's reputation will suffer if, as was reported by one project manager, you have to tell prospective clients that you "don't really know" what courses are being offered by the IT training division.

## Assignment 6.4

You are the human resources officer for a national organization in Ottawa. Over the past year, you have received numerous complaints from members in Vancouver who complain that "No one answers our calls after 2 p.m. (PT)." You have decided to propose that one IT specialist and one research officer (there are seven research officers and three IT specialists on staff) change their working hours to accommodate the Vancouver office.

# Web References

### A Practical Guide for Writing Proposals

http://www.members.dca.net/areid/proposal.htm

This site is maintained by Alice Read, an instructor at the University of Delaware, and contains a useful discussion and template for proposal writing.

### Reports and Proposals

http://www.personal.ecu.edu/southards/prepts.html#information

This site is maintained by East Carolina University and contains an interesting proposal writing exercise.

### The Online Communicator: Proposal Writing

http://www.online-communicator.com/writprop.html

This site contains a short online course on proposal writing.

# C H A P T E R · 7 ·

# Analytical Job Progress and Job Completion Reports

## LEARNING OBJECTIVES

In this chapter, you will learn

- what the nature and purpose of analytical job progress and job completion reports are;

- how to avoid tense errors when writing analytical job progress and job completion reports;

- what the structure and components of analytical job progress and job completion reports are;

- how to use Purpose and Focus Questions to organize, develop, and write analytical job progress and job completion reports that meet your reader's needs and level of knowledge.

## PRELIMINARY *exercise*

You are a recent graduate of a public relations program and have been hired by Morgana Consulting, which has just won a contract from Milly's Soft Ice Cream, a Vancouver-based ice-cream company considering moving into the Ontario and Manitoba markets. You see the article in Figure 7.1 and realize that your supervisor, who is away at a conference, will probably miss it. You cut it out and attach it to your summary.

**FIGURE 7.1**

### KRISPY KREME TO CLOSE SIX TEST STORES IN WAL-MARTS

CHARLOTTE, N.C. (AP) - Krispy Kreme Doughnuts Inc. is scrapping its test of bakery stores in Wal-Mart stores.

The beleaguered Winston-Salem, N.C., doughnut maker will close five outlets in Wal-Mart stores around the United States as of Sunday, and the sixth in April, according to a company spokeswoman. "It was a test, and we've made a decision right now that the concept is not viable, but we're going to continue our great relationship with Wal-Mart with our wholesale business," spokeswoman Amy Hughes said Wednesday.

More than 500 Wal-Mart stores carry doughnuts made in Krispy Kreme's own factory-style stores as part of its wholesale business.

A representative for Wal-Mart Stores, Inc. said the retailer doesn't comment on relationships with tenants or suppliers.

Stores in Wal-Marts in Charlotte, N.C., Mount Airy, N.C., Virginia Beach, Va., Maysville, Ky., and Garland, Texas, will close as of Sunday, Hughes said. A store in Hutchinson, Kansas, will close in April.

Asked if the closings are related to Krispy Kreme's financial situation, Hughes said, "That has nothing to do with it." She also said they are unrelated to Dunkin' Donuts' move, announced in May, to open its own shops within 10 Wal-Mart stores. Dunkin' Donuts is a unit of Allied Domecq PLC, a British spirits and wine company.

Krispy Kreme began rolling out stores with Hot Doughnuts Now signs in Wal-Marts in September 2003 as a test.

Company executives a year ago said the first test store, in Mount Airy, N.C., was generating about $20,000 US a week in sales, on average. That was well below the company's average at the time of around $69,000 but profitable, given the lower startup and operating costs, executives said then.

Krispy Kreme has more than 400 company-owned and franchise stores in the United States, Canada, Mexico, Australia, South Korea and Britain.

Its shares began a sharp decline in May 2004 from lofty levels, after the company issued its first profit warning in its four-year history as a public company. That profit warning has since come under regulatory and legal scrutiny amid concerns about its accounting for franchise repurchases.

*continued*

Krispy Kreme faces a possible default of that credit agreement Friday, and investors are awaiting word on the company's financial situation and prospects.

Krispy Kreme shares rose 28 cents, or 3.2 per cent, to close at $9.15 Wednesday on the New York Stock Exchange. On a 52-week basis, there was a low of $5.05 on Feb. 24 and a high of $35.35 last March 30.

## QUESTIONS TO CONSIDER

Before summarizing the article, answer the following questions:

1. What is the article about?
2. Who is the intended reader?
3. What are the major divisions in the text?
4. Does every one merit inclusion in a summary?
5. Are there any direct quotes that should be included in the summary?
6. Who is Amy Hughes?
7. What does Ms. Hughes say about the relationship between the closing of the stores and Krispy Kreme's recent financial problems?
8. What has happened to Krispy Kreme's stock over the past year?

# Introduction

Although analytical job progress and job completion (or status) reports have been written for decades, especially in engineering, construction, and similar areas, they have become even more widespread and important because the way work is organized has changed. Traditionally, work was structured in specific, well-defined, more or less measurable tasks that employees were expected to carry out under supervision. For the most part, few workers worked anywhere but at their employer's premises and they worked as one member of a group of individuals with a series of defined tasks.

Today, employees are just as likely to be working in teams assigned to a specific project—from developing a customer relations policy to designing websites to integrating entire divisions or companies. While a team has a leader and reports to a manager, its members are not under the level of supervision that characterized workplaces as late as the 1960s. But, since the manager is typically not part of a team's day-to-day activity, status reports are needed periodically to show that progress is being made. At the end of the team's work, there will likely be a job completion report.

Just as the use of teams to organize work has risen, so too has the number of people who work away from their employers' premises. For many of these employees, the natures of their jobs mean working off-site—sales, deliveries, inspection, construction, consultants. Still others telecommute from home. Not all off-site workers provide progress or job completion reports, but many have to do so precisely because they are away from the workplace. Much will depend on the type of work being done—routine, repetitive, or well-defined versus project-oriented, technological, or managed remotely.

This chapter teaches you how to write analytical job progress and job completion reports. You will learn that both are factual narratives. Both types of reports discuss (1) the purpose of a project; (2) the proposed schedule and budget; (3) any problems encountered and the solutions to these problems; and (4) the reasons for any changes to the schedule and budget. In addition, job completion reports contain a critical assessment of the success of the project. You will learn how to use the Purpose and Focus Questions to define your reader's understanding of the project and, especially, of the reasons for any schedule or budgetary changes. You will also learn how to avoid tense problems in your job progress and job completion reports.

# Editing Practice One

Sean McCutchen is an education consultant with Nova Scotia Corporate Trainers. Using his project completion report (Figure 7.2) and the Questions to Consider on page 168 as guides, examine Tom's job progress report in Figure 7.3. Tom Furbush is the communications director for the National Association of Hardware and Building Supply Stores; he is reporting on an advertising campaign designed to raise the profile of such stores.

**FIGURE 7.2**

## JOB COMPLETION REPORT

### Nova Scotia Corporate Trainers

*Literacy and Numeracy Are Workplace Issues*

TO: Eudora Carlson, Vice President of Operations, Shelburne Steel

FROM: Sean McCutchen, Education Consultant, Nova Scotia Corporate Trainers

DATE: June 28, 2007

SUBJECT: Job Completion Report For Shelburne Steel And Die's Literacy Upgrade Project

### Introduction

The Literacy Upgrade Project begun on February 1, 2007, was completed on April 12. The two-week delay was caused by the participants' unexpectedly weak numeracy skills, which necessitated the addition of two math classes. The final cost of the project is $50,000, $5,000 more than was originally budgeted.

### Purpose

The purpose of the Literacy Upgrade Project was to upgrade the literacy and numeracy skills of the Shelburne Steel work force. On January 10, 2007, Shelburne Steel accepted Nova Scotia Corporate Trainers' proposal to provide 36 hours of literacy training divided over nine weeks (four hours per week) to 110 employees. The employees were grouped into classes of 20, which were taught by either Melvin Andrews or me in facilities provided by Shelburne Steel and Die.

### Schedule

The original schedule called for the testing of the participants using the Morrison–Pearson Industrial Reading Test. These test scores were required to establish a benchmark against which to measure the efficacy of the literacy training:

- 65 percent of participants scored between 2 and 3 on a 5-point scale;
- 25 percent scored between 3 and 3.5.
  (Note: 4 is classified as competent for industrial readers)

*continued*

Following an analysis of the test scores, Mr. Andrews and I designed the teaching schedule that was submitted to you in the progress report dated February 3. The schedule called for nine weeks of teaching, divided as follows:

| Week | Topic |
|------|-------|
| 1 | Understanding Paragraph and News Story Structure |
| 2 | Understanding Report and Document Structure |
| 3 | Understanding Who Is Speaking |
| 4 | Understanding Difficult Sentences |
| 5 | How to Bring What You Know to What You Read |
| 6 | Understanding Turns of Phrase |
| 7 | Reading Technical Documents (with Numbers) |
| 8 | Reading Is Writing in Reverse—How Would You Want to Be Written To? |
| 9 | Testing and Feedback |

During the second week of classes, we discovered that some participants (we suspected as many as 30) were incapable of understanding technical documents with statistics or mathematical formulas. With your approval, we addressed this problem by changing the schedule and adding two classes: one in basic algebra, the other in the basics of statistical reasoning.

The final schedule (new sessions indicated in *italics*) of the Literacy Upgrade Project was divided as follows:

| Week | Topic |
|------|-------|
| 1 | Understanding Paragraph Structure and News Story Structure |
| 2 | Understanding Report and Document Structure |
| 3 | *Basic Algebra* |
| 4 | *Basic Statistical Reasoning* |
| 5 | Understanding Who Is Speaking |
| 6 | Understanding Difficult Sentences |
| 7 | How to Bring What You Know to What You Read |
| 8 | Understanding Turns of Phrase |
| 9 | Reading Technical Documents (with Numbers) |
| 10 | Reading Is Writing in Reverse—How Would You Want to Be Written To? |
| 11 | Testing and Feedback |

### Project Analysis

The additional weeks of instruction extended the project from 9 to 11 weeks and, hence, from 36 hours to 44 hours of instruction. The additional material covered, however, allowed the project to meet its goals as measured by standardized reading tests, participants' comments, and feedback from their managers.

*continued*

Results on the Morrison–Pearson Industrial Reading Test had much improved.

| Before Instruction | After Instruction |
|---|---|
| 65 percent scored between 2 and 3 | 15 percent scored 3.5 |
| 25 percent scored between 3 and 3.5 | 60 percent scored 4 |

10 percent scored between 4.5 and 5

(A score of 4 is considered competent)

Feedback from participants and, even more importantly, comments from managers were positive. On March 30, the production line managed by Mark Holmes had to be stopped because of a malfunctioning computer-operated drill press. According to Mr. Holmes, standard procedure in such situations is to revert to manual override until the production run is finished, at which point the computer problem is dealt with. He told us that prior to the course, the line would be down for about an hour because production staff had trouble reading the manual and working out the formulas needed to direct the drill press. The line was down for less than a half-hour because, he said, "The team did not have trouble understanding the manual and working out the formulas in it."

### Financial Analysis

The original budget of $45,000 for the Literacy Upgrade Project called for nine weeks of instruction to 110 students (divided into four groups that would each receive four hours of instruction per week). On February 13, I informed you that notwithstanding the results of the first Morrison–Pearson Industrial Reading Test, a large majority of participants required additional training in numeracy skills. We agreed that the courses necessary to address these problems would add $5,000 to the original budget.

| Original Budget | $ 45,000 |
|---|---|
| Numeracy Classes | +$  5,000 |
| Final Budget | $ 50,000 |

Encl: Participants' feedback forms.

FIGURE 7.3

## EDITING PRACTICE ONE: JOB PROGRESS REPORT

**A poorly written job progress report**

# NAHB National Association of Hardware and Building Supply Stores

TO:      Melissa O'Reilley, Vice President of Communications

FROM:    Tom

DATE:    February 10, 2007

SUBJECT: How the Ad campaign is going

Given all the problems we had getting going, the ad campaign is progressing really good. The missing ads will be only two weeks late, which means we can get them on air before the end of campaign. Unfortunately, they will not be able to air the number of times we wanted them too, unless we purchase more ad time.

As you know, the schedule called for Morley Productions to produce seven different advertisements supporting our members by January 15. The campaign itself was to begin on January 20 and run until the end of February. We booked airtime on CBC, CTV, Global, and several cable TV redistributors for this period.

We had three ads on time. Morley Productions reported delays in shooting the other four for a variety of reasons. One was the snowstorm that paralyzed Toronto in early January. Another was the strike by sound crews in Vancouver in late January. I can't remember the other reasons they gave.

On January 16 I spoke with Patricia Louks, the head honcho at Morley's commercial division, and she assured me that the commercials would all be in our hands by the end of the month. They did not arrive then and we did not get an e-mail or call.

I telephoned Ms. Louks on the next Monday and reminded her that we contracted for these commercials and the campaign was planned to present a continuing narrative and that without the other parts of the story the campaign would flop. She assured me that she understood this and says that the we would have the commercials by yesterday.

*continued*

Yesterday, two arrived. I viewed them with Jenny and Messel, who like them. I sent them off to the networks and cable stations.

According to Casey Mariah, response to the ads has been very favourable. She told me that we have received lots of calls praising them from both members and non-members. The polling numbers are said to look good too; something like 60 percent of people Casey asked have responded favourably to them. So it looks as if they are raising the industry's profile in the community.

The only concern I have is with the last two advertisements. Ms. Louks says that they will not be ready until next week. If that is true, then we will not be able to get them on-air for the last two weeks of the campaign. The problem with that is that they continue and wind up the story told in the other advertisements. If they are not on air for the entire last two weeks, then we can assume that they will not have been seen by the viewer population we are aiming at and not seen as many times as we planned for. It will probably be necessary to purchase more airtime to ensure that our plans are made real.

---

## QUESTIONS TO CONSIDER

1. Is this job progress report written in a professional tone?
2. Is the subject line clear?
3. Is it proper for the author of this report to write his name simply as "Tom"?
4. Are all of the tenses correct?
5. Should Tom have begun the report with the phrase "Given all the problems we had ..."?
6. Should Tom have begun the second paragraph with the phrase "As you know ..."?
7. When Tom mentions the reasons given by Morley Productions for why the commercials were not finished on time, should he have written "I can't remember the other reasons they gave"?
8. Is it proper to refer to Patricia Louks as the "head honcho"?
9. Are there places where Tom should have given specific dates?
10. The paragraph that deals with Casey Mariah is missing key information; what is it?
11. Does Tom present Ms. O'Reilley with enough budgetary information?
12. Does Tom present Ms. O'Reilley with a good analysis of the timing question?
13. Is this job progress report free of grammatical, punctuation, spelling, and usage errors?

# The Process of Writing Analytical Job Progress and Job Completion Reports

Analytical job progress and job completion reports are forms of informative writing. Job progress reports tell a manager how a project has been progressing and indicate when it will be completed. If there are problems that will affect the expected completion date, the progress report must detail these and indicate when the project will be finished. The job completion report summarizes the entire history of a project, including problems and solutions. Both types of reports contain sections that give the financial history of the project; that is, they show if the project is under budget, on target, or over budget. Both types of reports are based upon facts; namely:

- the project's established schedule;
- the project's actual course over time in relation to the original schedule, including a discussion and analysis of problems encountered and solutions found;
- the project's established budget.

## SPECIAL TENSE PROBLEMS OF ANALYTICAL JOB PROGRESS AND JOB COMPLETION REPORTS

Analytical job progress and job completion reports are not, of course, the only reports that span different time periods. The proposal details a situation in the present (the analysis of which requires the use of information from the past; for example, the problems encountered last week when the phone system failed) and discusses a solution to be implemented in the future. However, because job progress and job completion reports narrate events over time, some of which are further in the past than others and some of which will occur after a closer future, writers of these reports must pay special attention to their use of verb tense.

Tense indicates time. Tenses can be broadly grouped into three categories: *past*, *present*, and *future*. On a timeline, they look like this:

| Past Progressive | Progressive | Present | Future Perfect |
|---|---|---|---|
| Past Perfect | Past | | Future |

### Present

Verbs conjugated in the **present tense** tell readers that you are talking about events that are occurring right now or about habitual actions in the present. Thus, the sentence "The delivery is six hours late" tells the reader that *right now* at 3:00 p.m. (at the moment you are writing) the delivery that was supposed to arrive at 9:00 a.m. has not yet arrived. Since most business writing does not involve such immediacy, this form of the present tense is rarely used in business reports.

However, another form of the present tense, that which speaks of a habitual action, something that occurs over and over again or continuously, is quite common in business writing. There are two ways to write about these habitual actions. The first uses a verb conjugated into the **simple present**: "He *reads* three books a week." The second uses the present tense of the verb "to be" and a present participle—a verb conjugated in "ing," such as *considering*—which creates what grammarians call the **present progressive**: "The board *is considering* the proposal."

The sentence "The steel mill *produces* 3.8 million dollars' worth of product every hour" describes a state of affairs that occurs every hour. Although it is a form of the present tense, this use of the present actually speaks about the past, the present, and the (near) future (hence the use of the term "habitual"). Use it when you are sure that the action, in this case the production of steel valued at 3.8 million dollars, has been going on for a reasonable length of time (say, since the introduction of the third production line) and will continue for some time to come. The sentence "The company *is losing* five million dollars a year" describes an action that has been going on for a period of time and can be expected to continue (unless some action is taken).

### Past

Writing about the past is more complicated. English divides the past four ways, only three of which are of interest to business writers.

The **simple past** (sometimes called the historic past) is formed by conjugating verbs into the past tense, which for regular verbs means adding "ed" to it; it describes an action that began in the past and has finished. Hence, you would write, "The marketing plan *resulted* in an increase of five percent in sales," if after the marketing plan has run its course, sales went up by five percent. For the irregular infinitive "to find," you would write, "The survey *found* that 26 percent of our listeners have visited our website."

The **past progressive** tense (formed by combining the past tense of the verb "to be" with a present participle) indicates that an action occurred over a period of time before something else happened. Thus, in the sentence "The project *was proceeding* according to schedule until our computers crashed," the use of the past progressive ("was proceeding") indicates that the action came to an end at the time the second action ("the crash") occurred. The second action, which was finished before the sentence was written, is conjugated in the simple past. When two actions occurred at the same time in the past, as in the sentence "Three weeks later, while the commercials *were running*, we noticed that sales *were increasing*," both verbs are conjugated in the past progressive form.

The **past perfect** tense is used to express an action that was *completed* in the past before some other past action or event. In English there are two ways of forming the past perfect. The first is formed by combining the auxiliary verb "had" (or "have") with the past participle of the verb as in the following example: "The project team *had failed* to complete a full analysis, but it still *submitted* its report on time." This sentence makes it clear that the failure occurred before the submission was made. In some cases, you can use the simple past twice without losing the sense of one action coming before another; for example, "The project team *failed* to complete its full analysis before it *submitted* its report."

## Future

Two forms of the future tense are used most often in business writing. There are two ways of forming what is called the **simple future** tense. The first is by using the auxiliary "will" or "shall" before a verb: "I *will* finish tomorrow." The second is by putting "am/is/are" before the word "going" (the present participle of the verb "to go"), which is then followed by the infinitive that defines the action: "I am *going to finish* the report by tomorrow."

The second future tense used often, properly called the **future perfect** (or future anterior), is similar in logic to the past perfect. The future perfect signals that two activities will occur in the future, one before the other. Hence, in the sentence "The team *will have planned* its next move by the time all the data is in," "will have" signals that "the plan" is the first action and will be followed by the arrival of the data. To construct the future perfect, use "will have" followed by the past participle of the verb.

## THE STRUCTURE OF ANALYTICAL JOB PROGRESS AND JOB COMPLETION REPORTS

Although the structure of analytical job progress and job completion reports is quite similar, there are some differences. The introduction of the job progress report discusses the past and present, and predicts the future; by contrast, the introduction of the job completion report discusses the past (the course of the project including problems and changes to the schedule). The analysis section of the progress report indicates how you expect the project to proceed, while in the same section of the job completion report, you will discuss only the past. Similarly, the job completion report reports on the final cost of the project, while the job progress report reports on the cost to date and projects a final cost (which, of course, takes into account the financial impact of any problems).

## Box 7.1

### Job Progress Report

**Introduction**
- starts with a summary judgment statement that indicates how the project has been progressing
- includes a short sketch of problems, if any, and their ramifications (e.g., time and cost)

**Purpose**
- explains the purpose of the project and any relevant background information (e.g., the improvement of electronic linkages by the installation of fibre optics)

**Schedule**
- outlines the schedule as it was established either at the beginning of the project or in the last progress report*
- tells whether the project is on schedule
- details both causes of and solutions to any problems encountered

**Analysis**
- discusses whether the problems will alter the future of the project
- explains how the problems and their solutions will likely affect the project's budget

### Job Completion Report

**Introduction**
- starts with the assertion that the project is complete
- briefly indicates whether the original schedule (or the date of a subsequent schedule) and budget (or subsequent budget) were adhered to

**Purpose**
- explains the purpose of the project and any relevant background information (e.g., the improvement of electronic linkages by the installation of fibre optics)

**Schedule**
- outlines the schedule as it was established at the beginning of the project and any revisions made in the last progress report*
- tells whether the project was completed according to the last established schedule
- details both causes of and solutions to any problems

**Analysis**
- discusses how problems delayed the project (if it was delayed)
- explains how the problems and their solutions affected the project's budget

* If the schedule is changing, a second schedule—with changes indicated in italics—must be included.

## A SAMPLE JOB COMPLETION REPORT

The job completion report in Figure 7.4 was written by Ibrahim Sousa, the installation project manager for Optic-Tech, hired by Western Stock Trading to install fibre optical cable and 5 DPT servers at its headquarters in Vancouver. The report is to J. Wallace Feathstonehaugh, VP, Operations, for Western Stock Trading.

Before sitting down to write the report, Mr. Sousa made sure he had copies of both the original schedule and, because the schedule was altered after the installers encountered a major problem, the revised schedule that Feathstonehaugh agreed to during the project. He also took a copy of the final financial report from the file. Although he had written many such reports, Sousa began as he always did, by answering the Purpose Questions (PQs) and Focus Questions (FQs) that he taught his own employees to use when writing reports.

### Purpose Questions

1. What is my goal?
   Report on the completion of the Western Stock Trading project.
2. Who is going to read this job completion report?
   J. Wallace Feathstonehaugh, Western Stock Trading's VP, Operations.
3. What does my reader already know about the topic/issue?
   Everything. He was there for the entire project and we discussed the problems and solutions.

### Focus Questions

Next, Mr. Sousa scrolled down the page and saw the FQs for job completion reports.

1. Is the project complete?
   Yes.
2. What was the purpose of the project?
   To install fibre optical cable and five servers.
3. Did the project accomplish the objectives established at the outset?
   Yes.
4. What evidence supports a "Yes" response to the previous question?
   The fibre and servers have been installed and have passed their testing.
5. If the response is "No," why not?
   N/A
6. When did the project begin?
   May 2, 2006.
7. Did the project follow the original schedule?
   No.
8. If not, when was the new schedule for the project drafted?
   Revised schedule agreed to on May 5.
9. What was the expected completion date before the final schedule was produced?
   May 10.

10. What was the actual completion date?

May 12.

11. What unanticipated problems were encountered during the course of the project (e.g., delivery delays, procedural delays, construction delays)?

Discovery of support beams on 3rd and 4th floors that blocked the pathway of the cable.

12. Did these problems necessitate a major change in the schedule?

Yes.

13. Did these problems result in a change of plans (e.g., additions to or deletions from the plans)?

Running a trunk-line to an unused pneumatic tube that gave access to 3rd and 4th floors.

14. Were there any problems that did not change the schedule?

Yes.

15. What were they?

One computer was formatted incorrectly.

16. Did the project come in on budget or under budget?

Over budget.

17. If not, what is the cost overrun?

$4,000.

Mr. Sousa paused before beginning to write. He looked back over his answers. His answers to the PQs seemed fine, until he noticed that he had forgotten to include in the answer to the first PQ information that was in the 11th and 12th FQs. *My goal*, he thought, *is not to report on the project alone. Rather, I have to report that the project has been successfully completed and explain why it came in over budget.*

Mr. Sousa then checked the FQs and realized that while he had answered FQ 13 by saying they had run a trunk-line through an old pneumatic tube to get to the 3rd and 4th floors, he had forgotten to indicate that, since the tube was in a different location than the original trunk-line was, cable had to then be run to the left and right of the hubs. Accordingly, he changed the answer to "Running a trunk-line to an unused pneumatic tube that gave access to the 3rd and 4th floors. From the hubs on the 3rd and 4th floors, running cable both to the left and the right."

### Purpose Statement

Mr. Sousa drafted his purpose statement: "My purpose is to explain to J. Wallace Feathstonehaugh that the Fibre Optic and Server Project, which has been completed, went over budget." Satisfied with his purpose statement, Mr. Sousa then wrote the job completion report in Figure 7.4.

**FIGURE 7.4**

## JOB COMPLETION REPORT

TO:      J. Wallace Feathstonehaugh, VP, Operations, Western Stock Trading

FROM:    Ibrahim Sousa, Installation Project Manager, Optic-Tech

DATE:    May 30, 2006

SUBJECT: Job Completion Report For Installation Of Fibre Optics And 5 DPT Servers

### Introduction

The Fibre Optics/New Server Installation Project begun on May 2, 2006, was completed on May 12. The two-day delay in completion was caused by unexpected difficulties in running fibre-optical cable through the walls of 145 East Macdonald Street; the plans provided to Optic-Tech did not indicate the presence of five support beams that blocked the pathway along which cables were to run from the second floor hub to the hubs that were to be on the third and fourth floors, and from each to the workstations on the third and fourth floors. The final cost of the project is $102,000, $7,000 more than was budgeted.

*Sousa summarizes the reasons for the change in the schedule.*

*Sousa summarizes the reasons for the increase in the cost of the project.*

### Purpose

The purpose of the Fibre Optics/New Server Installation Project was to upgrade Western Stock Trading's (WST) IT network and servers. On February 11, 2006, WST accepted Optic-Tech's proposal to install fibre-optical cables throughout WST's building at 154 East Macdonald Avenue and to install five DPT servers, two of which were to be dedicated to the company's intranet and three to be Internet portals. The project was to take seven days and employ six linesmen, two computer technicians and one foreman.

*Sousa explains the purpose of the project.*

*Sousa provides breakdown of the planned work.*

*Sousa indicates how many workers were to be working on the project.*

### Schedule

The original schedule called for stringing and testing of cable to take five days, beginning on May 2, 2006. The installation and testing of the DPT servers was to have begun on May 9 and was to be completed on May 10. The original schedule was divided as follows:

*Sousa explains the two parts of the original schedule.*

*continued*

| Day | Activity |
| --- | --- |
| Tuesday, May 2: | Run optical fibre from basement to room 130, computer room |
| Wednesday, May 3: | Run optical fibre to offices and workstations on 1st floor |
| Thursday, May 4: | Run optical fibre to floors 2, 3, and 4 |
| Friday, May 5: | Run optical fibre to offices and workstations on 2nd floor |
| Monday, May 8: | Run optical fibre to offices and workstations on 3rd and 4th floors |
| Tuesday, May 9: | Set up DPT servers in computer room |
| Wednesday, May 10: | Test intranet and Internet connectivity |

Late in the morning of May 8, we discovered that we could not run cable from the hubs installed on the third and fourth floors to the workstations and offices on these floors. On each floor, a support beam blocked the intended path. Neither beam was indicated on the building plans provided to Optic-Tech by WST. I reported this problem to you before noon on May 8. You asked if we could run the cable around the floor in the other direction. I told you this was not possible because of the elevator shaft.

You then agreed to my plan to run the trunk line 25 metres through the front wall (facing East Macdonald Street) and to then use an old pneumatic tube to run the cable up to the third and fourth floors and from there run the branch lines.

The time needed to run the cable through to the pneumatic tube, reinstall a hub on each floor, and run the cable through the walls (one trunk-line going right from the hub and one going left) to the offices and workstations on the third and fourth floors, respectively, added two days to the project. The final schedule (new activity indicated in *italics*) of the Fibre Optics/New Server Installation Project was as follows:

| Day | Activity |
| --- | --- |
| Tuesday, May 2: | Run optical fibre from basement to room 130, computer room |
| Wednesday, May 3: | Run optical fibre to offices and workstations on 1st floor |
| Thursday, May 4: | Run optical fibre to floors 2, 3, and 4 |
| Friday, May 5: | Run optical fibre to offices and workstations on 2nd floor |
| Monday, May 8: | *Run optical fibre through front wall of 2nd floor* |

*continued*

| Tuesday, May 9: | *Prepare pneumatic tube and run optical* |
| | *fibre to floors 3 and 4.* |
| Wednesday, May 10: | Run optical fibre to offices and worksta- |
| | tions on 3rd and 4th floors |
| Thursday, May 11: | Set up DPT servers in computer room |
| Friday, May 12: | Test intranet and Internet connectivity. |

Sousa provides the second plan of work, detailing the changes in *italics*.

## Analysis:

The unexpected presence of support beams on the third and fourth floors of 154 East Macdonald Avenue increased the time needed to complete the Fibre Optics/New Server Installation Project by two days and increased its cost by $7,000. The use of the old pneumatic tube to run cable to the third and fourth floors, and the decision to run cable both to the left and right of the hubs on the third and fourth floors allowed for successful completion of the installation part of the project.

Sousa begins his analysis by drawing attention to the problem and how it affected both the project's schedule and cost.

Sousa tells how the problem was solved.

The installation of the DPT servers on May 11 went smoothly. During the testing of the servers and network on May 12, it was discovered that one of the DPT servers that should have been formatted as an intranet server had incorrectly been formatted as an Internet server. Reformatting it as an intranet server took 45 minutes. After it had been reformatted, testing of the network continued. At 4:00 p.m., the final test of the network indicated it was working as designed.

Sousa reports that another problem, which did not affect the schedule, was encountered and solved.

Sousa indicates that from a technical standpoint, the project was successfully completed.

As important as technicians' tests are to determining the functioning of an IT network, equally important is feedback from its users. On Monday, May 15, I met with Ms. Sally Wilcox, WST's online trade manager, Mr. Allan Violet, who is in charge of WST's website, and Ms. Louise Marseau, a data input clerk. Each indicated that the network either met or exceeded their expectations. Ms. Wilcox said that she was especially impressed with the speed with which confirmations of trades are generated and sent to clients.

Sousa presents different data—a manager's testimonial—to demonstrate the project was a success.

## Financial Analysis

The original budget of the Fibre Optics/New Server Installation Project was $95,000. On May 8, I informed you that because of beams that were not indicated on the plans WST supplied to Optic-Tech, we could not run cable to the third and fourth floors by the planned route. We agreed that the cable should be run through an old pneumatic tube, a decision that required running the trunk-line through the west wall of 154 East Macdonald Avenue. This change in the pathway added two days and $7,000.00 to the project. You approved these changes on May 8.

Sousa begins by reminding Feathstonehaugh of the original budget.

Sousa explains how the problem encountered on May 8 affected the budget.

Sousa underscores the fact that Feathstonehaugh approved of the changes to the schedule and budget.

| Original Budget | $ 95,000 |
| Revised Budget | + $ 7,000 |
| Final Budget | $102,000 |

Sousa provides the math, which shows the final budget.

# Editing Practice Two

Martha Caccias is an on-site operations manager for Tech Alarms. She is currently overseeing the installation of alarms at a garden supply company and has sent a job progress report (see Figure 7.5) to John Simpson, President of Tech Alarms. Using the Questions to Consider on page 179, edit her report.

## FIGURE 7.5

### EDITING PRACTICE TWO: JOB PROGRESS REPORT

**A poorly written job progress report**

## Tech Alarms
*Our Business Is Protecting Business*

Memorandum

TO:      John Simpson, President

FROM:    Martha Caccias

DATE:    March 9, 2007

SUBJECT: Progress Report On Installation Of Alarm System At Pine's Trees
         Bushes, And Plants

The installation of the alarm system at Pine's Trees, Bushes, and Plants is on schedule, about half of the work is now done. The budget has not been gone over as of now. However, we had to rearrange the work schedule because of some delivery delays.

The project was contracted for on February 28 when Mr. Oscar Pine agreed to the proposal that he asked for. The contract called for us to do several things. First, we had install an alarmed fence around the perimeter of his lot that is 160 metres long. Second, we had to install alarms on his building's doors and windows. Third, he wanted us to install motion detector and fire alarms in his building.

The schedule said that this work would take two weeks and that we would have a crew of four working on the project. During the first week we were supposed to install the alarmed fence. But we were not able to finish the job and haven't yet.

*continued*

The reason for this is that we did not have enough alarmed fence when we started. The engineer at Misconi Fencing assured me that we would get a shipment of more fence on the Wednesday we needed it. We didn't, which meant that by Wednesday afternoon we ran out of fence. About half the fence had been put up by then.

I called Misconi Fencing and told them that it was an emergency that we had to get more fencing. They said they understood but that it would not be possible to get more until Friday or Monday. I told them that that was not acceptable and they said there was nothing we could do about it. I spoke to you about this and you said that you would deal with the matter later.

Because we couldn't do any more fencing until next week, the crew and I turned to alarming Mr. Pine's building. The building has three doors in front, on the side, and in the back. We installed Ring True alarm systems on each door. The building has 10 windows; we installed a window break on each one. As well, we installed Night See motion detectors facing each window, door, and in the hallways. Next to the motion detectors in the hallways, we installed several Sniff Alert fire detectors. We have not yet installed the control panel beside the front door.

The fence is supposed to arrive Monday morning. When it does, we will finish the fencing before turning to completing the wiring of the control panel.

Had it not been for the problem with the fencing we would have had no problems. Luckily, this delay did not delay the project and we should able to continue with other work next week.

The project costs have not exceeded the budget of $35,000.

Mr. Pine says he is very happy with the installation and complemented us on our speedy and clean work, especially when we had to drill holes in his walls.

---

## QUESTIONS TO CONSIDER

1. Is the From line correct?
2. Are there any tense faults in the report?
3. The first sentence of the report ends with the phrase "about half of the work is now done." Is this a proper way of writing in a job progress report?
4. In the introduction, should Ms. Caccias have indicated exactly what was delayed?
5. Would this report be easier to read if Ms. Caccias had used subheadings?
6. Is the first sentence of the second paragraph clear?
7. According to the third sentence in the second paragraph, how much fencing needs to be installed?

8. Should Ms. Caccias have used dates as well as days to indicate when the fence was needed and when it would be delivered?
9. How many doors does Mr. Pine's building have?
10. Should Ms. Caccias have indicated how many Sniff Alert fire detectors had been installed?
11. Should Ms. Caccias have ended the memo with the report of Mr. Pine's satisfaction?
12. Is the job progress report free of grammatical, punctuation, spelling, and usage errors?

# Editing Practice Three

Craig Wood is a public relations researcher. His job completion report in Figure 7.6 details the results of a consumer satisfaction survey he conducted for the Credit Unions of Newfoundland and Labrador. Using the Questions to Consider on page 182, edit Mr. Wood's report.

### FIGURE 7.6

EDITING PRACTICE THREE: JOB COMPLETION REPORT

**A poorly written job completion report**

Credit Unions of Newfoundland and Labrador

Memorandum

TO:       Leon Portelance, Vice President, Regulatory Law

FROM:   Craig Wood, Researcher

DATE:    November 11, 2006

SUBJECT:   Job Completion Report Of The Customer Satisfaction Survey

Introduction
The analysis of the results of the Customer Satisfaction Survey carried out over the summer is now complete. Although we encountered some problems with tabulating the data, mainly due to incompletely filled-out forms, and a delay caused by computer glitches, the project has been completed on time. Rental of replacement computers, however, has added $1,000 dollars to the original budget.

*continued*

## Purpose

The Customer Satisfaction Survey was begun after the board of directors of the Credit Unions of Newfoundland and Labrador asked for it. We were directed to survey our clients to determine their satisfaction with present service and to test reaction to several ideas presently being considered: online banking, expanded investment services, and pilot projects for "cashless" communities.

## Schedule

The survey was designed and tested during the late spring of this year. Optical scanner versions were mailed out to 10,000 members chosen according to standard polling techniques. Another 2,000 members were asked to fill out a form that was posted on our website; we contacted these members by e-mail. Still another 2,000 members were asked to fill in their surveys by telephone interview.

The original plan called for the surveys to be sent out by June 30 and to be returned by August 15. In order to have reliable data, we required 50 percent of 10,000 mailed-out surveys to be returned by this date. We received 57 percent. We similarly required that at least 45 percent of members contacted online respond by the same date; we received more than 60 percent of the responses. Finally, the telephone interviews were conducted from August 15 to September 10. We received a 75 percent response rate.

Once the data had been collected, we began analyzing it. Quickly we discovered that 4,000 of the mail-in responses would not be readable by the optical scanner because they had not been filled out properly. Specifically, the ovals had not been filled in completely.

To correct this problem, I contracted with our temp agency for two temps to go over every answer and fill each in with a number two pencil. This took the better part of a week.

Once we were able to run the mail-in responses through the scanner, we discovered an additional problem with the mail-in responses. The survey questions were designed so that we could double-check responses. For example, question 4 asked if the client had ever thought he or she needed additional services while question 10 asked if the client thought our services were insufficient. Polling theory tells us that for the data to be reliable, more than 75 percent of respondents should answer such questions the same way.

The fact that we did not reach this response rate meant that for the mail-in response we could not consider these questions reliable. To make up for the shortfall in data, we had to reprogram the computers to tabulate questions 12 through 24 (which ask about specific services that could be introduced) and then match those answers against the answers for questions 4 and 10. After a

*continued*

conference call with Decimal Polling, we decided to assign an answer to these questions according to this formula: if a client answered yes to question 4 and no to question 10 but answered yes to three-quarters (8) of the questions between questions 12 and 24, we assigned a yes for both questions. We did the reverse in the reverse situation.

Additionally time was lost when the computer we had planned to use to tabulate the data failed. Trying to get it up and running took one day. The following day we rented a computer from Tech Computer Rentals, which once loaded with the proper software, worked very well.

Analysis

We received a total of 8,000 mail-in responses, 1,200 online responses, and 1,834 telephone responses for a total of 11,034 responses. Of these, 83 percent said that they were satisfied with our services. However, a total of 87 percent said that they thought we should expand services to the Net and increase products. The products that received the highest level of support were investment products, specifically mutual funds.

The total response to the questions about pilot "cashless communities" was 65 percent supporting. However, the total of online respondents who supported this idea was 89 percent. The total of telephone respondents was much lower, 10 percent. The percentage supporting it who mailed-in their responses was 20. Correlating these answers with the answers to questions 15, 16, and 17, which asked about use of Interac cards and experience with online financial services was fascinating. It turns out that the majority of respondents who support a pilot project on "cashless communities" are regular uses of Interac and have ordered merchandise over the Net. There was also an age correlation, with younger respondents generally supporting the idea.

Financial Analysis

The budget for the Customer Satisfaction Survey was $35,000. We had built in a contingency fund of $2,000 that was used to pay for the temps needed to correct the mail-in responses. The rental of the computer to replace the one that failed was $1,000 for the week. Accordingly, the project cost $36,000 or $1,000 over budget.

---

## QUESTIONS TO CONSIDER

1. Should the last sentence of the first paragraph say what the budget now is?
2. Is the first sentence of the second paragraph too obvious to be bothered with?
3. Is the second sentence of the fourth paragraph of the schedule section that says "This took the better part of a week" precise enough?
4. Are the fifth and sixth paragraphs of the schedule section clear?

5. Should Mr. Wood have included a chart in the analysis section?
6. Should Mr. Wood have included the "raw numbers" with the percentages in the analysis schedule?
7. Is the job completion report free of grammatical, punctuation, spelling, and usage errors?

# Editing Practice Four

Daniela Guerrero is a project manager at Canadian Public Relations, Inc. Her job progress report in Figure 7.7 details the progress of the Reads Across Canada promotional campaign. Reads Across Canada is a federal program designed to get boys between the ages of 9 and 14 to read more. Although Guerrero addresses the report to Tyron Charlton, the vice president of the accounts department, she knows that it will be read by the officials of the Ministry of Social Development in Ottawa. Using the Questions to Consider on page 186, edit Mr. Guerrero's report.

**FIGURE 7.7**

EDITING PRACTICE FOUR: JOB PROGRESS REPORT

**A poorly written job progress report**

TO:        Tyron Charlton, Vice President (Accounts)

FROM:    Daniela Guerrero, Project Manager

DATE:     June 1, 2006

SUBJECT: Boy Reading is Cool Progress Report

Introduction
Reads Across Canada reading promotion program begun on March 1, 2006, is both on time and on budget. Minor delays with production of television spots that were scheduled to run during the first week of April were accommodated without effecting the project's overall budget or projected timeline. The cross-country tour of hockey and football players scheduled for the third

*continued*

week of April had to be delayed three days because of the snowstorm that closed Pearson Airport in Toronto on April 21 and 22. The costs associated with this delay were covered by the $10,000 contingency fund, which presently has $5,000 left in in it. Production of the movie trailers scheduled to run between May 1 and June 1 was completed on time and, thankfully, under budget. Unfortunately, production of the Boy, Reading is Cool website ran significantly over budget. As of now we can forecast that when the Boy Reading is Cool project ends at the end of June, it will be $50,000 over budget.

## Purpose

The purpose of the Boy, Reading is Cool reading promotion project is to entice boys between the ages of 9 and 14 to read more. On September 6, 2004, the Federal Ministry of Social Development called for tenders for a national publicity program that would use television and movie theatre PSAs, and public appearances by hockey and football stars (and in Toronto baseball and basketball stars, and Vancouver basketball stars) to drive home the message that "reading is cool." The program is meant to combat the growing trend of boys in these ages to not read. Over the past 15 years, the number of boys who say they "read for pleasure" in this age group has dropped 20 points. Over the same period, the reading scores of boys in this age group have declined greatly. Canadian boys are more than 2 times more likely to be considered "reading risks" then are boys of most of the OECD nations.

## Schedule

The original schedule called for the production of television spots and the program's website to be completed by February 15. The television spots were then to begin airing on March 1 with the website becoming available the same day. Next, the cross-country tour of hockey and football (and other sports) stars was to begin on April 21; the stars were scheduled to go to schools to read to kids and some public readings were organized in large venues. Production of the PSAs that were to run in theatres was to be completed by May 1, with their first viewing date to be May 11. The last viewing date was June 1.

## Original Schedule

| Activity | Date Begun | Date Completed |
|---|---|---|
| Production of TV Spots | January 5, 2006 | February 15, 2006 |
| Production of Website | January 5, 2006 | February 15, 2006 |
| Airing of TV Spots | March 1, 2006 | June 1, 2006 |
| Website Go Live | March 1, 2006 | March 1, 2006 |
| Cross-Country Tour | April 21, 2006 | May 5, 2006 |
| Production of Movie Theatre PSAs | April 1, 2006 | May 1, 2006 |
| Airing of Movie Theatre PSAs | May 11, 2006 | June 1, 2006 |

*continued*

On January 19, 2006, I was informed by Alistair O'Reilly, Photography Director, that due to the malfunction of the mixing board on January 16, he was not going to be able to present the finished PSAs on February 1, as he had originally planned. Fortunately for him, the overall project completion date for the TV PSAs was not until February 15, a date he made.

The production of the Reading is Cool website was finished on time. In his report of January 22, (attached) Wilbert Kennedy, Coordinator of Online Services, informed me that the original budget for the website would not be enough. I informed you of this fact by e-mail on January 23. The problem, as you know, is that after he presented the mockup of the web site, which included 6 interactive games, video clips of films keyed to the text in books and clues for the National Reading Treasure Hunt, the Ministry of Social Development decided that the website should have 10 interactive games, more videos, a Flash statement from the Minister and several other features. These changes all cost a great deal of money and required that the website be redesigned almost from ground up. The Website was completed on-time but only because of a great deal of overtime by both programmers and web-content workers. The total for the website is $125,000, almost $50,000 more than was originally budgeted. There were no problems with the Go Live of the Website.

Further problems arose at the start of the sports stars Cross-Country Tour. On April 21, Toronto was hit by a snowstorm that closed Pearson Airport for 36 hours. By the time the backlog of flights had been cleared and the Cross-Country Tour begun, with a flight to Halifax, Boy, Reading is Cool had accumulated several unexpected expenses, including putting the Stars up at hotels, rebooking rooms in Halifax for the 23 that were originally booked for the 21 and similar rebooking issues at the other cities that were going to be toured that week. In order to get the schedule back on track, instead of finishing the first week on Friday, the stars agreed to meet with students in Montreal and Moncton on Saturday and Sunday. The second and third weeks of the Stars tour went as scheduled.

The PSAs for the movie theatres were produced on time and on budget.

## Project Analysis

The success of the Boy, Reading is Cool program will be judged against three criteria. First is the number of boys who attend scheduled events. As of today, more than 20,000 boys have attended events; this number matches the projections laid out in the Request for Proposal.

*continued*

The second criterium is the number of hits on the program's web site. To date, there have been more than 200,000 hits. More than half of this number have stayed on the site for at least 5 minutes and about the same number have played one or more of the games. There have been 30,000 entrants into the National Reading Treasure Hunt.

The third criterium is next year's National Reading Test. Since it has not yet been run, nothing can be said about it.

Had it not been for the April snowstorm, all parts of the Boy, Reading is Cool project would have been started and completed on time.

### Financial Analysis

The original budget for the Boy, Reading is Cool project was $575,000. As a result of the demands for additions to the Web site by the Ministry of Human Resource Development, the Web site, which was budgeted at $75,000 cost $125,000. The dislocation caused by the April snowstorm was accomodated by monies in the $10,000 contingency fund.

| Original Budget | $575,000 |
|---|---|
| Revised Budget | + $ 50,000 |
| Final Budget | $625,000 |

---

## QUESTIONS TO CONSIDER

1. In the introduction, should Ms. Guerrero have indicated how much over budget the website was?
2. In the purpose section, is the sentence that refers to the sports stars clear and concise?
3. Should Ms. Guerrero have named the stars?
4. In the schedule section, should Ms. Guerrero have given at least a few examples of where the sports stars were going to meet the boys?
5. Should this report have indicated when and on which networks the TV PSAs were scheduled?
6. Should this report have indicated which films the other PSAs were going to be paired with?
7. Should Ms. Guerrero have included a second itemized schedule?
8. Should Ms. Guerrero have introduced the criteria by which the project was going to be judged earlier? If so, in which section?
9. Is the job progress report free of grammatical, punctuation, spelling, and usage errors? Is the spelling and usage consistent?

# Summary

Analytical job progress and job completion reports are factual narratives that explain the course of a special project. Both types of reports contain sections that explain (1) the purpose of a project; (2) the proposed schedule and budget; (3) any problems encountered and the solutions to these problems; and (4) the reasons for any changes to the schedule and budget. In addition, the job completion report presents a critical assessment of the success of the project. Because these reports relate events over time, writers must be careful to ensure that they are using the proper tense, especially when writing about past events.

# Discussion Questions

1. What is the purpose of a job progress report?
2. What is the purpose of a job completion report?
3. How do job progress and job completion reports differ?
4. Why must both reports include discussions of changes to the original schedule?
5. Are these types of reports written only for technical projects?
6. Why must each type of report indicate whether a project is under/on/over budget?
7. Why do these reports raise special tense problems?
8. Why is it important to present numbers and percentages clearly (and in a comparable format)?
9. What are the types of errors that editing your reports will correct?

# Writing Assignments

## Assignment 7.1

Samantha Mandova, an editor at Bridge Publishing, a major publisher of textbooks, has just finished a study of Bridge Publishing's psychology textbooks. Her analysis included a survey of both professors and students who use the textbooks. She found, perhaps not surprisingly, that professors' and students' opinions differed. Professors' ratings tended to be influenced by coverage (e.g., did the text discuss a large number of psychological theories) and fidelity to original sources (e.g., lots of quotes). Students, by contrast, liked those books with simpler writing, visuals, cartoons, and running titles. You may create other data that supports this difference.

The study took two months. Ms. Mandova surveyed 160 professors and 3,000 students across Canada. While a large number of responses were late, the project was completed on time. Write Ms. Mandova's job completion report.

## Assignment 7.2

You are Carlo Giannani, Project Manager for Natural Horticulture, a large horticultural contractor in your city. You are overseeing the installation of greenery (grass, flowers, trees, shrubs) in the park that surrounds the new city hall. The project is scheduled to take three weeks. You have eight workers. Everything went according to schedule for the first two days, during which time your crew removed old grass, trees, and shrubs. Part of the project includes installing underground piping for the automatic sprinkler system. On Wednesday morning, your crew is digging a trench in which you are laying pipe. About halfway across the front lawn, the crew hits a concrete barrier that is not indicated on the plans. You have the crew unearth the top of the slab, which turns out to be seven inches thick, and then have the crew continue digging. They run into another such slab nine metres farther and another one nine metres beyond that.

The slabs are too thick to break with the hammers you have with you. You will have to rent jackhammers to break through them. You call Tools-for-Rent and reserve the equipment you need for Friday. Breaking through the slabs will take all day, which means that the project will be delayed one day. Renting the jackhammers and paying the salaries of your workers will put the project $2,500 over budget. Write this report to Zachary Getty, Natural Horticulture's accounts supervisor.

## Assignment 7.3

You are Mary Lise Merali, the executive assistant to your college's resident doctor, who requested you oversee the rewriting of all of the college's health-related pamphlets to ensure that they were presenting up-to-date information in readily accessible formats. After you requested help from your college's public relations and advertising programs, the instructors in these programs agreed to allow students to work on the pamphlets as part of field placement assignments. Printing was contracted out. Write the job completion report; be sure to include at least two unexpected delays.

## Assignment 7.4

Write a project report in which you tell one of your professors how a research or other project progressed. Be honest and include a problem.

# Web References

### Online Technical Writing: Progress Reports

http://www.io.com/~hcexres/tcm1603/acchtml/progrep.html

This site is maintained by Austin Community College in Austin, Texas, and contains several models of several different kinds of progress/completion reports.

## Engineering Writing Centre: Progress Reports

http://www.ecf.utoronto.ca/~writing/handbook-progress.html

This site is maintained by the University of Toronto and contains useful information about writing technical progress reports.

## Taking Care of Business: Progress Reports

http://www.prenticehall.ca/rogers/1_5.html

This site is maintained by publishing company Prentice Hall and contains a useful guide and example of a memo-form progress report.

# C H A P T E R  • 8 •

# Writing for Newsletters

## LEARNING OBJECTIVES

In this chapter, you will learn

- what the purpose of a newsletter as a means of transmitting information is;

- how to write news reports, feature articles, opinion columns, and promotional stories for newsletters;

- what the requirements of writing for newsletters are;

- how to use Purpose and Focus Questions to organize, develop, and write material for newsletters that meet your reader's needs.

# PRELIMINARY *exercise*

You are the assistant to Harold Homel, Community Relations Manager of InterProvince Treatment, a national waste disposal company. The nature of the company's business means that it is concerned about maintaining good relations with the communities where its plants are situated. Mr. Homel has asked you to summarize an article entitled "About Community Relations" (see Figure 8.1) for distribution to the InterProvince management team prior to a meeting on the company's community relations.

## FIGURE 8.1

## ABOUT COMMUNITY RELATIONS

### New strategic directions

Over the last ten years, IBM has been one of the largest corporate contributors of cash, equipment, and people to nonprofit organizations and educational institutions across the United States and around the world. In all our efforts, we help people use information technology to improve the quality of life for themselves and others.

IBM's contributions target a few key areas and leverage our expertise in technology. In our efforts, we strive to underscore the role of technology as a tool to address societal issues; demonstrate IBM's reputation as a solutions provider; and focus IBM's philanthropic programs to enhance relationships with customers and employees. This policy of strategic investments has benefited communities by bringing IBM experts from all over the world to address their concerns, and has engaged our employees more fully in the important mission of corporate citizenship.

We believe the same information technology innovations that are revolutionizing businesses can provide important breakthroughs for public and nonprofit organizations. These technologies have potential to help organizations deliver better services, manage costs, maximize effectiveness, and implement exciting new programs.

Our commitment to solutions-oriented innovation requires that we go beyond simple chequebook philanthropy. We are working hand-in-hand with public and nonprofit organizations to design technology solutions that address specific problems. This kind of partnership requires our grantee organizations to make significant commitments to us—to go beyond business as usual, to set clear benchmarks, and to focus on measurable results.

## QUESTIONS TO CONSIDER

Before summarizing the article, answer the following questions:

1. What is the article about?
2. Who is the article about?
3. Who is the intended reader?
4. What is the tone of the text?
5. What are the major divisions of the text? Does every one merit inclusion in the summary?

# Introduction

This chapter deals with writing newsletters. Though they share much in common with newspapers—articles can range from news reports or features to opinion columns—newsletters are not written for general audiences, as are, for instance, *The Globe and Mail* and Vancouver's *Province*. Rather, newsletters are written for more specific audiences. Some newsletters, such as *Local Lines*, the faculty union newsletter at Algonquin College (Ottawa), are written for a limited, internal readership. Others, such as the Canadian Civil Liberties Association's online newsletter, *Newsnotes* (http://www.ccla.org/news) are written for a larger, external (though self-selected) readership. In either case, newsletters are an economical way of providing information to a well-defined audience that an organization considers important enough to communicate with on a regular basis—customers, shareholders, employees, stakeholders, or organization members.

Newsletters differ from other types of writing covered in this book. Though accident reports and proposals, for example, are written with an eye to the fact that they could be read by individuals other than the person to whom they are addressed (e.g., an insurance company in the case of the accident report), newsletter articles are written for readers other than the newsletter's editor. Writers of newsletter articles must be aware that their readers

- seek information directly relevant to them;
- want to obtain information as quickly as possible;
- will not bother to read articles if the content is not easily accessible;
- will likely read the newsletter at their convenience.

This chapter teaches you how to write for newsletters. You will learn three different types of writing—news reports, feature articles, and opinion columns—and the requirements of each. You will learn how to write an engaging lead. You will learn the role of the newsletter editor, the meaning of "house style," and the editor's expectations of writers. You will learn how to use the Purpose and Focus Questions to define your readers and their knowledge.[1]

---

[1] This chapter does not deal with newsletter design and layout.

# The Process of Writing for Newsletters

Newsletters respond to their readers' need for concise, easily accessible, and useful information. They do this through their physical design—a layout that makes for easy reading with plenty of headings and no long, dense columns of text—and through writing style.

While we have referred to newspapers and will refer to how newspaper articles are written, it is important to understand how newspapers and newsletters differ. Put simply, no one need read a newsletter. True, there is no law requiring Canadians to read their city's morning paper. But doing so (or at least skimming the feature and a few other stories) is a convention practised by most adults. Newspaper editors take pains to make sure their papers contain stories relevant to people with different interests: thus, the sports, entertainment, and business sections—as well as the books and TV sections. Unless there is a major story, such as the tsunami that hit South Asia on Boxing Day 2004, the cover page usually carries a mix of international, national, and local news.

Although newsletters are more focused, the information in the articles, while nice to know, is less than immediately necessary. To our knowledge, no one has ever said at the office water cooler, "Did you see the story on page two of the company newsletter?"

Newsletter articles compete for their readers' attention against the myriad demands on readers' time, as well as whatever else is going on in the office. Accordingly, writers of newsletter articles must not only choose topics that are going to be of interest to their readers but they must write about them in engaging ways.

## SHORT NEWS ARTICLES

News writing focuses on providing readers with answers to the five Ws (Who? What? Where? When? Why?) and How? A news article consists of a lead—an opening paragraph that contains the most important information about the subject of the article—and subsequent paragraphs that support the lead by giving details and, where necessary, background about the story. The length of the article depends on the importance of the story and the amount of space available.

A good lead makes the reader want to continue into the article but at the same time summarizes everything the reader needs to know about the content of the article. You must find the newsworthy element of the story—the thing that makes it of interest to readers—summarize it in a sentence or a few words, and then try writing it out in a way that will immediately grab a reader's attention. This will probably take several attempts but, with practice, developing a lead will become easier and quicker (see Box 8.1).

You will find that usually—but not always—the most interesting and newsworthy part of a story revolves around who is involved and what they did or what happened to them. On the whole, what interests people is other people, especially those who have some connection to them.

## Box 8.1 COMING UP WITH THE LEAD

### Writing Tip

A common technique used by journalists for writing a lead is to write, "I want to tell you that" followed by the key information that will be of concern to their readers. A journalist will write and rewrite the complete sentence until satisfied and then delete "I want to tell you that."

For example, you may be writing a lead for a story in a company newsletter about the postponement of the opening next month of a new plant in High Falls, Alberta, due to changes in the international market and higher raw material costs, and the fact that 350 new positions will be on hold.

As a first attempt, you could write, "I want to tell you that the new plant scheduled for High Falls will not open as scheduled." To create a better continuation of "I want to tell you that," you might focus on three things that readers would want to know: the plant will not open; the causes are the changing market conditions and costs; and the effect will be 350 new jobs put on hold.

Thus, your revised sentence would be "I want to tell you that increased costs and unexpected decline in sales have delayed next month's scheduled opening of the new High Falls, Alberta, plant and the 350 new jobs that had been expected."

Now delete the first six words and you have your lead:

> Increased costs and unexpected decline in sales have delayed next month's scheduled opening of the new High Falls, Alberta, plant and the 350 new jobs that had been expected.

While there are three ways of organizing the body of news articles—inverted pyramid, chronological, and climactic—most news stories follow the inverted pyramid style. The inverted pyramid style owes its origins to the press release format developed by Secretary of War Edwin Stanton during the American Civil War (1861–1865); during such battles as Gettysburg, July 1–3, 1863, Stanton kept up a constant stream of press releases, with the latest battlefield reports coming at the top of his releases. While newspapers will typically make each sentence a different paragraph (at least for the first few paragraphs of a story), newsletter writers have a bit more leeway and can "chunk" information into two- or three-sentence paragraphs.

### ANALYSIS OF AN INVERTED PYRAMID STORY

In the news report in Figure 8.2, the news item for the New World Advertising company newsletter announces the appointment of Maria Jelinek to the position of creative director of Web-based advertising. The report answers the five Ws and How:

1. Who?
   Maria Jelinek.
2. What?
   Ms. Jelinek's appointment as creative director of the Web-based advertising division.
3. Where?
   Edmonton.
4. When?
   January 17, 2007.
5. Why?
   Creation of the new division.
6. How?
   Decision of the New World Advertising's board of directors.

## FIGURE 8.2

NEWS REPORT

*Vol. V, No. 3 Winter Issue (2007)*

New Creative Director Appointed to Head New Web Division

Maria Jelinek, currently Senior Project Manager of T. M. Lalle, an advertising company based in Regina, has been appointed to the post of Creative Director of New World Advertising's Web-based Advertising division. She will begin working at New World's Edmonton office on January 17, 2007.

Lead
• Who: Maria Jelinek
• What: Appointed to post
• When: January 17, 2007

After graduating from East Coast College's advertising program in 1995, Ms. Jelinek went to work at Halifax Advertising as a copy and graphics editor. Two years later, she took the position of Project Manager at T. M. Lalle, in Toronto. In 2000, she was named Senior Project Manager responsible for new technologies.

Body I
Details her
• education
• early career
• most recent position

Ms. Jelinek's appointment was announced by New World's chair, Robert Zellner, at the employee appreciation dinner on December 15, 2006. Mr. Zellner said that he and the search committee were confident that Ms. Jelinek's expertise would help New World position itself as a leader in Web-based advertising.

Body II
• Tells who announced her appointment
• Relates hopes for her future success

## FEATURE WRITING

A feature is a story that emphasizes some aspect of the news likely to be of interest to readers. The topics for a feature are as wide as potential reader interest and obviously will be determined by the type of newsletter (large international company, small association or government department), its readership, and the editor's preferences. A feature may be a story on a particular part of a company or department and what it does, an article on employees raising money for charity, a profile of a staff member, or an article on a topic of general interest such as travelling with pets. Like a "straight news" story, a feature requires crafting a good lead and organizing the body of the story in an appropriate way.

## A HUMAN INTEREST STORY (CHRONOLOGICAL)

The feature article in Figure 8.3 was written by Aadad Annan, an executive assistant at Moveable Caterers, a British Columbia food service company that runs cafeterias at colleges, universities, and hospitals. The feature tells the company's 2,000 employees about their new boss, Edouard Lachappelle, who has recently been appointed Vice President, Corporate Contracts and Nutrition. To help him organize this feature, which must outline Mr. Lachappelle's personal background, summarize his schooling, describe his business experience, and ultimately make Mr. Lachappelle more than simply another executive's name, Mr. Annan clicked on the file that contained the Purpose Questions (PQs) and the Focus Questions (FQs).

*Purpose Questions*

1. What is my goal?
   Answer everybody's questions about Mr. Lachappelle's personal and business background—make them feel as if they know him.
2. Who is going to read this?
   Employees of Moveable Caterers.
3. What do my readers already know about this topic/issue?
   They know Mr. Lachappelle has been appointed.

*Focus Questions*

1. What information do I need?
   - Mr. Lachappelle's birthplace
   - Something "personal" about him (hobbies/anecdotes)
   - Education
   - Previous work experience
   - Reason for wanting to come to work at Moveable Caterers
   - Any thoughts on coming to British Columbia
2. Where will I get this information?
   - Company fact file
   - Ask company president about him

- Interview Mr. Lachappelle for quotes about his life and education and plans for Moveable Caterers

3. How can I best structure this information for my readers?
   - Tell them about Lachappelle's education and career

Mr. Annan looked over his answers to the PQs and FQs and realized that the answer to the third PQ was incomplete. *True enough*, he thought. *Everyone knows he's been appointed. But the purpose of this profile is to give information to people who don't know anything else about him.* He changed his answer to the third PQ from "They know Lachappelle has been appointed" to "They know he's been appointed, but, with the exception of a few people in the main office in Victoria, no one has met him."

Mr. Annan then realized that his answer to the third FQ was also insufficient. *Yep, I have to tell them about Mr. Lachappelle's past, but the question is what form my article should take.* After a minute's thought, he wrote, "Use chronological order—because I'm writing about his career."

## Box 8.2 NEWS AND FEATURE WRITING REQUIREMENTS

### Writing Tip

Below are some of the key requirements of news and feature writing:

- Accuracy—make sure the facts are correct.
- Completeness—make sure that all the relevant facts are present.
- Quotes—be careful to quote individuals or extracts from other sources of information accurately.
- Simplicity—use short, concise sentences, paragraphs, and words.
- Concreteness—use specific, definite, and descriptive words and phrases.
- Brevity—make articles as brief and compact as possible.
- Acronyms and abbreviations—always spell out what acronyms (words formed from the initials or parts of a multi-word name) and abbreviations (the shortened form of a word or phrase) mean the first time you use them in your piece.
- Vocabulary—use a dictionary to check the spelling or definition of any word of which you are unsure.
- Organization—review the lead and structure you have used to organize and set up the story to ensure that readers can quickly and easily grasp the content.

## TONE

Mr. Annan now turned to writing the lead. Since the previous company newsletter had carried a news report announcing Lachappelle's appointment, he did not want to repeat the lead:

> Edouard Lachappelle, currently Vice President of Universal Cafeterias, will become Vice President of Corporate Contracts and Nutrition as of November 11, 2006. Mr. Lachappelle has 20 years' experience in the food service industry. He will be succeeding Paula Mantis, who is retiring.

Profiles, he knew, could be written in a somewhat more conversational or personal tone. Indeed, since the purpose of the profile was to tell Mr. Lachappelle's future employees something about him as a person (to make them feel as though he's not a complete stranger), his readers would expect a less formal tone. So, he looked back at his notes to see if he could find a good quote or a nice personal anecdote to use in his lead, one that would catch his readers' interest and let them feel as though Mr. Lachappelle was talking to each of them individually.

## FIGURE 8.3

### FEATURE ARTICLE

Vol. V, No. 3 Fall Issue (2006)

**Lead**
• Annan ends the lead with a personal detail designed to suggest Lachappelle's character.

### Edouard Lachappelle

Edouard Lachappelle, newly named Vice President (Corporate Contracts and Nutrition), likes to tell his friends that the business side of the food service industry may eat up most of his time but when visiting his company's cafeterias, he always makes time to eat.

Mr. Lachappelle was born in St. Eustace, Quebec, in 1955. He attended the Université de Montreal, graduating with a B.Comm. in 1976. "My plan," he recalls, "was to become a banker. But shortly after I joined what was then called the Dominion Bank of Canada, I realized that it wasn't for me." Lachappelle surprised his

*continued*

**Body I**
• Annan begins Lachappelle's biography with his birth then moves to his education.
• Annan includes Lachappelle's first job because the fact that he left it for the food service industry is interesting.

- Annan includes this (the quote about Lachappelle's grandmother) as a personal touch.

- Annan includes this quote to link the two parts of Lachappelle's career together.

Body II
- Annan moves to Lachappelle's connection to the Calgary Olympics because it is more interesting than being a restaurant chef.
- Annan allows Lachappelle to tell this part of his story.
- Annan includes this reminiscence because Moveable Caterers' employees will be able to identify with Lachappelle's memory of learning about new foods.

friends—not to mention his family—when he left the bank to study at Le Cordon Bleu cooking school, which had just opened in Montreal. "I was a pretty good chef. Even my grandmother liked what in Quebec we call tourtieres [meat pies]." But what he really excelled at was restaurant and events planning. "I guess the business discipline I learned at university couldn't be denied."

After graduating from Le Cordon Bleu in 1980, Mr. Lachappelle took a position as assistant catering chef at Montreal's prestigious Old Port Hotel. Four years later, he was offered a similar position at the Banff Springs Hotel, where he worked often with the committee organizing the 1988 Olympics in Calgary. "I was organizing a dinner for the International Olympic Committee in 1986 when one of the members of the Canadian committee asked me if I knew anyone who would be interested in becoming the chief nutritionist for the Olympics. I loved working at Banff, so I was surprised to hear myself say, 'Yes. Me.' Before I knew it, I found myself behind a desk dealing with suppliers from all over the world and learning how to prepare foods I'd never heard of. The Olympics was like a 25-day banquet. Balancing the nutritional demands of high-performance athletes with their training schedules and the need to ensure that their food was tastefully presented was a real challenge."

After the Olympics, Mr. Lachappelle became Vice President of Universal Cafeterias. Based in Toronto, Universal Cafeterias services more than 1,000 clients throughout Ontario, Western New York State, and Michigan. "I was at Universal for what's probably been the most exciting time in North America's food industry. When I started, cafeterias served meat and potatoes and spaghetti. Then came the salad craze, then North Americans discovered Mexican food. Setting up a kitchen so you could make 1,000 burritos when a year or two earlier no one would have eaten one took some doing," Lachappelle recalls. "Actually, the challenge was one thing, but from a nutritional standpoint I could not have been happier. Meat and potatoes are good for you, but so are salads and beans."

His latest appointment brings Mr. Lachappelle to Canada's West Coast. "I see it as the completion of a journey I began when I went to Banff," he says. His title, Vice President of Corporate Contracts and Nutrition, is a new one at Moveable Caterers. "I insisted on the title being changed from corporate vice president because I wanted to underline to everyone that, while I am responsible for the business side of things, the only reason Moveable Caterers exists is to provide nutritious foods." He's looking forward to visiting our cafeterias. And though he'll be wearing a business suit, he's more than likely to ask to borrow a white coat and chef's hat. If you're lucky, he might even surprise you by showing you how to make a tourtiere.

Body III
- Annan allows Lachappelle to tell about the difficulties of keeping up with changing food tastes—something that his employees must deal with every day.
- Annan includes this point on meat and potatoes to show to Moveable Caterers' employees that Lachappelle is interested in the nutrition part of the food service industry.

Close
- Annan brings Lachappelle's story up to the present.
- Annan includes Lachappelle's demand that the VP title be changed in order to underline his interest in nutrition.
- Annan ends the article with a personal touch.

**FIGURE 8.4**

## SAMPLE NEWSLETTER

CHALLENGES AND CHAMPIONS
An Insurance Bureau of Canada publication
Volume 5 Issue 4 July 2003

### Getting the Message...

By Terri MacLean, Executive Vice-President, Information & Investigations

Insurance fraud is a crime. It costs law abiding Canadians billions of dollars each year. IBC statistics show that auto theft accounts for $600 million in insurance premiums and costs Canadians a total of $1 billion each year. Bodily injury fraud is conservatively estimated at another 15 per cent of insurance claims.

More and more, evidence points to the involvement of organized crime in the commission of fraud, with the potential connection to active terrorist groups. Easy access to the proceeds of insurance fraud and auto theft is funding other criminal activies, such as drug and weapons trafficking.

The P&C industry recognizes the severity of the problem and the challenges ahead. IBC has played an important role in not only investigating fraud, but also in raising awareness among the public, government agencies and police forces that these are not victimless crimes. There are several specific steps IBC is taking on behalf of the industry in the fight against insurance fraud.

IBC is strengthening its capabilities in fraud prevention by expanding its ring investigation units nationally, with new units in Alberta, Quebec and the Atlantic region. This will sharpen the focus on organized crime groups involved in injury fraud and auto theft in key regions.

Investigators using technology called VisiCais and VisiLink can search information from across the country to identify links between claims. They can also produce graphics to illustrate connections and produce case briefs for Crown prosecutors.

A new crime analyst has been hired to support IBC and insurance company investigators. The analyst will search for trends and patterns in IBC databases and other sources of information. This work will improve the early identification of staged accident rings and organized crime involving stolen vehicles.

There are encouraging signs that police and government agencies are taking these crimes more seriously. IBC has entered into official agreements with many police agencies across the country, and has strengthened its ties with the National Insurance Crime Bureau (NICB) in the U.S. and the North American Export Committee (NAEC). IBC is expanding its involvement with the Canadian Association of Chiefs of Police and provincial Chiefs of Police Associations to enlist their support in the fight against fraud. In addition, international agreements with China, Panama and Lithuania, to name a few, are making it easier to recover stolen vehicles.

Toronto Police Services has got the message about the importance of auto theft, as shown in its commitment to Project HEAT. "Help Eliminate Auto Theft" began on June 5 and was a five-week project involving 30 officers throughout the Greater Toronto Area. The officers focused entirely on auto theft crime during this period. They watched

*continued*

for drivers who left their keys in cars while running errands. These drivers would receive a stern lecture or a fine, and would receive pamphlets with information produced by IBC. The officers also focused on specific regions to target auto thieves. Since the project began, there have been over 100 stolen vehicle recoveries, more than 30 arrests and many ongoing investigations of related crimes involving drugs and weapons found in vehicles.

Toronto Police Services has also been the first to work with IBC in using AutoVu technology to locate stolen vehicles. This technology, mounted on the roof of a police vehicle, scans licence plates and immediately checks those plates against a database of stolen vehicles. Over a six month period, more than 270 cars have been recovered, worth over $2.6 million. Toronto Police Services is putting a second vehicle on the road and many other police forces will follow suit shortly, partnering with IBC to use this equipment.

IBC is also making headway in recent discussions with Ontario Attorney General Norm Sterling. IBC has been promoting the appointment of a dedicated prosecutor in Ontario and other regions to handle insurance crime cases. The goal is to ensure that when the P&C industry and police work together to bring charges forward, prosecutors are sufficiently knowledgeable to obtain a conviction. In too many instances, these cases are plea-bargained and the criminal receives little more than a slap on the wrist. A knowledgeable prosecutor would work harder to educate the judiciary on the need for stiffer penalties.

The Ontario Attorney General agrees it's critical to provide more education and training for prosecutors on insurance crime. He has requested the Chief Crown work with IBC in developing a training program for prosecutors and an ongoing forum for exchanging information with the industry. This commitment on the part of the Attorney General will go much further than one single dedicated prosecutor in the province, who could not possibly handle all of the work. IBC will work with the Chief Crown to monitor the effectiveness of this initiative.

The key to an effective fight against insurance crime is the sharing and analysis of appropriate data. This month IBC will roll out its latest product to help insurers contribute information to the IBC database. Web Claims Submission allows adjusters and investigators to immediately download detailed claim information to IBC over the Internet, and includes the facility to flag files as suspicious. Once submitted, the claim information is available to any member company using Web Claims Search to access claim history data.

All these initiatives and efforts demonstrate that fighting fraud is a complex challenge that has to involve insurers, government agencies, police and the legal system. The focus in the months ahead has to be on education, communication, co-operation and commitment. Together we are making a difference!

Source: MacLean, Terri. "Getting the Message." *Challenges and Champions*. Issue 5, Vol. 4, July 2003 <http://www.ibc.ca/pdffiles/publications/newsletters/challenges_and_champions/july2003.pdf>. Insurance Bureau of Canada. Reproduced with permission.

# The Process of Writing an Opinion Piece

As in newspapers, opinion (or editorial) writing is normally done by the editor of a newsletter, regular columnists, or guest columnists. Editorials present the views of the newsletter (or more accurately those responsible for it) on topics it considers important and of interest to its readers. Editorials are traditionally unsigned, but in many newsletters the editor writes a signed column. A newsletter may also include columns by one or more other writers or reprint an opinion article from elsewhere if it expresses views that the editor or the organization publishing the newsletter believes readers should see. A "Letter from the President" is a common type of column in company newsletters. Some editors deliberately set out to create interest by inviting readers to express their views on controversial topics in a column or opinion forum.

Opinion writing is harder than it looks and is usually done by editors and professional writers employed by an organization's communications or marketing departments. Editorials and opinion columns are examples of persuasive writing and as such share much in common with proposals and even cover letters. Opinion columns seek to persuade readers to agree with the writer's point of view. They are products of *reasoned judgment*—not personal predilections. They are based on facts. They set out a clearly stated and logically structured chain of reasoning that leads the reader step by step to the conclusion desired by the author.

When writing an opinion column, follow these rules:

1. Clearly understand the topic on which you are being asked to give your views.
2. Research the topic.
3. Obtain advice about any sensitive or controversial aspects of your topic (editors will normally help you with this).
4. Do some hard thinking about what you want to say (remember, your readers do not want to read just the accepted, common opinion; they want to hear something new and interesting).
5. Draft and redraft to arrive at a concise, tightly structured, and logical argument supported by relevant facts.
6. Have someone (a coworker, friend, or supervisor) read your draft for clarity, coherence, and, if appropriate, sensitivities before giving it to the editor (you should do this for any type of writing).

## A SAMPLE OPINION COLUMN

The opinion column in Figure 8.5 was written by Nosmo King, a technologist at Can Light Technologies, a Vancouver-based company that designs and manufactures handheld computer devices. Mr. King was moved to write after the British Columbia government announced it would be bringing in legislation to ban smoking in all public places, including restaurants' outdoor patios. Before starting to write, he went on Can Light Technology's website and read the information on the newsletter's "Submissions" page. Since his topic, opposition to the proposed antismoking bill, fell under the heading "Community Issues" and all such submissions must be approved before being submitted, he sent an e-mail to Jason Talbot, the newsletter's editor, outlining his position. Talbot e-mailed back telling him to go ahead and, to help Mr. King organize his piece, he sent him a list of Purpose and Focus Questions, which Mr. King then used to help him organize his writing.

## Purpose Questions

1. What is my goal?
   To stop the government's bill.
2. Who is going to read this article?
   My coworkers.
3. What does my reader already know about this topic/issue?
   They know that smokers like me are really upset.

## Focus Questions

1. What is the present situation?
   - Smoking is legal in some restaurants and bars.
   - It is legal on restaurant patios.

2. What is the proposed change?
   - Ban smoking everywhere.

3. Who/what is proposing this change?
   - The government.
   - Antismoking fascists.

4. What is/are the argument(s) given for the proposed change? (What is/are the argument(s) given for keeping things as they are?)
   - Government says secondhand smoke is dangerous.
   - Government says people don't want to be around smoking.

5. What is the basis of the argument(s) in FQ # 4?
   - Some studies.
   - Lots of rhetoric.

6. Is there an historical example of a similar type of proposal from which something could be learned about how this proposal will work in the real world?
   - Yes, prohibition of alcohol.

7. What is my position?
   - Against.

8. What is the basis of my position?
   - Don't believe government should tell us what to do—civil liberties.
   - Don't believe portrayal of smokers as "evil" and "stupid" is fair.
   - Don't believe all the hype.

After finishing the PQs and the FQs, Mr. King got up from his desk, walked to the elevator, went down to the main floor, and walked outside of the building for his afternoon smoking break. When he was finished, he returned to his desk and read over his answers to the PQs and the FQs.

*This is an opinion piece in a company newsletter,* he thought when he read his answer to the first PQ. *I might want to stop the government's bill, but this piece in this newsletter won't do it. My real goal is to raise awareness among my coworkers in the hope that they will either write to their Members of Provincial Parliament to oppose the bill or at least that when they speak to their friends and family they will convince them to be against the bill.* Then he realized that his answer to the third PQ was overstated. The government might like to ban smoking everywhere, but that is not what is proposed in the bill. *If I overstate my case, my readers will think that I don't know what I'm talking about. Better change that answer to "public places like bars and restaurants."*

Mr. King was happier with his answers to the FQs. The answer to the third one, however, stuck out. *The antismoking crowd is surely vocal. And they might remind me of fascists, but anyone who knows the history of the fascists in Italy or Spain will point to the use of this word to discredit me. A better choice is "fanatics."* Mr. King then wrote his opinion piece entitled "Banning Smoking in Public Places—Health Measure or Social Control?" (Figure 8.5).

# Points for Newsletter Writers

## THE EDITOR

Newsletter editors do the job of editors of newspapers like *The Globe and Mail* and *Le Devoir*—setting the tone of the paper, deciding on content, and assigning stories—and they do the job newspapers normally assign to assistant editors or copy editors; for example, proofreading, editing proper (e.g., cutting a story to fit the space available), and arranging for graphics. As well, since most writers of newsletter stories are not professional writers, newsletter editors provide instructions to authors about such issues as the subject, length, and approach to be taken for the story.

## HOUSE STYLE

Many organizations have developed what is known as a "house style" to ensure consistency in the presentation of information; for example, the use of Canadian versus American spelling (e.g., labour versus labor), how the date is written, whether paragraphs are indented or not, and so forth. Some organizations develop their own style guides and require their staff to follow them.

Likewise, newsletters usually have either their own style guides or use guides produced by and for other organizations such as *The Canadian Style* (Government of Canada) or *The Globe and Mail Style Book* (*The Globe and Mail* newspaper). In Canada, a country with two official languages, it is particularly important to have a consistent approach to dealing with French phrases, the use of accents, and the names of Francophone organizations and communities (e.g., always use the official French-language name of a municipality such as *Lac des Deux Montagnes* even if it is often referred to by its English version, Lake of Two Mountains; see Appendix II).

**FIGURE 8.5**

<small>OPINION COLUMN</small>

# **ATM** CANADA BULLETIN

Vol. V, No. 3 Fall Issue (2005)

## IN MY VIEW
By Nosmo King

### *Banning Smoking in Public Places— Health Measure or Social Control?*

So. You like to go out for a social evening with friends. Maybe go to a restaurant for some dinner or to a pub for a drink and a chat. Unremarkable. Yes, but you smoke, and suddenly you are a miscreant, a purveyor of antisocial behaviour.

The official word is that secondhand smoke may (emphasis on the *may*) harm others and so smokers should be banned from indulging in their wretched habit in public places such as pubs, theatres, restaurants, malls, and the workplace. This is reminiscent of the great crusade to prohibit the sale and use of alcohol in the late 19th and early 20th centuries.

The prohibitionists wanted and succeeded in obtaining a complete ban on alcohol sale and consumption in the United States and, for the most part, in Canada. The product was portrayed as harmful to society, families, and individual health, and the opponents portrayed as agents of the big liquor companies, shadowy but evil empires whose corrupting tentacles were everywhere.

Opposition to prohibitionist fanaticism—which included laws allowing police to raid private homes on suspicion that alcohol was present illegally— became politically incorrect. Anyone raising arguments for moderation was demonized as being in favour of the evils of alcohol and against morality.

Any of this sound familiar? As we know, the evils prohibitionist extremists sought to cure were in the end far outweighed by the evils they caused—the rise of organized crime, the trampling of civil liberties, and the immense diversion of state resources and energies into a dead end.

But most of what prohibition was about had less to do with dealing with the effects of alcohol abuse and much more with reforming human nature and making sure that the unreformed conformed. Historians and sociologists tell us that prohibitionists as much as anything else were very concerned that the masses were not behaving appropriately; that is, in the way that they thought people ought to behave. Booze was a major contributor to this lack of respectable lifestyle that, if left unchecked, could threaten the very foundations of society.

So now it's tobacco. And the same strategies and tactics are being wheeled out, and the same lack of moderation and common sense in the name of curing an evil, redeeming us sinners who smoke, and bringing us and society to the promised land of the smoke-free world. Just as there was a problem with alcohol that required and requires regulation, so there is a health issue with tobacco. But what we now have in response to the problem is another attempt at control and conformity by those who use health as the stalking-horse for imposing their view of how we and society ought to be.

*Editor's Note:* Nosmo King is a technical analyst in the Integrated Systems Sector head office in Longeuil, Quebec. "In My View" is a column for readers who have an opinion on a topic of current interest and want to share it with others. Readers are welcome to write to the editor if they have comments on Mr. King's views.

## Box 8.3 A Sample Bilingual Newsletter

All federal government newsletters and many national organization newsletters are bilingual. The following article comes from *Nagano Eh?* the Official Team Canada Newsletter of the Canadian Special Olympics (2005 Winter Games: Vol. 1).

### Summer Training

You are following a training program this summer. It is also important for a winter sport's athlete to drink water. What's different though? It is important to drink a little more water. If during winter time you are losing a little less water through perspiration, it is still important to hydrate yourself adequately. We will talk about that this winter.

During summer time, it is important to **drink before being thirsty**! A few sips every 15 to 20 minutes should be enough. It is possible though and even risky to drink too much. If you need to go to the toilet more than once every hour, you might drink too much.

You should not drink just anything. Avoid soft drinks or sweetened drinks. Energy drinks like Powerade or Gatorade are not useful unless you train for more than 2 hours. Water is enough for most of your training sessions.

Here is an easy thirst quencher recipe:

1 can of unsweetened frozen orange juice
1 can of frozen white lemonade (they all contain some sugar)
1 litre of sparkling mineral water or lemon-lime soda (facultative)

Prepare orange juice and lemonade as recommended. Mix everything.

Good training!

### Entraînement d'été

Vous vous entraînez cet été. C'est important pour un athlète de sport d'hiver. Qu'est ce qui change cependant? C'est important de boire plus d'eau. Si en hiver on perd un peu moins d'eau par la transpiration, il faut tout de même bien s'hydrater. Nous en reparlerons à l'hiver.

En été, il faut s'assurer de **boire avant d'avoir soif**! Quelques gorgées à toutes les 15 ou 20 minutes devraient suffire. Il est possible et même risqué de trop boire. Si vous avez besoin d'aller à la toilette plus d'une fois par heure, vous buvez peut-être trop.

Il ne faut pas boire n'importe quoi. Il faut éviter les boissons gazeuses ou sucrées. Les boissons énergisantes genre Powerade ou Gatorade ne sont utiles seulement si vous faites plus de 2 heures d'activité. De l'eau est nettement suffisante pour la majorité de vos entraînements.

Voici une recette simple et très désaltérante :

1 boîte de jus d'orange congelé non sucré
1 boîte de limonade blanche congelée (elle contienne toujours un peu de sucre)
1 litre d'eau minérale gazéifiée ou boisson citron-lime (facultative)

Préparez les jus selon la recette recommandée. Mélanger le tout.

Bon entraînement!

Source: From *Nagano Eh?* the Official Team Canada Newsletter of the Canadian Special Olympics (2005 Winter Games; Vol. 1), <http://www.slam.canoe.ca/CanadianSpecialOlympics04/05winter01.pdf>. Reprinted with permission.

## WRITING FINISHED STORIES

Editors rightly dislike getting stories that have gaps or items labelled "statistics to follow," "reference coming," "see last week's press release," and such like messages. As the author of a story, it is your responsibility to turn in a finished product, complete and ready for editing.

## EDITING

A newsletter editor will usually review any material submitted and edit for grammar, punctuation, style, clarity, and content. This means that your story may well appear changed, perhaps significantly, from what you originally wrote. It is rare that anyone writes a story or any piece of business writing that cannot benefit from editing, and, in any event, space limitations or other more important content may mean cutting the length of your piece.

## CHECKING FACTS AND REFERENCES

As the author of a story for a newsletter, it is your job to ensure that what you write is accurate. You are responsible for checking the facts and figures that you use in your piece and the accuracy of any references to sources of information, including quotations.

## NEWSLETTERS AND THE WEB

The World Wide Web presents newsletter writers with both an opportunity and a challenge. By putting a newsletter on the Web, potentially many more people will see it.

---

**Box 8.4**   QUESTIONS TO ASK YOUR NEWSLETTER EDITOR

### Writing Tip

If you are asked to write for a newsletter and do not receive any specific instructions, ask your editor the following questions:

1. What is the newsletter's purpose? What are its objectives?
2. Who is the audience? Are there several audiences, and, if so, are there any priorities among them?
3. What kind of piece is wanted—news, feature, opinion, promotional?
4. How many words are wanted?
5. Are there any sensitivities to be aware of?
6. What should be the tone of the piece?
7. Is there a style guide and, if not, which standard Canadian style guide should be used?
8. Is there a headline or title needed or will the editor write this?
9. Which word processing package is preferred?
10. Are there any guidelines for story writing?
11. Are there similar previously published stories to which you can refer?

---

Readers can do a quick scan on-screen as well as download articles of interest. Also, if the newsletter is properly indexed, back issues can be made accessible through the website. However, writing for the Web is not the same as writing for print, and simply transferring a newsletter to the screen may not be as effective as designing an online version. See Chapter 12 for more about writing for the Web.

# Editing Practice One

Violet Turner is the editor of the Old Priority newsletter. Peter Morgan submitted the newsletter article in Figure 8.6. Using the Questions to Consider on page 209, edit the article.

## FIGURE 8.6

EDITING PRACTICE ONE: NEWSLETTER ARTICLE

**A poorly written newsletter article**

 Old Priority Condo Association Newsletter

March 2007

Board and Members Meeting

The last meeting of the association board with members brought forth many new things for members to consider including whether or not we should increase the fees. The Treasurer, Martha Delisle, spent some time explaining about the need for more revenues to cover increased costs.

There was much discussion of the fees since many people could not understand if there would be more increases after last year. In addition, the cost increases to be dealt with by the fee increases were challenged by some members. The question of replacement of patches of the parking lot floor and lighting had been scheduled for last year but had not been completed leading to issues of use of funds.

It was pointed out that the monies raised last year had been properly used for roof repointing and other jobs that had had to be done as the winter approached. In particular, the furnace had had to have several parts replaced and carpeting in the entrance had worn much more quickly than specified.

*continued*

Finally, the building superintendent, Mr. Sommers, had been taken ill for several weeks during which illness a contract company had had to be used to replace him.

Several people raised lighting questions, especially concerning the approaches to the parking and the entrance. They were assured that this was being dealt with and the steps taken were explained by Harry Rawlinson, board member responsible for maintenance and safety.

The social centre is being redecorated with new furniture. The fitness room has new machines coming and the pool is also getting a face-lift in the changing room area. Likewise, the lawn and garden outside the pool is being upgraded and a special children's area put in for younger visitors.

The meeting adjourned after much discussion which had meant that not all items could be covered. The meeting will continue on Wednesday next and their will be coffee and donuts served.

---

## QUESTIONS TO CONSIDER

1. Is there a clear lead in this article?
2. Does the article have a clear structure? Is there a logical progression of individual items?
3. Is the content easy to understand? Are there items that require more details or explanation?
4. Would headings help the reader? If so, what headings?
5. How would you rewrite this article? Is there further information you would include?
6. Are there grammatical, punctuation, spelling, or usage errors?

# Editing Practice Two

You are on a work term at the Upper Dryden River Association. Your manager has assigned you to "get the newsletter out as fast as possible." Shirley Gwyn submitted the article in Figure 8.7. With the help of the Questions to Consider on page 211, you determine that it is not publishable and decide to redraft it.

FIGURE 8.7

EDITING PRACTICE TWO: NEWSLETTER ARTICLE

A poorly written newsletter article

## Waterroads
### Upper Dryden River Association
#### —————— NEWSLETTER ——————

September 2006

The Navigation Study Public Workshops held from Deeville to Rogers Falls indicated strong turnouts of people interested in maintaining and improving a viable river system. Participants in both the Deeville and Grovetown meetings were pleased of the opportunity to talk face-to-face with environment activists and the others who attended also.

In Deeville an estimated 200 to 250 people turned out and an estimated 75 were in Bowles Hills Community College for the Manitoba event. Those interested in maintaining and improving the river infrastructure came from commodities groups, farm organizations, and local elevator organizations. It was particularly really encouraging to see the numbers of individual agricultural producers who took time during a very busy time to attend. During the meetings, navigation supporters were able to refute, on the record, some of the misstatements of fact and assertions by some that the river system benefits only large grain companies.

UDRA, ARC 2000 and others at the meetings were supporting what has come to be known as Alternative B. B is one of five alternatives put out by the Environment Ministry for public review and comment. The Alternative includes locks on the lower Dryden, 1,200-foot locks at LaHaye and Walopston, on the Minama feeder streams, and 1,200-foot guide wall extensions at locks 4–8 on the Lower Dryden.

Among the points raised by Alternative H supporters were strong ecological arguments including well-established environmental advantages of moving bulk commodities by barge Environment Ministry figures which show lower emissions from towboats than rail or trucks, estimates of air emission clean-up costs that would accompany a modal shift, fuel savings brought about by 1,200-foot lock chambers, and studies which indicate no significant environmental impact from increased barge transportation. Additionally, those who depend on the river for transportation were able to point out that towboats are about 10 decibels quieter than trains or trucks and that barge transportation is the safest transportation mode.

On top of that, it was pointed out that rehabilitation and flood control projects have been demonstrated to work, whereas many of the allegations of possible environmental damage are based on opinions, not established facts.

## QUESTIONS TO CONSIDER

1. Is there a clear lead in this article?
2. Does the article have a clear structure? Is there a logical progression of individual items?
3. Is the content easy to understand? Are there items that require more details or explanation?
4. Would headings help the reader? If so, what headings?
5. How would you rewrite this article? Is there further information you would include?
6. Are there grammatical, punctuation, spelling, or usage errors?

# Editing Practice Three

Constance Jordan is an intern at Western Canada Credit Unions, a consortium of credit unions across Western Canada. Using the Questions to Consider on page 212, edit the profile of Paul Herkimer she submitted to the newsletter of Western Canada Credit Unions in Figure 8.8.

**FIGURE 8.8**

EDITING PRACTICE THREE: NEWSLETTER ARTICLE

**A poorly written newsletter article**

Western Canada Credit Unions

Vol. V, No. 3 Fall Issue

Paul Herkimer—"A WCCU Lifer"

Paul Herkimer, our brand-new VP of the Integrated Systems Sector, is a self-confessed Western Canada Credit Union "lifer" whose long career has taken him all over the world. But, he says, it's great to be back in BC, his home province—just in time to get the guest room ready for the 2010 Olympics.

Born in Victoria in 1947, Herkimer whizzed through school before attending UBC, leaving in 1969 with his degree. A stint as a summer intern at the Victoria WCCU office grew into a something more—an offer to work at the WCCU office in Calgary. "Leaving my home province and being associated with the rough-and-tumble world of oil finance really opened my eyes to the different parts of banking."

*continued*

After four years in Calgary, Paul was offered the chance to move to Toronto where he would serve as WCCU's liaison officer with some of the big chartered banks that dominate finance in Canada. He knew Toronto from a couple of visits as a student but again found himself in a new and challenging milieu. He remained in Toronto for 11 years, and met and married his wife, Sonia.

From Toronto, Herkimer was transferred to Paris, where he served as vice president of WCCU's International Investment Division. "I had nine wonderful years in Paris," where two of his four children were born. From a very small overseas portfolio, he increased WCCU's international holdings a whopping 4,000 percent. "I couldn't have done it without a superb team."

In 1999, Herkimer move again, this time back to Canada, to Kingston, Ontario, where, at WCCU's expense he completed an Executive MBA and then a Ph.D. at Queen's University, specializing in electronic business practices.

Paul's now moved here. He says this appointment brings him full circle back to Vancouver—well, almost full circle since he started in Victoria. "WCCU's been great to me, a boy from Victoria. Because of it and the growth of the company and its faith in me, I've been able to see a great deal of the world."

---

## QUESTIONS TO CONSIDER

1. Should Ms. Jordan have written "whose long career" in the first sentence?
2. Ms. Jordan included the reference to "getting the guest room ready for the 2010 Olympics" because it is a running joke in BC. However, this profile will be distributed to all WCCU employees via the company's e-newsletter. Given this, should she have included this reference?
3. Should Ms. Jordan have indicated what degree Herkimer left UBC with?
4. Should Ms. Jordan refer to "Paul" at certain points in the profile and to "Herkimer" in others?
5. Ms. Jordan ends the first sentence of paragraph three by writing "he would serve as WCCU's liaison officer with some of the big chartered banks that dominate finance in Canada." While what she says is true, is her tone appropriate? Is the phrase "would serve" correct?
6. In paragraph four, Ms. Jordan writes that "he increased WCCU's international holdings a whopping 4,000 percent." Should she have included the dollar figures?
7. Should Ms. Jordan have written "at WCCU's expense" in paragraph five when she is telling of Herkimer's studies at Queen's University?
8. Are there other sentences that are too "cute"?
9. Are there grammatical, punctuation, spelling, or usage errors?

# Summary

Organizations use newsletters to communicate economically with important, specific, well-defined audiences. Newsletters employ design, layout, and writing style to make it easy for readers to access concise, useful information of direct interest to them.

There are four types of newsletter writing: news reports, feature articles, opinion columns, and promotional stories. News writing focuses on answering the Who? What? Where? When? Why? and How? of a situation and begins each story with a lead (an opening paragraph containing the most important information about the subject of the article). The rest of the article (the body) supports the lead and is organized in chronological order, to build to a climax at the end, or as an inverted pyramid with paragraphs in descending order of importance. A feature story emphasizes some aspect of the news likely to be of interest to readers and uses a similar structure to news writing. Opinion (or editorial) writing is done by newsletter editors or regular or guest columnists and presents the newsletter's or writer's views on topics it considers important, using a clearly stated and logically structured argument backed up by supporting facts. Promotional writing in newsletters covers product promotion and is usually done by marketing and communications specialists.

Newsletter editors manage the publication, decide on content, assign stories, give writers instructions, check and cut stories (to fit space available), and oversee layout and graphics. Newsletters have their own style guides, often produced by other organizations, to ensure consistency in spelling, punctuation, and presentation of information. Editors expect to receive finished stories that have been checked for accuracy.

# Discussion Questions

1. What are the role and purpose of newsletters?
2. What are the four types of newsletter writing?
3. What are the requirements for writing news reports, feature articles, and opinion columns?
4. What are the particular characteristics of the newsletter as an information and communications medium?
5. What is the process of organizing, writing, and publishing material in a newsletter?
6. What are the types of errors that editing your newsletters will correct?

# Writing Assignments

## Assignment 8.1

Haribundi Inc. is a manufacturing company with plants in Quebec and Nova Scotia. The company has just signed a major contract with a customer in Asia that will provide significant business over the next five years and create new jobs. As a member of the business development division, you have been assigned to write an article of 400 to 500 words on the new contract for *HariNews*, the company newsletter. You have been given a memo (see Figure 8.9) on the new contract as basic information and told that you can seek other information from the business development division as well as any other relevant sources.

---

### FIGURE 8.9

MEMORANDUM

 Haribundi Inc.

Memorandum

TO:       Charles Farnesworth, Vice President, Operations

FROM:     Bumpta Smuts, Vice President, Business Development

DATE:     August 18, 2006

SUBJECT:  Contract With OMG Technologies Inc.

This is to confirm that Haribundi Inc. has successfully completed negotiations with OMG Technologies Inc. for the contract for delivery of the XTM 5000 product range. This will mean a great deal of work for us and the opening up of the market in Southeast Asia. As you know, OMG headquarters is in India (Bangalore), and we expect that several staff will need to be on site to ensure liaison and train local personnel in the product range use.

At this point, we project a five-year commitment of 100,000 units starting at 15,000 this year (2006) and growing to 20,000 for each of the following three years and 25,000 in year five. The total contract value in final price terms is $50 million at current exchange rates.

*continued*

To meet this order will require immediate hiring of 15 new technicians and 20 assemblers. It is likely that another 20 will be needed over the life of the contract.

We are confident that OMG will increase its present order if the XTM does as well as we believe it will in the Indian market. Indeed, OMG has agreed in principle, subject to market performance in India, to distribute the XTM in the rest of the region. If this takes place, there will be continued growth in company hiring and operations.

## Assignment 8.2

Miriam Walsh, Director of Communications for Pavilion PermaComp, a large computer supply company, has assigned you to cover and write a 600-word feature article for the company staff newsletter, *Pavilion Portrait*, on the annual company headquarters staff summer picnic and children's parade. The picnic will be held in a few days on the beautiful company campus in Kanata, Ontario, and is usually attended by some 500 employees and their spouses and children. The children's parade is organized by the company's staff social and service club, the Serverites, and features many prizes given out by the president, Arva Hensick, and the chair of the club, Francesca Robertson. The food is always commented on since the event is catered by Bistro 345, a highly regarded local restaurant. Using your imagination to add any details, write the article for submission to Ms. Walsh.

## Assignment 8.3

Write a 350-word newsletter profile of your professor. The newsletter is for your department and school; the main readership is your fellow students.

## Assignment 8.4

Take the role of one of your professors and write a 125-word newsletter article for the faculty newsletter explaining why Reading Week is being pushed back one week this year.

## Assignment 8.5

Take the role of an expert in your field of study. Write a 300-word article in which you explain how a new computer program makes things much easier (or harder).

# Web References

### 101 Newsletter Answers

 http://www.101newsletteranswers.com/n_2index.htm

This is a commercial site that contains some very useful information on newsletter writing and templates.

### Got Marketing

 http://library.gotmarketing.com/bd-documents/
documents/5_Writing_Tips.pdf

This is a commercial site that contains useful information on writing e-mail newsletters.

### Christian Newsletters

 http://www.gospelcom.net/guide/resources/newsletters.php

This site is maintained by an evangelical Christian outreach organization. It contains very useful information on writing newsletters.

# PART 3

## External Writing

# C H A P T E R   • 9 •

# Routine and Good News Business Letters

## LEARNING OBJECTIVES

In this chapter, you will learn

- how good news and routine business letters are important to an organization's image;

- what the basic structure, main parts, and conventions of a business letter are;

- when to use direct organization of information in a business letter;

- how to use Purpose and Focus Questions to organize, develop, and write business letters that meet your reader's needs and level of knowledge;

- why style, tone, and sensitivity to readers' cultural and linguistic backgrounds are important in business letters.

# PRELIMINARY *exercise*

You are a communications adviser in the corporate communications department of Functional Wire and Cable, Ltd. Dominic DiAngelo, the department manager, has given you Anthony Mitchell's article "Writing Style Guide for E-Mail and E-Commerce" (Figure 9.1) and instructed you to prepare a summary for transmission to George Reeves, the corporate vice president. Mr. Reeves is concerned that company e-mail has recently become something of a free-for-all.

## FIGURE 9.1

## WRITING STYLE GUIDE FOR E-MAIL AND E-COMMERCE

A company or any other organization can define and adopt its own writing style for e-commerce and e-mail applications, whereby every Web page and e-mail conveys a sense of stylistic consistency.

A specific style sheet can be distributed to everyone within an organization to promote professionalism and uniformity.

Popular style guides such as Strunk and White's 1918 classic *The Elements of Style* and the original 1906 *Chicago Manual of Style* were published before the advent of computers or e-mail. As such, their rules are not always relevant to the exigencies of e-commerce and electronic business communications.

Updated style guidance is needed for the era of e-commerce and e-mail if we are to avoid projecting an unprofessional image and alienating both colleagues and customers. The guidance offered herein initially focuses on both e-commerce Web sites and e-mail, and then on e-mail only. It takes into account recent social changes and the advent of e-mail security technologies.

### Professionalism, Uniformity

Each organization can define and adopt its own unique style for e-commerce and e-mail applications, whereby every Web page and e-mail conveys a sense of stylistic consistency. Large organizations might designate a style committee or an individual style czar. A style sheet can be distributed to everyone within an organization to promote professionalism and uniformity.

There is no contemporary style guide applicable to the modern demands of e-commerce and e-mail communication. The ones that come closest are those published by the American Psychological Association. Their style is less restrictive and faster moving than competing approaches, which enhances its suitability for e-mail and e-commerce applications. They recommend using active verbs. The American Psychological Association's materials include guidance on how to properly cite electronic media.

### Community, Ethnicity, Gender

The American Psychological Association has issued the following guidance on removing ethnic and racial bias from language, guidance that is relevant to both e-mail and e-commerce Web sites:

*continued*

"Authors are encouraged to write in accordance with the principles of cultural relativism, that is, perceiving, understanding and writing about individuals in their own terms. Thus, indigenous self-designations are as important as designations by others, although authors must be cognizant of the fact that members of different groups might disagree about their appropriate group designation and that these designations might change over time."

The American Psychological Association recommends being specific about which community or ethnic group is being referred to. Their policy on spelling is as follows:

"Racial/ethnic groups are designated by proper nouns and are capitalized. When names of colors are used to refer to human groups, they are capitalized (e.g., Blacks instead of blacks; Whites instead of whites). Hyphens are not used in multiword labels (e.g., Mexican Americans instead of Mexican-Americans)."

In distinguishing between aggregations of men and women, the American Psychological Association recommends that the word gender be used rather than sex. Their advice on removing gender bias in writing is detailed at http://www.apastyle.org.

If you do not update your style, particularly as it relates to ethnicity, race and gender, then you risk alienating people who are different from you. You also risk alienating people who are similar to you but who do not want to be too closely identified with someone who might unwittingly be embarrassing themselves.

**Religious Content**

The American Psychological Association's style guides do not provide advice on minimizing religious faux pas in business communications. However, in a rapidly globalizing economy where organizations are becoming increasingly heterogeneous, it often makes sense to review and minimize the religious content of business communications.

In most Western business environments, the presence of an individual who becomes too extreme in their religious evangelism in normal business communications can cause unnecessary distractions. It risks creating a poor image for an organization.

Exceptions to the aforementioned guidance on evangelism are expected, however, if your organization is openly identified with a particular religion and you are communicating with others for the purpose of promoting or underscoring your faith. In such organizations, standard business etiquette regarding religion would obviously be modified, but hopefully with a stylistic consistency apparent throughout the organization.

Professionalism means avoiding ostensibly humorous or disrespectful remarks about an established religion in normal business communications.

**E-Mail Naming Conventions**

There are two parts of an e-mail address, as shown in this fictional example:

"Bugs Bunny" bugs@internationalstaff.net

In the business e-mail addresses that you use, confirm that your personal name (shown within the quotation marks in the address above) is both professional and consistent with how you would like to be addressed (minus titles, in most cases) and how you would like to appear within others' e-mail address books. A common error is for people to write their personal name in all lowercase or all uppercase letters.

In e-mail communications with someone who uses one name for business and another for some aspects of his or her personal life, make sure that you use his or her business name for business communications, particularly when that e-mail might be read by other individuals. In the U.S., it is not uncommon for women to use their maiden name as their business name—with their married name used outside the workplace.

*continued*

Both men and women might have personal names or nicknames that they would prefer not to have used by or shared with their business colleagues. It is important to respect and safeguard the privacy of people's personal names and personal e-mail addresses in a business context.

Figure out what personal salutations are appropriate for each person with whom you communicate. Use those salutations. When in doubt, ask.

Use a professional e-mail address for your business communications. Avoid free e-mail addresses for professional purposes.

### E-Mail Composition, Style

Do you compose within your e-mail client? How often do you use your e-mail client's spell checker?

For important communications, you can compose within a word processing program, spell check using that program's dictionary, then cut and paste the text into your e-mail client. The content can be saved as a text file or other type of document file, with the date and time (and time zone) noted at the top of the text. Replies can be appended above the original e-mail. Such documents can be stored alongside related correspondence such as chat records and document attachments.

E-mail security measures often strip out graphics and HTML from e-mail text. To use graphics and HTML, you might need to send them in an attached file.

Some e-mail recipients do not scroll down to read beyond what initially appears when they open an e-mail. For non-scrollers, place all essential information at the beginning.

The type of writing style that is most appropriate for non-scrollers or impaired scrollers is concise literature, borrowed from the abstracting field. Examples of concise literatures are found in the Future Survey monthly abstract service on science and technology, published by the World Future Society.

---

## QUESTIONS TO CONSIDER

Before summarizing the article, answer the following questions:

1. What is the article about?
2. Who is the intended reader?
3. What is the tone of the text?
4. What are the major divisions of the text? Does every one merit inclusion in the summary?
5. What is the claim made by the American Psychological Association?
6. According to Mitchell, how can religious "evangelism" affect business communication?
7. What is Mitchell's point about humour?
8. Should nicknames be used in corporate e-mail?
9. What is a "scroller"?

# Introduction

This chapter deals with good news and routine business letters. Good news business letters are written for a variety of reasons, from confirming understanding of a conversation to responding favourably to a complaint. Business letters differ from business memos and reports because normally they are written to individuals *outside* the company or organization in which the writer works.

Readers of business letters receive two messages. The first is relatively straightforward: Yes, DiscoMat will replace your broken MP3 player, or No, DiscoMat will not replace your broken MP3 player.

The second is a little more difficult to see but, in today's highly competitive marketplace is, perhaps, even more important. Companies from international powerhouses like Sony and Dell to local pizza shop or even dental offices spend considerable sums of money on logos and corporate stationery or the like. No matter how beautiful the stationery or impressive the paper and printing, a badly written, poorly organized letter with spelling or grammatical mistakes or an inappropriate tone reflects on the writer and the organization concerned. Indeed, educated clients/customers are likely to take such errors as also reflecting the company's attitude toward consumers in general.

This chapter teaches you how to write routine and good news letters. You will learn that business letters are written for many reasons and that they send a message about the writer and the organization. You will learn the various types of business letters, their basic three-part structure, and how to organize their content as well as how to use the Purpose and Focus Questions to define your objectives and your reader's needs. You will also learn to take into account cross-cultural and linguistic factors in writing business letters and how to determine the appropriate tone and style. Finally, you will learn to use the standard components, conventions, and formats for business correspondence.[1]

# Editing Practice One

Karla Seimans is the customer service manager for Jiffy Spot Dry Cleaning. Using her good news letter (Figure 9.2) and the Questions to Consider on page 225, examine Barry Yzerman's good news letter (Figure 9.3). Yzerman is the manager of Canadian Books.

---

[1] Since Microsoft Word, the most common word processing program, defaults to block letter style, the examples that follow are in block letter format. Examples of modified block and indented can be found in Appendix II. As well, Appendix II contains examples of how to properly address an envelope.

## FIGURE 9.2

KARLA SEIMANS'S GOOD NEWS LETTER

 **Jiffy Spot Dry Cleaning**
64 Alistair Dr., Unit 102, Charlottetown, PE C1A 1H9

November 4, 2006

Mr. Horace Dalton
145 Pine Street
Charlottetown, PE  C1E 5H5

SUBJECT:   Refund For Sports Jacket Damaged During Dry Cleaning

Dear Mr. Dalton:

We are sorry to hear that the sports jacket you entrusted to us for cleaning on October 25, 2006, was returned damaged. To compensate you for your loss, Jiffy Spot Dry Cleaning is enclosing a voucher valued at $150.00 redeemable at Men's Formal Wear at 490 E. Main Street.

As you are aware, we take great pride in our work and have over our many years in business endeavoured to keep abreast of the latest developments in dry cleaning. One of the greatest challenges in our business is balancing our customers' cleaning needs with new environmental regulations concerning dry-cleaning products. An added complication in our business is keeping up-to-date on the qualities and requirements of new fabrics and blends.

Six months ago, Jiffy Spot began using a new dry-cleaning formula marketed by Alliance Chemical, a formula that is considered the most environmentally friendly cleaner available. Over the six-month period we, and more importantly, our customers, were extremely pleased with the results.

Your jacket is a blend of wool and Zylon, a synthetic similar to Orlon. The cleaning technician who was on duty when your jacket came to be cleaned had been working for us for four months and was not aware that he should have checked to see if the blend was on the list of fabrics to be placed in a separate cleaning batch, which would then be double-checked against the products' specifications. We have taken steps to prevent this mistake from occurring again.

I hope that this explanation has restored your faith in Jiffy Spot's commitment both to a clean environment and, of course, to cleaning and protecting the clothes entrusted to our care. Enclosed is a $150.00 voucher redeemable at Men's Formal Wear at 490 E. Main Street. Please ask to speak to Ms. Kanaami. I have called her and described the jacket that was damaged, so that she can help you find a suitable replacement.

Sincerely,

*Karla Seimans*

Karla Seimans, Customer Service Manager

**FIGURE 9.3**

## EDITING PRACTICE ONE: BARRY YZERMAN'S GOOD NEWS LETTER

### A poorly written good news letter

*Canadian Books*

100 Bellevue St.
Markham, ON
L2S 9R2

August 3

Mason
3336 Green Rd.
St. Boniface, MB  R4A 1B9

SUBJECT:  Your damaged book

Dear Customer:

I have been informed that your *Canadian Summer's Cookbook* arrived with its cover half ripped off. I agree that this should not have happened. We will give you a new book to make up for it.

Just as soon as I received your letter, I went to the warehouse to find out how something like this could happen. After I spoke to the the shipping and receiving guys, I figured it out. Instead of wrapping your book in heavy bubble wrap, for some unknown reason, they wrapped it in the lighter bubble wrap. That wrap is very good for lighter books, like the ones we print in soft cover. It's not very good, as you can tell, for heavier books.

I'm sure that this problem wont happen again. The shipping guys assured me of that.

Since the book you payed for is not usable, I have told the warehouse to ship you a new one. This time, I assure you, it will be wrapped correctly.

Let me close by saying that we here at Canadian Books thank you for being interested in our books.

Sincerely,

Barry Yzerman,
Manager

## QUESTIONS TO CONSIDER

1. Is the date line correct?
2. Is the inside name correct?
3. Does the subject line clearly indicate what the letter is about?
4. Is it correct to write "Dear Customer" in a response to a complaint letter?
5. Does the first paragraph establish a professional tone?
6. Should Mr. Yzerman have waited until the third sentence of the first paragraph to say that the damaged book will be replaced?
7. The intent of the second paragraph is to explain to Mrs. Mason how the mistake that damaged her book happened—and that steps have been taken to prevent such problems in the future. Does the paragraph succeed in this aim?
8. Should Mr. Yzerman have written "for some unknown reasons" in paragraph two?
9. Is the third paragraph written in a professional tone?
10. Is the fourth paragraph written in a professional tone?
11. Is the letter free of grammatical, spelling, punctuation, and usage errors?

# The Process of Writing a Good News Business Letter

Mark Twain's famous quip "I didn't have time to write a short letter, so I wrote a long one instead" perfectly captures the business letter writer's dilemma. Although one might spend more time with pen in hand or in front of a computer screen when writing a long letter, that time is usually not well spent. Nor, we hasten to add, is it appreciated by the reader—who has to spend more time reading a long letter.

Twain's point is that a good short letter takes time. Time spent planning and organizing one's thoughts so that they are clear, concise, and presented in a way that is useful for the reader. No one, especially in a busy office, wants to wade through difficult prose and muddy thought processes. The point of writing a business letter is to make one's points quickly and convincingly.

## DEVELOPING LETTER CONTENT, TONE, AND STYLE

Using Purpose Questions (PQs) and Focus Questions (FQs) to write a letter will help you clarify

- whether the letter is routine or good news;
- what the main idea you need to communicate to your reader is;
- what information the letter should contain;
- how to use direct organization;
- what the appropriate style and tone should be.

*Purpose Questions*

1. What is my goal?

   Start with what you want to achieve with the letter: Ask yourself why you are sending this letter; what you want the recipient to do or not do; what result you want to obtain.

   The goal may be quite straightforward. The goal in replying to a routine request for information is to provide the information sought by the writer in a timely fashion. The goal in sending a routine letter ordering a product is to obtain the product at the stated price when it is needed. The goal in writing to a company to request a replacement under a product warranty is to have the company honour the warranty and provide the replacement.

   Whatever your immediate goal, you have another—to maintain a positive image for your company or organization with whomever is going to read the letters you write.

2. Who is going to read this letter?

   Identifying your reader's needs is essential. When we speak of "needs" we mean two things:
   • What does your reader need to know immediately?
   • What are your reader's sociological characteristics (e.g., reading level)?

   A customer who has gone to the trouble to pack up her scratched CD and send it to Record Spinning Inc. needs to know that it has been received and that it is going to be replaced; hence, the information in the opening is direct:

   > We are sorry that your All the World's Songs CD was defective
   > and hope you enjoy the one that is enclosed with this letter.

   A letter that is answering a request for information is equally straightforward:

   > Thank you for your letter and questions of September 12, 2006,
   > concerning the differences between motor vehicle and airplane
   > tires. We hope you find these answers useful.

   When we speak of sociological factors, we do not, of course, mean that you are going to interview your reader with a clipboard in hand. Rather, there are several sociological factors that you likely already know: job status, educational status, perceptions (about your company or organization), age, and cultural background. These are not hard-and-fast categories—age, for instance, can determine education level—but they are useful rules of thumb.

   a) **Job status**—What position does the reader occupy? First and foremost, this position is *outside your company or organization.* This means that even if you are writing to a person who occupies a position equivalent to yours, you cannot write to him or her the same way you would to an internal colleague. Writing even to individuals who are junior to you who work for other organizations must be more formal than if you were writing internally.

You would also write differently if you were writing to a communications company's CFO than if you were writing to its vice president, Technical Services, to complain about the new telephone/Internet system. In the first case, were you making a complaint, you would emphasize the financial/organizational problems the defective computer-and-phone system has caused your company, though, of course, you would mention the technical issues. In the second case, you would mention the financial/organizational problems and stress the efforts of your technical people to "get the system up and running" and the company's ongoing failure to do so.

## Box 9.1 LETTERS FOR TRANSMITTING A DOCUMENT OR PRODUCT

The simplest form of routine letter is a transmittal letter, used to accompany and signify the transfer of a document or product from one person or organization to another. A transmittal letter may be very short or it may include some commentary on the document or product that it accompanies.

### COMMUNICATIONS L'IMAGIE

4576, rue de la cimetière
Montréal, QC C9C 8J8
Tel. (514) 497 2975 Fax. (514) 346 7845
www.limagie.com

September 5, 2006

Mr. Jerzy Lopski
Sales Manager
JBM Inc.
2370, La Transcanadienne
Dorval, QC  C7C 2N2

Dear Jerzy,*

Attached is an advance copy of the new product brochure the sales team will use this year, which you asked for yesterday.

Best wishes,
Hélène Turcotte
Head Writer

Encl. Brochure

---

*Turcotte uses Lopski's first name not because she knows him well. Rather, she uses it because this is a routine positive response to a request made at a meeting they were at the day before. Were she writing a letter demanding that a late payment be made immediately, she would have written "Dear Mr. Lopski."

b) **Educational status**—What you assume to be your reader's level of education affects the way you write. For example, were you responding to a claims letter about a flashlight built into an action figure and the complaint letter was hand-written and contained several misspellings and incorrect word choices, you would be justified in assuming that the complaint was written by a child or young teen. Answering him or her with a letter with a sentence that said, "Before receiving your missive, we had received no indications of malfunctions similar to the one you describe" would be both incorrect and boorish. If, however, a complaint letter about an expensive TV with a built-in CD player has phonetic spellings, you would be justi-fied in assuming that the writer is an adult and that English is not his or her first lan-guage. We hasten to add that in making this statement we are not stereotyping, which has everything to do with prejudging the behaviour or beliefs of individuals based on their racial, ethnic, or religious background. Rather, our point is sociological: people who spell phonetically are likely not native speakers of English, which means their reading level is likely lower than the societal norm.

## Box 9.2    JUDGING THE READING LEVEL OF YOUR WRITING

Both Word and WordPerfect allow you to check the reading level of your writing. Normally, business writing should be at about grade 10, though, of course, highly technical documents will be at a higher level and, when neces-sary, writing can be simplified. A good way of ball-parking your writing is to compare it to newspapers. Papers in the Sun chain are written at about a grade-six level; the *Ottawa Citizen,* grade 10; and *The Globe and Mail,* grade 12 (the business section is higher).

When writing to individuals whose English is weak, it is necessary to write as simply as pos-sible, without patronizing your reader.

- Avoid using slang, acronyms, or abbreviations.
- Avoid using culturally specific references or expressions.
- Express one idea per sentence using direct, concrete language.

c) **Perceptions**—What perceptions of your company does the reader likely have? Do you know how your organization is perceived by the market or by particular audi-ences? Will the reader expect a personal approach to his or her concerns rather than a form letter or an impersonal, formal letter?

d) **Age**—How old is the reader? Most of the time, age has little relevance, but responding to an information request from a child will require a different letter than responding to one from an adult. Likewise, responding to an older person who is unfamiliar with technology is different than responding to someone in their 30s, 40s, or 50s, who can be assumed to be, for example, Net savvy. Thus, a letter telling a 70-year-old client how to check his banking online should contain many more pictures of screens so that the process can easily be followed.

e) **Cultural background**—Does the reader belong to a culture with a high level of formality and more elaborate style of writing. Readers in Japan, for instance, expect more formal writing than do Canadians or Americans. The same is true for Germans. A French businessperson would end a formal letter with the following sentence written in French:

"Please accept, sir, the expression of my highest regards."

When writing to anyone you think might come from another culture or speak a different language, ask yourself if your letter
- contains words that might not be known by your reader;
- contains expressions that might confuse your reader;
- refers to events that might not be known by your reader;
- refers to individuals and/or job titles that might not be familiar to your reader;
- assumes cultural knowledge that your reader might not have.

**Box 9.3** BUSINESS LETTERS AND CULTURAL CONTEXT

## Writing Tip

Most of your business letters will be written to people in Canada or the United States. The increased multicultural nature of our society, however, means you may find yourself writing to individuals whose origins are Asian, African, South American, Eastern European, or Middl e Eastern. Be aware that while such individuals may live by the Gregorian calendar, which is most common worldwide, their holy days may not coincide with Christmas, Easter, or the (oh, so Canadian!) "August long weekend." If you are writing to someone whose name suggests that he or she may not celebrate Christian holidays, it is confusing to refer to the "Christmas vacation"; instead, write, "The office will be closed from December 23 through January 2."

3. What does the reader already know about the subject of the letter?
   If you are responding to a request or a claim, your reader already knows what has malfunctioned or gone wrong. What he or she does not know, of course, is the action you will take. This is why good news letters begin by stating that the claim will be honoured or the information sent. Even though your customer's main interest is in getting the malfunctioning or damaged product replaced, it is good business practice to

explain the reasoning behind your agreeing to honour the claim. Remember, he or she took the time to write, and he or she wants to see that you took the time to consider the problem—not just call Shipping and tell them to send out another widget.

### Focus Questions

Focus Questions help to define what information is needed in a letter. While they will vary with the circumstances specific to each letter, the following three FQs apply to preparing any letter:

1. What are the relevant facts? What are the facts that you need to be able to write the letter? What facts should be included in the letter?
2. What are the factors that must be taken into account? Are there company policies that will determine or influence a decision about a request? Are there special circumstances that should be put forward in making a claim?
3. What is the information the reader must have to achieve the goal of the letter? The information the reader needs may be completely factual; for example, facts provided in response to a request for information about a company or its products. But the facts may need to be interpreted and analyzed and the results included in the letter to enable the recipient to have a full understanding of a situation or a decision.

### Purpose Statement

Using the PQs and FQs enables you to arrive at a purpose statement that will guide you in writing your letter. The purpose statement (one to three sentences) briefly sets out what you wish to accomplish in writing the letter and the main idea you want to get across to the reader. The following are purpose statements that could have been written for some of the examples of different types of letters.

Karla Thomaset's response to Jeremy Dalton's routine claim request:

> The purpose of my letter is to keep Mr. Dalton as a customer by telling him that we are honouring our warranty and that we regret the inconvenience caused to him by the defective product. The main idea is that we are a company that stands by its warranties and values its customers.

John Grant's good news letter to Veronica Chapley:

> The purpose of my letter is to keep Welforteck as a customer by telling Ms. Chapley that we have accepted her claim, that her arguments are correct, and that we are immediately sending replacement furniture. The main idea is that her claim is valid and that we value her company as a customer.

## Box 9.4  BUSINESS LETTER STYLE

### Writing Tip

Business letter style:

- one paragraph for each idea
- short paragraphs
- bullets
- short sentences
- the active rather than the passive voice
- simple, concrete, and direct words and phrases
- no jargon
- positive rather than negative ways of expressing ideas

## BASIC STRUCTURE OF A GOOD NEWS OR ROUTINE BUSINESS LETTER

Good news and routine business letters are divided into three parts:

### Opening

Since there is no need to be concerned that a reader will react negatively when starting to read the letter, routine and good news letters normally present their main idea in the opening.

> Thank you for filling out the online survey we sent you on November 4, 2006. As a token of our appreciation, we are pleased to send you a free sample of X-Remove stain remover.

> Your request for information about the number of Canadians who have served in the medical corps of the Canadian Forces since 1980 has been forwarded to the Director of National Defence.

> I am attaching the information about November sales that you asked for at the planning meeting last Tuesday morning.

> We are sorry to hear that the Canadian Cooking cookbook you ordered on January 5, 2007, arrived damaged. A replacement book has already been dispatched from our warehouse.

*Body*

The body of a good news or routine business letter supports the main idea expressed in the letter opening. In the information request letter, the specific information requested is set out:

> I require information about Canadian business analysts who were not entranced by the dot-com boom of the late 1990s.

In the routine claim request letter the body provides the details of and justification for the claim:

> The XRL sound system was set up according to the instructions provided. When it was tested, however, we immediately heard the shriek of feedback. After checking to make sure that all connections were correct, our technicians tested the system again. Once again, moments after turning it on, there was feedback.

The body of a good news letter that is responding positively to a claim explains what actions are being taken to ensure that the problem does not occur again. This is important because it shows the complainant that you are taking seriously his or her time and effort in writing to you:

> After receiving your complaint and the damaged cookbook that you sent back to us, I met with our shipping department. We found that the book had been wrapped in bubble wrap designed to protect our smaller softcover cookbooks. We have put in place procedures to prevent this mistake from reoccurring.

*Close*

The close of a letter is its final element. The close emphasizes the value of the customer and the expectation of a future relationship.

If a claim is being met, the close looks forward to a continuing relationship and future business:

> We are sorry for the inconvenience the malfunction of the LRG speaker caused you, and we thank you for giving our products another opportunity to prove themselves to you.

The close of an information request letter asks for action, gives a deadline for receipt of the information, and expresses thanks in anticipation.

> Let me close by thanking you for your time and reminding you that I require the information by September 2, 2006.

## LETTERS THAT TRANSMIT GOOD NEWS

A good news letter gives a positive response to a complaint, a request for a refund or adjustment, a job interview, a warranty extension, or a similar matter. Any positive answer to a request is a good news letter, including positive responses to routine requests. However, we emphasize in this section the good news letters that are not routine since they respond to requests that raise questions or issues that require making a decision as to whether to accept or reject the case being made. Writing these good news letters may mean taking into account various factors, including, for example, customer satisfaction, the impact on the organization of responding positively to similar requests in the future, or even possible legal implications.

## A SAMPLE ROUTINE LETTER

In writing the letter in Figure 9.4 to Agafix Ltd., seeking timely replacement of damaged goods shipped to his company, Mario Lacoste, a purchasing officer with OEM Inc., began by entering his Purpose Questions and answers.

### Purpose Questions

1. What is my goal?
   My goal is to get the damaged goods replaced as soon as possible.
2. Who is going to read this letter?
   Doreen Keyes, the Agafix sales representative, is going to read this letter.
3. How much does my reader know about the subject of the letter?
   My reader knows a great deal since we spoke about the matter on the telephone today.

### Focus Questions

Mr. Lacoste then asked himself a series of Focus Questions to help develop the content of the letter to Ms. Keyes. Mr. Lacoste answered each question as follows:

1. What has happened?
   Three out of five cases of Grade A printing paper we ordered from Agafix on September 5 are damaged and unusable.
2. When did it happen?
   The paper arrived yesterday, September 10, 2006.
3. What is the result or consequence?
   We will be unable to meet our production schedule in two days.
4. What action needs to be taken?
   We need to receive three replacement cases of paper.
5. Who should take the action?
   Agafix Ltd.—Doreen Keyes.
6. When should the action be taken?
   Immediately.

*Purpose Statement (First Version)*

Given the information he had developed, Mr. Lacoste wrote a purpose statement.

> The purpose of my letter is to ensure Doreen Keyes sends us replacements for the damaged paper as soon as possible. The main idea is that the paper arrived damaged and must be replaced immediately.

Then he wrote a first draft (see Figure 9.4) of his letter to Ms. Keyes.

*(This is only a first draft and not to be used as an exact example.)*

## FIGURE 9.4

### Routine Letter—First Draft

3256 Hutton Street
Ottawa, ON K2N 7T4 Canada
Tel: (613) 456 3487    Fax: (613) 456 2390
E-mail: oem@cynpo.ca    www.oemco.ca

**OEM Inc.**

9-11-2005

Ms. Doreen Keyes
Agafix Ltd.
3200 Sullivan Boulevard
Denton, Manitoba

Dear Doreen:

I'm writing after our phone discussion yesterday about the three cases of damaged printing paper we received from you.

As pointed out yesterday, we need replacement for these cases immediately in order to maintain production. Could you arrange for this to happen, please? Thanks.

Best regards,

Mario Lacoste

Mr. Lacoste reviewed his draft and then realized that he had not fully answered his PQs and FQs. The goal of his letter was to make sure that production was not disrupted, not simply to get three replacement cases of paper, and to make sure that Agafix knew that the cases had arrived damaged and that OEM should not be charged for them. While his letter was routine—supplies were sometimes damaged and Agafix always replaced them once informed—Mr. Lacoste nonetheless felt that his letter should give full information to avoid any misunderstanding or delay. He also realized that although when he phones Agafix, he asks to speak to "Doreen," since this is a claims letter, he should not refer to her by her first name. He rewrote his purpose statement as follows:

> My goal is to have Agafix deliver three replacement cases of Grade A paper to OEM Inc. within two days, without charge, to avoid disruption to production. I am writing to Doreen Keyes, who already knows about the problem I want resolved.

While Ms. Keyes was aware of the subject of the letter, Mr. Lacoste needed to have everything clearly on record and he needed to think about the matter from her perspective as his reader—how might she react to what he wrote, both the content and the tone?

In reviewing his draft, Mr. Lacoste also realized that he had not

- stated when the paper had arrived at OEM or specified what kind of paper (Grade A) was involved;
- properly set out what would happen if the paper was not replaced immediately—in two days, OEM would not be able to meet its production schedule—so that Ms. Keyes fully understood the situation;
- given an order number for reference to ensure that OEM and Agafix could properly record and track everything and make certain that OEM was not charged for the damaged paper.

### Purpose Statement (Final Version)

Mr. Lacoste wrote a revised purpose statement:

> The purpose of my letter is to avoid disrupting production by having Doreen Keyes process our claim and send us replacements for the damaged paper within two days. The main idea is that the paper arrived damaged and must be replaced immediately without charge.

As he considered what he had to write in light of his revised purpose statement, Mr. Lacoste began to think about how he could organize the content of his letter. The first paragraph of his revised letter should tell Ms. Keyes immediately that OEM had received damaged goods that needed to be replaced and that he had discussed the matter with her earlier in the day.

He also wanted to provide Ms. Keyes with the information he had put together in answering his FQs to back up his opening sentence. He remembered that in a business letter, each paragraph should deal with one topic and that the topics and paragraphs should follow each other in a logical order so that the reader could easily follow the points being made. Moreover, in such a letter it was quite acceptable for a paragraph to be only one sentence long. Mr. Lacoste knew that long sentences or dense paragraphs more than 10 or 12 lines long may be misread or even skipped completely.

---

## FIGURE 9.5

### ROUTINE LETTER—FINAL DRAFT

3256 Hutton Street
Ottawa, ON K2N 7T4 Canada
Tel: (613) 456 3487    Fax: (613) 456 2390
E-mail: oem@cynpo.ca    www.oemco.ca

**OEM Inc.**

September 11, 2006

| | |
|---|---|
| *Lacoste uses Keyes's full name and makes sure to include her position in the company.* | Ms. Doreen Keyes<br>Sales Representative<br>Marketing and Sales Division<br>Agafix Inc.<br>3200 Sullivan Boulevard<br>Denton, MB  R1X 3V5 |

*Inside address is complete.*

*The subject line announces the topic of the letter and includes the order number.*

SUBJECT:  Replacement Of Damaged Cases Of Grade A Paper: Order # 2006/09/0987

*Although Lacoste knows Keyes as Doreen, because this is a formal letter, he addresses her by her last name.*

Dear Ms. Keyes:

*Opening*
*Lacoste opens the letter by referring to their earlier conversation.*

I am writing following our telephone conversation earlier today in which I requested that Agafix replace three damaged cases of Grade A paper.

The three damaged cases were part of a shipment of five cases of Grade A paper ordered on 5 September 2006. The shipment arrived at OEM on 10 September 2006, when, upon inspection, three cases were found to be damaged and unusable.

*Body I*
*Lacoste identifies the product and when it was delivered, and explains the sequence by which damage to paper was discovered.*

*Body II*
*Lacoste sets off the effects that this problem will have on OEM in its own paragraph so that information stands out.*

As I noted in our telephone conversation, OEM's production schedule will be interrupted unless we receive replacement cases within 48 hours for those damaged.

*continued*

- Lacoste asks for action.
- Lacoste makes clear that he believes that the expense must be borne by Agafix.

I would appreciate receiving confirmation that the damaged cases will be replaced at no charge and new cases delivered to OEM Inc. by 13 September 2006.

Yours sincerely,

Lacoste signs off the letter with the standard polite business form.

Mario Lacoste
Purchasing Officer

Lacoste uses his full name and title.

Lacoste indicates that there are four documents enclosed with this letter (order, bill of lading and two damaged pieces of paper as samples.)

Encl. 4
cc M. Crumble, Purchasing Manager, OEM Inc.

cc stands for carbon copy; it tells Keyes that OEM's purchasing manager has been sent a copy of this claims letter.

## A LETTER RESPONDING POSITIVELY TO A CLAIM

The good news letter in Figure 9.6 was written by Andrew Mann to go out under the signature of John Grant, ErgoDrive's vice president of client relations. The purpose of the letter is to tell Ms. Chapley that ErgoDrive will be replacing furniture that was delivered damaged—and that action to prevent such problems in the future has been taken.

Before writing the letter, Mr. Mann took a few moments to answer the Purpose Questions and Focus Questions that Mr. Grant had given him when he started working for ErgoDrive.

*Purpose Questions:*

1. What is my goal?
   To tell Ms. Chapley that she'll be getting replacement furniture.
2. Who is going to read this letter?
   Ms. Chapley.
3. What does my reader already know about this topic/issue?
   She knows her furniture arrived broken and that she has the right to demand its replacement.

Since he had not written a letter like this before, Mann paused for a moment to look over his answers. Then he looked at the notes he had jotted down in Mr. Grant's office, answered the FQs, and wrote the letter.

## FIGURE 9.6

## GOOD NEWS LETTER

**ERGODRIVE BUSINESS FURNITURE** ● ● ● ●

369 Essex Street, Fredericton, New Brunswick X8B 8V5 Canada

Tel. (506) 345 7690    Fax. (506) 345 7755    amann@ergodrive.ca

Mann writes the date clearly.

June 24, 2007

Mann makes sure to use Chapley's title.

Mann spells out Newfoundland because his company's letterhead spells out New Brunswick.

Ms. Veronica Chapley

Vice President, Finance

Welforteck Ltd.

346 Reedy Street

St. John's, Newfoundland

A5S 9D2

Mann uses subject line to do more than simply tell Chapley that this letter is about her complaint; he tells her what is going to be done about her complaint.

Subject:    Shipment Of Furniture To Replace Damaged Furniture
(June 21, 2005)

Dear Ms. Chapley:

Direct Opening Mann lets Chapley know immediately that this letter is a positive response to her complaint.

Thank you for your June 21, 2007, letter detailing the damage suffered by the furniture delivered to your company last week. You will receive replacements for the damaged items within three working days.

The detailed inventory of damage and the individual item numbers as well as the photographs you provided helped us greatly in assessing the situation and determining what had gone wrong. You are quite correct in noting that the packing and shipping instructions provided to Central Transportation Inc. were imprecise and that the result of this was the damage suffered by the furniture Welforteck ordered. We have confirmed this through our own investigation and revised our procedures to ensure that this type of error does not occur again. In fact, your letter has enabled us to identify and rectify deficiencies in our procedures. The replacement items are being assembled now and carefully packed for immediate dispatch to you.

Body
- Mann mentions "item numbers" and "photographs" to show that he is aware of the facts Chapley presented in her letter.
- Mann agrees with her analysis of the problem.
- Mann points to further investigation to show that ErgoDrive has used her information.
- Mann details action being taken to prevent this problem from occurring again.

*continued*

I regret the inconvenience that has been caused to you and Welforteck. We can remain in business only if our clients are certain that we will provide them with excellent products, and we strive to do this. This is why we appreciate you giving us the opportunity to demonstrate this commitment and hope to serve you again in the future.

Yours sincerely,

John Grant
Vice President, Client Relations

cc D. Winchester, Shipping Manager

# Editing Practice Two

Dwayne Oskosch is a senior sales associate with Boots for Walking Inc., a major boot manufacturer. He has drafted a letter giving a positive response to a customer complaint. Using the Questions to Consider on page 241, edit the letter in Figure 9.7.

**FIGURE 9.7**

EDITING PRACTICE TWO: GOOD NEWS LETTER

A poorly written good news letter

## Boots for Walking Inc. "The Boot People"

1300 West 54 Street, Regina, SK N9X 0T8 Canada
Tel. (306) 234 7651    Fax. (306) 435 2398    www.bootswalk.com

October 9, 2006

Mr. Arthur Porter
Apt. 456
1700 Bayview Street
Toronto, ON  M5W 7Y7

Subject: Extra-Soft Mark IV Boots

Dear Mr. Porter:

Thanks for your letter about the above subject. We really appreciate hearing from our customers because, of course, without them, we would not be in business.

You wrote to us in the autumn about the problems you were having with your new Extra-Soft Mark IV Boots. These are as you know a fine product and used by hikers all over Canada and the United States that form what we at Boots For Walking hear through our customer feedback mechanisms major customer satisfaction. In fact, I believe that our boots have been recently issued to firefighting crews because of their special qualities and superior strength.

Needless to say, we were somewhat surprised to learn of your difficulties with the Extra-Soft Mark IV but after our specialists examined them in-depth we decided that we would allow your claim. I'm pleased to say that we are sending you a new pair of Extra-Soft boots as you requested and these should be with you shortly in time for you to pursue your excursions this autumn.

We at Boots for Walking hope that profit from our superior product to have many miles of walking enjoyment and we look forward to being able to serve you again to meet all your outdoor footwear needs.

Yours truly,

Dwayne Oskosch
Senior Sales Associate

## QUESTIONS TO CONSIDER

1. Is Mr. Oskosch's letter organized appropriately?
2. In which part of the letter does he deliver his good news?
3. Is the opening of the letter effective?
4. Is the closing effective?
5. What is the tone of the letter?
6. Would Mr. Porter feel that Boots for Walking respects him or the company's customers?
7. Does Mr. Oskosch's letter contain unnecessary or inappropriate information?
8. What impressions might Mr. Porter gain from the letter?
9. Are there grammatical, punctuation, spelling, or usage errors?
10. How would you rewrite this letter to make it more effective?

# Editing Practice Three

Karla Thomaset is the general manager of Flexomatic Ltd., a manufacturer of weight training and muscle building equipment. Using the Questions to Consider on page 243, examine her letter (Figure 9.8).

FIGURE 9.8

## EDITING PRACTICE THREE: RESPONSE TO A ROUTINE CLAIM REQUEST

**A poorly written response**

# Flexomatic Ltd.

36 Hull Road, Ottawa, K3V 909 Canada

**Tel:** (613) 436 9988  **Fax:** (613) 453 2254  **E-mail:** flexomatic@trace.ca

November 21, 2006

Mr. Jeremy Dalton
17 Chapel Avenue
Ottawa K1N 9S2
Subject:   <u>Refund</u>

Dear Mr. Dalton:

We, here at Flexomatic, were very upset by your letter of November 12, 2006, in which you told us of your unhappiness with the Muscle Expander machine you had bought from us. You should receive a new Muscle Expander by special delivery.

Our products are manufactured to the highest quality levels, but sometimes bad things happen in the manufacturing process. We are concerned that the Muscle Expander you bought did not operate as specified.

We value our customers. As you know, when a company values its customers, it treats them well. This is why we are going to replace your Muscle Expander. Being completely satisfied is what we want.

I hope that you will enjoy your new Muscle Expander and thank you for your confidence in Flexomatic.

Yours sincerely,

*Karla Thomaset*

Karla Thomaset
General Manager

## QUESTIONS TO CONSIDER

1. Is the company address written correctly?
2. Does the subject line clearly identify what the letter is telling Mr. Dalton?
3. Is the first sentence written in a professional tone?
4. Is Flexomatic's "upset" the point? Does it "ring true"?
5. Does the second sentence indicate clearly when Mr. Dalton can expect to receive the replacement machine?
6. Is the first sentence of the second paragraph written in a professional tone?
7. Is the third paragraph written in a professional tone?
8. What is "Being completely satisfied is what we want" supposed to mean?
9. Is the letter free of grammatical, spelling, punctuation, and usage errors?

# Editing Practice Four

Malcolm Chesnutt is technical director for Northern Pet Foods, Inc. Using the Questions to Consider below, edit his inquiry letter (Figure 9.9), addressed to Ian Jackson, Director of Sales for Innovative Plastics Solutions.

## QUESTIONS TO CONSIDER

1. Does the first paragraph clearly indicate what information Chesnutt is looking for?
2. Should Chesnutt have indicated the measurements of the packages Northern Pet Foods, Inc. will need?
3. Is the second paragraph clear?
4. Is the second sentence of the fourth paragraph, "The easiest time for deliveries ..." written in a professional tone?
5. Is the fourth paragraph clear?
6. Should Chesnutt have put the information in the fifth paragraph earlier?
7. Is the second sentence of the sixth paragraph, "Since you probably will have some questions ..." written in a professional tone?
8. Is the letter free of grammatical, spelling, punctuation, and usage errors?

## FIGURE 9.9

### EDITING PRACTICE FOUR: INQUIRY LETTER

**A poorly written inquiry letter**

**NORTHERN PET FOODS, INC.**
1550 FIRST AVENUE
ETOBICOKE, ONTARIO
M1U 5T8

*Only the Freshest Ingredients for YOUR 4-legged Friends*

October 30, 2006

Mr. Ian Jackson
Director of Sales
Innovative Plastics Solutions
77 Innovation Drive
Winnipeg, MB  R7L 7I8

Dear Mr. Jackson:

This spring Northern Pet Foods will be bringing to market a new product. This product is single-serving size gourmet foods for canines. I am looking for a provider of plastic packages.

I would like to see an information package that describes your products and your design team's abilities. Do you have such a package?

We will require three different designs because we have three different types of dog foods:
- Young dogs
- Older dogs
- Dogs requiring low-ash diets

The designs can be structurally different or they can be visually different.

NPF operates six days a week. We are located in a busy industrial park in Etobicoke. The easiest time for deliveries would be Thursday afternoons. This is not an absolute requirement but can you let me know if you cannot ship the packages so that they will arrive on Thursday between 3 and 5 p.m.?

We will require at first a total of 30,000 packages per week; 10,000 for each type of dog food.

I require a response by November 20 because I have to submit the final proposal to my management committee by December 1. Since you probably will have some questions about this project, we should speak on the phone. Please call me.

I look forward to your response.

Sincerely

Malcolm Chesnutt
Technical Director

# Summary

Business letters are written for many reasons and may be transmitted by surface post, e-mail, or fax. Letters provide information and through their content and presentation also send a message about the writer and the organization. A key element for an organization's success is the image it projects—a badly written letter reflects poorly on the writer and the employer. Writing letters today is more challenging since there is less time, no support staff to check drafts, and more people responsible for producing their own correspondence. While technology both helps and hinders letter writing, no program or website can replace the sensitivity and skills required to produce the right content and message in a letter.

Good news business letters include routine letters (e.g., requests for information about a product), acceptance of a claim for a refund, and letters of transmittal. Good news letters have a basic three-part structure—opening, body, and complimentary close—that remains the same regardless of the type of letter concerned. These letters are written using the direct organizational form.

It is vital when drafting a letter and choosing an approach to understand as much as possible about the recipient and to take into account cross-cultural and linguistic factors. Reader knowledge will also determine the appropriate tone—formal, semiformal, or informal—and style. Business letter style generally favours one idea per paragraph, short sentences, use of the active voice, plain language, brevity, positive rather than negative expression of ideas, and clarity. Letters must use and follow standard components and conventions, such as the date, inside address (recipient's), salutation, subject line, complimentary close, signature, enclosures, copies, and distribution, and employ one of the several recognized formats, such as block or indented.

# Discussion Questions

1. What are the different types of business letters and their uses?
2. What is the difference between direct and indirect organization of a business letter?
3. When should you use direct and indirect organization for a letter?
4. What are the three parts of a business letter?
5. Why are a letter's tone and style important?
6. How can you use PQs and FQs to determine a business letter's goal, main idea, information, organization, presentation of the main idea and information, and tone and style?
7. What are the components and conventions of a business letter?
8. What are the types of errors that editing your letters will correct?

# Writing Assignments

## Assignment 9.1

Write the first lines of the following letters:
1. Fulya Olka is a public relations agent. She is writing an inquiry letter to NewsSwift, a news-clipping service that promises to provide clippings from 20 major newspapers by 6 a.m.
2. Mark Chabalis is a bank manager. He is writing an apology letter to a client whose bank account was closed by a computer glitch.
3. Julie Dawson is a manager of a florist's. She is writing to accept an invitation to speak to the Boy Scouts about small business administration.
4. Mohammad Rakis is the owner of a small barber shop. He is writing to confirm a conversation he had with HairCare suppliers, which accidentally sent him two boxes of women's hair care products—and no hair care products for men.

## Assignment 9.2

You are the marketing associate for OmniAll Enterprises Ltd., a novelty product company that supplies other businesses with products for promotions. The company has received a letter from OmegaNet Inc., a Canada-wide, rapidly growing high-technology company. OmegaNet's promotions manager, Marty Stephanson, is seeking a refund for an order he placed for 20,000 T-shirts for a promotion involving a new product launch. Mr. Stephanson claims that the T-shirts had the wrong date on them and so could not be used. However, you know that OmniAll shipped the order according to the specifications provided by OmegaNet, including the date to be printed on the T-shirts.

Draft a response to Mr. Stephanson's letter for your boss, Mark Merx, Director of Marketing.

## Assignment 9.3

Write a letter of inquiry to a company of your choice seeking information about its products.

## Assignment 9.4

BDER Ltd. has received a shipment of five personal computers, keyboards, monitors, and printers from DOM Computer Supply Inc. Two computers, one monitor, a keyboard, and a printer are faulty. You are the purchasing officer of BDER. Write a letter to the sales manager at DOM, Anthea Greenstone, seeking immediate shipment of replacement equipment.

## Assignment 9.5

Write a letter of transmittal that covers the Annual General Sales Report of VeJet Plumbing Corporation.

## Assignment 9.6

You are the customer service coordinator for a small electrical appliance manufacturer. Mrs. T. Overlander has returned a toaster, which she reports burns her toast. Write a letter telling her that a new toaster has already been shipped. Explain to her the malfunction that caused her toast to be burned.

# Web References

### Writing an Effective Business Letter

http://www.business-letters.com/business-letters.htm

This site is maintained by Business-letters.com and contains a short discussion of the strategies used to write effective business letters.

### Writing Business Letters

http://writing.colostate.edu/references/documents/bletter/index.cfm

This site is maintained by Colorado State University and contains detailed discussions about the strategies used to write different kinds of business letters as well as several excellent examples.

### OWL Online Writing Lab—Business Letters

http://owl.english.purdue.edu/handouts/pw/index.html#sub7

This site is maintained by Purdue University in Indiana and contains extremely useful information on how to write business letters.

# CHAPTER • 10 •

# Letters That Persuade (Bad News and Sales Letters)

## LEARNING OBJECTIVES

In this chapter, you will learn

- how bad news, persuasive, and sales letters are important to an organization's image;

- what the basic structure, main parts, and conventions of a persuasive business letter are;

- when to use indirect organization of information in a business letter;

- how to use Purpose and Focus Questions to organize, develop, and write sales and other persuasive letters that meet your reader's needs and level of knowledge.

# PRELIMINARY *exercise*

You are the assistant to the vice president (international) of Steel, Tool, and Die, a large international steel and die manufacturer with plants and offices across Europe, Asia, and North America. You know that there is a meeting next week to discuss how to use e-mail more efficiently. You clip this article (Figure 10.1) and attach a point form summary to it.

## FIGURE 10.1

### EUROMAIL: WHAT GERMANS CAN TEACH US ABOUT E-MAIL

North America and Europe are two continents divided by a common technology: e-mail. Techno-optimists assure us that e-mail–along with the Internet and satellite TV–make the world smaller. That may be true in a technical sense. I can send a message from my home in Miami to a German friend in Berlin and it will arrive almost instantly. But somewhere over the Atlantic, the messages get garbled. In fact, two distinct forms of e-mail have emerged: Euromail and Amerimail.

Amerimail is informal and chatty. It's likely to begin with a breezy "Hi" and end with a "Bye." The chances of Amerimail containing a smiley face or an "xoxo" are disturbingly high. We Americans are reluctant to dive into the meat of an e-mail; we feel compelled to first inform hapless recipients about our vacation on the Cape which was really excellent except the jellyfish were biting and the kids caught this nasty bug so we had to skip the whale watching trip but about that investors' meeting in New York ... Amerimail is a bundle of contradictions: rambling and yet direct; deferential, yet arrogant. In other words, Amerimail is America.

Euromail is stiff and cold, often beginning with a formal "Dear Mr. X" and ending with a brusque "Sincerely." You won't find any mention of kids or the weather or jellyfish in Euromail. It's all business. It's also slow. Your correspondent might take days, even weeks, to answer a message.

Euromail is also less confrontational in tone, rarely filled with the overt nastiness that characterizes American e-mail disagreements. In other words, Euromail is exactly like the Europeans themselves. (I am, of course, generalizing. German e-mail style is not exactly the same as Italian or Greek, but they have more in common with each other than they do with American mail.)

These are more than mere stylistic differences. Communication matters. Which model should the rest of the world adopt: Euromail or Amerimail?

A California-based e-mail consulting firm called People-onthego sheds some light on the e-mail divide. It recently asked about 100 executives on both sides of the Atlantic whether they noticed differences in e-mail styles. Most said yes. Here are a few of their observations:

"Americans tend to write (e-mails) exactly as they speak."

"Europeans are less obsessive about checking e-mail."

"In general, Americans are much more responsive to e-mail–they respond faster and provide more information."

One respondent noted that Europeans tend to segregate their e-mail accounts. Rarely do they send personal messages on their business accounts, or vice versa. These differences can't be explained merely by differing comfort levels with technology. Other forms of electronic communication, such as SMS text messaging, are more popular in Europe than in the United States.

The fact is, Europeans and Americans approach e-mail in a fundamentally different way. Here is the key point: For Europeans, e-mail has replaced the business letter. For Americans, it has replaced the telephone. That's why we tend to unleash what e-mail consultant Tim Burress calls a "brain dump": unloading the content of our cerebral cortex onto the screen and hitting the send button. "It makes Europeans go ballistic," he says.

Susanne Khawand, a German high-tech executive, has been on the receiving end of American brain dumps, and she says it's not pretty. "I feel like saying, 'Why don't you just call me instead of writing five e-mails back and forth,'" she says. Americans are so overwhelmed by their bulging inboxes that "you can't rely on getting an answer. You don't even know if they read it." In Germany, she says, it might take a few days, or even weeks, for an answer, but one always arrives.

Maybe that's because, on average, Europeans receive fewer e-mails and spend less time tending their inboxes. An international survey of business owners in 24 countries (conducted by the accounting firm Grant Thornton) found that people in Greece and Russia spend the least amount of time dealing with e-mail every day: 48 minutes on average. Americans, by comparison, spend two hours per day, among the highest in the world. (Only Filipinos spend more time on e-mail, 2.1 hours.) The survey also found that European executives are skeptical of e-mail's ability to boost their bottom line.

It's not clear why European and American e-mail styles have evolved separately, but I suspect the reasons lie within deep cultural differences. Americans tend to be impulsive and crave instant gratification. So we send e-mails rapid-fire, and get antsy if we don't receive a reply quickly. Europeans tend to be more methodical and plodding. They send (and reply to) e-mails only after great deliberation.

For all their Continental fastidiousness, Europeans can be remarkably lax about e-mail security, says Bill Young, an executive vice president with the Strickland Group. Europeans are more likely to include trade secrets and business strategies in e-mails, he says, much to the frustration of their American colleagues. This is probably because identity theft—and other types of hacking—are much less of a problem in Europe than in the United States. Privacy laws are much stricter in Europe.

So, which is better: Euromail or Amerimail? Personally, I'm a convert—or a defector, if you prefer—to the former. I realize it's not popular these days to suggest we have anything to learn from Europeans, but I'm fed up with an inbox cluttered with rambling, barely cogent missives from friends and colleagues. If the alternative is a few stiffly written, politely worded bits of Euromail, then I say … bring it on.

*Thanks to Pierre Khawand for research assistance.*

---

## QUESTIONS TO CONSIDER

1. What are the article's major divisions?
2. Should you include the examples ("Hi," "Bye") the author uses to show Amerimail is chatty?
3. Should you include the examples to show that Euromail is stuffy?
4. What is meant by "brain dump"?
5. Are there any quotes that should be kept?
6. Would a chart be useful for showing the times different cultures spend on e-mail?

# Introduction

This chapter deals with bad news, sales, and other persuasive letters. As are the good news and routine letters studied in Chapter 9, bad news and sales letters are written to someone outside the company or organization in which the writer works.

Readers of bad news letters receive two messages.[1] The first (though, as we'll see, not the first part read) is the news that Window-Shades-and-Walls is not going to replace Mrs. Mildred Fife's window shade that she claims has yellowed prematurely. The second message is less obvious, but, perhaps, even more important. Does Window-Shades-and-Walls show respect for Mrs. Fife, even as it refuses her request? Demonstrating respect for the customer is accomplished by writing style, sensitivity, and clear reasoning.

Readers of sales letters see three messages. The first, obviously, is the offer of sale of an item or service. The second is how this product or service will fill his or her needs. Thus, a sales letter written by Found Money will explain that the company's accountants are specialists in finding tax savings, government rebates, and GST savings in tax returns up to seven years old. The letter will also indicate Found Money's fees and some idea of its success rate. The third message the letter sends concerns respect: does the letter demonstrate respect for the reader?

This chapter teaches you how to write bad news and sales letters—letters that seek to persuade. You will learn that these letters are written for many reasons and that they send a message about the writer and the organization. You will learn the various types of business letters, their basic three-part structure, and how to organize their content, as well as how to use the Purpose and Focus Questions to define your objectives and your reader's needs. You will also learn how to determine the appropriate tone and style. Finally, you will learn to use the standard components, conventions, and formats for business correspondence.[2]

# Editing Practice One

Jason Law is a customer service supervisor with Electro-Grills. Using his bad news letter (Figure 10.2) and the Questions to Consider on page 254, examine Malcolm Cranston's bad news letter (Figure 10.3).

---

[1] For the sake of clarity, we have divided this chapter in two. The first part will deal with bad news letters, the second with sales letters. All assignments and Web links are gathered together at the end of the chapter.

[2] Since Microsoft Word, the most common word processing program, defaults to block letter style, the examples that follow are in block letter format. Examples of modified block and indented can be found in Appendix II.

**FIGURE 10.2**

BAD NEWS LETTER

## Electro-Grills

85 John St.
Carstairs, AB  T0H 3K0
**www.electro-grills.com**

July 25, 2006

Mr. C. Chase
7905 Prium Cr.
Whitehorse, YK  Y3B 6G2

SUBJECT:  Your Letter Concerning Your Electro-Grill

In a climate such as Canada's, the grilling season is short. This is why Canadians can be seen grilling while wearing toques and even, we are told, by flashlight.

Electro-Grills has tried to help Canadians grill by providing them with a quick and clean source of heat with which to cook wieners, hamburgers, fish, and vegetables. In an Electro-Grill, the heat does not come from a flame but from a patented electrical coil controlled by a microprocessor (really, a small computer) that precisely calibrates the heat required to prepare different foods. The heart of this system is, therefore, like a CD player or digital camera, susceptible to damage if it is immersed in water, as yours was when you cleaned it. Proper cleaning procedures, which are explained in both the User's Manual that accompanied your Electro-Grill and on the side of the grill itself, clearly warn against immersing the heating and control unit in water.

We know you purchased your Electro-Grill secure in the knowledge that it is manufactured to the highest standards and that, under normal conditions, it would provide years of trouble-free service. To help you continue to enjoy your outdoor cooking, I am enclosing a $30.00 gift certificate redeemable at any Canadian Tire store for the purchase of grilling tools.

Yours sincerely,

Jason Law, Customer Service Supervisor

FIGURE 10.3

## EDITING PRACTICE ONE: MALCOLM CRANSTON'S BAD NEWS LETTER

### A poorly written bad news letter

*Shawbridge* ♣ *Stores*

240 King St. Halifax, NS    B4T 0N9
**www.shawbridge.ca**

12/2/06
Mr. Carson Groves
R.R. #1
Mabou, NS  B1B 4P2

SUBJECT:  Why you didn't pass the credit check

Dear Mr. Groves:

I am writing to tell you that you did not pass the credit check required to get a Shawbridge credit card.

I'm sure this is a big shock to you. As you know, only those customers who have an A rating with the Credit Bureau are eligible for Shawbridge cards. The reason for this is because unlike other credit cards, Shawbridges card is at an lower interest rate. This is because our customers are better credit risks.

The report from the Credit Bureau said that your debt is higher than the amount that is allowed by Shawbridge. The report also said you have two many cards. Finally, the report indicated that you are a B credit risk, fully 3 steps below what is necessary for our card.

We would be happy to consider you're application for credit in the future. Our policy, which is applied to all who are unable to pass the first credit check, is that you must wait a year before applying for again. If you want to pass the credit check next year, I suggest you improve your credit rating. To help manage your affairs better, I am enclosing a little booklet entitled "How to Improve Your Credit Rating," published by the Credit Bureau.

I know you are disappointed. Carrying a Shawbridge credit card is something worth striving for. I look forward to hearing from you next year.

Sincerely,

Malcolm Cranston, Credit Officer

## QUESTIONS TO CONSIDER

1. Is the date written correctly?
2. Is the subject line written correctly?
3. Does the subject line show that Mr. Cranston is sensitive to his reader's needs?
4. Bad news letters are supposed to ease their readers into the issue; does the first paragraph show that Mr. Cranston understands this?
5. Should paragraph two have begun by saying "I'm sure this is a big shock to you"?
6. What is Mr. Groves's likely reaction to the last sentence in paragraph two?
7. Mr. Cranston included paragraph three to clearly explain to Mr. Groves why he was denied a credit card. Could the information in this paragraph have been presented more tactfully?
8. Should Mr. Cranston have written, "Our policy, which is applied to all who are unable to pass the first credit check"?
9. What is Mr. Groves's likely reaction to the second part of paragraph four: "If you want to pass ..."?
10. In the place of Mr. Groves, how would you respond to the sentence "Carrying a Shawbridge credit card is something worth striving for"?
11. Is the letter free of grammatical, spelling, punctuation, and usage errors?

# The Process of Writing a Bad News Letter

Bad news letters can include refusals of a request for information, credit, a job or job interview, an order, a favour, or an invitation. Other bad news letters may announce price increases, termination of service, closure of a plant, or the end of a contract. All these letters tell someone something he or she *does not wish to learn*; namely, that his or her request—whatever it was—has been refused or that there is about to be a change that affects them negatively.

After reading a bad news letter, most readers would, naturally enough, be upset. In many cases, this emotion could turn into anger at and result in a negative view of the organization sending the letter. The writer of a bad news letter seeks to avoid this by taking into account the reader's feelings. Such letters begin with general statements that ease readers into the issue. The writer's goal is to get some agreement before informing the reader of the bad news. The writer's hope is that having agreed with the first point the letter makes, the reader will be receptive to the logic of the rest of the letter.

### BAD NEWS LETTERS USE INDIRECT ORGANIZATION

Generally, business people prefer direct communication, whether written or oral. It saves time and is less likely to lead to misunderstanding.

Bad news, however, is disappointing and possibly upsetting to the recipient, and the impact on and likely reaction of the reader must be considered in organizing the content of letters that deliver refusals of requests or other such bad news. A successful bad news letter is one that communicates the negative decision while at the same time maintaining the organization's relationship with the reader. This is most commonly achieved by using the indirect approach to presenting the main idea.

To avoid upsetting the reader before he or she has had a chance to read fully your reason, a bad news letter opens with a neutral statement rather than with a straightforward refusal. You want the recipient to read the reasons you cannot give a positive response or why a change must be made, and thereby increase the likelihood that the reader will at least understand the context and logic of the decision. This may preserve some goodwill toward your organization. You are seeking to minimize the risk of the recipient either not reading all of your letter or being so upset by reading bad news first that he or she immediately becomes antagonistic to the reasons set out in the rest of the letter.

Experience in business communication shows that the best way of organizing bad news letters is a neutral or positive (without being misleading) opening followed by a body that sets out the reasons why the request is being refused. Obviously, any reader will expect the reasons you put forward to be valid, coherent, and, as required, properly supported by facts and analysis. The bad news follows and then any possible alternative courses of action or suggestions are outlined. This indirect approach allows the reader to read why a request is being refused or an unwanted change is being introduced before receiving the bad news.

## BASIC STRUCTURE OF A BAD NEWS BUSINESS LETTER

*Opening*

In order to avoid upsetting the reader immediately, bad news letters usually open in a pleasant neutral tone that does not refer to the letter's substantive content. A letter denying a credit increase could open with:

> You have been a valued customer of Shawbridge's for several years....

A letter turning down a job application might begin with:

> Thank you for your application to JetStar Communications....

*Body*

The body of a bad news letter is the place where the bad news is introduced, explained, and specifically delivered. Depending on the particular circumstances, it may also offer alternatives or suggestions. The structure of the body of a bad news letter is designed to avoid alienation by bringing the reader to an understanding of the reasons for the refusal of a request and thus it aims to minimize ill-feeling.

The body of a letter turning down an article submitted to *The Canadian Journal of Independent Business* (a journal for small- and medium-sized businesses) could say:

> Your article, "Getting the Hip and Hop from e-Commerce," was very well written. Our editorial staff found your argument about the importance of music on websites especially interesting; the over-40 crowd here had never realized that youth always have their computers' speakers turned on. However, while some of our readers would find your work interesting, most do not have websites—and those who do have basic click-and-order sites. I regret, therefore, to inform you that we will not be able to accept "Getting the Hip and Hop from e-Commerce" for publication.
>
> I wish to reiterate that the article was well written and interesting. I would be happy to look at another of your articles that is better suited to our readers.

The body of a letter turning down a claim that the Drivertec 300 computer platform has malfunctioned could read:

> The Drivertec 300 is the result of an intensive research and development effort undertaken by SoloDrive. This effort included a multi-platform approach that would allow the Drivertec 300 to run on a range of systems and platforms. These systems and platforms are identified in the instructions that accompany the product. Any system or platform not specified may or may not be able to run the application. Your system is not among those specified and, while the Drivertec 300 you bought and installed was able to operate, there was a strong possibility that the longer it was used, the greater the chance that it would degrade and cease to function properly.

### Close

Businesses do not seek to create ill will; you never know if sometime in the future the recipient of a bad news letter will be in a position to help or hinder either you or your business's activities. Since bad news given in the body of a bad news letter is apt to be upsetting, the close of such letters seeks to "lessen the blow" by accentuating the positive or, as is the case in this close of a bad news letter that turns down replacing an electric grill (because it was immersed in water during cleaning), saying:

We know that people like you purchase our Electro-Grills secure in the knowledge that they are manufactured to the highest standards and that, under normal conditions, they provide years of trouble-free service. To help you continue to enjoy your outdoor cooking, I am enclosing a $30.00 gift certificate redeemable at any Canadian Tire store for the purchase of grilling tools.

**Box 10.1** AVOIDING THE NEGATIVE AND STRESSING THE POSITIVE

## Writing Tip

Experience shows that successful business letters, those that achieve their goal, focus on positive rather than negative wording and ideas. People generally tend to react negatively to negative messages:

- Avoid, to the extent possible, negative words such as *stop, no, cannot, deny, unable, failure,* and *mistake.*
- Emphasize what can be done in a given situation rather than what is not possible.
- Use an indirect approach to soften or modify the perception of negative information.
- Generally strive for a positive and pleasant tone.

## SAMPLE BAD NEWS LETTER

Before writing the bad news letter in Figure 10.4, which turned down a request from customer Stuart Hay, Arthur Kennedy, a customer relations associate with Grobart Supplies and Equipment Ltd., answered the following PQs and FQs.

*Purpose Questions*
1. What is my goal?
   To turn down Mr. Hay's request.
2. Who is going to read this letter?
   Stuart Hay, customer with complaint.
3. What does he know about the problem/issue?
   He knows his paints have faded. He knows we have a replacement policy (though he thinks it is more than 2 years).

He then turned to the Focus Questions:

*Focus Questions*

1. How do I acknowledge receipt of the request?
   Refer to letter and specific request.
2. What is the basis of the request?
   Mr. Hay claims Olivia paints have yellowed.
3. What is the legal basis of request?
   Mr. Hay points to our warranty.
4. Is the customer's reading of the terms of the warranty/guarantee/contract correct?
   No.
5. Is the claim made within the legal time limits stipulated (if not, how long after)?
   No (3 years, not 2).
6. Is the product being used as it was designed to be used?
   No.
7. If not, what is the limit (what is the use)?
   Used beyond 2-year technical limit common to paint industry.
8. Has the product been used beyond generally accepted industrial limits?
   Yes.
9. How would customer know the technical/warranty time limit?
   Pamphlet gives both.
10. Is there anything we can do to build goodwill?
    Yes, give a gift certificate.

After finishing these PQs and FQs, Mr. Kennedy read the guidelines he had prepared for writing bad news letters. Although several of the FQs used the word "legal," Mr. Kennedy remembered that he should not use this term in his letter because it tends to upset people. *No use in getting into a fight about the small print*, he thought. He also remembered that while businesses might get many refusal letters a week, it was more than likely that Mr. Hay would get only one during the week. He would want to be treated as an individual and not find himself being lumped in with others. Thus, Hay looked at other words he should not use:

- policy;
- company policy;
- the same treatment for all.

Successful bad news letters keep customers while turning down the specific request. Accordingly, Kennedy also decided against using:

- we must refuse;
- we must deny;
- we cannot accept.

Finally, Mr. Kennedy wrote his purpose statement as follows:

> My purpose is to retain Mr. Hay as a customer by explaining tactfully to him why we cannot give him a refund and offering him a $50.00 coupon as a token of goodwill. The main idea is that the paints are high quality and work as expected when used according to published instructions.

## FIGURE 10.4

BAD NEWS LETTER

### GROBART SUPPLIES AND EQUIPMENT LTD.

*222 Onslow Drive, Vancouver, BC V6C 9B8 Canada*

*(604) 435 6521 (T)  (604) 435 6698 (F)  www.grobart.ca*

June 23, 2007
Mr. Stuart Hay
34 Avenue Road
Victoria, BC  B3B 9X4

Dear Mr. Hay:

Thank you for your letter of June 17, 2007, concerning a refund for hardened oil paints bought from us.

I am pleased to learn that you have had such good results from our Olivia oil-based paints over the years. We consistently try to ensure that the Olivia range of colours is of the high quality required to meet the varied needs of artists and we are concerned that you have encountered the difficulties set out in your letter.

*continued*

**Opening**
- Kennedy politely thanks Hay for his letter.
- Kennedy states Hay's complaint to make sure Hay knows he's been heard.

**Body I**
- Kennedy begins the body with a noncommittal but sympathetic opening.
- Kennedy underscores Olivia's commitment to quality.
- Kennedy refers again to difficulties detailed in the complaint letter.

- Kennedy appeals for Hay's agreement about price and known quality of Olivia paints.
- Kennedy states technical limit for paints.
- Kennedy states warranty limit. *(Note: Kennedy does not use the word "warranty"; he does not want to have to point out to Hay that his reading of the legal terms is wrong. To do so would build ill will, not goodwill.)*
- Kennedy shows that the paints were beyond warranty limit.

Close
- Kennedy directs attention away from the problem and toward Hay's interest in painting.
- Kennedy gives him a gift certificate in an attempt to keep Hay's goodwill.

As you note, Olivia paints are among the more expensive on the market and that is why the quality process we use is designed to ensure that Olivia paints meet a high quality standard. Part of this standard is that the paints are capable of being used for up to at least two years from the date of purchase. The set of paints that you bought in April 1999 were tested against and met that standard.

As is pointed out in the pamphlet that accompanies the Olivia paint set, after two years, the paints may become either too dry to provide a good colour or may fade very quickly after being applied to the canvas. I am afraid that this is what you found; namely, that after applying the paints for the first time two weeks ago they had faded from the canvas after a couple of days. As far as we know, the type of chemical reaction that caused the paint to fade after use is common to all similar oil-based paints and unfortunately no one has been able to come up with a solution that would allow such paints to be used after being stored for long periods.

Since you have recently taken up your painting again, I am enclosing a certificate for $50.00 that can be used toward the cost of any of our oil paint products. Good painting!

Yours sincerely,

*Arthur Kennedy*

Arthur Kennedy
Customer Relations Associate

Encl. 1

Body III
- Kennedy directs Hay to pamphlet that indicated the two-year time limit.
- Kennedy refers to the fading in neutral, technical terms common to the industry.
- Kennedy refers to industry standards and research. *(Note: There is no direct refusal of Mr. Hay's claim.)*

Encl. is short for Enclosure; in this case, the gift certificate.

---

## Box 10.2   TESTING BAD NEWS LETTERS

### Writing Tip

A test for bad news letters is to ask how you would react if you received the letter you have drafted and to consider its tone, style, and content.

If you were the recipient, would you feel

- dissatisfied perhaps, but at least you understand the reasoning for the decision?
- patronized?
- that the language used is pleasant or neutral in tone?

What image would you have of the organization that sent the letter?

# Sales and Other Persuasive Letters

Sales letters and persuasive claim letters also use the indirect approach. This approach is based upon businesspeople's, and particularly salespeople's, experience in communicating to persuade others to accept an idea, product, or service. A persuasive letter writer assumes that the reader is likely to resist accepting the request, suggestion, product, or service being offered and that this resistance must be overcome by relevant arguments and reasons. The challenge is to ensure that the reader actually reads these arguments and reasons—and is in a frame of mind to consider them. Putting the main idea first as in the direct approach risks a reader simply ignoring the rest of the letter.

Persuasive letters are designed to lead their readers to make a decision and, as a result, to take the action that the writer wants. They present arguments and supporting information to convince the reader to agree with the request being put forward. Persuasive letters include sales letters, claim letters, collection letters, requests for service, proposal letters, and letters seeking a favour, such as the contribution of staff time to a charity fundraiser. Use a persuasive letter when you expect some resistance or you need to justify the action you want the recipient to take.

## BASIC STRUCTURE OF A PERSUASIVE BUSINESS LETTER

A persuasive business letter has a basic three-part structure:

### Opening

Since people are not usually focused on the topic you are writing to them about, persuasive letters use an indirect opening designed to catch their attention. The first step, therefore, is to engage the reader's interest with an appropriate opening. A sales letter announcing a new computer-screen cleaning product could begin

> What part of your computer do you use the most? Your keyboard? Your mouse?
>
> No. Here's a hint: you're looking at it. It's your screen.

Only after the reader has been "hooked" can a sales letter move on to its main idea, the announcement of the product or service.

A persuasive claim letter (e.g., one in which a complaint is made) may begin

> For 10 years we have been pleased with the travel/hotel planning provided by Calgary East Travel.

## Box 10.3   On Modes of Persuasion

Since the purpose of persuasion is to convince people to perform an action or to agree with a position that they at first do not want to perform or agree to (i.e., to move them from point A to point B), persuasion raises certain ethical concerns. As far back as Ancient Greece, philosophers have tried to define the ways and means of legitimate argumentation. Both Plato and Aristotle considered the Sophists, who used tricks of language and rhetoric to make false claims seem real, illegitimate. In *Rhetoric*, Aristotle famously divided persuasion into three types:

- *ethos*, where the claim depends on the known character of the speaker;
- *pathos*, where an audience's emotions are stirred by a speech;
- *logos*, where a truth is proved through a reasoned argument.

Today, these types of persuasion are normally called

- *testimonial*, used in advertisements that feature either the user of a product or a celebrity;
- *emotional*, used when appealing to a consumer's desire to look better, run faster, or smell nicer;
- *rational*, used in letters in which a reasoned, logically based argument built on relevant facts convinces a reader to inquire about your product/service.

### Body

The body of a sales letter is where the writer presents logically organized arguments and reasons the reader should be interested in the product or service being offered. Sales letters are not commercials and hence do not rely on images or emotion-laden dialogue. Though in some cases, such as a sales letter for an emergency computer power supply, it would be legitimate to write:

> Five-Minute Protector ends the fear of the power going off and your data going with it. Five-Minute Protector gives your computer five minutes to run. Enough time for you to save, back up, and properly shut down your computer.

In sales letters, the body is carefully organized to show readers why and how the product or service meets their needs and to convince them to buy. Only after you have demonstrated that your product or service is reasonable and required, should you introduce the question of its cost.

## Box 10.4 Features and Benefits of Products and Services

### Writing Tip

It is easy to confuse features and benefits. Readers are less interested in a product's or service's features than they are in what it can do for them—its benefits.

- Features are the various characteristics of whatever you are selling (product-centric perspective).
- Benefits are the advantages the customer will obtain from whatever you are selling (reader/buyer-centric perspective).

In writing a sales letter, the reader/buyer-centric perspective is key. Features must be clearly translated into benefits that the reader/buyer can easily understand.

The body of a persuasive claim letter provides the facts that back up the argument that the product or service is defective. A letter written by a graphic design company requesting replacement of a defective printer would say:

> After installing the printer according to the manufacturer's instructions, we found that the printer would not print a test file. Our technicians then followed the "Troubleshooting" procedures detailed in the manual on the CD-ROM. Every one of the tests indicated in the manual came up positive: the printer was initialized, the printing program could "see" it, and the drivers were uncorrupted. After the technicians worked on this problem for 45 minutes, I told them to uninstall the program and repackage the printer for shipment back to you.

> As you can understand, the loss of a high-speed colour printer created a serious problem for a graphic design company like ours. Our customers expect that our proofs will be of the highest quality and that they will be ready on time. We, in turn, expect that the equipment we purchase will work—the first time it is installed. Had we not been able to use our old printer, which was scheduled to be donated to a local charity, we would have not been able to fulfill a contract with a long-standing client.

*Close*

The close of a persuasive or sales letter motivates the reader to act by clearly stating what you want him or her to do. Since it is you who wants the reader to act, it is up to you to make it as easy as possible by giving such information as your phone number, e-mail address, or fax number, or by providing an order form that can easily be filled in. The close of a sales letter for an office-cleaning company could say

> Apex Cleaning has a 20-year record of providing reliable—and safe—cleaning services. Our workers are all bonded, which ensures you that your office equipment is in safe hands when you are not there. Our environmental engineers ensure that only the safest chemicals are used in your work environment. If you would like an estimate, please contact me at 902-123-4567.

The close of a persuasive claim letter also asks for action. However, since the desired action is to be performed by the company receiving the complaint, it is important to underline what you see as that company's responsibility. A letter written by a dentist's office requesting a replacement for an order of toothbrushes that were not embossed with MedPath's name could read

> We would like our excellent working relationship with OralFix to continue. I look forward to hearing that a shipment of toothbrushes embossed with MedPath's name (address, telephone number, and e-mail) will be couriered to us by June 1, 2007.

## A SAMPLE SALES LETTER

In a sense, all business letters are "sales" letters because they transmit an image and "sell" the organization from which they originate. In large companies, like Future Shop or KPMG International Accounting, it is rare for new and relatively inexperienced staff to be given the task of writing sales letters. They are usually written by marketing and sales professionals. Sales letters are often part of an overall marketing and sales strategy and designed to respond to various corporate objectives and needs. In small companies, however, it is common for a sales letter to be assigned to the best writer in an office. Knowing how to prepare a sales letter and how to write persuasively are assets in any career or workplace.

Since a sales letter is designed to persuade its reader to decide to buy and act on the decision, it uses indirect organization to bring the reader to the point of decision and action. Price, thus, is not usually introduced until the end of the letter, after the information and arguments that will hopefully convince the reader to buy what is being offered.

## Box 10.5 ETHICS AND PERSUASION

### Writing Tip

- Don't distort facts.
- Don't choose facts selectively.
- Don't make false claims for products/services.
- Don't make blatant emotional appeals.

Before writing the sales letter in Figure 10.5 on page 267 to Willomena Philpotts, Vice President, Corporate Services, of Wadenda Corporation, a medium-sized manufacturing enterprise, Wellesley Mancini, an account representative with Deltasource Inc., a company selling payroll outsourcing services to companies, answered the PQs and FQs that he used to help him organize his writing.

*Purpose Questions*

1. What is my goal?
   To motivate Ms. Philpotts to call to inquire about our payroll service.
2. Who is going to read this?
   Ms. Philpotts and the chief accountant.
3. What does my reader already know about this topic/issue?
   They know that such services exist, but they likely know nothing about ours.

*Focus Questions*

1. What product/service are we selling?
   Payroll.
2. What are the components of this produce/service?
   - Biweekly pay deposits
   - Pension deposits
   - Issuing T4s and other tax information

3. What problem(s) does this product/service solve?
   - Keeping up with bank's Web/modem changes
   - Keeping up with changes to tax code

4. Will this product/service save the consumer money?
   Yes.
5. How will it save money?
   - Reduction in payroll services (clerks)
   - Reduction in time spent with bank

Body V
- Mancini compares Deltasource's cost to a single employee's salary.
- Mancini sketches out Deltasource's intriguing policy whereby its payments are a percentage of savings.

Deltasource can give you a worry-free and cost-effective outsourced payroll system for less than the annual cost of a payroll clerk. We offer several payment options, including a percentage of agreed-upon anticipated savings and a direct monthly fee for service approach.

Deltasource is so sure we can save you money that we will provide a free, no-commitment, confidential initial evaluation of your payroll organization to estimate what level of savings might be realized. In other words, you have nothing to lose and potentially a lot to gain simply by calling me at (604) 397-3487 to have our experts look at your payroll arrangements. I look forward to hearing from you.

Close
- Mancini offers free estimate.
- Mancini tries to motivate Philpotts by saying, "you have nothing to lose and ... a lot to gain."
- Mancini closes with personal statement.

Yours sincerely,

Wellesley Mancini
Account Representative

---

## A SAMPLE PERSUASIVE CLAIM LETTER

Diane Marleau is the finance manager at the Centre for Advanced Communications (CAC), a national training and human resources company. Following a stay at Hotel Alpha-Costa, where she received extremely poor treatment, she told Jonathan Oboto, and he asked his assistant, Greta Howell, to draft a persuasive claim letter that would go out under his signature. Before drafting the letter (Figure 10.6), Ms. Howell took her notes and recast them into answers to the PQs and FQs she used to organize her writing.

### Purpose Questions

1. What is my goal?
   To demand a refund from Hotel Alpha-Costa.
2. Who is going to read this letter?
   Mr. Gerry Smart, Manager, Guest Services.
3. What does he know about this topic/issue?
   Nothing.

### Focus Questions

1. Where did the event occur?
   Hotel Alpha-Costa's check-in.
2. What was the date/time of the event?
   May 2.

3. Who from CAC was there?
   D. Marleau.
4. Who from (fill in the blank) was there?
   "Myra" and "Henry."
5. How did the incident begin?
   Ms. Marleau was told that her suite was not booked.
6. Had we properly ordered/booked/arranged for (fill in the blank)?
   Yes.
7. After the incident began, what then happened?
   Alpha-Costa could find no record of her booking—even when given D.M.'s credit card number.
8. What was the result of the problem/issue?
   Ms. Marleau had no room at Alpha-Costa.
9. Did (fill in the blank) act quickly and politely to try to rectify the situation?
   No. They acted only after Marleau insisted.
10. What did (fill in the blank) do to try to rectify the situation/alter arrangements?
    Call other hotels in the city.
11. Was the effort successful?
    Yes.
12. Were there other problems with the service?
    Yes, Alpha-Costa's staff did not help Ms. Marleau get a cab to the other hotel.
13. What action(s) do we require?
    • apology
    • refund
14. Action if we do not get #13?
    Cancel further use of Alpha-Costa hotels.

Before beginning to write the letter, Ms. Howell reviewed her notes and the printout of answers to the PQs and FQs. She noticed that she had left out demanding an apology from her answer to the first PQ and she pencilled it in. Then she saw that she had written "May 2" as her answer to the second FQ; she pencilled in "11:45 p.m.," because she knew that the time, especially because it was at night, was important. A moment later, she drafted the following purpose statement and then she began writing the letter.

*Purpose Statement*

> My purpose is to demand an apology and refund for the treatment D. Marleau received at Hotel Alpha-Costa, 11:45 p.m. on May 2, 2007, when her reservation was lost and she received little help in finding alternative accommodations. It must be clear to the hotel that if it does not issue both the apology and refund, CAC will cancel its contract with it.

## FIGURE 10.6

### Persuasive Claim Letter

 **THE CENTRE FOR ADVANCED COMMUNICATIONS INC.**
3479 Malmsley Avenue, Toronto, ON M5C 9N7 Canada
(647) 770 4444 (T)    (647) 770 4566 (F)    cac@cybon.ca

May 18, 2007

Mr. Gerry Smart
Manager, Guest Services
Hotel Alpha-Costa
1067 Booth Street
Toronto, ON  M4C 1N8

Dear Mr. Smart:

**Opening**
- Howell opens with a positive statement designed to get Smart's agreement and acknowledges the ongoing business relationship between the hotel and CAC.
- Howell politely introduces the problem and intimates that if it is not dealt with properly, CAC will "pull its business" from Alpha-Costa.

As I am sure you know, the Hotel Alpha-Costa has a well-deserved reputation for comfort and outstanding service. Certainly, the Centre for Advanced Communications Inc (CAC) has found this to be the case, and visiting executives are routinely booked into the Alpha-Costa. However, the recent experience of Ms. Diane Marleau, CAC's executive vice president, has led us to question whether our confidence in your hotel is misplaced.

On 2 May 2007, at 11:45 p.m., Ms. Marleau arrived at the Alpha-Costa after a long flight from Los Angeles. She was told that the suite she expected was not available despite her guaranteed reservation and was, in fact, required to produce evidence of her reservation to show that she had any claim upon a room at all. The only "evidence" Ms. Marleau had was her credit card number, but the front desk personnel, Myra and Henry, could find no record of this.

**Body I**
- Howell states time event occurred.
- Howell mentions the "long flight," because it indicates how tired Marleau would have been; this is a legitimate appeal to sympathy.
- Howell details sequence of events. By putting "evidence" in quotation marks, Howell gives a sense of how the staff spoke to Marleau.

**Body II**
- Howell tells of Alpha-Costa's unsuccessful effort to find a room.
- Howell tells what happened next— that Marleau had to insist that Alpha-Costa call around for an available room, underscoring the fact that Marleau received no help from Alpha-Costa's employees.

Upon Ms. Marleau's insistence that a room be provided for her, she was told that a special effort would have to be made since the hotel was full. Only after Ms. Marleau insisted did the staff telephone other hotels to see if accommodation was available. At 12:15 a.m., the Hotel Marchand gave Ms. Marleau a room, and she was given directions how to reach it. Ms. Marleau then had to take her luggage to the front door and get a cab herself, arriving at the Marchand at 12:30 a.m. Her room was not the equivalent of a suite at the Alpha-Costa.

Ms. Marleau and the CAC were shocked by the treatment she received from your hotel. Unless appropriate action is taken, we will have to reconsider continuing using your hotel.

*continued*

**Body III**
- Howell makes clear CAC's unhappiness.
- Howell indicates restorative action is expected.

We would expect a full refund of the various costs related to Ms. Marleau's stay at the Marchand as set out in the enclosed list and receipts. In addition, we would expect an apology to Ms. Marleau.

We hope that our previous excellent relationship with the Alpha-Costa can be continued and I look forward to hearing from you. I can be reached by telephone on my direct line at (647) 770-3458.

Yours sincerely,

Jonathan Oboto
Finance Manager

Encl. 5
cc Ms. D. Marleau

Body IV
• Howell tells what is expected:
  – refund
  – apology

Close
• Howell returns to a cordial tone and restates CAC's desire to continue to use Alpha-Costa hotels.
• Howell indicates how restorative action can most easily begin.

# Editing Practice Two

Collette Dawson, Director of Member Services for a major health club, has written a letter refusing a customer's claim for a refund of her annual fee (see Figure 10.7). Using Ms. Howell's letter and the Questions to Consider on page 273 as guides, examine Ms. Dawson's bad news letter.

## FIGURE 10.7

### EDITING PRACTICE TWO: BAD NEWS LETTER
**A poorly written bad news letter**

*Form Fitness and Health Club Inc.*

*2400 Henry Boulevard, Ottawa, ON K4S 9F2 Canada*

*Tel. (613) 256 7639     Fax. (613) 346 3498     www.formhealth.ca*

November 12, 2006

Ms. Vera Jensen
3498 Lakethorn Drive
Kanata, ON  K2E 1X3

Subject: Annual Fee Refund Claim

Dear Ms. Jensen:

It is indeed regrettable that we must correspond under the present circumstances, as you point out in your letter and I am afraid that you may consider that the circumstances have not improved since I must regrettably inform you that we are unable to process your request for a repayment on your annual club fee.

We do quite clearly state in the club membership form that the annual fee is not normally refundable either in whole or in part. I have enclosed a copy of your application with the relevant section highlighted for your attention. You will note that the wording is quite clear and that there are no allowances for refunds under any conditions. It is, I am afraid, in the nature of our business that the volume of memberships may vary significantly over any given time period and this means that our cash flow must be stabilized in order to meet both ongoing operational requirements and amortize the heavy capital investment that allows us to provide our members with superior facilities and the highly qualified staff for the high quality programs we offer. We simply could not offer these benefits to members if we could not be assured of a reasonably stable revenue stream.

Naturally, we hope that you will understand why we are unable to accede to your request and nonetheless continue to use our club once you have recovered from your broken ankle. If this is as you expect, you would still have several months left on your membership for this year and I know that our staff would be delighted to see you again and to give you all the benefits of our excellent facilities and programs that you have enjoyed until recently.

Yours sincerely,

Collette Dawson, B.Phys. Ed., Dip. Kin., C.D.R.S.
Director of Member Services

Encl. 1

## QUESTIONS TO CONSIDER

1. Is Ms. Dawson's letter organized appropriately?
2. In which part of the letter does she deliver the bad news?
3. Is the opening of the letter effective?
4. Is the closing effective?
5. What is the tone of the letter?
6. What would Ms. Jensen's attitude likely be toward Form Fitness and Health Club Inc. after reading Ms. Dawson's letter?
7. Does Ms. Dawson's letter contain unnecessary or inappropriate information?
8. What impressions might Ms. Jensen gain from the letter?
9. Are there grammatical, punctuation, spelling, or usage errors?
10. How would you rewrite this letter to make it more effective?

# Editing Practice Three

In his letter in Figure 10.8, Reginald Scrubb is seeking to persuade Fantastik Systems Inc. to provide him with what he considers appropriate service for a computer system he bought from the company. Using the Questions to Consider on page 274, examine Mr. Scrubb's letter.

---

**FIGURE 10.8**

EDITING PRACTICE THREE: PERSUASIVE CLAIM LETTER

**A poorly written persuasive claim letter**

34 Samuel Johnson Crescent
Peterborough, Ontario
K9D 8S9

August 29, 2006

Fantastik Systems Inc.
1993 Fielding Drive
Humber Business Park
Vancouver, BC V7A 9B3

Subject: Your Company's Useless ZXD 1100 Computer System

I do not know who to address this letter to but frankly, given that I have been waiting for a response form you for almost two weeks to my telephone message, it probably would not make any difference.

*continued*

---

The ZXD 1100 computer system I bought from your store in the Campbelford Mall three months ago has caused me nothing but trouble since I got it home. I have had to use your so-called technical help line several times in order to deal with a variety of problems. This is why I left you a message on your general customer service line but have not heard a word from anyone. What kind of operation are you running? After all, you claim in your advertising that your company puts its customers in front and that your products and service are guaranteed quality. I have seen no evidence of any of this so far.

My system crashes often and not all the installed software works as it should despite my efforts with your technical support line. One of my colleagues from our company's systems unit has looked at the computer and tried to fix things but in his opinion the defects are inherent in the system itself and there is nothing much that can be done. So, I want either a new system and proper support from you or a complete refund.

I assume that you do care about your company's customers and its reputation. I can assure that depending upon the response I receive from you, that reputation may certainly not be very high with me or for that matter my family, friends, and colleagues.

In hope everlasting,

Reginald M. R. Scrubb

---

## QUESTIONS TO CONSIDER

1. Would Mr. Scrubb's opening likely get attention?
2. What would be the probable reactions of an employee to the letter?
3. Does Mr. Scrubb provide enough information to allow for a decision to be made about his request?
4. Does the letter make a convincing case for a refund or a new system?
5. How well does Mr. Scrubb organize his arguments?
6. In which part of the letter does he make his request?
7. Is the closing effective?
8. Does Mr. Scrubb's letter contain unnecessary or inappropriate information?
9. Are there grammatical, punctuation, spelling, or usage errors?
10. How would you rewrite this letter to make it more effective?

# Editing Practice Four

Tom Haig, Sales Director of Customer Management Solutions Inc., wrote the letter in Figure 10.9 to persuade Ed Pierce, the president of the Bowman Group Inc., to buy his company's customer relations management product.

## FIGURE 10.9

EDITING PRACTICE FOUR: SALES LETTER

**A poorly written sales letter**

**Customer Management Solutions Inc.**
4560 des Pins, Laval, QC H4S 6F1 Canada
Tel. (450) 439 6655    Fax. (450) 328 2240    www.cms.ca    cms@ergo.ca

May 4, 2007

Mr. Ed Pierce
President
Bowman Group Inc.
3487 Pearson Avenue
Waterloo, ON   N5T 9Y2

SUBJECT: New Customer Relations Package

Dear Ed Pierce:

I would like to take a few minutes of your time to tell you about an exciting new product that we believe will enable you to put your business significantly ahead.

You've probably heard of us. We supply more standard correspondence and customer relations management software systems to small- and medium-sized business than any other similar company in the country. In fact. We are proud to say that we have helped and are helping entrepreneurs across this land to prosper and grow and thereby create jobs and wealth for us all everywhere.

Our software is tried and tested and is constantly being updated and improved as a result of the feedback we get from our satisfied customers. Its no surprise then that we want to offer you an exciting new customer relations management system that you can easily install on your system with a

*continued*

minimum of effort or disruption. Even if you do find something challenging with the package—CustomeRel—you just call our help line and we'll deal with it. But its so easy to use we doubt that you'll need to contact us.

You can get the package from us, in stores or directly from the Web at our site. It's a very reasonable $655.00 with subsequent upgrades available at a discounted price for existing users.

We know that good customer relations management is a key competitive advantage in a highly competitive world and so I urge you to give us a call at the above number or send us an e-mail now. If you act before May 31, 2007 we'll sell you CustomeRel for only $300.00.

Yours sincerely,

Tom Haig

Sales Director

---

## QUESTIONS TO CONSIDER

1. Does the opening sentence effectively get the attention of the reader?
2. Does Mr. Haig describe the features of CustomeRel?
3. What are the benefits of CustomeRel that Mr. Haig sets out?
4. Does Mr. Haig clearly demonstrate to Mr. Pierce why the product meets his needs?
5. Does Mr. Haig effectively stimulate action in his last paragraph?
6. How well does Mr. Haig organize his arguments?
7. Does the letter contain unnecessary or redundant information?
8. Are there grammatical, punctuation, spelling, or usage errors?
9. How would you rewrite this letter to make it more effective?

# Summary

Bad news, sales, and other persuasive letters are routine forms of business writing. Bad news letters are especially challenging because through them organizations say "no" to clients and customers—individuals whom the organization does not wish to alienate. To avoid alienating the recipient of a bad news letter, writers use the "indirect approach." Since this approach does not state the purpose of the letter at the beginning, it is likely that its recipient will read the entire letter, thus giving the writer time to clearly show the logic for the refusal. Writers of bad news letters strive to find areas of agreement with the person to whom they are saying "no." Bad news letters always end cordially.

Sales letters also use the indirect approach. These letters begin with an opening designed to "grab attention." They then go on to describe a product/service's features. Sales letters demonstrate how the product/service will benefit the recipient of the letter. Only after the benefits have been established does the sales letter indicate the price of the product/service. Sales letters seek to generate an order or, at least, an inquiry from the recipient.

Persuasive claim letters are written to convince a company to refund money either under an established warranty or because of poor service. These letters use the indirect form because it allows the writer to establish at the beginning that he or she values the business relationship and, all things considered, would rather not see it ruptured. The letter then goes on to detail the problems. Special care must be taken to include dates and times and, if the product or service is technical, all relevant technical information.

Whichever one of these letters you are writing, each is an advertisement for your company. Informing a client that you are not going to issue a refund because the warranty date is passed is, most likely, already expected. What the recipient of the letter does not want to experience is a poorly written, badly organized letter couched in an insulting or patronizing tone.

# Discussion Questions

1. What are the types of persuasive business letters?
2. What is the difference between direct and indirect organization of a business letter?
3. When do you use indirect organization for a letter?
4. What are the three parts of a business letter?
5. Why are a letter's tone and style important?
6. Why are the costs of a product or service mentioned toward the end of a sales letter?

# Writing Assignments

## Assignment 10.1

Write the first lines of the following letters:

1. Candace Yerksa is an office manager at La Presse Francophonie, a company that publishes French newspapers across Canada. She is writing a letter on behalf of editor Margaret Wright rejecting an article on identity theft on the Internet.
2. Michael Van Cornwall is an organizer of rock concerts. Yesterday, the hottest act around came to town; when he took the band to check into the Posh Suites Hotel, he was told that there was no booking for their suite. He is writing a letter to the hotel.
3. Fred Smith is the customer service manager for Davidson Heating and Cooling. He is writing to Mrs. M. Pickle telling her that she will not be receiving a refund on her broken water heater because the guarantee expired two years ago.
4. Martha Banks is a business service manager at Star Bank. She is writing a sales letter to Shelby Landholdings, which, in addition to owning the building in which her bank's branch is located, owns many buildings around the city. Her goal is to interest Shelby Landholdings in Star Bank's new online accounting service.

## Assignment 10.2

You are a business development associate with InterLink Training Inc., a communications company offering marketing communications training courses and workshops for business personnel. InterLink has developed a new workshop on customer communications but wants to test and, if necessary, adjust it in the field. You intend to approach the personnel director of Virtual Digit Inc., Paula Yates, to propose that her company receive the workshop for no cost, providing that Virtual Digit staff who take the workshop evaluate it for InterLink. Draft a letter to Ms. Yates, with whom you have never corresponded.

## Assignment 10.3

You are the IT supervisor for Bits and Bytes, a company that upkeeps corporate computers, e-mail, and Internet systems. Write a bad news letter explaining why you are unable to honour the warranty on the system you installed at the Canadian Association of Community Groups. The reason you cannot honour the warranty is that someone at the CACG downloaded unauthorized information, which corrupted the Web server.

## Assignment 10.4

Write a bad news letter from your place of employment to a customer or supplier.

## Assignment 10.5

Write a persuasive claim for luggage lost by an airline.

# Web References

## Writing an Effective Business Letter

http://www.business-letters.com/business-letters.htm

This site is maintained by Business-letters.com and contains a short discussion of the strategies used to write effective business letters.

## Writing Business Letters

http://writing.colostate.edu/references/documents/bletter/

This site is maintained by Colorado State University and contains detailed discussions about the strategies used to write different kinds of business letters, as well as several excellent examples.

# C H A P T E R  • 1 1 •

# Cover Letters and Résumés

## LEARNING OBJECTIVES

In this chapter, you will learn

- what the value, essential content, and purpose of an effective cover letter and résumé are;

- what the reader of a cover letter and résumé is looking for;

- what the structures and appropriate writing style for an effective cover letter and résumé are;

- how to use Purpose and Focus Questions to organize, develop, and write cover letters and résumés that meet your reader's needs;

- how to use alternative formats for cover letters and résumés, including those for online job applications.

You are part of a team charged with preparing a pamphlet entitled "How Not to Get That Dream Job" to be put out by the students' association of your college or university. You volunteered to find out what experts have said about job interviews. Your search engine brought you to the online version of an article published in the *Journal of the American Library Association* (see Figure 11.1). Though the article is written for American students of library science (note the reference to the First Amendment, which guarantees the right of free speech), you decide that it is worth summarizing.

## FIGURE 11.1

## DO NOT WEAR A TONGUE RING TO YOUR JOB INTERVIEW

In November I gave you tips on interpreting library job ads. Last month I taught you how to write a résumé. If you followed my advice, you have probably already been called for an interview. Don't blow your chances now! One *faux pas* at the interview and you're history, because the interview is where you can make your strongest impression on the employer. Work this opportunity to your advantage by following these nine simple tips:

- Don't eat beans 24 hours before the interview. The most important advice I can give you to put yourself at ease physically. The week or day before the interview is not the time to plunge into an exercise frenzy to improve your personal appearance. Also, avoid going on crash diets, especially those featuring legumes that will result in either a fainting spell or an embarrassing case of flatulence.
- Dress like a normal human being. This, I realize, is difficult for some librarians to do. As our nation's staunchest defenders of the First Amendment, we greatly value our right to self-expression not only in speech but also in dress. The job interview, however, is not the place to celebrate this form of personal freedom. Stay away particularly from the retro '60s hippie look and the "3P" look of the '70s—plaid, purple, and polyester. Also, exercise some caution with accessories. Most library employers are frightened by lip gloss on men and combat boots on women. Tongue rings are also not conducive to a comfortable verbal give-and-take. Finally, stay away from dangling earrings and necklaces, because if you're nervous you'll end up sounding like a human wind chime.
- Be yourself unless you are a completely obnoxious person. Don't try to psychoanalyze the employer and attempt to playact the personality type that you think he or she is seeking. Most librarians are conscientious, polite, and honest, and coincidentally those are the personal qualities that most employers are looking for. So just be yourself and let your innate goodness show through naturally.
- The only buttons you should wear are the kind that keep your shirt on. You only have to mill around at an American Library Association's annual conference to discover that librarians are button people. We like to wear our feelings in writing on our lapels. I think it is another of our First Amendment idiosyncrasies. Unfortunately, we tend to be naive and think that everyone will respect us for our openness,

especially other librarians. This is not always the case. A man wore a button to an interview that I was conducting that said "Question Authority." I wondered if he would be able to get along with his boss, so I asked him why he wore the button. He responded, "I am philosophically opposed to authority." Guess who didn't get the job.

- Do not quote library-school professors. Even though you may be going right from a library school classroom to the interview, try to deprogram yourself from library-school bull. The kind of practicing librarians that you will be interviewing with will not be impressed with how some library-school professor who has not worked the reference desk in 20 years sees the world. Think about the life of the average professor. You have job security for life, you have quasi-dictatorial powers, and day in and day out everyone in your class writes down everything you say. It's a perfect formula for losing touch with reality.

- Do not snicker when your interviewer tells you the starting salary. This is difficult advice to follow, but hey, before you get too cynical, consider the cost of living. There are some less expensive areas of the country where the average library salary does not put you below the poverty line.

- Do not wad up pieces of paper and shoot them at the Nerf™ hoop that hangs in your interviewer's wastebasket. I did this once and it was a big mistake. The guy interviewing me challenged me to a game and I beat him decisively. Guess who didn't get the job.

- Do not ask "When does that dinosaur who runs reference plan to retire?" This may be important information to you, especially if you're planning a career in reference, but you're much better off getting the answer through less formal, back-channel sources of information.

- Do not give your interviewer an organizational chart of how you think the library should be reorganized. This should wait until you've been on the job for at least two weeks.

Source: Manley, Will. "Do Not Wear a Tongue Ring to Your Job Interview." *American Libraries.* Vol. 28, No. 2. February 1997: 136. Reprinted with permission.

## QUESTIONS TO CONSIDER

Before summarizing the article, answer the following questions:

1. What is the article about?
2. Who is the article about?
3. Who is the intended reader?
4. How many main points does the article contain?
5. Will you keep the tongue-in-cheek tone?
6. If you answered "yes" to question five, which example(s) of such language would you retain?
7. How would you "Canadianize" the reference to the First Amendment of the *Constitution of the United States of America*?

# Introduction

A well-written cover letter and résumé is an excellent investment—the 700 or so words in a one-page letter and two-page résumé are worth thousands of dollars. A job with a $30,000 starting salary and an annual two percent increase provides more than $150,000 after five years. The cover letter and résumé that helped you get the job are worth something like $215 a word.

Although most positions are advertised via word of mouth (traditional newspaper want ads and their Web-based cousins account for only a fraction of available jobs), almost every position involves providing a cover letter and résumé. There are two reasons for this. One is legal: Federal and provincial human rights legislation requires that companies maintain files of applicants so that they can demonstrate that their hiring decisions were made in accordance with established regulations. The other reason is practical: Even if you are the niece or nephew of the company's vice president, it is unlikely that members of a selection committee would be familiar with your education and work history; still less so if you were the friend of the computer programmer who tells you of an opening in the marketing division.

Unlike other business writing, cover letters and résumés are primarily about yourself. This does not mean you can ignore your reader's interest—in this case, deciding whether your application should be added to the "Let's Interview" list. Quite the contrary—readers of cover letters and résumés are not usually interested in you, the person, but, rather, *you as a potential employee or colleague*, capable of pulling your weight in the organization. Accordingly, these readers care more about your education, training, work history, and accomplishments than they do about your hobbies and how much of a "people person" you are; if true, this last will be evidenced at your interview.

This chapter teaches you how to write cover letters and résumés. You will learn that the purpose of a cover letter and résumé is to get you an interview. You will learn how to use the Purpose and Focus Questions to define your reader and to organize your cover letter so that you demonstrate that you have the qualifications for the position. You will learn how to write two different types of cover letters and résumés. As well, you will learn how to prepare a scannable e-mail résumé and cover letter.

# Editing Practice One

In June, Oscar Lyman will finish the first year of his two-year photography program at Canada College in Orillia, Ontario. He is applying for a position as assistant photographer at the MotoPictures in-store kiosk at SuperGrocers in Orillia. He addressed his cover letter, however, to Mr. Peter Quill, the human resources director at MotoPictures' corporate headquarters in Toronto. Using Lyman's letter (Figure 11.2) and the Questions to Consider on page 287, examine Claire Davis's cover letter and résumé in Figures 11.3 and 11.4; she is applying for the position of assistant advertising manager at Heritage Furniture, a chain of 15 upscale furniture stores across Western Canada.

FIGURE 11.2

## COVER LETTER

16 Antares Drive
Orillia, ON  L3M 2B9

Mr. Peter Quill
MotoPictures
67 Front Street
Toronto, ON  M6T 2T1

March 15, 2007

SUBJECT:  Application For Assistant Photographer Position (Online Jobs,
March 15, 2007)

Dear Mr. Quill:

I am writing to apply for the Assistant Photographer position in the MotoPictures kiosk in the Orillia, Ontario, SuperGrocers, advertised on *Online Jobs* on March 15, 2007. My education and work experience qualify me for this position.

By this June, I will have completed the first year of the two-year photography program at Canada College in Orillia. I have learned how to use both 35mm and digital cameras to take portraits. My final assignment for my portraits class consisted of 15 portraits of children, five of them under five years of age. In my lighting class, I learned how to use lighting to both soften and highlight facial features. In my business communications course, I learned how to listen actively and how to put customers at ease.

My work experience has prepared me for the position of Assistant Photographer. Over the past three years, I have worked part-time at Mellon's Meats in Orillia. After working at the deli counter for 18 months, I was promoted to Assistant Weekend Manager. Among my other responsibilities, which include closing the cash and ensuring that the alarm is armed, is dealing with the complaints that originate over the weekend. During the summers of 2002 and 2003, I was the Arts Animator at Camp Wassinipee, near Midland, Ontario; the final staff/camper talent show featured a 20-minute Camp Wassinipee's funniest moments video produced by the 12-year-old campers under my guidance.

Due to my school and work schedules, I can most easily be reached on Tuesday afternoons or by voice mail. Likewise, I am most easily available for an interview on Tuesday afternoons. Let me thank you in advance for your time.

Sincerely,

*Oscar Lyman*

Oscar Lyman

---

## FIGURE 11.3

## Editing Practice One (I): Sample Cover Letter

**A poorly written cover letter**

May 22, 2007

Heritage Furniture
11 Main Street
Regina, SK   S5A 5U9

To Whom It May Concern:

I am very interested in your job. I would be perfect for it.

I really enjoyed going to school and learning all about advertising. We learned how to plan and run campaigns. In the required media course, we studied layout and design which I was good at. I helped organize the United Way Campaign at School which everybody liked.

I am a people person and have always worked with people. In my job at Morgan's Pharmacy, I helped people every day. I also did stock there and arranged for Mr. Morgan to donate money to the local school.

I know that you will find me a bright, energetic member of your team when you meet me. Contact me for an interview.

Sincerely,

*Clare Davis*

Claire Davis

FIGURE 11.4

## Editing Practice One (II): Sample Résumé

### A poorly written résumé

1400-10 West Way
Regina, SK  S9T 3G5
(306) 223-4567
clairedavis@internet.com

**Education**

| | |
|---|---|
| Calgary Centre Junior High School | 1997–1999 |
| Central Calgary High School | 1999–2003 |
| Morgan College | 2003–2006 |

**Work**

| | |
|---|---|
| Floor Worker<br>Morgan's Pharmacy<br>Regina, Saskatchewan | 2004–2006 part-time work |
| Waitress<br>Davis Donuts<br>Regina, Saskatchewan | 2002–2004 part-time work |
| Camp Counsellor<br>YMCA<br>Regina, Saskatchewan | 2001 July and August |
| Babysitter | 1998–2001 |

**Computer Knowledge**
WordPerfect 8

Excel

**Foreign Languages**
None

## QUESTIONS TO CONSIDER

1. Does the cover letter follow standard form for inside addresses?
2. Is the cover letter written in a professional tone?
3. What is the meaning of the sentence "I am very interested in your job"?
4. Does the first paragraph of the cover letter make clear what the letter is about?
5. Do the subsequent paragraphs of the cover letter support the claim the first paragraph makes?
6. Does the cover letter address the concerns of the reader?
7. Is the résumé easy to follow?
8. Does the résumé follow the standard form for listing schools and work experience?
9. Should Ms. Davis have included the foreign language section in the résumé?
10. Is Ms. Davis's cover letter free of grammatical, punctuation, spelling, and usage errors?

# The Process of Writing a Cover Letter and Résumé

You may have laboured for hours crafting a letter that shows how you fit perfectly the advertised position of collections agent. However, the person charged with reviewing the cover letters and résumés received (which can often number more than 100) is less concerned with giving your life experience its due than with giving the manager a list of 20 names that can then be cut down to a shortlist of six people to be interviewed next week.

Studies show that résumés and cover letters are looked at for as few as 27 seconds before the judgment is made whether to discard or read them carefully.[1] In these few seconds, the reader is looking for three things: basic qualifications; correct writing; and synthesis.

- Basic qualifications. Does the applicant have the basic qualifications for the position? For most students this usually means do they have the required college diploma and certifications such as CPR or a bonding number.
- Correct writing. Are the résumé and cover letter marred by grammar, punctuation, spelling, usage, or formatting errors? A reader doing the first screening of applications is likely to assume that an applicant who cannot be bothered to properly write and present 700 words will be equally careless in the office.
- Synthesis. Does the applicant have the ability to link previous experience to the position's requirements? The reader of a cover letter wants to determine if an applicant is able to synthesize (summarize and present in a way appropriate to the position) education, work, and life experience. For example, a former mechanic seeking a new career appropriate to a business computer networking diploma program could emphasize that a successful mechanic utilizes many of the same problem-solving skills as a computer specialist. Moreover, successful mechanics demonstrate the kind of attention to detail and human relations skills needed in the computer management field.

---

[1] E-mail resumes may be looked at for even less time, for when the file opens in Word or WordPerfect, the misspellings and ungrammatical sentences are underlined.

Successful cover letters and résumés appeal to the interest of the prospective employer. Appealing to the interest of the employer means that you have understood both your reader's needs (e.g., good clear writing and easy-to-read layout) *and* what the employer is actually looking for in an employee. The employer, you must remember, is trying to fill a position, which means the company has a gap in its portfolio of skills. A gap, we hasten to add, that you want to be given a chance to fill.

Whether found in newspapers or online, want ads are designed to tell you what skills and what kind of person an employer is looking for. A want ad that says, for example, "retail experience wanted," is not asking you to only list your sales jobs. It is asking for that and for you to show via a concrete example that you are a good salesperson. You might, for instance, say that you won the award for selling the most widgets during the Christmas season.

Claire Davis's cover letter (Figure 11.3 on page 285) is too perky by half. Instead of saying, "I helped people every day," she might have said, "I was responsible for helping seniors shop for over-the-counter medication and cosmetics on the Seniors' Shopping Days held every other Tuesday."

## THE PURPOSE OF A COVER LETTER AND RÉSUMÉ

Notice we have not used the word "hired." There is a good reason for this. Big box stores and fast-food outlets may hire on the basis of a résumé or application. By contrast, "positions" such as nurse, junior advertising account executive, collections agent, or network manager, are almost never filled on the basis of a résumé and cover letter alone. These and other positions are filled by applicants who, on the basis of their cover letters and résumés, are interviewed and then chosen.

The purpose of a cover letter and résumé is not, then, "to tell them you are interested in the job." In a job market in which there are often 100 applicants for each position, the reality is that *they* simply don't care that *you* may be interested in the position.

The purpose of a cover letter and résumé is to interest the reader in interviewing you for the position. In other words, you must think of the cover letter and résumé not as your pitch for the position but for an interview for the position. And your task is to tailor your cover letter and résumé to meet the prospective employer's needs. In other words, your résumé and cover letter are going to be read, not from your perspective but from the perspective of the organization or company to which you are applying. The human resources department simply does not care about what you enjoyed studying or what you have enjoyed at work. It is interested in discovering what skills and knowledge you have that *meet the company's or organization's needs.*

## BASIC STRUCTURE OF A COVER LETTER

A cover letter is made up of four parts:

- Introduction: announces your interest in the position and states your belief that you have the requisite qualifications.

- Education: details how your education qualifies you for the position; gives details of specific courses and/or projects that demonstrate your unique training or academic experience.
- Work: explains how your work history demonstrates your suitability for the position.
- Closing: thanks the reader for his or her time and indicates if there are any limitations on your availability for an interview.

## Box 11.1  WHAT THE LAW SAYS

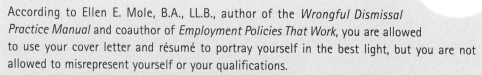

### Writing Tip

According to Ellen E. Mole, B.A., LL.B., author of the *Wrongful Dismissal Practice Manual* and coauthor of *Employment Policies That Work*, you are allowed to use your cover letter and résumé to portray yourself in the best light, but you are not allowed to misrepresent yourself or your qualifications.

"Canadian courts have held that 'mere puffery' is allowed. However, if an employer finds that you have misrepresented your qualifications by, for example, claiming education or work experience you do not possess, you can be fired for cause. For instance, if you claimed on your résumé that you had completed one year of a B.A., when in fact you had withdrawn before even taking the final exams in the first semester, your employer might be able to fire you without notice and without pay.

"Courts in Nova Scotia, Ontario, Saskatchewan, and Alberta have gone so far as to award costs to the companies that fired the employee who misrepresented him- or herself. In 1992, for example, the Saskatchewan Court of Queens Bench in *Werle v. SaskEnergy* ruled that an employee was dismissed for just cause for falsely claiming that he had a B.Comm. degree at the time of his hiring and for remaining silent about the truth during the (short) time of his employment, despite knowing that the company had issued a number of announcements about his hiring, which included references to his educational background. He had to pay SaskEnergy's court costs, including its legal bills."

Source: Based on an interview with Ellen E. Mole, B.A., LL.B.

## A SAMPLE COVER LETTER

The cover letter in Figure 11.6 was written after David Margoles, who will be graduating with a marketing diploma in June, saw the want ad in Figure 11.5 in his hometown newspaper.

FIGURE 11.5

## WANT AD

If You Like to Get People Talking about Books, We Want to Talk to You

We are
- a large book retailer, national in scope
- a company with room for you to grow as we grow
- concerned with local issues and improving literacy
- developing one of Canada's largest e-commerce divisions
- not so big that we can't order that book on the history of darning you want to give to your favourite aunt for Christmas

You must
- have a diploma in marketing
- have demonstrated competence in developing partnerships between business and public institutions such as schools or hospitals
- have extensive volunteer experience in Eastern Ontario
- be energetic, willing to travel throughout Eastern Ontario
- be able to solve problems
- have excellent communications skills

Send cover letters and résumés to:
Director of Human Resources
Books, Books, and More Books
Box 299, Station A
Kingston, ON K1P 5T9

---

At first Mr. Margoles thought he could reuse the cover letter and résumé that he used last summer. *They worked pretty well; got lots of offers*, he thought but then realized he hadn't written anything about his communication skills and his willingness to travel. *Maybe I can just put in a sentence here and there*, he concluded. He looked at last year's letter, shook his head, and thought, *I'd better rewrite the whole thing and the résumé, too.* He started with a cover letter.

### Purpose Questions

Mr. Margoles clicked on his word processing program and quickly entered the Purpose Questions (PQs) that guide business correspondence and then answered them.

1. What is my goal?
   To get the job.
2. Who is going to be reading this cover letter and résumé?
   The HR director.

3. What does my reader already know about the topic/issue?
   Not much about me.

After thinking for a moment, he realized that these answers were of little help and he began again. This time, he answered the first PQ by writing, "To make my cover letter and résumé stand out so I can make the shortlist for interviews."

Answering the second PQ took more time because the advertisement did not give a name. Since he was at his computer, he clicked on to his Web browser, entered the company's name, brought up its site, and then clicked on Departments. A moment later he wrote, "Diane Pelchick, Director of Human Resources."

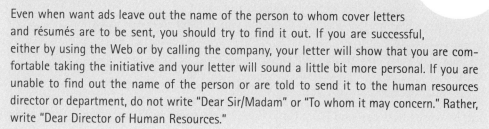

## Box 11.2   KNOW TO WHOM YOU ARE WRITING

### Writing Tip

Even when want ads leave out the name of the person to whom cover letters and résumés are to be sent, you should try to find it out. If you are successful, either by using the Web or by calling the company, your letter will show that you are comfortable taking the initiative and your letter will sound a little bit more personal. If you are unable to find out the name of the person or are told to send it to the human resources director or department, do not write "Dear Sir/Madam" or "To whom it may concern." Rather, write "Dear Director of Human Resources."

After he read the third PQ, he remembered that employers are not interested in prospective employees' personal lives; they are interested in filling a position, a position that represents certain needs of the company. He then wrote down, "Ms. Pelchick knows nothing about me, but she knows what she is looking for." She needs someone with

1. a marketing diploma
2. partnership experience
3. volunteer experience
4. a willingness to travel
5. good writing skills
6. problem-solving skills

### Focus Questions

Now that Mr. Margoles had his audience clearly in mind, he asked himself the three Focus Questions (FQs) for cover letters and résumés.

1. What have I done in school (e.g., presentations or special projects) that makes me a better candidate for this position than anyone else in my class?

2. What in my work experience demonstrates that (a) I have the skills required for this position or (b) I am a quick learner and good worker?
3. Do I have any relevant volunteer experience?

He started to answer the first FQ by thinking, *I've studied marketing for three years and liked it a lot*, but then realized that most of the other 29 students in his class could say the same thing. Then he thought, *I like working with people and I like books*, but then realized that it would be strange not to write that when applying to work in public relations for a chain of bookstores.

Mr. Margoles paused for a moment, looked back at his answer to the third PQ, "What does my reader already know about the topic/issue," and then with the first FQ in mind thought, *We may all have studied marketing, but I was the only one to work on a partnership. I got the local video stores to donate their old stock to the local hospital, and I was part of the committee that planned the announcement of the computer lab that is being supported by X-Tel.* Before long he had the following list:

1. Worked on video stores/hospital partnership
2. Planned computer lab/college announcement
3. Volunteered as hockey coach in Kingston and as baseball coach in Ottawa
4. Sat on student council
5. Obtained A's in advertising copy class
6. Tutored English in high school
7. Held field placement with Website Analysis

Next, he turned to the second FQ: "What in my work experience demonstrates that (a) I have the skills required for this position or (b) I am a quick learner and good worker?" After thinking for a moment, Mr. Margoles decided that his experiences at Records, Yes Records in Kingston, Ontario, demonstrated that he had the skills needed for this position. "I got the New Music Evenings up and running," he keyed in. A moment later he added, "At Sports R You, I was the person who worked with amateur teams to make sure that underprivileged kids had equipment."

Mr. Margoles looked next at the third FQ: "Do I have any relevant volunteer experience?" For a moment he thought he would write that he used to volunteer as a hockey coach but then decided against it. *I already have enough to say about my skills and what I've done*, he thought. *The letter will get too long. It would be important only if I had not already shown through my work and school experience that I'm a good employee and that I have a lot of initiative.*

## ALWAYS USE ACTIVE VERBS

Before writing his purpose statement, Mr. Margoles looked over the following list of active verbs that he had found in a file marked Cover Letters/Résumés that he had saved on his hard drive.

| | | | |
|---|---|---|---|
| achieved | budgeted | constructed | designed |
| administered | built | coordinated | developed |
| analyzed | compiled | created | directed |

| edited | installed | planned | tracked |
| evaluated | investigated | presented | trained |
| founded | maintained | programmed | wrote |
| implemented | managed | researched | |
| increased | monitored | solved | |
| initiated | organized | supervised | |

**Box 11.3** WHAT TO DO IF YOU DO NOT HAVE ANY RELEVANT EMPLOYMENT EXPERIENCE

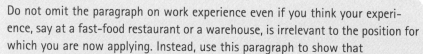

## Writing Tip

Do not omit the paragraph on work experience even if you think your experience, say at a fast-food restaurant or a warehouse, is irrelevant to the position for which you are now applying. Instead, use this paragraph to show that

- you are a reliable employee;
- you have worked for an employer for a number of years (thus showing that you were worth keeping on);
- you have progressed in positions or responsibility even in your part-time or short-term jobs;
- you were serious about working even while going to school;
- you were trusted with management or assistant management responsibilities or with money.

If Nathalie Bergeron—who had worked for three years at Burgers and Fries, rising from fill-up girl to assistant manager, and for three years as a part-time medical secretary—were applying for the same position as David Margoles, she would write the following paragraph about her work experience:

> My work experience, both at Burgers and Fries and as a medical secretary, demonstrates my ability to work with the public and the fact that I am not frightened by a challenge. At Burgers and Fries, although I began as the fill-up girl (responsible for making sure that cups, cartons, and other things necessary for serving the public were filled), within three months I was assigned to the cash. During the summer of 1997, I was promoted to assistant evening manager, responsible for customer relations, employee relations, and contests. Over the past three years, I have been a part-time medical secretary for Dr. Sandra Levine. My responsibilities included organizing Dr. Levine's PowerPoint presentations, ensuring that conference organizers had booked the proper equipment for her, and editing her newsletter.

## Box 11.4 TIME AND TENSE

### Writing Tip

Note how the active verbs are all conjugated in the simple past tense. The reason for this is that when speaking of your work experience, you are referring to the past. This is true even for your present job or position because your task is to say what you *have* accomplished. (If you were referring to an ongoing project of which a significant portion had been completed, you may, of course, conjugate any of these verbs into the present perfect tense; for example, "For the past three months I have edited the company newsletter.") See Chapter 7 for further discussion of tense.

*Purpose Statement*

Mr. Margoles then wrote, "My purpose is to write a cover letter and résumé that will stand out from other applicants' and make Ms. Pelchick want to interview me."

He paused over the words "stand out" and imagined a cover letter that would grab attention. *Maybe I should use bright blue paper and start with a real catchy sentence, something like, "I'm exactly who you are looking for."* Then, he thought, *I could write a paragraph about all the things I did at Algonquin College.*

> I worked very hard at Algonquin, as you can see by my high grades, especially the A in my advertising copy class, higher than anyone else's. I also worked hard on the partnership between the hospital and the stores, and it was really worth it to see how happy the patients were to get all those films. I worked on the press kit that was part of the announcement about the partnership with X-Tel computers.

He looked at this sketch and realized that for someone who was trying to demonstrate that he was a good communicator, he had written a disorganized and unprofessional paragraph. *The paragraph sure doesn't show I am a synthetic thinker,* he thought. In fact, he realized it did not even have a clear topic sentence. Putting himself in the shoes of a human resources officer pressed for time, he asked himself, "What do you mean by 'handled' press releases. Did you write them? Distribute them?" Even the first sentence is a mess, he decided. "Why should Ms. Pelchick care about the grades of other kids in the class?"

Cover letters are something like persuasive essays, he remembered learning in his business-writing class. They argue for your point of view, in this case that you should be interviewed. Then he recalled that, though not a business document in the same sense as a proposal, a cover letter must nonetheless make a business case for you. In other words, a cover letter must present information about you that shows how you fit the position.

Mr. Margoles thought for a few moments more then deleted what he had written and produced the cover letter in Figure 11.6.

## FIGURE 11.6

### COVER LETTER

1198 West Street
Ottawa, ON  K1B 3E5

April 13, 2007

Ms. Diane Pelchick
Director of Human Resources
Books, Books, and More Books
Box 299, Station A
Kingston, ON  K1P 5T9

SUBJECT:  Application For Marketing Position (#1454)

Dear Ms. Pelchick:

I am writing to apply for the position of marketer, advertised in *The Kingston Whig-Standard* on 10 April 2007 (#1454). I believe my education and work experience qualify me for this position.

As indicated on my résumé, I will be graduating from Algonquin College (Ottawa) in June with a three-year diploma in marketing. I learned how to plan and implement a business partnership in my Special Business Projects class, for which I developed a program that saw local video stores donate old stock (for example, *Mary Poppins, Star Wars,* and *Annie Hall*) to the video collection of the Queensway–Carleton Hospital in Ottawa. As well, I designed the press kit and wrote the press release that announced the college's partnership with X-Tel computers on June 12, 2005. During my field placement at Website Analysis, I proofread and reformatted documents that I then placed on corporate websites.

*continued*

Margoles uses a subject line in his cover letter to ensure that it is filed correctly.

Margoles states his "thesis."

If it is given, cover letters should always include the competition number.

This paragraph demonstrates Margoles's ability to identify salient points of his education and then use them to support his claim that his education has prepared him for this position.

Margoles includes
information to
show his
knowledge of and
links to the
Kingston arts
community.

My work experience has prepared me for a career in marketing. In addition to the regular responsibilities of a salesperson, at Records, Yes Records in Kingston, I ran and organized the publicity for the "Introducing New Music Evenings," a program that was praised by Queen's University's campus radio. Part of my responsibilities at Sports R You included liaising with local amateur teams and leagues to ensure that underprivileged children had equipment.

Margoles includes
information to
show that he has
experience dealing
with many different
types of
organizations and
groups.

Let me thank you in advance for your time. I am available for an interview at your convenience.

Sincerely,

David Margoles
(613) 224-9876
dmargoles@internet.ca

---

## BASIC STRUCTURE OF A RÉSUMÉ

A résumé is made up of the following sections:

- Education: lists the names and locations of schools, dates of attendance, major fields of study, and degrees, diplomas, and certificates received.
- Work History: details your employment history, including employer's name, dates of employment, most important job title, and significant duties, accomplishments, and promotions.
- Skills: describes special skills or capabilities, such as the ability to use computer programs, office equipment, and other languages.

## A SAMPLE RÉSUMÉ

Mr. Margoles also rewrote his résumé as shown in Figure 11.7.

**FIGURE 11.7**

## Résumé

David Margoles
1198 West Street
Ottawa, ON K1B 3E5
(613) 224-9876
dmargoles@internet.ca

### Education

| | |
|---|---|
| 2004–2007 | Algonquin College (Marketing Diploma, expected graduation June 2007) Ottawa, Ontario |
| 2000–2001 | Carleton University (General Arts Program) Ottawa, Ontario |
| 1996–2000 | MacDonald High School Kingston, Ontario |
| 2006 | Field Placement/Co-op Proofreader/Webmaster Website Analysis Ottawa, Ontario |

Résumés always list education and work experience in reverse chronological order.

Abbreviations should not be used in résumés.

### Work History

| | |
|---|---|
| Summer 2004–Present | Salesperson Sports R You Ottawa, Ontario |
| Summers 2002/2003 | Salesperson Records, Yes Records Kingston, Ontario |
| June 2001–August 2002 | Coordinator YMCA Camp Ottawa, Ontario |
| 1998–2000 | Various part-time jobs |

To save space, Margoles uses descriptive titles. He addresses his specific duties and accomplishments in the cover letter.

Margoles groups together his part-time work experience.

*continued*

**Volunteer Experience**

Winter 2000

Assistant Hockey Coach
YMCA
Kingston, Ontario

Summers 2003/2004

Baseball Coach
Ottawa West League
Ottawa, Ontario

**Computer Programs**
WebMaster
Adobe PageMaker
Word
WordPerfect 8
Excel
ACCPAC (basic)

References available upon request.

---

## HOW TO CUSTOMIZE YOUR RÉSUMÉ

The résumé in Figure 11.7 is designed to be used by college and university students, which is why it begins with Education and highlights Field Placement. If your college or university training does not include field placement, do not include this heading. Similarly, if you know only WordPerfect and/or Word, do not create the heading Computer Programs, just as you would not indicate that you know how to type.

You can add categories as needed. For example, were Mr. Margoles to speak Spanish as well as French and English, he would have created a heading for Languages:

**Languages**
English (mother tongue)
French (speak, read, write)
Spanish (speak)

You will have probably noted that this résumé does not contain a category entitled Hobbies. The reason for this is that people often mistakenly assume they can write "reading, movies, playing baseball, and skiing" under this heading, the last two supposedly indicating, we have been told many times, "that I can work in a group." Human resources officials, however, tell us something different. They see such a list as filler, unless the items listed somehow link to the position itself. For example, Mr. Margoles could have written "Going to poetry readings" because this activity would be relevant to the publishing business.

## THE ORDER OF SCHOOL AND WORK PARAGRAPHS

As is the case for most college students, the basis for David Margoles's application is his college diploma. Accordingly, he has put the paragraph synthesizing his education experience before the one that deals with his work experience. If, in three years, he decides to apply for a position that requires three years of work experience in the field, he will reverse the order of these paragraphs and, of course, emphasize what he has accomplished during his three years of employment.

## AN ALTERNATIVE FORMAT FOR COVER LETTERS

Even if it is illegal for employers to discriminate on the basis of age, older students often feel that they would be better off using a functional résumé that does not draw attention to their age (which can usually be deduced by the year you graduated from high school). Experts are divided on whether students are correct. Many think that instead of switching résumé formats, which a human resources official notices immediately, older students are better off addressing the age question in the cover letter and, if possible, turning it to their advantage.

Note, for example, how in her cover letter to Dr. Diane Lachance (see Figure 11.8), Dawn Rogers, who will be graduating with a diploma in dental hygiene, addresses the 10-year "gap" in her résumé created by the fact that she stayed home with her two children until she returned to school two years ago.

## FIGURE 11.8

### COVER LETTER (ALTERNATIVE FORMAT)

15 Elm Street
Ottawa, ON  K4U 4Y6

March 29, 2007

Dear Dr. Lachance:

I am applying for the position of pediatric dental hygienist in your practice.
I believe my education, work, and life experience qualify me for this position.

As you can see from my résumé, I returned to school two years ago to study
dental hygiene. My intention, to build on the training I received as a pediatric nurse at Red River College, has been fulfilled, as indicated by the A
grade I received in my field placement at the pediatric dental division of
Mercy Hospital. Although I was required to deliver only one oral presentation
for my public health class, Immigrant Services asked me to deliver the presentation to several different groups of immigrants.

Although I have never worked in a dental office before, my experience as a
pediatric nurse and as a mother involved in the school health committee
have prepared me to deal with both children and parents frightened by the
medical–dental environment. As a pediatric nurse, my job involved easing
children's fears and explaining procedures to parents as much as it did traditional nursing. As a member of the school health committee, I organized
health awareness programs and was called upon to explain health issues,
including the mass inoculation of children for meningitis in January 1992 to
both parents and older students.

Let me thank you in advance for your consideration. I am available for an
interview at your convenience.

Sincerely,

Dawn Rogers

## AN ALTERNATIVE FORMAT FOR RÉSUMÉS

Sometimes older students who have been out of the work force for a number of years or students who have either never worked or who have held only a series of short-term or part-time jobs find that the chronological résumé Mr. Margoles used does not fit them. The most common alternative is the functional résumé.

Instead of listing school, work, and volunteer information in reverse chronological order, the functional résumé lists skills, abilities, and achievements under headings that are appropriate to the position in question. A functional résumé for a position in an accounting department would organize information under the following seven headings:

1. Education (in reverse chronological order)
2. Accounting Experience
3. Computer Skills
4. Communication Skills
5. Other Office Skills
6. Volunteer Experience (if applicable)
7. Work Experience (in reverse chronological order)

A functional résumé (see Figure 11.9) for Dawn Rogers would be divided into the following nine headings:

1. Objective
2. Education (in reverse chronological order)
3. Dental Hygiene Skills
4. Dental Assistant Skills
5. Applicable Nursing Skills
6. Computer Skills
7. Communication Skills
8. Work Experience
9. Volunteer Experience

**FIGURE 11.9**

## Résumé (Functional Format)

Dawn Rogers
15 Elm Street
Ottawa, ON  K4U 4Y6
(613) 797-0923
drogers.2@linkup.com

(Bilingual: English/French)

### Objective
- Work in a pediatric dental office that sees clients of all levels of difficulties

### Education
- 2005–2007, Algonquin College, Ottawa, Ontario (Dental Hygiene Diploma expected)
- 1991–1994, Red River College, Winnipeg, Manitoba (Registered Nurse)

### Dental Hygiene Skills
- Scaling
- Polishing
- Radiographs
- Apply pit and fissure sealants
- Impressions (mouth guards and bleaching trays)
- Assess periodontal condition
- Dental hygiene assessment
- Oral hygiene education and instruction

### Dental Assistant Skills
- Crownal polishing
- Chairside assisting
- Sterilization
- Placement and removal of rubber dam

### Applicable Nursing Skills
- Medical pediatric practice
- Advanced first aid and CPR
- Overall assessment
- Preliminary diagnostic
- Public health education

*continued*

## Computer Skills

- Office Med
- Med-Staff (Institutional)
- Medications Schedule
- Patient Monitor Office Pro

## Communication Skills

- Communicated medical information to parents/children
- Explained medical issues to groups
- Developed lesson plans for primary-school classes
- Designed outreach program for sex education for teens

## Work Experience

- 1994–1999, Pediatric Nurse, Red River Hospital, Winnipeg, Manitoba
- 1997–1999, Health Care Aid, County Old Age Home, Winnipeg, Manitoba

## Volunteer Experience

- 1999–2003, Parents' Health Committee, MuchMore School

---

## FONT AND PAPER

Word processing programs offer students a myriad of fonts, as well as the ability to put words in *italics*, to **bold** or underline them or even to do all ***three*** at the same time. However, as the preceding sentence indicates, far from making your meaning clearer and more forceful, inappropriate use of these options makes reading difficult, which is likely to increase the odds of your letter being discarded.

Similarly, office supply stores now carry printer paper that ranges from plain white to cream to turquoise and beyond. When writing a cover letter that you wish to have stand out, you might be tempted to print it on your favourite-coloured paper or on one you think will somehow complement you. However, in a busy office, your intended reader is likely not interested in colour schemes. Indeed, your reader will likely find anything but standard bond white or off-white paper a bother.

Accordingly, unless you need to use a video to show a particular skill (related to video making) or you are asked for a portfolio of your work (e.g., sketches of a window design), we suggest you avoid the temptation to be flashy and, instead, "play it down the middle." Remember, you are trying to convince whoever is going to read your cover letter and résumé that you should be interviewed for a salaried position. Thus, you want to appear businesslike and professional. Make sure you

- use standard bond or like paper;
- use a clean font such as Times New Roman 12 pt, Arial 11 pt or Stone Sans 8.5 pt;
- make a clean printed copy for each position for which you are applying.

## Box 11.5 WHAT NOT TO PUT IN A COVER LETTER OR A RÉSUMÉ

The following statements on a cover letter or résumé are likely to redirect it to the recycling bin. To increase your chances for an interview, make sure you don't make the same or similar mistakes!

"My salary expectation is at least $45K, anally."

"Do I have to be nice to stupid customers?"

"I am only available for an interview this Friday afternoon. I will phone for an interview."

"When you phone me for an interview, if a man answers, hang up."

"I have the ability to access problems and provide quick solutions."

"I demand a salary commiserate with my extensive experience."

"I have lurnt WordPerfect 6.0 computor and spreasheet progroms."

"Received a plague for Salesperson of the Year."

"Wholly responsible for two (2) failed financial institutions."

"Reason for leaving last job: maturity leave."

"It's best for employers that I not work with people."

"Let's meet, so you can 'ooh' and 'aah' over my experience."

"You will want me to be Head Honcho in no time."

"Am a perfectionist and rarely if if ever forget details."

"I was working for my mom until she decided to move."

"Marital status: single. Unmarried. Unengaged. Uninvolved. No commitments."

"I have an excellent track record, although I am not a horse."

"I have become completely paranoid, trusting completely no one and absolutely nothing."

"My goal is to be a meteorologist. But since I possess no training in meteorology, I suppose I should try stock brokerage."

"I procrastinate, especially when the task is unpleasant."

"Personal interests: donating blood. Fourteen gallons so far."

"As indicted, I have over five years of analyzing investments."

"Instrumental in ruining entire operation for a Midwest chain store."

"Marital status: often. Children: various."

"Reason for leaving last job: They insisted that all employees get to work by 8:45 a.m. every morning. I couldn't work under those conditions."

"The company made me a scapegoat, just like my three previous employers."

"Finished eighth in my class of ten."

Source: SaskNetWork. Government of Saskatchewan <http://www.sasknetwork.ca/html/JobSeekers/ lookingforwork/coverletters.htm#notput>. Reprinted with permission.

# E-MAIL RÉSUMÉS

If you are applying to an employer that requests an e-mail application, you will most likely be asked to send your cover letter and résumé as an attachment file formatted in ASCII (American Standard Code for Information Interchange) or in RTF (Rich Text Format, Microsoft Word). When printed, ASCII documents are in "plain text" format, which means that neither italics nor accents appear in either the on-screen or printed version of the document. Accordingly, you should put quotation marks around titles. Cover letters and résumés formatted in RTF maintain both italics and accents.

Whether or not the company or organization to which you e-mail your application gives an office e-mail address or simply gives you the company's general e-mail delivery address, both your résumé and cover letter will be batched by a program that scans your résumé for key words. These résumés must, therefore, do part of the job normally assigned to the cover letter. Where applicable, for example, you will include more than just the title of your position.

For example, had Mr. Margoles worked at an ice cream shop instead of the YMCA from June 2001 to August 2002, he would have written server/cashier instead of coordinator. Since the duties of a server/cashier are well understood, he would not have had to list his duties. The same would not be true of his job at Records, Yes Records. For, as you see from the cover letter in Figure 11.6, he did more than help customers find CDs and work the cash register, duties that would be expected of a salesperson at a music store.

In order to indicate his other duties at Records, Yes Records, he would have to rewrite that section as follows:

**Work History**

Summers 2002/2003          Salesperson/Public Relations
                           Records, Yes Records
                           Kingston, Ontario
                           Duties: Sales
                           Project Coordinator
                           Public Relations
                           Concert Coordinator

## Box 11.6 SKILLS RÉSUMÉ

A skills résumé stresses skills you have learned and the abilities you have demonstrated at work or in a volunteer position.

Begin writing a skills résumé by matching your strongest skills with the requirements of the position for which you are applying. Select details from your work and volunteer experience that show you employing these skills. Remember to include your work history at the end of the skills résumé.

---

## FIGURE 11.10

### SAMPLE RÉSUMÉ

**A poorly written résumé**

Angel A. Smith
609 North Fifth Street
St. Peter, Minnesota 56082
(507) 931-4821

**Professional Objective**
A career in human resources management involving training, coordinating, communicating, and researching

**Education**
St. Cloud State University, St. Cloud, MN

Date of Graduation: May 1997
B.S. in Interdepartmental Speech Communication
B.A. in English

**Computer Competency**
Word processing and database programs, Lotus 1-2-3, Electronic Compugraphic MCS System

**Skills Training**
- Created and presented two-hour workshop, "Persuasive Writing Strategies for Promotional Materials," to 18 volunteer coordinators: United Way Voluntary Action Center
- Designed and presented one-hour workshop, "The New Look in Resumes," to 26 high school seniors
- Provided on-the-job training to writing consultants: The Write Place

*continued*

- Contributed writing techniques, story ideas, time management guidelines, and format and production procedures to the Write Place newsletter staff
- Motivated individuals toward healthy lifestyle by teaching aerobic dance classes to groups of 20–40 people: Learning Exchange, Shoemaker Hall–SCSU, Whispering Hills Girl Scout Camp

## Coordinating

- Supervised and established Speech Communication Week idea, events, program time schedule, budget allocations, delegated responsibilities to faculty, community members, and students
- Planned and organized SCSU Shoemaker Hall 1994 Spring Formal Dinner–Dance for 200: location, entertainment, transportation, menu, beverages, invitation, decorations, advertising
- Coordinated Writing Consultants' Ink newsletter production; assisted in implementing newsletter purpose, content, and format: The Write Place
- Organized, promoted, and participated in fundraising event during annual community summer festival: United Way Voluntary Action Center
- Directed and organized Drama Night and Synchronized Swimming Show: Whispering Hills Girl Scout Camp

## Communicating

- Performed administrative responsibilities and resolved potential personal problems: The Write Place
- Wrote budget development proposal, final report, and internal–external correspondence: Speech Communication Week
- Edited and contributed articles to newsletter; developed, typeset, keylined student manual and promotional brochure: The Write Place
- Wrote weekly newspaper column for local newspaper; wrote news releases and promotional materials: United Way Voluntary Action Center
- Assisted in writing and creating media kits promoting Speech Communication Week
- Explored printing options, expense estimates for fundraising project by making phone call and personal visits to area print shops and lumber companies: United Way Voluntary Action Center
- Presented Write Place services information to groups of 20–30 students in SCSU classes

## Researching

- Completed extensive research pertaining to word processing and revision; had article published in national newsletter: The Write Place
- Researched promotional writing strategies and resume writing techniques for two workshops: United Way Voluntary Action Center and The Write Place

*continued*

### Volunteer Experience

- Special Event Coordinator, Speech Communication Week, SCSU (1996)
- Editor, Writing Consultants' Ink, The Write Place, SCSU (1995–1996)
- Assistant Communication Intern, United Way Voluntary Action Center, St. Cloud, MN (summer 1996)
- Public Relations Assistant, The Write Place, SCSU (1995–1996)
- Coordinator, Shoemaker Hall Spring Dinner–Dance, SCSU (1994)
- Hall Council Representative, Shoemaker Hall, SCSU (1993–1994)

### Employment

- Writing Consultant, The Write Place, SCSU (1995–1997)
- Communications Representative, Handicapped Services, SCSU (1995)
- Receptionist, Learning Resource Center, SCSU (summer 1994)
- Aerobic Dance Instructor (certified), Learning Exchange, SCSU (1994)
- Camp Counselor, Whispering Hills Girl Scout Camp, Rushford, MN (summer 1993)
- Waitress/Hostess, County Kitchen Restaurant, St. Peter, MN (1991–1992)

### References
Available Upon Request

---

Source: Leo: Literacy Education Online, Saint Cloud State University <http://leo.stcloudstate.edu/resumes/analyresum7.html>. Reproduced with permission.

# Editing Practice Two

The cover letter in Figure 11.11 and the résumé in Figure 11.12 were written by Amy Pal for a position as office manager at a national lobbying organization. Using the Questions to Consider on page 311, edit Ms. Pal's cover letter and résumé.

**FIGURE 11.11**

## Editing Practice Two (I): Cover Letter

### A poorly written cover letter

May 15, 2007
770 Glenwood Rd.
Winnipeg, MB  R2J 7W7

Dear Director of Human Resources:

I am interested in the advertised position. I think you will find that my work experience and my schooling make me a good candidate for it.

As you can see on my résumé, I will be graduating from Red River College's office managing program soon. In this program we studied Organizational Behaviour, Office Systems, Law I and II, Business English, Computers, etc.... I did very well, especially in courses that show I am a team leader. In high school also I took courses in team building.

You may be wondering what I did for the year betwcen high school and college. Well, you will be impressed to know that I worked at a Baskin Robbins, first as a server and than as the weekend manager, which shows that I am a leader. During the summer of 2005 I helped manage Trinkets, A Store Where You Can Find Things.

My work and school schedule keep me very busy, so if you want to interview me you have to call on Thursday afternoons. I know you will be very impressed with me.

Sincerely,

Amy Pal

FIGURE 11.12

## Editing Practice Two (II): Résumé

### A poorly written résumé

Amy Pal
770 Glenwood Rd.
Winnipeg, MB R2J 7W7
(204) 123 3456

**Education**

| | |
|---|---|
| 2005–2007 | Red River College<br>Winnipeg, Manitoba |
| 2001–2003 | Portage High School<br>Winnipeg, Man. |
| Field Placement | None |

**Jobs**

| | |
|---|---|
| 2005–now | Assistant to Weekend Manager<br>Perkins<br>Winnipeg, Manitoba |
| 2004–2005 | Assistant Manager<br>Baskin Robbins<br>Winnipeg, Manitoba |
| 2003–2004 | Server<br>Baskin Robbins |

**Languages**
English

**Hobbies**
Skiing
Bike riding

## QUESTIONS TO CONSIDER

1. Is the return address of the cover letter complete?
2. Should this cover letter have a subject line?
3. Does the first sentence of the first paragraph clearly state the letter's purpose?
4. Does the second paragraph make clear when Ms. Pal will be graduating?
5. Is the list of courses in the second paragraph necessary?
6. Does Ms. Pal demonstrate (i.e., provide evidence for the claim) that she is a "team leader"?
7. If you were a busy human resources official charged with reading 100 cover letters and this was the 50th, how would you respond to the beginning of the third paragraph, "You may be wondering what I did ..."?
8. Does Ms. Pal use concrete words to describe her duties?
9. Should Ms. Pal use abbreviations?
10. Are Ms. Pal's cover letter and résumé free of grammatical, punctuation, spelling, and usage errors?

# Editing Practice Three

The cover letter in Figure 11.13 was written by George Sapocolopolis, who will be graduating in June with a diploma in business administration, for a position advertised by a small plastics manufacturing company. Using the Questions to Consider on page 313, examine Mr. Sapocolopolis's letter.

**FIGURE 11.13**

## EDITING PRACTICE THREE: COVER LETTER

**A poorly written cover letter**

Mr. Morgan
Moncton Plastics
Moncton, NB E1T 5U9

George Sapocolopolis
1110 rue du Fort
Montréal, QC
H4R 3I9

Date:      November 15, 2006

Subject:   Office Manger's Position

Dear Mr. Morgan:

I am writing to apply for the position of Manager, Business Operations with your firm. My résumé will show that you are looking for someone like me.

By the time I graduate college in June, I will have studied all aspects of business operations from computers to payroll. While most of my classmate focused on large companies, I concentrated on studying what small companies like yours need to perform better in tomorrow's global marketplace. Note how my field placement at Plastique de Montréal manufacturing, would have prepared me for a company like yours; there I saw lots of things that could be improved by the methods we studied.

Since I have always been a full time student, I have never had a full-time job. But my summer jobs have show that I am a good worker. When I was in high school, I worked at a landscaping company, first as a gopher and later as an assistant landscaper. For the past two years, I have worked at Lilly Electronics' distributing department. The first year I was a shipping clerk and last year I worked in the office, where I helped introduce new computers.

I am sure that I can be an asset to your company. I would love to speak to you about the job.

Sincerely,

*George Sapocolopolis*

George Sapocolopolis

## QUESTIONS TO CONSIDER

1. Does the subject line announce what this letter is about?
2. How would Mr. Morgan likely react to the tone of the second sentence of the first paragraph, "My résumé will show that you are looking for someone like me"?
3. How would Mr. Morgan likely react to the end of the second paragraph: "… there I saw lots of things that could be improved by the methods we studied"?
4. What does Mr. Sapocolopolis mean when he writes, "I helped introduce new computers"?
5. Is the closing line, "I would love to speak to you about the job," appropriate to a cover letter?
6. Is Mr. Sapocolopolis's cover letter free of grammatical, punctuation, spelling, and usage errors?

# Editing Practice Four

The cover letter in Figure 11.14 was written by Carly Price, who has a B.Ed. and has spent the past four years as an interpreter at the Vancouver Aquarium; she is applying for a senior historical interpreter's position with Parks British Columbia. Using the Questions to Consider on page 315, examine Ms. Price's cover letter.

FIGURE 11.14

## EDITING PRACTICE FOUR: COVER LETTER

**A poorly written cover letter**

Xia Ping, Personnel Director
Parks British Columbia
Vancouver, BC  V8U, 7H2

Carly Price
304 Ivy Avenue
Vancouver, BC  V6A, 5H6

Date:      September 21, 2006

Subject:  Application for Senior Historical Interpreter's Position

Dear Mr. Ping:

I am writing to apply for the position of Interpreter advertised by Parks British Columbia. Both my work and education make me a really good applicant for it.

For the past four years I have been an Interpreter at the Vancouver Aquarium. My responsibilities have included organizing field trips, designing teaching materials, animating groups as well as general public relations duties. I am especially proud of the school unit I designed for the high school students. I received Employee of the Year award for the brochure I wrote for the Aquarium.

My education at UBC was very useful at the Aquarium and it will be too for your Interpreter's position. In addition to learning how different learners learn, we learned how to create lesson plans that sizzle; this is especially important for someone who is going to supervise Interpreters. I also learned how to develop interactive learning stations—something that can easily be adapted to historical interpretation sites.

Perhaps the most important thing we were taught was that in order to make learning come alive, the presenter must make it relevant to the learner. This belief was the key to my success at the Aquarium and will be my guiding light as the Senior Historical Interpreter at Parks British Columbia.

I look forward to hearing from you soon.

Sincerely,

Carly Price

## QUESTIONS TO CONSIDER

1. Is the subject line written correctly?
2. Should Ms. Price have indicated where the position was advertised?
3. Does the second sentence of paragraph two, "My responsibilities ..." provide her reader with enough detail of what Ms. Price actually did at the aquarium?
4. Should she have explained what the "school unit" contained?
5. Should she have discussed the brochure and, perhaps, attached a copy of it to this letter?
6. Is the first sentence of paragraph three, "My education at UBC ..." clear and logical?
7. Should she have written "we learned how to create lesson plans ..."?
8. Are the last two sentences in paragraph three, "Perhaps the most important thing ..." clear?

# Summary

Cover letters and résumés are likely the most important business documents you will ever write. For if they are not well written, it is likely that you will not be interviewed and thus not hired. The purpose of a cover letter and résumé is not to "get you the job," but, rather, to *get you the interview*.

Cover letters and résumés must be oriented toward the needs of the reader, the person doing the first cut. They must establish that (1) you have the basic qualifications for the position; (2) you are a clear and concise writer who pays attention to details such as spelling and grammar; and (3) you have the ability to synthesize (i.e., summarize) your relevant experience. You must make a "business case" for why you (out of hundreds of applicants) will best "fit" the position. A good way to show initiative is to find the name of the person to whom you are writing (unless the advertisement specifies "Department of Human Resources").

There are two types of cover letters and résumés. The first type of cover letter, generally used when applying for a position directly out of school or another job, emphasizes your relevant education and work experience. The second, generally used by individuals who have been either out of the job market for several years or who have held a series of short-term positions, emphasizes skills acquired over time. The first type of résumé presents a list (in reverse chronological order) of your education and your work experience. The second type of résumé (commonly know as the skills or functional format), which is used with the second form of cover letter, presents a similar list but also contains a section that highlights your work-related skills.

Established case law in Canada allows you to present yourself in the best light. You commit a fraud, however, if you claim skills, education, or work experience that you do not possess.

# Discussion Questions

1. What is the purpose of a cover letter and résumé?
2. What are readers of cover letters and résumés looking for?
3. How much can cover letters and résumés be worth to you?
4. Can you lie in your cover letter or on your résumé?
5. Why is it important to be able to prepare a cover letter and résumé that can be transmitted electronically?
6. How do the programs that scan résumés and cover letters sort them?
7. How do you use active verbs to sharpen your focus?

# Writing Assignments

## Assignment 11.1

Diana Primo is 22 years old. She will be graduating in June with a diploma in small-business administration. She is going to apply for a position with a local small high-tech firm that designs and manufactures chemical sensing systems. She has no special background in computers or technology; however, she studied chemistry for two years at university. Though she did well in university, she decided that "pure science" was not for her. As well, she has worked as a volunteer for a local environmental organization monitoring industrial effluent. Her field placement was with a printing plant that had recently installed a central computer-directed printing system.

Write a cover letter for Ms. Primo in which you turn her university experience from a "negative" to a "positive." Remember to stress her volunteer work. Make the best use you can of her field placement.

## Assignment 11.2

Almost certainly, you have learned either new skills or specific procedures while working at your present or most recent job. For example, if you are a server at an ice cream store, you have learned to work the cash, use the Interac machine, keep track of stock, deal with the public, and, of course, to make certain ice cream dishes. If you are a part-time landscaper, you have learned how to operate machinery, read plans, deal with customers, and anticipate and solve technical or design problems.

Put yourself in the position of a human resources officer who will be writing the want ad and conducting the interview to fill your present or most recent position. Make a list of the skills that you have learned on the job that you, as the official, would want candidates to have *before* they start to work. Then write the cover letter in which you show that you have these skills.

## Assignment 11.3

Take the role of a harried human resources officer. Give yourself two minutes to decide whether you will keep your classmate's cover letter and résumé. Be prepared to defend your reasoning.

## Assignment 11.4

Write your own cover letter and résumé.

# Web References

### Monster.ca: résumé centre

http://resume.monster.ca

This site is maintained by Monster.ca and contains useful discussions of cover letters and résumés. Samples can be found at http://resume.monster.com/archives/samples.

### CareerJournal.com

http://www.careerjournal.com/jobhunting/resumes/index.html

This site is maintained by *The Wall Street Journal* and contains useful articles on cover letters and résumés.

### SaskNetWork—Cover Letters

http://www.sasknetwork.ca/html/JobSeekers/lookingforwork/coverletters.htm

This site is maintained by the Government of Saskatchewan and contains useful examples of cover letters and résumés.

# C H A P T E R · 1 2 ·

# Writing for the Web

## LEARNING OBJECTIVES

In this chapter, you will learn

- the characteristics of the Web as an information and communications medium;

- the requirements of writing for the Web;

- how to use Purpose and Focus Questions to organize, develop, and write material for the Web that meets your reader's needs.

## PRELIMINARY *exercise*

You are the communications assistant to Veneta Bishop, Manager of Corporate Communications for RunQuick Couriers Ltd., a Toronto-based courier company. Part of your job is to prepare documents for the company's website and to generally keep Ms. Bishop abreast of Web developments. You see the article in Figure 12.1 and decide to write a summary of it for Ms. Bishop.

**FIGURE 12.1**

### INFORMATION TECHNOLOGY: PICKING UP WHERE SEARCH LEAVES OFF

The time-saving trend of "tagging" is luring legions of Web surfers—and Yahoo!

Joshua Schachter used to be a lot like the rest of us online. When he surfed the Web, he'd zip through interesting articles only to find that days later he couldn't remember where he had seen the stories or sites that had caught his interest. Unlike most of us, though, the 30-year-old New Yorker is a software programmer—so he did something about this lapse in memory. A little over two years ago, Schachter created a program that let him tag Web links using words he would remember and then store them for easy access. So when Schachter saw a story about, say, the music videos of Icelandic singer Bjork, he would slap a "music" tag on it and file it away.

At the end of 2003, Schachter opened a Web site, del.icio.us, to let anyone use the technology. With del.icio.us, people are able to tag any link they choose for easy retrieval later. What makes tags more powerful than a Web bookmark is that they can be shared easily with other people. If someone tags a story on Iraq, for example, that link is added to a list on del.icio.us of other Iraq content. Anyone on the service who wants to read about Iraq can then find a list of stories that have been tagged and see who tagged them. Today more than 85,000 people are using the free service. "Tagging is about the most important tool of last year," says Clay Shirky, an adjunct professor at New York University's Interactive Telecommunications Program.

Indeed, the practice is catching on fast. The blog index Technorati Inc. and corporate portal developer Plumtree Software Inc. (PLUM) are adopting the technology. Amazon.com Inc. (AMZN) announced in February an investment in tagging startup 43 Things. And in March, Net giant Yahoo! Inc. (YHOO) paid an undisclosed sum for Flickr, a year-old photo-sharing service that attributes its success in luring 420,000 subscribers to its use of tagging. While Yahoo won't discuss specific plans, it's expected to sprinkle tagging throughout its Web properties. "I hope [Flickr's co-founders] become part of our vanguard to help us as we venture boldly and somewhat blindly into this [new world]," says Jerry Yang, co-founder of Yahoo.

There's a good reason Yahoo is taking tagging seriously. The trend represents a new approach to organizing and finding information online, and industry watchers expect it to draw people away from the traditional Net search offered by Yahoo and Google Inc. (GOOG). Tagging won't replace Google et al. But people may turn to tags more frequently over time, reducing their use of established search engines.

The risk? It could cut into the search-advertising revenues that are all-important to Google and Yahoo. No one has estimated the potential toll, but losing even a few minutes of people's time each day could be costly. "Search is no longer the only way to find things," says Howard Rheingold, author of *Smart Mobs: The Next Social Revolution.*

Search engines, for all their advances in recent years, have a glaring drawback: No matter how many pages they index or how quickly they bring back results, they can't put those results into context. They can find a specific word, but they can't figure out what the word means. An example: Look up the word "python" on Google, and the list of results throws together sites about the reptile, the programming language, even Monty Python. You have to sift through pages of irrelevant results to find what you want. To help avoid the confusion, Web sites often manually label their pages with category titles, a version of tags called metadata. But mass search engines, such as Google, don't use metadata because they can contain spam or misleading descriptions.

## A "LAYER OF SOCIAL KNOWLEDGE"

Tagging, however, lacks the algorithmic wizardry of search engines. But it lets people work together organically to create the context traditional search typically misses. Blogger Thomas Vander Wal coined the word "folksonomy," a combination of the words folk and taxonomy, to describe this joint work. It's like a grassroots Dewey Decimal Classification System for the Web. The essence: The combined work of people busily tagging content creates another way to make sense of the mountains of information online.

People are using tags to share their work and their whimsies. At del.icio.us, groups are adopting specific tags to help them collaborate on projects. For instance, in January a group of bloggers interested in applying technology to nonprofit groups adopted the "NPTech" tag. They file links to that tag, creating a bibliography of research that contains more than 900 articles, Web links, and blog posts. At Flickr, individuals often create a tag meant to inspire others to take and share photos. An example: Under the "What's in your bag?" label, users have posted photos of the contents of computer bags, knapsacks, and purses. "What has me really excited is this layer of social knowledge that's being created," says David Weinberger, a fellow at Harvard University's Berkman Center for Internet & Society. "We can't even anticipate yet what kind of research we will be able to do or the services that will develop."

The rising popularity of tagging is spurring debate about potential problems. Already, spam is being posted within tags at Technorati. Flickr and Technorati use a combination of automatic filtering and manual removal to combat these early marketing attempts. Still, if spam can't be held in check, it will undermine the usefulness of tags. "Every healthy ecosystem has parasites," says David L. Sifry, founder and CEO of Technorati. "We're trying to take into account what we learned from e-mail spam."

Another worry is whether tagging could collapse under its own weight because it isn't a standardized system created by professionals. In the free-flowing tagging world, one person might apply the tag "camera phone" to photos taken with a mobile phone, while someone else uses the words "mobile phone," undermining the whole point of sharing valued information. People also might use overly broad words as tags, say, Paris or wireless, resulting in too much information to plow through.

Tagging proponents such as Shirky maintain that no one company can afford the cost of applying standard tags to everything on the Web—that only many individuals tagging every day could help structure the vast reaches of Net content. And these individuals and businesses are devising ways to make it easier to find just the right information via tags. For instance, Technorati recently copied Flickr in offering lists of related tags when someone does a search on a generic one. So while tagging may look unorganized, there is logic to this avalanche of virtual Post-its.

People are providing their own likes and dislikes as guideposts to help others pick their way through cyberspace. Tagging is bringing a new kind of order to the chaos of the Web.

---

Source: Green, Heather, and Robert D. Hof. "Picking Up Where Search Leaves Off." *Business Week* 11 April 2005. Reprinted with permission.

1. What is the article about?
2. Who is the intended reader?
3. What is the tone of the text?
4. What are the major divisions of the text? Does every one merit inclusion in the summary?

# Introduction

This chapter teaches you how to write for the Web. You will learn the differences between writing for the Web and for traditional printed documents, and how to organize, present, and write material for a website.

Although you may write mainly for individuals or other quite specific audiences—memos to your manager, drafts of letters and memos for him or her to send to others, reports to colleagues, or letters to individual customers—you may well be asked to produce material to be posted on the organization's Internet or intranet site.

Websites have their own challenges and requirements for effective writing and communication—above all, readers usually want to get specific information quickly and easily. Unless they really want to read an item, readers won't hang around on a site that makes it difficult for them to access information. According to Dr. Jakob Nielsen, an expert in making websites accessible and usable, "A continued problem that has always been bad and continues to be bad is the writing on websites."[1]

The Web is an expanding technology—new applications are constantly being developed and its technical capability constantly enhanced. We take ease and speed of access to information for granted now, as we do search engine capacity, and we expect to be able to quickly "look it up on the Web" no matter what type of research we are doing. We read texts differently on the Web and we write differently for the Web—we are conditioned to expect to be able to find information immediately and, with blogs, we write now for immediate consumption and effect. We also expect information provided by organizations to be current and up-to-date—once again, immediate. The mindset we bring to the Web and its content is quite different from that which readers brought to books and other printed material before the Web.

In an Internet-networked world, it's unthinkable for any company or organization that wants to be taken seriously and wants to communicate with its customers and clients not to have a website. Having a website makes it much easier to keep information up-to-date and to provide in-depth, supplemental material to site visitors. It's worth noting that Web audiences tend to be quite specific for most organizations—visitors to the Canadian Wood

---

[1] Interview. *Digital Web Magazine* 13 November 2002 <http://www.digital-web.com/articles/jakob_nielsen>.

Company site are likely to be interested in the company as such, in the wood industry as a whole, or in finding a job with the company. Writing for a website means dealing with its characteristics as a communication and information tool and the expectations Web users have developed as the technology continues to evolve.

Building an effective website is a matter of combining content valuable to users with excellent design that makes it easy to navigate the site and find information. However, we are *not* dealing in this chapter with Web design and layout. You will find useful references to these topics in the Web Links section at the end of this chapter.

# Editing Practice One

Edward Collins is the safety officer at Delorco Textiles, a fashion company designing and producing men's clothing for the Canadian market. Using his accident memo (Figure 12.2) and the Questions to Consider on page 323, examine the memo posted on the intranet site of another company, Barrk Chemicals, by Lottie Tuvald in Figure 12.3.

---

**FIGURE 12.2**

WEB PAGE MEMO

**A poorly written Web memo**

**IT'S YOUR LIFE—SAFETY AND YOU**

**by Ed Collins, Company Safety Officer**

Last Wednesday, April 3, 2007, one of our colleagues was badly injured in the cutting section. She almost lost her arm when a power cutter was left running and unattended by a member of her work team.

Fortunately, prompt medical attention meant her arm was saved. She still faces months of recovery and physiotherapy.

Why did this happen? Because someone was careless and didn't follow our standard safety procedures for working in the **cutting section**.

We train everyone before they start work here in Delorco's general safety procedures and in the specific procedures related to their jobs. And we hold retraining sessions and workshops and inspections all the time.

We expect—and your colleagues expect—everyone, regardless of job, to follow the procedures for their own and everyone else's safety. If you don't, or if you get careless or lazy, people suffer. Needlessly.

If you want to know more, check our **Safety FAQs** or contact me at the **Safety Office**.

---

FIGURE 12.3

## Editing Practice One: Web Page Memo

**A poorly written Web memo**

BARRK CHEMICALS INC.

OFFICE OF SAFETY AND SECURITY

Calgary, Alberta

REMINDER

The company has seen a disturbing increase in safety violations over the last few months. More particularly, and the reason for this notice, some days ago one of our employees was injured on the job and sustained significant harm. It is unlikely the employee in question will be able to return to work for some time. This will, of course, result in disruption to the launch of the company's very important new CR345-ED7 product for the general industrial usages division. In other words, it could well involve significant costs.

As you know, the company takes safety extremely seriously and every employee is expected to read and digest the Barrk Chemicals Safety and Procedures Manual provided to them once hired. The manual is also available online at barrksafety.com, and you are reminded that while the company is required by law to ensure that you are given a copy of the manual and made fully aware of its contents—this is why we have training sessions—you are also required to know and *to follow* the procedures laid down.

In the case of the injured employee referred to above, he did not follow the rules in mixing chemicals and nor did his coworkers, resulting in harm to the individual concerned. This type of carelessness cannot be allowed to continue in everyone's best interests. If you have any questions or wish to obtain further information, please contact my office.

Lottie Tuvald
Executive Director
Barrk Chemicals Office of Safety and Security

## QUESTIONS TO CONSIDER

1. Does the reader immediately understand what the subject of this posting is?
2. As a Web page, is the material presented in an easy-to-scan fashion?
3. Is the "Reminder" written as a Web document? If not, what is wrong with it?
4. Is the main message of the announcement clear and easy to understand?

5. Would a reader be likely to read to the end?
6. Is the tone appropriate?
7. Is the exact nature of the injury suffered by the employee clear?
8. What appears to be the greatest concern of Ms. Tuvald?
9. How would you rewrite the "Reminder"?

# The Process of Writing for the Web

The Web differs from the printed page as a medium for transmitting information in important ways, which, taken together, lead to a specific set of rules and requirements for effective writing of Web materials.

## PRINT VERSUS WEB DOCUMENTS

A printed document is normally complete and forms a whole—the report or memo you have drafted and printed out (or e-mailed) is a continuous piece of information with a well-understood structure. Readers know to and expect to treat it as a single item, and they normally start at the beginning and carry on until they have finished the entire document.

A Web document, however, is usually designed to allow for moving easily and instantly to other relevant information through built-in hyperlinks. Readers do not perceive it as a whole in the same way as a printed text and expect to read it in segments, moving backward and forward through the document on-screen to other linked information.

## READING ON THE WEB

Reading a Web document on a computer screen is significantly different from reading a printed document. Normally we read printed materials with the light coming from behind and above our eyes and falling on the page being read. In contrast, screens are backlit, which means that light is coming directly to our eyes—and with it, glare. The problems posed by glare are compounded by the resolution of computer screens. The resolution (a measurement of the density and clarity of images, such as letters on a page or screen) of type is lower on a screen than on a printed page.

Apart from light source and resolution, the optical mechanics of reading printed materials and reading from a screen are also different. We are generally about 18 inches away from a screen and staring straight ahead at it. But we tend to read printed documents by holding them about 12 inches from us and toward the floor, so that our eyes are focused downward. This is, it seems, the most comfortable way for our eyes to read (and to avoid the common neck ache that accompanies using a computer for long periods of time without a break).

In addition, we read from left to right in a downward progression to a break point, normally the end of the page, and then move upward to start a new page and return to the left to right downward progression. Reading from the screen involves moving the eyes continuously downward with no horizontal break or movement. More particularly, to go through a long document we have to scroll downward, and when text scrolls on-screen, our eyes then attempt to focus on it as it passes by. And, obviously, since new pages appear at the touch of a button, readers who read longer on-screen documents do not have the mental break provided by the time turning a page takes.

Reading from a screen is, then, some 25 percent slower than from the printed page. And many argue that, even with new flat-screen technology, reading from the screen is not enjoyable. In fact, most people *scan* a Web page rather than read each word. Most users download and print out after scanning four or five pages of a longer document. It's just easier to work with than constantly going up and down on a screen.

## Box 12.1 THE TRADITIONAL ESSAY VERSUS THE WEB PAGE

The following comparative table highlights the differences between the essay and the Web page.

**The Traditional Essay**
- provides context and then narrows its topic
- develops a single idea and approach (thesis)
- has a progressive, logical structure that moves toward a conclusion
- is presented in long, interconnected blocks of text (paragraphs) that clearly relate to each other

**The Web Page**
- immediately introduces its major point and then provides the reader with an overview of how the site will be organized
- is unified by a single theme and seeks to inform by creating link relationships between chunks of data
- arranges information in hierarchies but allows readers to decide what they want to read, allowing them to follow a particular line of inquiry, provide background information or definitions, or to learn about a topic in more depth
- connections by hyperlinks are encyclopedic, providing related information, definitions, or descriptions
- generally, chunks of text should be fairly short (one screen or less) and should stand alone

Prepared by Kristen Leaver.

Source: From "Writing for the Web." The Writing Centre, University of Toronto at Scarborough 18 January 2000 <http://tls.utsc.utoronto.ca/TWC/writeguides/webwriting.htm#traditional>. Reproduced with permission.

## USERS DRIVE THE WEB

A website is driven by and at the mercy of its users—if they don't find a piece of information, a site, or a page useful, they quickly move on. You do not have very long to attract and hold users' attention as they scan pages. Web users are often surprised and frustrated by how much time they spend searching for information on the Web (despite increased search engine power) and this adds to the perception of pressure and the need when scanning a site or page to very quickly "see" what information is present and determine its usefulness.

This fast movement may be somewhat different when users are connecting to a website for very specific information that they know is available on that site—for example, a product use instruction or a personnel policy or form on a company's intranet site (internal website accessible only to company personnel). Even here, however, the information has to be written and presented to match user needs and the demands of the Web as a medium. Users, who may be important to the organization as clients or who as employees should be aware of key company policies, may not stay on the site or may stay and get the information but become annoyed at having to spend time accessing it.

## COMPETING FOR ATTENTION

People can come to a website from anywhere in cyberspace looking—or rather scanning—for information. As a result, every site and every page is in this sense in competition for the attention of the user.

Organizations that are direct competitors compete through their sites as much as in any other area—price, quality, service, etc. A poorly written and organized site where it is hard for visitors to easily find information they seek will lose them to a competitor's more user-friendly site with direct consequences for revenues.

## THE IMPORTANCE OF TEXT AND CONTENT

The Web brings together text, graphics, and audio and there is no doubt that the "look" of a site can help attract users. However, while text may not be very interesting to many Web designers, it is the key factor for most users.

Studies have found that people generally come to (and stay on) a website for information, and that the visual or graphic aspect of a site is less important than the content. Other studies have shown that when a Web page comes up on the screen, people focus on the centre of the window and read the body text before they move to examine other elements such as header bars. And, when asked about a page, they tend to comment much more about content than other items.

This does not mean, of course, that good graphic design is unimportant—indeed the visual focus and approach of a site is one of a number of "usability" factors that must be taken into account. Rather, it simply underlines that the information the organization operating a site presents has to be communicated effectively to its intended audience. This means writing your texts to meet the needs of the Web and its users—after all, putting your words on the Web ensures that potentially vast numbers of people will see and judge you and your organization by the quality of its writing.

## ADAPTING INFORMATION FOR THE WEB

*Organization*

Given the nature of the Web, you have to organize the information you intend to put up on a site to respond to the need for

- easy scanning;
- maximizing "readability";
- quick understanding of the subject and content of the page or site.

It helps to think in terms of

- tables of contents and levels of information—a table of contents presents the material in a report or book so that the reader can easily and quickly see the main divisions of the text, (e.g., sections or chapters), which are the most important or guiding elements, with supporting subsections at lower levels of sequence and importance;
- linkages between different levels of information that offer readers the ability to choose what information they wish to access as they read;
- bulleted lists setting out what information is available.

## Box 12.2   AN EASY-TO-NAVIGATE SITE

Visit http://www.nurflugel.com/Nurflugel/Fauvel/e_index.htm to see an example of a well-designed website.

### Structure

- Break up long texts into easy-to-read segments and aim for smaller pages of text and information and again use bulleted lists where this allows readers to quickly scan the information. Apart from helping users perceive and read the content, shorter pages and lists take less time to load onto readers' screens.
- Use the inverted pyramid style of organizing information with one main idea to a paragraph, starting with the most important paragraphs and moving to the least important. Similarly, try to begin each paragraph with the topic sentence. The Web is a linking medium and writing for interlinked information elements is not the same as writing for start-to-finish, linear flows of text.
- Use summaries—outline what is in the document that follows so that readers can decide if they want to read it or move on.
- Use FAQs—Frequently Asked Questions—to help users quickly get standard information on your organization or subject, which is all many of them will want (you can link FAQs to more in-depth information if appropriate).

FIGURE 12.4

## Canada Revenue Agency FAQ on E-Filing

Frequently asked questions about EFILE

1. <u>What about your documents?</u>
2. <u>What if we need more information before we assess your return?</u>
3. <u>When can you expect your refund?</u>
4. <u>How can you get faster payments and income tax refunds?</u>
5. <u>What if you have a balance owing?</u>
6. <u>What if you need to change your return?</u>
7. <u>What if we review your return after we assess it?</u>

1. What about your documents?

   You have to show all your documents to your EFILE service provider. Neither you nor your EFILE service provider should send us a paper copy of your return unless we ask you to do so. Your service provider can give you more details.

   Keep all information slips, receipts, and other documents used to prepare your return, as well as a copy of your completed Form T183, *Information Return for Electronic Filing of an Individual's Income Tax and Benefit Return*, for six years. We may ask to see them.

<u>Top</u>

2. What if we need more information before we assess your return?

   We may need more information from you before we can assess your return. We will let your EFILE service provider know if your return has been selected for review. We use the same criteria to select both paper and EFILE returns for a more detailed review.

   If we do such a review, we will ask for supporting documents to verify the amounts you claimed. For example, we may ask to see your RRSP receipts. If your EFILE service provider has informed us that this service is provided, we will contact him or her with the request. Otherwise, we will contact you.

<u>Top</u>

3. When can you expect your refund?

   In most cases, we can process an electronic return in about two weeks since EFILE cuts out several manual steps.

   However, we ask that you wait four weeks before contacting your tax services office about your refund. Before you call us, check with your EFILE service provider to see if we have asked for any supporting documents. This review will delay processing of the return.

   You can visit <u>My Account</u> to get information about the status of your current-year refund.

*continued*

You can also contact your <u>tax services office</u> by telephone or in person. If you do, be ready to provide your name, address, date of birth, social insurance number, and specific information from your return.

We may also need to know the document control or confirmation number of your return. You can find this number in Part H of Form T183, *Information Return for Electronic Filing of an Individual's Income Tax and Benefit Return*. This is the form you will have signed to declare that the information reported on your income tax and benefit return was complete and accurate.

<u>Top</u>

4. How can you get faster payments and income tax refunds?

To get faster payments and refunds, ask your EFILE service provider about our direct deposit service. You can use this service for your income tax refund, your goods and services tax/harmonized sales tax credit payment, and your Canada Child Tax Benefit payments. Refunds and payments can be deposited directly into an account at your financial institution.

<u>Top</u>

5. What if you have a balance owing?

If you have a balance owing, you can make your payment in several ways. You may be able to pay by telephone, Internet banking, or automated banking machine. To find out, ask your <u>financial institution</u>. You can also make your payment free of charge at your financial institution in Canada. To do so, use Form T7DR(A), *Electronic Filing Remittance Voucher*. If you mail your payment to us, attach to Form T7DR(A) a cheque or money order payable to the Receiver General of Canada. Do not mail cash. You can file early, and you can postdate your payment for as late as April 30.

Because of the speed at which we process your return, your *Notice of Assessment* may not show your payment. As soon as we credit your account, we will send you a revised statement that shows your payment and your current balance.

To help us credit your payment properly, give your name, address, and social insurance number in the space provided on the form. Also write your social insurance number on the front of your cheque or money order.

<u>Top</u>

6. What if you need to change your return?

After we have acknowledged receiving your return, you cannot send us another version of your return. If you want to change your return, you can either send your request to us electronically using **My Account's** <u>Change my return</u> option, or you can send to the tax centre that serves your area a completed form <u>T1-ADJ T1 Adjustment Request</u>, or send a signed letter explaining the changes (including the years of the returns you want us to change), your social insurance number, an address, and a telephone number where we can reach you during the day. With the letter, include supporting documents for your original return and documents for the changes you want to make.

*continued*

Top

7. What if we review your return after we assess it?

We routinely review returns after we assess them, whether they are filed electronically or on paper. This does not mean that you or your EFILE service provider made any errors or omissions. If we select your return for review after we assess it, we will send a letter asking for receipts and documents to support your claims. If you receive such a letter, please read it carefully and send the information we request.

If you completed Part E of Form T183, *Information Return for Electronic Filing of an Individual's Income Tax and Benefit Return*, you authorized your EFILE service provider to represent you. In this case, we will send a letter to the electronic filer asking for the information to support your claims.

Source: Canada Customs and Revenue Agency. Reproduced with permission of Minister of Public Works and Government Services Canada, 2005.

Use hypertext links to

- move less important material to secondary pages so readers can move to it as they wish;
- move important but detailed material to other pages—this avoids having to summarize or set out the material since you can simply link to the original;
- connect the main sections of a longer document such as a report—for example, on each final page of a section of a report, ensure links to the other sections of the report are present;
- allow the reader to proceed at his or her own pace and sequence to access other information connected to the main text.

Avoid too many links since this may be a nuisance and possibly confusing for many readers—you have to judge what information is important to place in the main text and what should be placed on subsidiary pages and linked to.

**Box 12.3** GOVERNMENT OF CANADA INFORMATION AND SERVICES ON PUBLIC SAFETY

**Internet Safety**

http://www.safecanada.ca/topic_e.asp?category=3

**Hacking**

http://www.safecanada.ca/link_e.asp?category=3&topic=28

**Identity Theft**

http://www.rcmp-grc.gc.ca/scams/identity_e.htm

## Box 12.4  EVALUATING WEBSITES

There are a variety of elements involved in evaluating a website; for example:

- identity (Is it clear who "owns" the site?);
- purpose (Is the site seeking to inform? entertain? sell? spread an idea?);
- information quality (Is the information accurate? current? objectively presented?);
- accessibility and usability (Is it easy to quickly reach the information content? Are there icons, menus, and/or symbols that facilitate moving through the site? Does the print size make the text easy to read? Do the links make for easy navigation? Do the graphics help or hinder getting at the information?).

All of these elements have to be considered collectively to arrive at a judgment about a site. Since writing is key to a site's utility, to evaluate it we need also to focus on elements that make for good writing. Use the following questions to help you judge a site's writing:

- Is the text free of grammatical, spelling, and sentence structure errors?
- Does the text present its information in a concise form? Are paragraphs or sections of information each approximately 130 words or less?
- Does each paragraph present only one idea? begin with a topic sentence? use an inverted pyramid style (i.e., conclusions, news, the most important ideas are presented first, followed by details and background information)?
- Are summaries used before long texts?
- Is the style conversational, simple, and easy to understand, using short words and sentences without jargon or promotional/marketing fluff? (Style will depend upon the subject, the organization, and the audience concerned; government and legal information, for example, will require a level of formality and precision not present in a site aimed at stock car racing fans.)
- Is the text easy to scan—are the key points obvious?
- Are important points condensed and presented in bulleted text and lists?
- Are *italics* used for emphasizing points or words?
- Are quotes set out from the text and emphasized to get attention?
- Does the site make use of meaningful, clear titles or headings and subheadings, headlines, captions, summaries, large type, bold text, highlighted keywords, phrases and links, lists, graphics, captions, tables of contents?
- Are menus used to present content and structure? Is there a logical progression of topics?
- Is the hypertext structure logical and obvious, making it easy for a user to find more information?
- Are links clearly labelled and self-explanatory so that a reader will easily know where and what they lead to?
- Do the graphics complement the text and help a user find information? Are all graphics captioned?

Source: Jeff Lilburn. Mount Allison University Libraries and Archives.

## Style

Write concisely and simply. Particularly on the Web, users are quickly turned off by overblown ("marketese") or pretentious language. In general, you can expect to halve the word count of conventional texts. So write a text and then compress and cut it—keep asking yourself if you really need this word, phrase, sentence. It's better to cut first and add words later if needed.

Use an informal style but only to the extent allowed by the type of document you are preparing—a report is not a family letter and, for most organizations, a certain level of formality in written material is necessary for legal and operational reasons as well as corporate image.

Refer to the house style guide if your organization has one. This will help ensure consistency across your communications.

## Presentation

Use headings to indicate what information a reader is about to scan. Organize them to indicate the relative importance of a page or section of a text by using capital or lowercase letters, italics, boldface type, and varying font sizes. If it's acceptable practice in your organization, highlight particularly important text within the body of the document.

## Accuracy

Ensure that the information put up on the Web is accurate: check facts, references, and quotations just as you would for any other kind of written material.

If you are using the Web for research, you want to be sure that the information you find on a site is reliable. The Library of Mount Allison University in Sackville, New Brunswick, developed a list of criteria to evaluate website information reliability (see Figure 12.5).

## WRITING WEB PAGES

Merrillee Wright, an operations analyst with GRG Textiles and Fabrics Ltd., was assigned by her manager, Arthur Brough, to write a section for the company website on GRG's export activities. She was to provide general information but with references to the 15 countries to which GRG currently exports.

Ms. Wright went through the following process to prepare her text and the page.

## Purpose Questions

She brought up on her computer screen the three Purpose Questions (PQs) she used to help her develop texts: What is my goal? Who is my reader? What does my reader already know?

She answered each question as follows:

1. What is my goal?
   To provide information on GRG's export activities to visitors to the company website.
2. Who is my reader?
   Visitors to the GRG website.

**FIGURE 12.5**

## Criteria to Evaluate Website Information Reliability

### Purpose
What is the purpose of the site? Is the site intended to inform? Entertain? Influence? Satirize? Is the purpose clearly stated or can it be derived from the introduction or contents list?

### Audience
Who is the intended audience? What is the intellectual level of the information? Is it aimed at beginners or specialists?

### Authority
What experience or expertise do the authors have on the topic(s) covered? Is there a c.v. or list of publications provided? Is the content of the site peer reviewed? Is there an editor?

### Accuracy/Quality of the Writing
Can the accuracy of the information be verified in another source? Are any sources cited? Are they relevant? Reliable? Is the document well written? Well edited?

### Links
Are links to similar or relevant sites provided? Do they work? Does the site rely heavily on links or on original content?

### Point of View/Objectivity/Bias
Is the author arguing for or defending a particular idea or thesis? Does the author promote a particular point of view? Express opinions? Are all sides of the issue addressed and discussed? Is there an introduction or "about this site" section in which clues about point of view can be derived? What else has the author published? Does the site contain advertisements? How might these influence the site's content?

### Scope
Is coverage broad or narrow? Does the site try to cover too much? If broad, does it provide sufficient detail for your purposes? If narrow, is it too specific, too specialized?

### Relevance
Is the information relevant/important? Does it help further knowledge within the field? How does it compare to other sources? Is the information relevant to your specific information need? Is it the best source available for your purposes?

### Timeliness/Currency
Is there a bibliography or list of works cited? Are any recent sources cited?

## Box 12.5 CITING SOURCES FROM THE WEB

Citation is telling your readers where information you include in a piece of writing comes from—your sources. This shows you didn't make up facts and figures and allows interested readers to refer to your sources for more information. "Acknowledging Information Sources" in Appendix II deals with the use of footnotes and endnotes for detailing where you obtained information.

Traditionally, with printed documents, citation was fairly straightforward with established rules (although, in academic and scientific writing, complex rules). The arrival of the Web made it necessary to develop approaches for citing Web and other electronic sources, particularly given the often transient nature of Web pages (it's a good habit to print out at least the first page of any material you are citing from the Web so you have it available even if the site disappears completely or moves location).

There are various styles that can be used for citing references to a book, article, etc. but, in general, all include:

1. title;
2. author's name;
3. publisher's name;
4. where published;
5. when published; and, if appropriate,
6. specific page number or other specific reference.

So, you may, for example, refer to a book in a report to support a point you are making and cite it as

Winning Export Marketing Strategies. Bloggs, Charles A. Ballsov Inc., Toronto, 2004.

If you refer to specific pages or a specific section of the book, you add these:

Winning Export Marketing Strategies. Bloggs, Charles A. Ballsov Inc., Toronto, 2004: Chapter 3.

However, if you are citing information you have found on the Web, a given site is normally the reference point, and the protocol and address replace the publisher's name and place. Also, the author's name may or may not be given in the reference, and the title will possibly be a file name. Moreover, since the Web is "browsable" via keyword or key-phrase searches, there's not really much point in using a specific page reference within an electronic document. Finally, the mobile or transient nature of Web pages and sites may well mean that the only date available is the one on which you accessed a page.

It is a useful practice to attach the date of access to references. Thus, you will have both a printout of the first page of your Web source and the date of access.

The basic rule is: give readers more information rather than less on Web references and sources. If you have a reference's title, author, and other information and the website address where it can be found, set out everything you can:

- Holmes, S. H. "Serial Killers and Their Use of Cyberspace." Crime Facts, Inc. Calgary, Alberta. 30 Nov. 2005
  <http://www.crimefacts.com/documentation/Refs/serialkillers/holmes>.
- Wild, Brunehilda. "Hiring Staff and Human Rights Laws." 25 May 2005
  <http://www.edgertonbasslaporte.com/hrstaffing/2>.

3. What does my reader already know?
   The average reader would likely visit the GRG website because he or she had some interest in the company and its industry, but most visitors would not have detailed knowledge of GRG exporting activity. This means that the information provided cannot be too technical and should be able to be easily read by a general audience. However, it should also allow for people interested in individual countries to which GRG exports to be able to get more detailed information.

### Focus Questions

Ms. Wright then entered several Focus Questions to help her better define what she needed to do specifically to create the Web page.

1. What information will I need?
2. Where will I get this information?
3. How can I best organize and structure the information for my Web readers?
4. Who do I have to work with to create the Web page for my material?
5. Is there any other part of GRG that has a strong interest in what will be written?

Ms. Wright gave the following answers to her questions:

1. What information will I need?
   General information on GRG's export activities and specific data on the 15 countries to which GRG exports, including, for each country:
   - brief description (population, language, currency, size of gross domestic product (GDP);
   - year GRG began exporting;
   - types of products exported;
   - value in Canadian dollars of GRG exports for the current year;
   - a source of further information about each country to which text can be linked.
2. Where will I get this information?
   From GRG's export department, the Department of Foreign Affairs and International Trade Canada's website, and other relevant websites.

3. How can I best organize and structure the information for my Web readers?
   The first level of information will be general and cover GRG export activities as a whole. It will respond to the average reader's needs under such headings as History of GRG Exporting, Countries where GRG Exports, Facts and Figures, GRG Export Contacts. The History section would be a few paragraphs on the development of the company's export trade and plans for the future. Countries would be a list of the 15 countries, each with a link to a separate section on another Web page. Facts and Figures would give overall, non-sensitive statistical data on GRG exporting. GRG Export Contacts would provide information on the Export Department and details of its staff and how to contact them.
4. Who do I have to work with to create the Web page for my material?
   Don Smith, the GRG Webmaster.
5. Is there any other part of GRG that has a strong interest in what will be written?
   The export department.

### Purpose Statement

As she looked over the answers to her PQs and FQs, Wright wrote the following purpose statement: My purpose is to provide visitors to the GRG website with information on our export activities at different levels of detail appropriate to different needs.

Ms. Wright then assembled the material she needed, including latest export figures and details for each country, organized it into the structure she had decided upon, and completed a first draft of her different pages. She made sure to make a bulleted list of the 15 countries to which GRG exports in descending order of volume of sales.

Her main text written, she wrote and rewrote a summary introduction until satisfied that it provided a reader with a quick but complete overview of what he or she would find on the rest of the page.

Next, she looked at her main text and wrote the main and subsidiary headings to make it easier for readers to scan it.

Her basic writing completed, Ms. Wright e-mailed her text to the export department for checking for accuracy and, once it was returned, submitted it to Arthur Brough for his approval.

Following Brough's approval and making some changes he'd requested, she contacted the GRG Webmaster, Don Smith, to explain the project and when the text must be up on the company site.

After e-mailing Mr. Smith her draft text, Ms. Wright met with him to determine how the text would be visually presented on the site.

Upon completion of Mr. Smith's work, Ms. Wright reviewed a "shadow" page (a draft) and made a few suggestions to Mr. Smith.

Finally, she e-mailed Mr. Brough that the site was ready and asked him to review the "shadow" online, as well as a printout of the page she had delivered. Once Mr. Brough gave his approval by e-mail, Ms. Wright e-mailed Mr. Smith to tell him to put up the page on the GRG site.

## FIGURE 12.6

### Web Page

---

# Résumés on the Web

In an Internet world, the electronic résumé is increasingly used by both those looking for a job and employers looking to fill positions. Most people send a résumé to an employer as an attachment to or in the body of an email or to be stored on a job bank. Many companies now require job applicants to submit their personal and employment information online through a job application form on the company's site. Some people with their own personal websites make their résumé accessible via their site.

## WRITING A WEB RÉSUMÉ

A Web résumé is written in Hypertext Markup Language (HTML) and arranged using a Web structure to be easily scannable in terms of its basic and important details while allowing for access to more expanded information through its links. The level of first page information might vary, perhaps with simply basic details and then links to education, experience, and interests, where specific details would appear. These, in turn, could provide links to more detailed information.

FIGURE 12.7

## Web Résumé

**HALDEMAR DERWIN JACOBS**

Address:    435 Omara Street, Apt. 34, Capital City, Ontario J2N 2V4
Tel:    (712) 443-5732
E-mail:    1ambest@rover.com

Education    Experience    Accomplishments    Interests

**EDUCATION**
2005 Diploma in Nutrition Technology, Algonquin College

"Diploma in Nutrition Technology" would link to a list of courses that made up the program of study for the diploma and a further link to details for each course.

You could equally have a standard résumé with its normal off-line structure and headings but with links to allow for providing more in-depth information on specific work experience or projects undertaken.

A Web-based resume can, of course, also offer various multimedia features. It is likely not very useful for the average job seeker but in creative and professional sectors can provide a showcase for previous work and projects and project a particular desired impression.

Employers offering jobs or receiving applications in other areas probably won't want to receive a Web link to your site or to be bothered seeking HTML-based résumés with all sorts of bells and whistles. Indeed, whether a Web-based résumé would be useful to prospective employers at all is something that would need to be weighed against your professional objective.

### Other Résumés for Electronic Transmission or Posting

Online job banks or job boards usually offer various services but are essentially a mechanism for matching job seekers and prospective employers. There are several types of job board:

- industry or business-sector specific (for example, tourism, http://www.cooljobscanada.com);
- company specific—a company or organization has a website or, more likely, a part of its corporate site for receiving and storing résumés;
- regional—focused on jobs available in a given geographical area (for example, Saskatchewan, http://www.careers.gov.sk.ca);
- general in nature in terms of types of jobs and location (for example, http://www.hotjobs.com).

In terms of preparing a résumé, a standard, formatted version with clear bolded headings for its sections (Education, Experience, etc.) can be used without adaptation when sent as an e-mail attachment or to a job board that specifically allows this.

If you send a formatted version, include a plain text version and cover letter in the body of the e-mail and make sure the e-mail subject line clearly indicates what you are sending; that is, refer to the job you are applying for.

Some employers optically scan résumés into a database based on keywords specific to the job in question. Only résumés with such keywords are retained for further examination. If you are told to send a scannable résumé, this means essentially cutting out all bullets, italics, bold, and tabs, and use a font that is plain, like Arial.

# Editing Practice Two

Examine the following article and then determine how to organize and place it on a website, using the Questions to Consider on page 340.

**FIGURE 12.8**

EDITING PRACTICE TWO: NEWSLETTER ARTICLE

 Old Priority Condo Association Newsletter

March 2007

Board and Members Meeting
The last meeting of the association board with members brought forth many new things for members to consider including whether or not we should increase the fees. The Treasurer, Martha Delisle, spent some time explaining about the need for more revenues to cover increased costs.

There was much discussion of the fees since many people could not understand if there would be more increases after last year. In addition, the cost increases to be dealt with by the fee increases were challenged by some members. The question of replacement of patches of the parking lot floor and lighting had been scheduled for last year but had not been completed leading to issues of use of funds.

It was pointed out that the monies raised last year had been properly used for roof repointing and other jobs that had had to be done as the winter approached. In particular, the furnace had had to have several parts replaced and carpeting in the entrance had worn much more quickly than specified. Finally, the building superintendent, Mr. Sommers, had been taken ill for several weeks during which illness a contract company had had to be used to replace him.

*continued*

Several people raised lighting questions, especially concerning the approaches to the parking and the entrance. They were assured that this was being dealt with and the steps taken were explained by Harry Rawlinson, board member responsible for maintenance and safety.

The social centre is being redecorated with new furniture. The fitness room has new machines coming and the pool is also getting a face-lift in the changing room area. Likewise, the lawn and garden outside the pool is being upgraded and a special children's are put in for younger visitors.

The meeting adjourned after much discussion which had meant that not all items could be covered. The meeting will continue on Wednesday next and their will be coffee and donuts served.

---

## QUESTIONS TO CONSIDER

1. Will every word be displayed or will you summarize and then refer readers who want to learn more to subheadings?
2. Is there a clear lead in this article? Does the article have a clear structure? Is there a logical progression of individual items?
3. Is the content easy to understand? Are there items that require more details or explanation?
4. Are there grammar, punctuation, spelling, or usage errors?
   Would headings help the reader? If so, what headings?
5. How would you rewrite this article? Is there further information you would wish to include?

# Editing Practice Three

Organizations now frequently have websites (job boards) where prospective employees are encouraged (or required) to post their résumés. Organize your résumé for placing on a website. Consider the questions on page 341.

1. What are the most important items you want to place first?
2. How are you going to structure the information you want your reader to see immediately?
3. What headings are you going to use? What headings would a reader expect to see when accessing the page?
4. Is the content easy to understand? Are there items that require more details or explanation?
5. Are there grammar, punctuation, spelling, or usage errors?

# Editing Practice Four

Choose a website and evaluate it using the list in Figure 12.5 on page 333. Write a report on your evaluation.

# Editing Practice Five

Write text for a website about being a student at your school.

QUESTIONS TO CONSIDER
1. Who is your audience?
2. How much does the audience know about your college?
3. What do you want to tell them?
4. How will you organize your information?
5. How will you indicate to readers what information is on the site and what the most important information is?
6. What do you want a user to see as soon as they click on to your site?
7. Will you link to any information on other sites? Why these sites?

# Summary

Websites offer a presence in cyberspace and the ability to keep information up-to-date easily and provide in-depth, supplemental material. Writing for the World Wide Web, however, has its own specific requirements. Reading a Web document on a computer screen is significantly different from reading a printed document. Most people *scan* a Web page rather than read each word and for a longer document, they print it out after scanning four or five pages. Moreover, users scan a site or a page for relevant, useful information and quickly move on if their attention is not caught or the information is too difficult to access.

Websites compete and must attract users through good design and, most importantly, content. Information has to be written and presented to match user needs and the demands of the Web as a medium—easy scanning; maximizing "readability"; allowing for quick understanding of the subject and content of the page or site. It helps to think of tables of contents and levels of information allowing the reader to easily and quickly see the main divisions of the text and their sequence so they can make linkages between and access different levels of information as they wish. Bulleted lists, plenty of headings, and highlighted text help readers navigate, as does a simple, concise informal writing style.

Hypertext links can be used to move detailed material elsewhere in a document, let users move at their own pace, and connect parts of a long document. Long text can be broken into "readable" pieces and summaries, and use of the pyramid style of organizing texts can help readers focus on the most important information in the shortest time.

# Discussion Questions

1. What are the differences between reading print and Web-based documents?
2. What are the particular characteristics of the World Wide Web as an information and communications medium?
3. How should you write to take account of the Web's characteristics?
4. What is the process of organizing, writing, and putting up material on a website?
5. What types of errors will editing Web materials correct?

# Writing Assignments

## Assignment 12.1

As a new human resources specialist at InnoHorizon, a software development company, you have been given the following text by your boss, Svetlana Michaud-O'Higgins, Assistant Manager, Corporate Communications, to put up on the company intranet for use by employees. InnoHorizon, which has operations across Canada and in the United States and Europe, uses its intranet as the primary means of communicating standard information on personnel matters to its staff. You must now determine how to best organize and present this text for the Web.

## FIGURE 12.10

PERSONNEL MEMORANDUM

Personnel Policies: Leaves of Absence — Types of Leaves of Absence

Amendments to the Paid Sabbatical Leave Policy: Replaces

Present Paid Sabbatical Leave Policy Section as of October 20, 2006

### General Provisions

Employees may be granted salary and benefit continuation while on sabbatical leave if (1) such leave is requested of the employee by the Company in order for the employee to pursue training or other work experience that would further the effectiveness of the work of the employee at the Company, or (2) such leave is requested by the employee for the purpose of continued study or specialized professional work experience that will benefit the Company and is approved by the President.

### Eligibility

Employees shall become eligible to apply for a Sabbatical Leave of Absence after continuous full-time service of a minimum of six (6) calendar years. A recipient of a Sabbatical Leave shall become eligible for a subsequent Sabbatical Leave only after completing six (6) additional years of full-time service calculated from the date the employee resumes his or her duties at the Company. The duration of a Sabbatical Leave granted to an individual shall not be used to determine eligibility for application for a subsequent leave.

### Period of Sabbatical Leave

The period of Sabbatical Leave shall be determined in each instance by the validity of the request of the applicant and the needs and resources of the Company.

### Requesting Sabbatical Leave

Applications requesting Sabbatical Leave shall be submitted at least six (6) months before the requested Sabbatical would begin. The application shall, in addition to other pertinent data requested by the President, contain adequately detailed plans of the purpose and scope of the proposed professional activities for the period of Sabbatical Leave. The completed application shall be submitted to the employee's supervisor. Action of the President to deny a request for Sabbatical Leave shall cancel that application. Another application must be submitted for a subsequent request.

### Compensation for Sabbatical Leave

Compensation granted during a period of Sabbatical Leave shall be full salary for a leave of one (1) to three (3) months' duration, three-fourths (3/4) regular salary for a leave of four (4) to six (6) months' duration, and two-thirds (2/3) regular salary for a leave of seven (7) months to one (1) year.

*continued*

In the event the employee is to be engaged in remunerative employment of any kind during the period of time covered by a Sabbatical Leave, the President shall determine, at the time the sabbatical is granted, the rate of compensation to be paid by the Company, not to exceed the limits set forth above, with due consideration being given to additional expenses incurred by the staff member during the Sabbatical Leave.

Compensation shall be payable according to the payroll procedures of the Company.

### Continuation of Employee Status

Except as expressly provided above, Sabbatical Leave shall be treated as full-time service to the Company for the purpose of computing length of service for consideration for salary increments, promotions and assignments, insurance, retirement, and other benefits dependent upon years of service. Vacation and sick leave accrue as if the employee were working on a full-time basis.

### Termination of Sabbatical Leave before Expiration

Sabbatical Leave may be terminated prior to the expiration date only upon mutual agreement between the recipient and the President.

### Report of Achievement

A recipient of a Sabbatical Leave shall be required upon returning to the Company, to submit to the President through his/her supervisor, duplicate copies of a comprehensive written report outlining the recipient's experiences and achievements in keeping with the purpose for which the leave was granted. One copy of this report shall be retained in the recipient's personnel file.

### Obligation to Return

Employees on Sabbatical will return to the position held prior to the Sabbatical. Sabbatical Leave is granted with the expectation that the recipient has an obligation to return to the Company for an extended period of service. Before the leave is granted, the recipient shall agree in writing, that in the event of failure to return to at least one year of service after such leave, he or she will reimburse all sums paid by the Company during the period of the leave.

---

## Assignment 12.2

As a staff communicator at Haribundi Inc., you have just been told by your supervisor to write an item about a major new contract for the "Breaking News" section of the company's website. You have been provided with a memo (see Figure 12.11) and instructed to prepare an immediate posting to "Breaking News."

## FIGURE 12.11

MEMORANDUM

 Haribundi Inc.
MEMORANDUM

**To:** Charles Farnesworth, Vice President, Operations

**From:** Bumpta Smuts, Vice President, Business Development

**Date:** August 18, 2006

**Subject:** Contract With OMG Technologies Inc.

This is to confirm that Haribundi Inc. has successfully completed negotiations with OMG Technologies Inc. for the contract for delivery of the XTM 5000 product range. This will mean a great deal of work for us and the opening up of the market in Southeast Asia. As you know, OMG headquarters is in India (Bangalore), and we expect that several staff will need to be on site to ensure liaison and train local personnel in the product range use.

At this point, we project a five-year commitment of 100 000 units starting at 15 000 this year (2006) and growing to 20 000 for each of the following three years and 25 000 in year five. The total contract value in final price terms is $50 million at current exchange rates.

To meet this order will require immediate hiring of fifteen new technicians and twenty assemblers. It is likely that another twenty will be needed over the life of the contract.

We are confident that OMG will increase its present order if the XTM does as well as we believe it will in the Indian market. Indeed, OMG has agreed in principle, subject to market performance in India, to distribute the XTM in the rest of the region. If this takes place, there will be continued growth in company hiring and operations.

---

## Assignment 12.3

For your college, department, or program, develop a list of FAQ and answers for a website.

# Web References

### Writing for the Web

 http://www.useit.com/papers/webwriting

This site is maintained by Dr. John Morkes and contains both information about how people read on the Web and how to design documents that can be scanned and read easily.

### Writing for the Web

 http://www.sun.com/980713/webwriting

This site is maintained by Sun Microsystems Inc. and contains guidelines on how to write for the Web; topics covered include layout, how to write to be found (by a Web surfer), use of graphics, and how to organize layers of information.

### Web Pages That Suck

 http://www.webpagesthatsuck.com

This site is maintained by Vincent Sanders and offers daily examples of sites that do not work well for users, mainly from a design viewpoint.

# CHAPTER • 13 •

# Grant Applications

## LEARNING OBJECTIVES

In this chapter, you will learn

- what the various types of grant programs are;

- what the purpose of grant applications is;

- what steps are involved in preparing a basic grant application;

- how important it is to properly meet grant program eligibility requirements;

- how to structure the different parts of a grant application;

- how to use Purpose and Focus Questions to organize, develop, and write grant applications that meet your grant program requirements.

# PRELIMINARY *exercise*

As the business development associate with Oriana Technologies, a small firm in Brandon, Manitoba, you are responsible for assisting the business development manager, Ian MacDonald. Part of your work includes scanning the World Wide Web and the media for material relevant to opportunities for Oriana Technologies and providing summaries to Mr. MacDonald. You have noted an article on grant applications for business (see Figure 13.1) and must now prepare a summary for Mr. MacDonald.

## FIGURE 13.1

### USING HARD AND SOFT TYPES OF DATA IN DEVELOPING BUSINESS AND OTHER GRANT APPLICATIONS

A grant application proposal that works moves beyond simply stating claims of past or future success. The application offers information and facts and figures clearly and coherently set out. The jargon of sales and marketing does not need to be used.

To use facts, you must be well prepared for the application writing process. As with any other writing, you need source material, which in this case comes in two forms: hard data and soft data.

"Hard data" are whatever can be specified at some level, which normally means that it is quantified. Statistical information is the most common form of hard data in applications. Statistics give an air of validity to your application and imply that some rigorous procedures are being used at your organization, whether true or not.

"Soft data" are anecdotal, usually gathered in informal communications, and lack the rigour implied in statistical data. Soft data that are presented well, via quotes and anecdotes, add context and a particular and recognizable quality and tone to an application that can't be matched by any statistics.

An excellent application uses both hard and soft data. For example, if you were describing your organization to establish its credibility (usually the introduction or some title such as "applicant," "description of the applicant," or "qualifications of the applicant") you'd want to focus on your organization's background, activities, and, as appropriate, accomplishments specific to the application. It's where you demonstrate to the reader that you are skilled in performing the kind of work or undertaking the kind of project or activity for which you are seeking support.

Depending upon whether you are a commercial or a nonprofit organization, any or all of the following can be used to draw upon and should be kept easily available.

**Hard Data**

Statistics describing all aspects of your organization, its markets and clients, or community and clients; descriptions of each of your current and prior programs, with data on participant numbers and type of services offered; follow-up data on current and prior clients; copies of any formal or informal evaluations of your organization or its programs; list of previous grants and their agencies.

*continued*

**Soft Data**

Correspondence and verbal feedback from clients, former clients, suppliers; correspondence and verbal feedback from current and prior granting organizations; copies of newspaper or magazine stories about your organization, or stories in which it has been mentioned favourably; awards and commendations received by the organization, staff, and/or board members; data on visits paid to your organization by representatives of government or other granting agencies; information requests you have received from other professionals in your field.

You can start with this list and then build one that includes other data sources appropriate to your own situation. While situations differ, the correct use of the correct data in increasing your chances of making successful grant applications is always a plus.

Source: Nakatime, Windsor, Vice President, Institute for Business and Non-Profit Innovation. *IBNI News.* April 1998.

## QUESTIONS TO CONSIDER

Before summarizing the article, answer the following questions:

1. What is the article about?
2. Who is the article about?
3. Who is the intended reader?
4. What is the meaning of specialized terms such as hard and soft data?
5. What is the tone of the text?
6. What are the major divisions of the text? Does every one merit inclusion in the summary?

# Introduction

There are any number of programs operated by the federal government and provincial and municipal governments that offer financial assistance to Canadian businesses and other types of organizations. Some of these programs provide grants (funds that do not have to be repaid), while others may provide repayable forms of assistance.

The federal government's Canadian Studies Program, for example, provides grants to not-for-profit organizations, companies, and individuals to help them develop learning materials (print, audio, audio-visual, new media, multimedia, or combinations) on Canada for use by educators and the general public. The federal Language Industry Program offers grants to firms in translation and interpretation, language technology, and language training to help with the cost of marketing their products and services in Canada and abroad.

The City of Ottawa's programs include Affordable Housing, which provides funding to help construct, renovate, or convert properties for use as affordable housing. Community Funding offers annual funding to nonprofit agencies that deliver a range of health, recreation, and social services in the community.

In addition to direct financial assistance, there are programs that provide expert advice and help. We use "grant applications" here to cover applications to all of these programs.

There are also many private foundations and charitable organizations that provide help for a wide range of activities. Much foundation funding supports research on an incredible variety of topics—from investigating and seeking cures for illnesses to attempting to understand and address social problems. The Alberta Heritage Foundation for Medical Research funds basic, patient, and health research, for example, while the J. W. McConnell Family Foundation in Montreal supports programs in social and leadership development and arts and culture.

For the most part, foundations support nonprofit organizations (e.g., Big Brothers/Sisters) but may also help commercial enterprises, particularly in partnerships with the public and voluntary sectors. The same type of application procedure is used by foundations and charities and, again, while the exact nature of programs may vary, we use "grant applications" to cover these also.

Most programs that offer financial or other assistance have limited funds available. In some programs, applications must compete against each other and the highest ranked of the group will be funded from the money available. In other cases, individual applications are simply judged against the evaluation criteria used by the program and supported if they meet the criteria. Of course, if the available funds run out, then regardless of whether an application meets the evaluation criteria, it will not be funded. Competitive programs normally have specific deadline dates for receipt of applications whereas noncompetitive programs allow for submission of an application at any time.

Granting programs are set up with a specific purpose; for example, to provide assistance to companies making exploratory trips to foreign markets to assess export prospects, develop technology skills among the work force, encourage research to be done in various fields, develop community-based services and projects, and many other reasons. The purpose determines the program's eligibility rules; that is, who can apply to be considered for funding or other assistance, as well as whose application will be chosen as best meeting the purpose.

We focus on the "basics" of writing grant applications because, depending upon the program concerned, drafting applications to programs run by government and private foundations that might be of interest to a company or a nonprofit organization can be demanding. Indeed, "grantsmanship" has become a recognized area of expertise, with specialist writers available for hire and workshops in application preparation offered by companies and nonprofit organizations as well as granting program operators. In addition, there are many published articles and guides to grant writing and a large amount of information on the Web.

Grant applications are usually prepared by experienced staff, often the same people who develop and write proposals. Nonetheless, you may be called upon to write parts of an application or to do a first draft, particularly in small organizations where there are fewer people available.

This chapter teaches you how to prepare grant applications. You will learn that grant applications can be made to public or private sector organizations. You will be able to determine if your project is eligible under a grants program. You will learn about the different steps involved in preparing an application. Finally, you will also learn how to use the Purpose and Focus Questions to help focus, structure, and organize the content of an application.

**FIGURE 13.2**

## APPLICATION FOR COMMUNITY GRANT TO NON-PROFIT ORGANIZATIONS

Halifax Region Municipality
PO Box 1749
Halifax, Nova Scotia
B3J 3A5 Canada

### Application for Community Grant to Non-Profit Organizations in HRM 2005–2006
Application Deadline: Friday. April 1st, 2005

| | |
|---|---|
| 1. Name of Applicant Organization: | 2. Contact Person: <br> Telephone: <br> Fax: |
| 3. Mailing Address: | 4. Civic Address (if different from #3): |
| 5. NS Registered Joint Stock Number: | 6. Federal Charitable Status Number: |

7. Tier: Circle the description that best describes your organization: volunteer only or volunteer plus permanent full- or part-time staff and the budget range.

| | | |
|---|---|---|
| Tier I | Volunteer/Staff or No Staff | <$50,000 |
| Tier II | Volunteer/Staff or No Staff | <$250,000 |
| Tier III | Volunteer/Staff or No Staff | >$250,000 |

### Please include the following information with your application.

❑ Proof of current registration as a non-profit society: certificate number from the Registrar of Joint Stocks or Federal Charitable Registration number through Canada Customs and Revenue Agency. If you are in the process of applying for registration, include a copy of your application form.

❑ An accurate updated list of members of the Board of Directors with name, address, and telephone number.

❑ A financial statement or Treasurer's report from the last completed fiscal year.

❑ State the location of the project if different from the address listed above in boxes 3 or 4.

❑ State which grant category you are applying to; a complete list of eligible activities is included in the Community Grants Guide. Copies of the Guide are available from HRM Customer Service Centres or call HRM Call Centre at 490-4000.

❑ Include a covering letter if you want to tell the Grants Committee something about your organization and its goals. Please do not include binders, self-promotional materials or lengthy reports. If more information is required, staff of the Grants Program will contact you during the review process.

❑ List any grants received from any HRM Department, Program or Commission. List any other forms of assistance your organization receives from HRM such as leasing agreements, tax subsidies, services, etc.

**Time-frame: The review process usually takes 6 months.**

| Application for Community Grant 2004–2005 |
|---|

| 8. Check the category of the grant: |
|---|

8. Check the category of the grant:
   ❑ Environment          ❑ Emergency Assistance     ❑ Heritage
   ❑ Recreation           ❑ Emergency Shelters       ❑ Ethnoculture
   ❑ Affordable Housing   ❑ Social Supports          ❑ Arts and Crafts
   ❑ Social Housing

| 9. Amount of grant requested: <br><br> $ | 10. Other HRM assistance: property tax, rent subsidy, grant, in-kind, etc. |
|---|---|

11. Have you applied to other funding agencies for this project? Please list name and amount:

12. Describe the specific project that you are going to do (attach additional information if required):

13. Describe the people this project aims to serve (how will the public benefit?):

14. How will you measure the "success" of your project?

The following is a project budget (not your entire organizational budget), please see the Community Grants Guidebook 2005–2006 for help in completing this section.

| Project Budget | | | |
|---|---|---|---|
| **Estimated Income** | | **Estimated Expenses** | |
| Type of Project Income | $ Amount | Type of Project Income | $ Amount |
| HRM Grant Requested | $ | | $ |
| Other HRM Assistance | $ | | $ |
| Provincial Assistance | $ | | $ |
| Federal Assistance | $ | | $ |
| $ Share of Project Budget from Your Organization | $ | | $ |
| Project Income (fees, rental, admission, etc.) | $ | | $ |
| Other | $ | | $ |
| Other | $ | | $ |
| Other | $ | | $ |
| Total Estimated Income for the Project | | Total Estimated Cost of the Project | |
| Note: if $ are not confirmed mark with * | | Difference between income and expenses: $ | |

Reproduced with permission of the Halifax Regional Municipality.

# The Process of Writing Grant Applications

The writer of a grant application must attend to both the administrative and the substantive aspects of the application.

The administrative aspects generally include

1. responding to eligibility requirements;
2. assembling and attaching any supporting documentation;
3. making and enclosing the required number of copies of the completed application;
4. ensuring the application is signed by the appropriate people;
5. meeting any deadline date for submission.

The substantive aspects relate to the content of the application, where you set out

1. the project or activity for which you are applying for support;
2. how much or what you need;
3. how the funding or other assistance will be used and over what time period;
4. how and when you will report on your results;
5. who will be involved in running the project and their qualifications;
6. any other information required by the granting organization.

## STEPS IN PREPARING A GRANT APPLICATION

Usually, preparing an application requires proceeding through the following steps:

1. Determining if the granting program is the right one to apply to. Why and how can it help us achieve our objectives? What needs that we have can it help us meet?
2. Determining eligibility. Do we meet all the eligibility requirements?
3. Determining what information we need to provide to show eligibility.
4. Defining precisely the project or activity for which we are seeking support and how it relates to the objectives and interests of the granting organization/program.
5. Identifying who will be responsible for carrying out the project or activity.
6. Determining what information we need to fully deal with question 4.
7. Identifying who will be involved in preparing the grant application and what their roles will be (information gathering, writing specific parts of the application, editing, reviewing, approving, etc.).
8. Determining what the administrative requirements for the application are, including the deadline for submission, number of copies, supporting documentation such as résumés of those who will be undertaking the project/activity or corporate brochures, signatures required, and so forth.
9. Preparing and reviewing the first draft of the application and writing the final draft.
10. Assembling all the required documentation with the application for final review and signature and sending it to the granting organization.

Frequently, applications are prepared by teams, depending upon the size of the organization applying and the size and complexity of the project or activity involved. Each member of the team will take one aspect of the application and then work with the other members to review and complete the final application. Many organizations, especially those that rely on external support for much of their activity—for example, nonprofit organizations or companies with high research funding needs—have one staff member who specializes in writing grant applications.

Most granting organizations or agencies, government or nongovernment, provide full documentation on their program requirements and objectives, including application forms and guides to completing and submitting an application. However, while the information required is set out, it is the content of the application that will determine if it is successful. The quality of writing, then, will make the difference and this is even more important when there is no application form and you must develop and draft your own application.

**Box 13.1**   WRITING GRANT APPLICATIONS: POINTS TO REMEMBER

## Writing Tip

Remember the following points when preparing grant applications:

1. Read carefully. Check if the program is the right one for your needs. Follow any specific content and administrative process directions carefully.
2. Make a checklist. Go through the program documentation and construct a checklist of everything that is required and must be submitted. You can use the checklist to make certain that the application is complete before you submit it.
3. Demonstrate eligibility. Verify that you are eligible to apply and clearly demonstrate your eligibility. Remember, eligibility often includes submitting the application before a deadline date.
4. Make linkages. Clearly show how the project or activity concerned is relevant to the granting program's objectives and requirements, why it is worth undertaking, how it will achieve anticipated results, and how funds or assistance applied for will be specifically used.
5. Justify facts and assertions. Support any facts or assertions made using reliable sources or offer to provide support on request.
6. Be brief. Too much information may work against an application, especially when there are many to be reviewed.
7. Use plain language. Keep the language simple and straightforward; avoid jargon and technical terms unless directly linked to explaining the project or activity.
8. Use a style and tone that is neutral but confident. An application is not a sales pitch but it does have to persuade the granting agency that the organization presenting it is entirely capable of undertaking the project or activity concerned.
9. Present numeric data simply. Present numeric data in simple, easy-to-understand formats.

10. Reverse the role. Ask yourself, from the perspective of the granting organization, why your application should be funded as opposed to another—and then be sure that you have proven your case.
11. Get an outside review. Have an "outside" person review the proposal before submission. (Evaluating your own or your organization's work is difficult and an outsider will bring a fresh and unbiased eye and may both identify weaknesses and make suggestions for strengthening the application.)
12. Make a final check. Always do a final check of the application using the checklist to ensure that all required information, documentation, copies, and signatures are in place.

# Editing Practice One

Examine the information provided in May 2007 by Josephine Roberts for Topcode Inc. in Box 13.3 in response to the requirements of the Federal–Provincial Program for Export Assistance (FPPEA) set out in Figure 13.3. Then look at the information in Box 13.2 filed by Rodney Herrick, Export Development Manager for the InterSurvey Market Analysis Group Inc., for his successful June 25, 2007, request for funding to FPPEA. Compare the information provided in each application.

## Box 13.2 INFORMATION FILED BY INTERSURVEY

- A provider of highly sophisticated market analysis services to companies and organizations.
- Employs 45 people, mainly analysts and strategists.
- Incorporated federally, Canadian-owned, and located in Toronto.
- Completely Canadian services offered.
- Company has been operating for 12 years.
- Profitable, with most recent annual sales of $2.6 million; export budget of $75,000.
- Registered in the WIN Exports database.
- Seeking $7,000 for a market exploration visit by Mr. Herrick to Australia and to attend the Australian Business and Industry National Show and Exhibition.
- Received $6,000 in October 2003 for a marketing exploration visit to the United Kingdom.
- Business in the United Kingdom reached $350,000 last year.
- Reports on the United Kingdom trip were filed in October 2004 and October 2005.

Josephine Roberts, market development associate with Topcode, a supplier of specialized information systems support services, was surprised to receive a note from Harry Ghiz, Topcode's marketing manager, telling her that the June 1, 2007, draft application for financial assistance under FPPEA would be rejected as ineligible. Mr. Ghiz's note did not go into detail but asked Ms. Roberts to discuss the matter with him later in the day.

**Box 13.3**  INFORMATION FILED BY TOPCODE INC.

The relevant information Ms. Roberts had set out in the application was as follows:

Topcode is seeking $5,500 for a market exploration visit to Italy, including attendance at a trade show in Turin, and had received $7,000 assistance under the FPPEA program for a trip by Ghiz to Austria in December 2002. The $7,000 had been properly accounted for and reports filed as required by FPPEA within six months.

The company is a federally incorporated, privately owned enterprise located in Ottawa, Ontario, with annual sales of $1,560,000 and a mainly technical staff of 53. Its service is completely Canadian, and Topcode is a viable business that has been operating for over 10 years and is now starting to make its first export sales to Italy as a result of the previous trip and further work.

Ms. Roberts has consulted the FPPEA program information she had found on the Web (see Figure 13.3).

**FIGURE 13.3**

FEDERAL–PROVINCIAL PROGRAM FOR EXPORT ASSISTANCE

Contact your nearest Federal–Provincial Foreign Trade Office to apply.

The Program
FPPEA recognizes that many Canadian businesses do not have much active export experience or capability to export or to undertake the market research required to develop an international marketing plan. Usually this is because of insufficient corporate knowledge of exporting or insufficient in-house financial or human resources.

The FPPEA will help these companies to make one market visit or participate in a trade fair so they can decide whether to develop an export capability and/or if their product or service is exportable to a new market.

*continued*

## Limitations

- The FPPEA contribution per application is a maximum of $10,000.
- A company can have only one approved application in a 12-month period.
- Each application must be in a different market new to the company.

## Eligibile Applicants

Companies with annual sales greater than $300,000 and less than $12 million, and/or with fewer than 120 employees for a firm in the manufacturing sector or 60 in the service industry are eligible.

## Eligible companies must

1. be incorporated or an unincorporated firm of professionals, such as architects or engineers;
2. be established and operating in Canada;
3. demonstrate the capability to undertake the activity;
4. be financially able to successfully complete the activity;
5. have an exportable product or service with Canadian content of at least 60 percent;
6. have met reporting and repayment requirements of any previous government assistance.

## Ineligible Applicants

Nonprofit organizations, publicly funded and owned institutions, Crown corporations, Crown-owned companies, their subsidiaries and affiliates are ineligible.

## Eligible Costs

FPPEA will share up to 40 percent of return economy international airfare or equivalent transportation costs for a market identification visit or the cost of participation in an international trade fair held abroad.

## Ineligible Costs

FPPEA will not cover

1. the cost of goods/samples;
2. the cost of translation into English or French;
3. salaries;
4. commissions;
5. entertainment costs;
6. hospitality costs;
7. accommodation and meals;
8. sales taxes, including GST.

## Where/When to Apply

Applications must be submitted to your nearest Federal–Provincial Foreign Trade Office at least six weeks prior to the date of the proposed visit or trade fair.

Current financial statements must accompany the application.

*continued*

### Period for the Activity to Take Place

The activity period for an application is the time required to carry out the planned activity. The start date is date of approval of the application. The expiry date is eight months later.

The program covers eligible costs incurred only during the activity period.

### Sales and Revenue Reporting Requirements

The success of assisted marketing activities and whether there is a requirement for repayment of the FPPEA contribution is determined by sales and revenue reports. These reports must be submitted by the due dates set out in the FPPEA agreement and must include all revenue and sales made by the company in the targeted market. Reports are also used to evaluate future requests for assistance and to assess overall performance of the program.

Two reports must be submitted: the first, one year from the date of approval; the second, another 12 months later.

Even if there has been no revenue or sales, a "nil" report must be made under the agreement.

### Repayment

The repayment clause of the FPPEA agreement requires that repayment of the FPPEA contribution is based on 4 percent of revenue/sales made in the target market.

Repayment is due with each of the two Revenue/Sales Reports.

Companies are only required to repay up to the amount of the approved FPPEA contribution.

---

## QUESTIONS TO CONSIDER

1. Why did Mr. Ghiz consider that the application would be rejected as ineligible?
2. Was there any information required that Ms. Roberts did not provide?
3. Was there any information that she did provide that would make Topcode's application ineligible?

## A SAMPLE GRANT APPLICATION

The grant application in Figure 13.4 was prepared in several stages by Charles Broncevic, Vice President, Social Affairs and Development, of Capital City University Student Union. A major activity of the University Student Union is outreach work with underprivileged youth in the city to develop literacy skills.

Mr. Broncevic decided to apply for funding under the Community Together Program (CTP), run by the Capital City government and offering grants for projects designed to help communities strengthen their economic and social base. The application process was straightforward. The University Student Union had to meet the CTP eligibility criteria, show how it would use the money requested and why it needed the amount of money for which it was applying. There was no application form, so Mr. Broncevic was free to structure the application as he thought best. He decided to start with an introduction section but he would write it once he had finished the rest of the application.

Mr. Broncevic first reviewed the eligibility criteria and decided to write a specific Eligibility section showing how the Union met them. Eligible applicants had to be

- based in the community;
- nonprofit;
- well managed.

Other eligibility criteria included:

- applications had to be submitted at least three months before the start of the activity for which a grant was being sought;
- the maximum period of funding was 12 months;
- the maximum amount available was $50,000;
- a project or activity had to fall within the interests and aims of the CTP.

### Purpose Questions for Eligibility

Mr. Broncevic began with the three Purpose Questions (PQs) he normally asked when he had to write a report or letter:

1. What is my goal?
2. Who is my reader?
3. What does my reader already know?

His goal was "to demonstrate to the CTP that the University Student Union meets the eligibility criteria." His reader was the CTP staff member(s) who would check the application upon arrival to see if the Union was eligible. For the third question—What does my reader already know?—Mr. Broncevic reflected that he would have to carefully and concretely show his readers, who might know nothing about the University Student Union, why and how it met the CTP eligibility criteria.

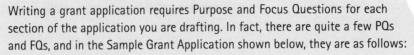

**Box 13.4** PQs and FQs for Grant Application Writing

Writing a grant application requires Purpose and Focus Questions for each section of the application you are drafting. In fact, there are quite a few PQs and FQs, and in the Sample Grant Application shown below, they are as follows:

### PQs FOR THE ELIGIBILITY SECTION
1. What is my goal?
2. Who is my reader?
3. What does my reader already know?

### FQs FOR THE ELIGIBILITY SECTION
1. Is the University Student Union community-based?
2. Is it nonprofit?
3. Is it well managed?
4. When do we want to start the project?
5. How much money do we want?
6. Does the project fall within the aims and interests of the CTP?

### PQs FOR THE PROJECT DESCRIPTION SECTION
1. What is my goal?
2. Who is my reader?
3. What does my reader already know?

### FQs FOR THE PROJECT DESCRIPTION SECTION
1. What do we want to achieve with our project?
2. What are the main elements of our project?
3. How will the project actually work?
4. Who will benefit from the project?
5. Who will be involved in the project?
6. How much will the project cost and what will the money be spent on?
7. How long will the project last?
8. How will we know if the project has worked and has achieved results?

*Focus Questions for Eligibility*

Mr. Broncevic moved on and set out and answered several Focus Questions (FQs) to help him deal with the specific content of the eligibility section. He realized that the application had to concretely show readers why and how the Union met the CTP eligibility criteria—readers who might have a limited amount of time to review each of the many applications they received.

1. Is the University Student Union community-based?
   It has been associated with Capital City since 1929 and has a tradition of working in the community since that time.
2. Is it nonprofit?
   The Capital City University Student Union is incorporated as a nonprofit corporation.
3. Is it well managed?
   The Union employs professional staff to support its elected directors and volunteers. Its directors are accountable to and removable by its members. It is audited annually, has never been in financial difficulty, and has been praised by the Canadian Management Faculties Association as an example of an excellently managed student union.
4. When do we want to start the project?
   In approximately four months' time.
5. How much money do we want?
   $40,000 to $50,000.
6. Does the project fall within the aims and interests of the CTP?
   To be demonstrated in setting out the project details.

Mr. Broncevic decided that he would use subheadings in the Eligibility section to deal with each item: incorporation; nonprofit status; nongovernment status; financial management capability; project start date; and amount requested.

## Purpose Questions for the Project Description

Mr. Broncevic decided to follow Eligibility with a section entitled Project Description. This was where he would detail what the University Student Union wanted to do—its proposal for using the CTP's money. Once again, he started by asking himself the basic PQs. He developed the answers bearing in mind that (1) he had to show program staff—and outside reviewers of the application who would be asked for their opinions—why the project was worth funding, and (2) he could not assume they would know anything about the Student Union and its outreach activities.

1. What is my goal?
   To ensure that CTP funds our application by demonstrating convincingly that it is worthy of support.
2. Who is my reader?
   CTP staff and the program's external reviewers.
3. How much does my reader already know?
   Nothing.

## Focus Questions for the Project Description

With his PQs in mind, Mr. Broncevic jotted down a series of Focus Questions (FQs) to help him organize and develop the detailed content of the Project section. He looked at the questions and put himself in the place of the people who would evaluate the application. After a couple of attempts at answers and reviews of what he had written, wherever he found information that was incomplete or unfocused, given the needs of his readers and the answers to his PQs, he ended up with the following:

1. What do we want to achieve with our project—its objectives and results?
   Our objective is to increase the employability of 40 underprivileged youth aged 16–18 in Capital City by providing training to upgrade their literacy skills.

2. What are the main elements of our project?
   Recruiting and choosing the course participants. Choosing the Capital City students to provide the literacy training. Arranging for the training facility. Giving the course. Providing post-course help to participants. Evaluating the course.

3. How will the project actually work?
   The current literacy outreach work undertaken by the Student Union will enable recruitment of participants, and the Union will also work with the local Social Development Canada (SDC) office, community, church, and other groups to ensure awareness of the project. The skills course will be delivered at a local community centre and will provide both in-class sessions and a high level of individualized attention. We will give participants counselling at the end of the course and evaluate the course with them.

4. Who will benefit from the project?
   Directly, those who are trained. Indirectly, their families and the community. Literacy skills will enable the youth concerned to obtain jobs, obtain better jobs, or continue with their education. This will bring benefits to the individuals concerned, their families, and the community in terms of reduced unemployment, higher income, less neighbourhood crime.

5. Who will be involved in the project?
   John Wills, the Union's outreach program coordinator, and 20 student volunteers; Duncan Soames, local SDC consultant; Isadora Trahan, community centre manager; and Denise Roberge, course evaluator.

6. How much will the project cost and what will the money be spent on?
   Each trainee will receive a workbook and a textbook costing $30, for a total of $1,200. Rental of a room and computers in the community centre, including Internet access for each student, and unlimited use of the machines for each individual will cost a total of $3,500. The course already exists so there's no cost for it. The course will be evaluated by an outside evaluator for $2,000, and there will be the costs of administering the project for CCUSU, the "overhead," about $3,000. The total would be $9,700.

7. How long will the project last?
   Four and a half months, including six weeks to organize and recruit trainees, two months to deliver the training, four weeks to evaluate and report.

8. How will the Student Union know if the project has worked and has achieved results?
   Each participant will be interviewed and tested at the end of the training. The project evaluation report will provide evidence and participants will receive a follow-up questionnaire three months after the training.

*Purpose Statement*

Mr. Broncevic reviewed what he had written and formulated a purpose statement: "My purpose is to tell the Community Together Program readers about the Capital City University Student Union, our project, the needs the project will meet, and the various benefits it will have, in such a way as to convince them to provide funding for the project."

As he looked at the questions and answers, Mr. Broncevic decided that it made sense to change the organization of the information. Following the introduction and the eligibility section, he would write a section called Project Objectives, next Project Description, then Project Costs, and finally a section on Project Personnel. This would allow him to list the cost items separately and clearly set out the roles of those from the University Student Union directly involved in the project.

Then Mr. Broncevic remembered that the foundation wanted reports on the projects it supported and he checked the CTP documentation. One progress report was required after half the project had been completed and another not less than three months after the project finished. He decided to include a section on Project Reporting to deal with this.

He realized as well that he could use subheadings in Project Description to organize his information on how the project would work. This would make it easier to show the various aspects of the project and how they were related and, therefore, easier for the CTP staff and external readers to go through the application.

But if he were to put all this information in the various sections what then, Mr. Broncevic asked himself, should go in the introduction? He thought that this was where he could introduce the Capital City University Student Union outreach program, explain what it did, and detail what it had accomplished since it started operating three years ago. The introduction, in fact, could provide both an understanding of why CCUSU was a good candidate for the foundation's help and a perspective for the readers and assessors as they went through the application.

Therefore, Mr. Broncevic decided that the final structure of the application would be

- Title Page
- Table of Contents
- Introduction
- Eligibility
- Project Objectives
- Project Description
- Project Costs
- Project Personnel
- Project Reporting
- Appendix A: Information on Capital City University Student Union
- Appendix B: List of Community Outreach Activities and Projects Undertaken by Capital City University Student Union.

The appendixes would support the information in the body of the application, especially the material showing the University Student Union's eligibility and experience.

Mr. Broncevic now wrote each section. The final application (see Figure 13.4), when approved by the University Student Union president, Arthur Farnesbarnovich, would be sent with a transmittal letter signed by Mr. Farnesbarnovich on Capital City University Student Union letterhead.

## FIGURE 13.4

### GRANT APPLICATION
### A poorly written grant application

Application by the Capital City University Student Union
for a Grant to Support a Literacy Outreach Project
Designed to Upgrade Unemployed Youth Literacy Skills
June 1, 2007

Table of Contents
Introduction
1.0 Eligibility
2.0 Project Objectives
3.0 Project Description
4.0 Project Costs
5.0 Project Personnel
6.0 Project Reporting
Appendix A: Information on Capital City University Student Union
Appendix B: List of Community Outreach Activities and Projects Undertaken by Capital City University Student Union

Introduction
Capital City University Student Union (CCUSU) represents and provides services to Capital City University students. CCUSU has a long tradition of community involvement and for the past three years has operated an outreach project with unemployed youth to help them improve their literacy skills. The project has brought together a small number of student volunteers and a literacy skills expert from the university staff.

An important part of CCUSU's approach is the use of student volunteers to work directly with underprivileged youth to teach the skills in a practical, applied manner, because youth relate better to youth. The present application is designed to obtain support to assist CCUSU in continuing its literacy skills outreach effort at an expanded level.

1.0     Eligibility
1.1     Incorporation
        Capital City University Students Union (CCUSU) is a provincially incorporated corporation with its legal office and headquarters in Capital City, Ontario.

*continued*

1.2       Nonprofit Status
          Capital City University Students Union is incorporated specifically as a nonprofit
          corporation.

1.3       Nongovernment Status
          Capital City University Students Union has no governmental status of any kind.

1.4       Financial Management Capability
          Capital City University Students Union's annual budget is $1.1 million. The Union
          employs professional staff to support its elected board of directors and volunteers.
          Its directors are accountable to and removable by its members. Financial adminis-
          tration is overseen by the vice president of finance and the Union's finance com-
          mittee. Annual audits are performed as required by law. The CCUSU has never been
          in financial difficulty and has been praised by the Canadian Management Faculties
          Association as an example of an excellently managed student union.

1.5       Project Start Date
          September 1, 2007.

1.6       Amount Requested
          $30,000.00.

2.0       Project Objectives
          The project is designed to increase the employability of underprivileged youth by
          upgrading their literacy skills through one-on-one training.

          The project will directly benefit the course participants and, indirectly, their fami-
          lies, by providing them with hope and encouragement and, eventually, with employ-
          ment income. Likewise, the community will benefit from a more highly skilled work
          force that will provide workers to local business. The project should also encourage
          other youth to seek training and will provide life experience and skills to the
          CCUSU student volunteers.

3.0       Project Description

3.1       Project Elements
          The project consists of the delivery of a specially designed, part-time two-month
          training course in literacy skills for 40 underprivileged, unemployed Capital City
          youth aged 16–18. At the conclusion of the course, participants will receive inten-
          sive job search counselling to develop their job search skills as well as to prepare a
          résumé through Social Development Canada (SDC).

          The project will be advertised through the Capital City Community Development
          Association, the Capital City Municipal Youth Outreach Office, Social Development
          Canada, the provincial government and the Inter-Faith Youth Ministry. Those who
          wish to be trained will be enrolled on a first-come first-served basis after regis-
          tering through the local SDC office.

*continued*

The CCUSU will use an existing and successful training course and will recruit trainers from among the Capital City University student body. Those students chosen who are without experience in delivering literacy training will be given intensive one-day "train-the-trainer" instruction by the project manager.

Course participants will be evaluated to determine their existing literacy skills level. A customized approach to learning will be developed for each person within the overall course framework and curriculum.

The course will be highly interactive and run in two sections of 20 trainees from 8:30 a.m.–12:30 p.m. and 1:20 p.m.–5:00 p.m. daily Monday to Friday. Each volunteer will work with two participants and be able to use the community centre's personal computers. Each participant will be provided with a textbook and a specially designed workbook.

3.2     Project Evaluation

Upon completion of the course, using a standard evaluation methodology, each participant will be interviewed using a questionnaire to evaluate the course's impact and the extent to which its learning objectives have been achieved. The project as such will be evaluated in terms of its operation and initial impact, but final success will depend on the ability of trainees to find employment relevant to their skills. A follow-up contact questionnaire will be sent to trainees three months after the course.

The overall project evaluation report, which will include the specific course evaluation, will be provided to the CTP as part of the required final project report. CCUSU will also make available the results of the follow-up questionnaire.

3.3     Project Management

Overall project direction and control will be provided by Charles Broncevic, Vice President, Social Affairs and Development, CCUSU. Project management by John Wills, CCUSU outreach program coordinator.

Timeline and Activities

| August 15–September 1, 2007 | Meet with and confirm cooperation with SDC, Inter-Faith Youth Ministry, community centre, and Ministry of Education and Skills Training. Contract with evaluator. |
| September 2–October 1, 2007 | Recruit and train student volunteers. Prepare course materials and community centre space. Recruit participants. |
| October 3–December 2, 2007 | Run training course. |
| December 5–December 18, 2007 | Course participant evaluation interviews, counselling and résumé preparation. |

*continued*

| December 18–January 10, 2008 | Project evaluation. |
| | Draft report preparation and submission to CCUSU. |
| January 10–January 30, 2008 | Reaction to report. |
| February 1, 2008 | Submission of final project report to the Community Together Program. |
| May 1, 2008 | Submission of follow-up report. |

3.4    Preliminary Activities

The CCUSU has approved the project and initial discussions have been held with SDC, the Capital City Inter-Faith Youth Ministry, the community centre and the provincial Ministry of Education and Skills Training office in Capital City. All have expressed their support for and willingness to participate in the project.

4.0    Project Costs

| | |
|---|---|
| Course materials (workbook and textbook costing $30.00) | $1,200.00 |
| Computer facility rental/Internet access | $3,500.00 |
| Course evaluation | $2,000.00 |
| Administration | $3,000.00 |
| TOTAL COST | $9,700.00 |

5.0    Project Personnel

| Individual | Role | Position and Organization |
|---|---|---|
| Charles Broncevic | Overall Project Direction | Vice President, Social Affairs and Development, CCUSU |
| John Wills | Project Manager | Outreach Program Coordinator, CCUSU |
| Duncan Soames | Consultant | SDC |
| Isadora Trahan | Manager | Community Centre |
| Denise Roberge | Evaluator | Dres Research Ltd. |

Summaries of project-relevant experience and résumés for Mr. Broncevic, Mr. Wills, and Ms. Roberge are attached and form part of this section.

6.0 Project Reporting

CCUSU will submit

- a Progress Report on November 1, 2007, detailing the project's progress against the timeline and activities set out in section 3.4 Timeline and Activities;
- a Final Project Report on February 1, 2008, that will include the results of the course evaluation and a statement of project expenditures against the amount granted.
- a Follow-up Report in May 2008 showing the results of a survey of course participants after three months.

# Editing Practice Two

Bearing in mind that the funding program personnel must determine from the written application whether a grant should be made, read the application in Figure 13.5, then answer the Questions to Consider on page 371.

---

## FIGURE 13.5

### Editing Practice Two: Grant Application Extract

**A poorly written grant application extract**

**Application to**
Industrial Innovations Assistance Program (IIAP)
**Applicant**
Dolortech Medical Technology Innovations Inc., Boudreau Business Park, Croston Harbour, New Brunswick.

**Eligibility**
We are eligible. We are a for-profit company with no previous experience of government funding assistance for innovation. We are under 50 employees and annual revenues are less than $5 million and we have been in existence for over one year.

**Project Title**
Premarket preparation of the XTM 5000 Electronic Pain Relief System (XTM 5000).
**Amount Sought (max. $20,000)**
$15,000.

**Project Description**
It is not our intention to mount a fully operationalized project at this time, but rather to explore simply the major aspects of the challenge available to us. In keeping with the program's intention to help small and developing companies to do proper innovation work before and as part of the stage leading up to determining product marketability, we expect that the funds that will be made available will be expensed into preliminary assessment of product technical feasibility. We have got assurances from a major testing organization that they will perform the necessary tests for stress and tolerances on the XTM 5000 electronic pain relief system. These tests will, of course, permit us to confirm the viability of the system preparatory to applying for Canadian Standards certification and once this is done then move to full prototyping of several examples of the product ready for field testing later this year. We are fully confident of the XTM's soundness and market attractiveness.

*continued*

**Use of Funds**
Payment to testing organization and associated costs.

**Personnel**
Mr. Albert Saunders and Mr. Lionel Richard are the company's principals and chief technical personnel. As well, Ms. Lucy Renault, the company's senior product engineering design specialist, will oversee the testing.

**Date Funding Required**
*Immediately. This is a highly competitive marketplace.*

**Corporate Profile**
A corporate profile is attached.

---

## QUESTIONS TO CONSIDER

1. What sort of questions do you think a reader might have in looking over the Dolortech application?
2. Is the information given under each heading on the application clearly set out? Does it answer the questions you have identified?
3. Is the Project Description section easy to read and understand? Does it clearly set out exactly what the project consists of and when it will take place?
4. Who will be working on the project? What will be their roles?
5. Are the style and tone appropriate?
6. Is the application free of grammatical, punctuation, spelling, and usage errors?

# Editing Practice Three

The grant application in Figure 13.6 is to a program that does not have a specific application form. Applicants are asked to describe themselves and their project and state the amount they are seeking and other relevant details.

Bearing in mind that the foundation personnel must determine from the written application whether a grant should be made, evaluate the application using the Questions to Consider on page 373.

## Editing Practice Three: Grant Application

### A poorly written grant application

Application to the Foribunda Institute for a Grant to
Provide Enhanced Street Youth Service

### Applicant

Youth Street Services of Saskatoon. We provide services to young people living on the city's downtown streets. These services include counselling, directing to emergency shelters, assisting to return home, and aiding with nutrition and employment. We've been working in this field for many years and currently employ five staff members and use a pool of volunteers to help us out. Many of these are professionals giving of their time. We work with social agencies, police, child protection agencies, and local service and business organizations.

### Program

Youth General Purpose Program.

### Project Description

Our project is to enhance our ability to find street youth temporary employment. Many of these youth need help to avoid lapsing into petty crime and prostitution to get money and most of them have little skills and in any event don't know how to present themselves.

There are many causal jobs and tasks that the city core local community and its business community have available: tidying up rubbish in business places and other sites; cleaning projects such as wall and floor washing in private and public spaces that are unsuitable for commercial or municipal service, distributing flyers and such like tasks. Many such tasks would only last a day or even a few hours but some could last longer.

Task duration is less important than providing something meaningful and remunerated for these youth, most of whom have little or no solid work experience or understanding of what paid work entails in terms of work ethic, sense of responsibility, etc. This of course makes it difficult for them to get work even when they are ready to try as well as the problem of the fact that few employers are ready to hire street youth, given their reputation and appearance and lack of fixed address.

Our project will deal with this. We will work with the local business and wider community and the street youth to place youth in temporary, casual employment. We will ensure that businesses know that there is a pool of people available for this type of work and that proper wages will be paid. We will help the youth to understand what is involved and teach them basic employability skills.

*continued*

The project will be supervised by the executive director, Ken Delorme, and directly run by our community liaison officer, Karen Wyzchynski. Karen has significant experience in this area. It will run from April to November at which point we will review the experience with our community partners and report to the foundation.

**Amount**
$15,000.

**Attachments**
Annual Report; staff résumés.

---

## QUESTIONS TO CONSIDER

1. What sort of questions do you think a reader might have in looking over the Youth Street Services application?
2. Is the information given under each heading on the application clearly set out? Does it answer the questions you have identified?
3. Does the Applicant section fully explain the organization and its activities? If not, what other details would you want before giving a grant?
4. Is the Project Description section easy to read and understand? Does it clearly set out exactly what the project consists of and when it will take place? Is there enough detail to justify funding?
5. Who will be working on the project? Is it clear what their roles and responsibilities will be?
6. Are the style and tone appropriate?
7. Is the application free of grammatical, punctuation, spelling, and usage errors?

# Editing Practice Four

FIGURE 13.7

EDITING PRACTICE FOUR: GRANT APPLICATION EXTRACT

Application to
Municipal Ecology Program (MEP)
Prince William County, Ontario

**Applicant**
Healthy and Respectful Communities Inc., 34 Main Street, South Copperston, Ontario.

**Eligibility**
As a local not-for-profit cooperative enterprise, incorporated for some 10 years, we are eligible under the program because also we are in the county. We had revenues of some $45,000 in our last year of operation. We have a Board which oversees operation and reports to members.

**Type of Assistance Sought**
We need assistance under the ongoing resource supplement part of the program since we want to hire a full-time project coordinator for the several very important projects we are running in the area.

**Total Amount Sought**
$40,000.

**Demonstration of Need**
The $40,000 will let us hire for one year a full-time project coordinator to back up the part-time staff, members, and volunteers. We have several projects that are clearly important to the community such as recycling encouragement/education ("Recycling Respects the Community"), wildlife conservation and protection ("Respect our Wildlife"—ROW) part of which is keeping watch for hunting violations and pollution threats to wildlife, "Greenspaces and Gathering Places" that encourages and works with children and schools to maintain and protect public spaces for residents and visitors, and Alert to Pollution (ATP) program where our members and volunteers observe and report pollution to the appropriate authorities.

There is no doubt that without these programs the threat to the ecology of our community from human misuse and pollution would be overwhelming. This would impact all the residents and of course tourism and local business. Preserving the quality of life in the county is vital.

**Person Responsible for Administering Any Funds Granted**
Kenworth Lecompte, President, Healthy and Respectful Communities.

*continued*

**Funding Period**
Fiscal year: April–March.

**Information on the Applicant Organization**
Annual Report attached includes financial statements and other relevant
details. More information can be provided if required.

---

## QUESTIONS TO CONSIDER

1. What sort of questions do you think a reader might have in looking over the Healthy and Respectful Communities application?
2. Is the information under each heading on the application clearly set out? Does it answer the questions you have identified?
3. Can you easily understand what the funds requested will be spent on?
4. Is there sufficient information on the person who will be responsible for any funds granted, Mr. Lecompte?
5. Is it appropriate to state that "More information can be provided if required"? How would you react if you were reviewing the application?
6. Is the information provided in the Demonstration of Need section sufficient and clear? Does it convincingly show why funds should be given to this applicant rather than another?
7. Is the application free of grammatical, punctuation, spelling, and usage errors?

# Summary

There are many government, private, charitable, and other organizations that offer various kinds of grants and other types of assistance to business and the nonprofit sector. However, funds are normally limited and often must be competed for. The goals and objectives of individual grant programs determine who is eligible to apply; but preparing an application usually involves several steps: checking the relevance of the program and eligibility to apply; relating the project for which funding is wanted to the granting organization's interests and objectives; detailing who will undertake the project; deciding who will prepare the application; determining administrative requirements such as supporting documentation required; and drafting and submitting the application. Often, organizations that rely upon external funding have staff specializing in application preparation. While granting organizations usually provide application forms and information, it is an application's content—and therefore its writing—that determines its success.

# Discussion Questions

1. What is the nature and purpose of grant applications?
2. What are the steps involved in preparing and submitting a grant application?
3. What is the purpose and what are the types of eligibility requirements?
4. What is the importance of eligibility requirements?
5. What is the difference between the eligibility and the content parts of a grant application?
6. Describe the steps in the process of writing a grant application.
7. How do using the PQs and FQs help to ensure that your application meets your reader's needs?
8. Why are the appearance and tone of an application important?
9. What are the types of errors that editing your applications will correct?

# Writing Assignments

### Assignment 13.1

Go to the World Wide Web. Click on the Canada site, http://www.canada.gc.ca. Select On-line Forms and Services and click on it, then select a Topic. If you prefer, click on a granting foundation site. Download the details of a program that is of interest and determine the eligibility requirements for applying to the program.

### Assignment 13.2

Go to the site of an agency or foundation that interests you and look for a program to which you might like to apply and identify the stages of developing and submitting an application. What would you have to do? In what sequence? What information would you need to gather?

### Assignment 13.3

Using the program you have chosen in Assignment 13.2, develop a checklist for ensuring that the application is complete and ready for submission.

### Assignment 13.4

You are the assistant marketing manager for Bentham Manufacturing Ltd., a medium-sized Regina, Saskatchewan, restaurant kitchen equipment company. You have been asked by your boss, Arthur Romanowski, to write the first draft of an application to the Program for Export Market Development  for assistance for attendance at a trade show in France in five months' time. The company has 90 employees and annual revenues of

$3.7 million. It has never used PEMD before and it does not receive any other federal or provincial government assistance. You can download the application form from the PEMD site at www.dfait-maeci.gc.ca/pemd/menu-en.asp.

# Web References

### Write Winning Proposals

http://www.writewinningproposals.com

This Canadian site contains a self-study course, which teaches proposal-writing techniques that have been used by nonprofit organizations to win government grants.

### Guide for Writing a Funding Proposal

http://www.learnerassociates.net/proposal

This Michigan State University site provides a how-to guide and examples of funding proposals as well as links to more resources.

### How to Write a Winning Proposal and Get Those Grants!

http://trc.virginia.edu/Publications/Grant_Writing.htm

This site is maintained by the University of Virginia and offers a beginner's guide to proposal writing for grants.

### Grantwriters.com

http://www.grantwriters.com

This site offers information on and training for writing grants and also supplies other useful sources for grant-writing information.

# APPENDIX I

## NOTES ON SPELLING AND GRAMMAR PROGRAMS

This appendix is not a full guide to spelling, grammar, punctuation, and usage. Rather, it is a short guide to using spell- and grammar-checking programs. A list of Web-based guides and tutoring programs appears at the end of this appendix.

## Understanding the Limitations of Spell- and Grammar-Checking Programs

Word processing programs such as WordPerfect and Microsoft Word have embedded within them spell- and grammar-checking programs. These programs are useful to business writers. However, since you are ultimately responsible for a memo you print and send to your manager or a report you e-mail, you should not rely on these programs alone.

Even after you have configured your spell-checking program to Canadian English, which must be done in order to prevent it from flagging col*our* or cen*tre* as errors, spell checkers will fail to recognize many words Canadian business writers use. Canada, Alberta, New York, Montreal, St. Lawrence, as well as Thomas, John, and Charles Dickens will be recognized. Abitibi, Red Deer, Research Triangle Park, N.C. (where Nortell has a large installation), as well as Rachel, Takis, and Margaret Atwood will not be.[1]

Nor can spell checkers prevent errors arising from confusing homonyms (their/there/they're) or similar-sounding words that are of the same part of speech (*accept* and *except*, or *affect* and *effect*).

Grammar-checking programs must also be configured. However, instead of telling yours to recognize Canadian spellings, you must set it so that it judges your document according to the correct linguistic/grammar scale. When you are writing reports, set the grammar-checking function to either "formal memo" or "very strict" style. If you are writing a newsletter, set it for "news writing" style. Just as spell checkers will flag Gaspé and the Kootneys, which are correct, grammar checkers will flag constructions that may be odd but are perfectly correct in their context.

For example, if your memo includes a direct quote from your CEO's answer to a shareholder's question, you might end up transcribing a passage that would be flagged for overusing the personal pronoun *I*.

---

[1] English spell checkers automatically read any word with accents, for example, *résumé*, as an error. Check to see if you can add words with accents to the program's database. If you can, add to your program a list of the most common French (or any other language's) words you use. If you cannot add words with accents, be sure to keep this list handy when you proofread your work.

I believe that our success over the past seven quarters is proof that our plan is working. I want to take the opportunity your question affords me to thank Frank Quarrels, the principle author of the plan. I think the record shows that the 30 percent growth rate I spoke of a few moments ago shows that despite the naysayers and the pain involved in downsizing, cutting back to our core business activities was the right thing for us to do.

However accurate the program might technically be (in written form this passage does lack style and variety), you should not correct it or accept the change suggested by your grammar checker. The reason is that this is a direct quote taken from spoken English, the rules of which are not quite as strict as they are for written English or, perhaps more properly, we should say that they are more context specific.[2]

Context matters also for other rules, such as the split infinitive. Ever since James Tiberius Kirk took command on the USS Enterprise, spoken English has been more accepting of split infinitives. "To boldly go where no man has gone before" was flagged by the computer for violating the split infinitive rule. This rule states that the two-word English infinitive—e.g., *to design*, *to calculate*, *to sell*—should not be split by an adverb such as *quickly*, *boldly*, or *carefully*. Although Captain Kirk's famous construction violates the rule promulgated by Dr. Samuel Johnson in the 18th century, it is more powerful than the suggested correction, "To go boldly where no man has gone before."[3]

Similarly, we endorse leaving the direct quote "the engineers hoped to quickly develop a patch" if that is what Amanda Coreson, your company's chief software engineer, said. However, for a progress report in which you are explaining how problems cropped up during the installation of specialized software, you should write, "the engineers hoped to develop a patch quickly," because the formal written reports should not violate the split infinitive rule.

## SPELL CHECKERS

Spell checkers are excellent at catching typographical errors. A jumbled version of *the* (t-e-h) or an "e" at the end of *potato* would either be automatically corrected by your program or flagged when you do a spell check. However, other errors, such as *form* for *for*, or *from* for

---

[2] Experts disagree on whether writers should change contractions that occur when someone is speaking (especially extemporaneously). The argument against changing *can't* into *cannot* or *hadn't* into *had not* is that the speaker him- or herself used the contraction: that is what was said. The other side, which we favour, argues that (1) since writers already provide the punctuation when reporting direct quotes, and (2) since writers almost never include slips of the tongue, we can silently change nonstandard usages such as contractions.

[3] Dr. Johnson, writer of the first complete English dictionary, based his rule upon Latin grammar. Unlike in English, in which the infinitive of the verb is two words—*to build*, *to manage*—in Latin (and hence in the Romance languages: French, Spanish, Romanian), the infinitive of the verb is one word (the French *danser* = to dance; *juger* = to judge). In the Romance languages the one-word infinitive cannot, of course, be split. Proper English usage follows this form, even though it is somewhat counterintuitive.

*frame*, will not be flagged, because the incorrect word *is* spelled correctly. Some grammar checkers can catch these errors; however, the only way to protect against such errors is by proofreading your documents carefully.

Proofreading on the screen is extremely difficult for two reasons. First, reading from the screen is unnatural. Second, since we are used to acting very quickly when on computers (think of how quickly you click the "Send" button when you've just drafted an e-mail), we are apt to read quickly. Although this suggestion flies in the face of the long-desired "paper-less office," we suggest that you print out a copy of everything you write so that you can proofread more effectively.

Even when set to Canadian spellings, which take account of the *-our* and *-re* endings we use for words like *colour* and *centre*, spell checkers remain fundamentally American. *Franklin Roosevelt* is recognized but not *Jean Chrétien* or *Ralph Klein*. Nor are many Canadian place names recognized; the program we use rejects Calgary, Edmonton, Victoria, Etobicoke, and Moncton.

Fortunately, adding words to these programs is usually easy. It is a good idea, therefore, to get into the habit of adding these names—correctly spelled, of course—to your program as you encounter them or when you start using a new program.

## CANADIAN PROPER NOUNS

GEOGRAPHY
British Columbia
Saskatchewan
Alberta
Manitoba
Ontario
Quebec
New Brunswick
Nova Scotia
Prince Edward Island (P.E.I.)
Newfoundland and Labrador
Yukon
Eastern Arctic
Nunavut
Northwest Territories
Skeena River
Mackenzie River
Kootneys
Vancouver Island
Red Deer
Regina
Terrebonne
Sherbrooke
Sarnia

BUSINESS
Bank of Montreal
Bank of Nova Scotia
Royal Bank
Toronto-Dominion Bank
National Bank
Vancity Credit Union
President's Choice Bank
[Your company]
[Other companies and organizations]
[Your industry's association]

TRADEMARKS
MasterCard
VISA
AMEX
Air Miles
Air Canada
Royal Airways
Alcan
Inco

POLITICS
Finance Minister Ralph Goodale
Leader of the Opposition Stephen Harper

| GEOGRAPHY CONT'D | POLITICS CONT'D |
| --- | --- |
| Etobicoke | Mayor [your local mayor] |
| Markham | Councillor [your local councillor] |
| Kanata | Member of Provincial Parliament [your local MPP] |
| Hamilton | Member of Parliament [your local MP] |

## FRENCH WORDS

Unlike our American counterparts, English Canadian business writers routinely have dealings with or write about business relationships with Francophone businesses and organizations. Spell checkers will automatically flag a French word, even a commonly used one, as being an error.

### Box A1.1 FRENCH SPELLING

In a country with two official languages, you must pay particular attention to the spelling of French names, whether individuals or organizations. Unlike English, French spelling includes accents that are easy to omit or use incorrectly. For example:

- *hôpital central*, not *hopital central*
- *caisse de dépôt*, not *caisse de depot.*

*Common French Words and Phrases*

Assemblée Nationale
Banque Nationale
Bombardier
Bourse de Montréal
Caisse de Dépôt et Placement du Québec
Chemin
Fédération des communautées acadiens et francophones du Canada
Hôtel de Ville
Ministere des petites et moyennes entreprises
Office de la langue française
Premier ministre du Québec (premier of the province, not the federal prime minister)
Province du Québec
Quatre Saisons (a television station)
Quebecor

Radio-Canada
Télé-Québec
RDI (Radio-Canada's 24-hour news station)
Rue
TVA (a television station)

## DOUBLE-CHECK SPELL CHECKERS

Spell checkers will not correct homonyms (*two*, *too*, and *to*) or sound-alikes with the same function (*accept*, *except*) that beginning writers and writers pressured by a deadline are apt to confuse. The only way to weed out these errors is by being on the lookout for them when proofreading your document.

### Words Often Confused

*Adverse* is an adjective:  Adverse weather conditions delayed the installation of the fence.
*Averse* is an adjective:   I am averse (opposed) to following your suggestion.

*Advice* is a noun:  The consultant gave us advice on how to redesign the system.
*Advise* is a verb:  We hired the consultant to advise us.

*Affect* is usually a verb:  The staff's moods were affected by the tension in the office.
*Effect* is usually a noun:  Downsizing has a negative effect on the morale of those who remain.

*Amount* is used when referring to things considered as a group or mass, cases in which counting is either impossible or makes little sense: The amount of steel produced continued to rise through the '90s.
*Number* is used when referring to things that could be counted but are not being counted: The number of complaints to the Consumer Safety Council has risen by 10 percent.

*Can* is a verb that denotes ability:  I can have the report ready by tomorrow.
*May* is an auxiliary verb that asks permission or states permission:  May I have your approval to ask for a formal quote?

*Disinterested* is an adjective that states neutrality:  The judge is a disinterested participant in the trial.
*Uninterested* is an adjective that reports lack of interest:  I am uninterested in your excuses.

*Farther* is usually an adverb that points to distance:  Winnipeg is farther from Ottawa than Toronto is.
*Further* is usually an adverb that means in addition to:  I will work further on this plan before submitting it.

*Imply* is a verb (the speaker may *imply*):  He implied that the Minister of Finance did not know what he was doing.
*Infer* is a verb (the reader or listener *infers* from evidence before him or her):  I inferred that he did not think much of the Minister of Finance's abilities.

(The two, however, can be used in the same sentence: I inferred from what he implied during his speech that the plan has been cancelled.)

*Its* is the possessive form of the pronoun *it*:  The company guards its patent.
*It's* is the contraction of the subject/verb combination *it is* (and hence should not be used in business writing unless it is in a direct quote):  It's generally considered by those who use the photocopier that automatic stapling would be a useful feature.

*Less* follows the same rule as *amount* and is used when referring to things considered as a mass or group:  There is less controversy this year about the advertising campaign than there was last year.
*Fewer* follows the same rule as *number* and is used when referring to countable items but when you are not actually reporting on the number counted: We encountered fewer problems with the software installation than we had expected.

*There* is an adverb that indicates place: The accident occurred over there. Or it can be used as a pronoun that serves as a function word, often in introductory terms: There are too many issues on the agenda; I propose that we split it and have two meetings.
*Their* is the possessive form of they: Their (referring to Tom's, Mary's, and Jean's) complaints are justified.
*They're* is the contraction of *they are* and hence should not be used in business writing unless it is part of a direct quote: "They're unable to agree on a schedule."

## UNDERSTANDING WHAT GRAMMAR-CHECKING PROGRAMS TELL YOU

Grammar-checking programs flag grammar faults and suggest alternative constructions. Often writers instantly recognize the problem the program has identified. Few writers would, for example, disagree that "After the program was installed" is a fragment and therefore incorrect. Other times, however, grammar checkers indicate a fault that requires you to make a decision that rests upon your existing understanding of grammar or, if you click on "Help," the explanation that the program itself provides.

The following is an explanation of the most common problem areas.

### ABBREVIATIONS
An abbreviation is formed either by taking the first letters of an organization, name, or title and grouping them or by shortening a single word. Some, such as D.D. (Doctor of Divinity), D.A. (District Attorney), Mr. (Mister), encl. (enclosure), require periods. Others that have become household names, so to speak—FBI, UN, km, cm—do not require periods; however, if your company uses a style guide, it's best to confirm its punctuation preference. Also, it is normal to spell out most abbreviations the first time they appear in a report ("United States," "Canadian Union of Postal Workers"); subsequent references can use the abbreviated forms: U.S., CUPW.

## ACRONYM

An acronym is a name formed by grouping the first letters of an organization's name, for example, and turning them into a word: NATO (North Atlantic Treaty Organization), CSIS (Canadian Security and Intelligence Service), scuba (self-contained underwater breathing apparatus). Acronyms should not be confused with abbreviations, which are not pronounced as words.

## ADJECTIVE

An adjective is a word (e.g., large) that modifies (adds information about) a noun.

> *large* company
> *small* market

## ADVERB

An adverb is a word (e.g., quickly) that modifies a verb (adds information about the action).

> dries *quickly*
> works *quietly*

## CLICHÉS

Clichés (from the French word for stereotype) are overworked expressions that should be avoided because they sound more like filler than original or critical thought. You can tell if a saying is clichéd if you can finish the saying in your mind before the speaker/writer gets to the end of it.

| | | |
|---|---|---|
| agree to disagree | at the end of the day | back to the drawing board |
| bite the bullet | bottom line | built-in safeguards |
| conservative estimate | finishing touches | give the green light to |
| goes without saying | grind to a halt | in close proximity |
| inextricably linked | in short supply | keep options open |
| marked contrast | moot point | peer group |
| powers that be | pros and cons | reliable source |
| selling like hotcakes | take the bull by the horns | |
| thrust of your report | wear and tear | |

## COLONS

Colons have eight uses.

1. They replace a period when the sentence ends with a list.

> The advantages of joining our Internet company are many: lower rates, faster service, better tech support.

(Note: a colon is not used if the list comes immediately after the verb.)

> The problems included poor planning and incompetent office management.

2. They replace a period when the sentence ends with a word or short phrase that both identifies an ambiguous noun in the sentence and by doing so intensifies the meaning of the sentence.

> In business, everyone is after the same thing: money.

3. They replace a period when the following sentence further explains the first by giving an example.

> Travelling to the Tree Top Conference Centre is easy: buses leave from Calgary's bus station every other hour starting at 9:00 a.m.

4. They separate an independent clause from a quotation.

> Everyone knows what the Leader of the Opposition, Stephen Harper, said in the Commons today: "Follow the money. Just follow the money and we'll find who profited from Adscam."

5. They appear between figures in time references.

> The summer work hours are 8:00 a.m. to 3:30 p.m.

6. They are used to set off the salutation in a letter.

> Dear Mr. Membeke:

7. They are used to indicate portions and ratios.

> The odds are 100:1 on there being another ice storm in the next 20 years.

8. They separate titles from subtitles.

> This year's surprise bestseller was Sandra Gwyn's *Tapestry of War: A Private View of Canadians in the Great War.*

COMMAS

In business, commas have four primary uses.

1. They set off introductory phrases or words.

> A sentence that begins with either a prepositional phrase or a dependent clause must include at least one comma.

> Under these economic conditions, our sales should have grown much faster.

> While we have been studying the market, our competitors have been trying out new products.

> As the car was spinning out of control, I hit my head on the steering wheel.

2. They separate items in a series.

> The company will have to upgrade the computers, telephone system, and locks.

> There are four items on the agenda: president's report, comptroller's report, report on the flooding of the basement, and a proposal to purchase a new phone system.

(American writers would generally not put a comma before the *and* in a series. British writers normally would. As usual, Canadian usage is somewhere in the middle. A good rule of thumb is to use the comma before the *and* if the items in the list are themselves rather long: e.g., report on the flooding of the basement. If your company has a style guide, it will likely specify whether commas should precede *and*.)

3. They are placed before coordinate junctions that join two complete sentences.

> Inflation has cut into our profits, yet we will still outperform last year's estimate.

4. They are placed around words, phrases, or clauses that contain nonessential information.

> Brian Mulroney, who was PM from 1980 to 1988, brought in the Free Trade Agreement.

> Canadian businessmen, myth has it, are less adventurous than their American counterparts.

## COMPARATIVES AND SUPERLATIVES

A comparative term compares two persons, things, or ideas, and can replace an often grammatically incorrect *more* + adjective construction.

> For our office, the Jiffy-Quick photocopier is *better* (more good) than the Photo-Sure photocopier.

> Investo Credit is the *younger* (more young) of the two companies.

A superlative compares two or more persons, things, or ideas, and can replace an often grammatically incorrect *most* + adjective construction.

> Investo Credit is the *youngest* (most young) investment company in this sector.

## COORDINATE CONJUNCTIONS

Coordinate conjunctions link two complete sentences together. Normally the second sentence amplifies or further explains the first. There are six different coordinate conjunctions that can be remembered with the mnemonic device FANBOYS:

> For
>
> And
>
> Nor
>
> But
>
> Or
>
> Yet
>
> So

When linking two sentences, be sure to place a comma before whichever one of the FANBOYS you are using.

The construction will be delayed, for the rain has prevented the pouring of the foundation.

## ELLIPSIS

An ellipsis (...) signals that you have omitted words from a direct quote.

> The CEO said, "Budgetary contingencies have forced us to reduce activity in public relations, product development ... and corporate travel."

## Exclamation Marks

The exclamation mark ends a sentence with a bang.

> Do not use in business writing!

(The exception to this rule is, of course, if it is in a direct quote.)

## Misplaced Modifiers

Modifiers are words or groups of words that reveal something (e.g., quality or action) about other words. They act as adjectives (i.e., they modify a noun) or adverbs (i.e., they modify a verb—literally, adding to the verb).

Modifiers must point clearly to the word that they are modifying.

> Watching from the gallery of the Toronto Stock Exchange, we were able to see the <u>first</u> trade of our <u>first</u> stock offering.

A misplaced modifier is one that does not point clearly to the word it is modifying.

> I could <u>almost</u> see the entire trading floor. (What is almost seeing?)

> Correct version: I could see almost the entire trading floor.

Note: "only" cannot modify a verb:

> Incorrect: The shoes only cost $75.00.

> Correct: The shoes cost only $75.00.

## Passive Voice

While not technically inaccurate, passive constructions are generally not used in business writing.

A passive sentence reverses the expected order of action.

> The new process was invented by Richard Bodkin.

Passive sentences are often used by writers who want to hide the actor of the sentence.

> The decision was taken to raise taxes.

These sentences should be rewritten in the active voice:

Richard Bodkin invented the new process.

The town council voted to raise taxes.

There are some instances when the passive is acceptable. If you are writing about something in which the *doer's identity* is unimportant, as in scientific testing, use the passive voice.

The experiment was conducted yesterday.

The passive can also be used when speaking of large historical events in which thousands or millions of people took part.

The West was settled by millions who fled poverty in Europe and Asia.

PARENTHESES

Parentheses are used to set off information that you want to give but want to de-emphasize.

The committee voted (6–2) for the proposal.

PERIODS

Periods have several uses.

1. They signal the end of a complete sentence.
2. They replace other letters in abbreviations: Ph.D. (Doctor of Philosophy), Q.C. (Queen's Council).
   (Note: Some well-known abbreviations such as the CBC, EU, or UN do not take periods.)
3. They signal the decimal place in numbers and percentages: 75.4%

POSSESSIVE

With the exception of the possessive pronouns (e.g., mine, yours, his), possession is signalled by adding an apostrophe followed by an s ('s) to a common or proper noun.

Canada's gross national product has grown steadily for the past decade.

If the noun is plural, as in *clients*, put the apostrophe (') after the "s." Do not add an additional *s*.

Our clients' firms are not doing well.

## PREPOSITIONAL PHRASES

A prepositional phrase is made up of a preposition followed by a noun: *beside* the river.

Prepositions are words such as *about, above, between, after, to,* and *on.* They can be thought of as indicating the direction of action of a sentence (I went *to* the office) or time *(Before* the meeting, the president met *with* the comptroller). Note that when a sentence begins with a prepositional phrase (Before the meeting) it is followed by a comma.

The subject of a sentence **cannot be in a prepositional phrase.** This means that if you are having trouble with your sentence's subject/verb agreement, you can reduce the number of words with which you are dealing. In long sentences—*During the meeting that was held after the fire at Wordsworth's Bookstore, the fire marshal reported that under the baseboard heater to the right of the main entrance, a wire melted, causing a short in the heating system*—it is sometimes difficult to determine the subject of the sentence. Is it "the meeting," "the fire marshal," or "the baseboard heater," which, after all, caused the fire?

Recognizing prepositional phrases allows you to narrow down the possibilities. Mentally cross out the prepositional phrases. *During the meeting that was held after the fire at Wordsworth's Bookstore, the fire marshal reported that under the baseboard heater to the right of the main entrance, a wire melted, causing a short in the heating system.* Thus, you are left with "the fire marshal reported that ... a wire melted, causing a short," which should be short enough for you to determine that "the fire marshal" is the subject of the sentence and that "reported" is the main verb.

### SOME PREPOSITIONS

| | | | |
|---|---|---|---|
| about | before | for | out |
| above | behind | from | over |
| across | below | in | through |
| after | between | inside | to |
| against | beyond | into | toward |
| along | by | near | under |
| among | despite | of | upon |
| at | during | on | with |

Note: When you begin a sentence with a prepositional phrase, for example, "After the movie," the prepositional phrase acts like a subordinate conjunction and must be set off by a comma.

After the movie, we went back to work to finish the project.

### PRONOUNS

Pronouns replace nouns (names of persons, places, things, and ideas). There are seven different types of pronouns.

1. Personal Pronouns: There are two types of personal pronouns.

Subjective: *I, you, he, she, it, we,* and *they* are subjective pronouns. When they appear in a sentence, they are either the subject of the sentence or part of a compound subject (i.e., a sentence with more than one actor).

> *You* are going to have to change the schedule to reflect the delays.

> Maurice and *I* are working on the project.

Objective: *Me, you, him, her, it, us,* and *them* are objective pronouns. They signify the recipient of an action.

> Give it to *him.*

2. Possessive pronouns: *Mine, my, yours, your, his, hers, her, its, ours, our, theirs,* and *whose* refer to a previously mentioned noun.

> Credit for this strategy is all *hers.*

3. Relative pronouns: *That, which, who, whom,* and *whose* refer to a previously mentioned noun.

> Reginald is the person *whom* we should thank for this project's success.

4. Indefinite pronouns: *Anyone, nobody, something, anything, each,* and *another* are examples of indefinite pronouns. They stand in for either individuals or individual events that you want to group together. Although readers understand that indefinite pronouns refer to a group of things or individuals, they are conjugated as singular nouns.

> Anyone who has any further thoughts on this project should e-mail them to Ovid.

5. Reflexive pronouns: *Myself, yourself, himself, itself, oneself, ourselves, yourselves,* and *themselves* are used either to emphasize the person being spoken about or to indicate that the doer of the action is also the receiver of the action. With the exception of sales letters, or when emphasizing the actor is of vital importance, they are not normally used in business writing.

> Ask *yourself* if you can afford to miss this savings opportunity!

> He explained the plans to me *himself.*

6. Demonstrative pronouns: *This, that, these,* and *those* refer to specific persons, places, or things that are established elsewhere in the text.

> So this is our plan....

7. Interrogative pronouns: *What, which, who, whom,* and *whose* ask questions.

> *Which* team should we assign to the Thompson account?

PUNCTUATION
See periods, commas, question marks, semicolons, colons, and exclamation marks.

QUESTION MARKS
The question mark signals that the sentence is a question.

> May I have your approval to investigate this project further?

REDUNDANCY
Redundancy occurs when words and phrases are unnecessarily repetitive. There is always an obvious *shorter* replacement.

| Redundant Words/Phrases | Replacement |
|---|---|
| absolutely essential | essential |
| actual experience | experience |
| adequate enough | adequate |
| advance planning | planning |
| any and all | all |
| avail ourselves of (the opportunity) | take |
| basic fundamental | fundamentals |
| close proximity | near |
| consensus of opinion | consensus |
| contributing factor | factor |
| current status | status |
| end result | result |
| finalize | finish/complete |
| filled to capacity | filled |
| foreign imports | imports |
| group meeting | meeting |
| in order to | to |
| in the amount of | for |
| in the event that | if |

| | |
|---|---|
| overall plan | plan |
| please find enclosed | enclosed is |
| pursuant to | regarding/about |
| qualified expert | expert |
| raise up | raise |
| rise up | rise |
| the reason is because | the reason is |

## RESTRICTIVE/NONRESTRICTIVE CLAUSE

Relative pronouns *which* and *who* are used to introduce modifying phrases that act as adjectives—adding interesting information about the subject or object of the sentence but no information that is vital to **identify** the subject or object.

In the sentence *Brian Mulroney, who was prime minister from 1980 to 1988, brought in the Free Trade Agreement,* the clause "who was prime minister from 1980 to 1988" is set off by commas, because, while interesting, it is not essential information that is needed to identify who Brian Mulroney is.

In contrast, in the sentence *Myth has it that the man who was Canada's fourth prime minister died while eating soup at Windsor Castle,* the clause "who was Canada's fourth prime minister" is not set off by commas because the information contained within it is necessary to identify who "the man" (Sir John David Thompson) was and why he is of some interest.

When "that" is used as a pronoun to introduce a phrase or clause, the phrase or clause is never set off by commas. The information within it is always essential to the meaning of the sentence.

> The product line that we decided to introduce last year has been a great success.

## RUN-ON SENTENCES

A run-on sentence, sometimes called a fused sentence, occurs when two complete sentences are joined together without a semicolon or coordinate conjunction.

*Profits are up in the fourth quarter, they will probably rise again in the coming first quarter* is a run-on because each clause—"Profits are up in the fourth quarter" *and* "they will probably rise again in the coming first quarter"—forms a complete sentence in its own right.

This fault can be fixed by inserting a semicolon or a conjunction (preceded by a comma) between the two parts of the sentence.

> Profits are up in the fourth quarter; they will probably rise again in the coming first quarter.

> Profits are up in the fourth quarter, and they will probably rise again in the coming first quarter.

SEMICOLONS
Semicolons have two uses.

1. They join two complete sentences, in which the second amplifies the meaning of the first.

> Canada's national debt is declining at a faster than expected rate; Finance Minister Ralph Goodale added $15 billion to the expected pay-down of $10 billion.

When a subordinate conjunction such as *however* or *therefore* introduces a second independent clause within a sentence, a semicolon must precede it.

> Indonesia has endured the punishment of countless tsunamis; however, the tsunami of December 2004 was its deadliest ever.

2. They substitute for commas in a list when items in the list already have commas within them.

> Our options are to continue with the existing product line, which is still generating respectable profits; acquire firms in areas close to our core business; develop new products in-house; or seek out strategic alliances.

SENTENCE
A sentence is a group of words that contains at least one subject and one verb.

> *We service* all makes and models.

Sentences can have different structures. Some of the most common are:

1. Subject—verb—object:

> I sent the package to your address.

2. Dependent clause—subject—verb—object:

> Because of what was said at the meeting, I decided to rework the numbers.

3. Prepositional phrase—subject—verb—object:

> After considering my options, I decided to turn down the proposed transfer.

4. Subject—prepositional phrase—verb—object:

> The marketing department, along with the consultants, created the following advertising campaign.

5. Verb—adjective—noun (used in instructions):

> Click on the house icon.

## SENTENCE FRAGMENTS

A sentence fragment is an incomplete sentence.

Most sentence fragments occur when writers mistakenly think that a long dependent clause is a complete sentence.

> Although the President's Executive Committee has been considering all the options relating to the replacement of the photocopier, phone system, and the security system.

This fault can be fixed by affixing this dependent clause to an independent clause.

> Although the President's Executive Committee has been considering all the options relating to the replacement of the photocopier, phone system, and the security system, *the PEC has not yet come to a decision.*

## SPLIT INFINITIVES

Unlike French, in which the infinitive of the verb is one word, as in *devoir*, in English the infinitive is made up of two words; e.g., *to work*. A split infinitive occurs when an adverb (e.g., quickly) is placed between the word *to* and the word *work*—*to quickly work*.

Splitting infinitives, unless you are quoting someone else's direct speech, is a violation of the rules of Standard Written English, even though the construction is not difficult to understand.

> The production team was able to work quickly on the problem (not *to quickly work*).

## SUBJECT–VERB AGREEMENT

In English, subject–verb agreement problems arise for two reasons.

• Confusion between the third-person singular (*he/she/it*) and third-person plural (*they*) in the present tense.

As you can see from the chart below, which shows the present, past, and future conjugations of the infinitive *to design*, with the exception of the present, the endings of regular English verbs (once they are formed into other tenses) do not change to align with the subject.

| Present | Past | Future |
|---|---|---|
| I design. | I designed. | I will design. |
| You design. | You designed. | You will design. |
| He/She/It **designs**. | He/She/It designed. | He/She/It will design. |
| We design. | We designed. | We will design. |
| They design | They designed. | They will design. |

Problems arise when writers are unsure about the number of people or other units that make up the subject of the sentence they are working on. For example, in spoken English, we are used to saying, "They are conducting a survey," even though we know from previous information in the conversation that the survey is actually being conducted by a single company, say Ipsos Polling. The sentence should have been "*It* is conducting a survey."

- Confusion caused by the use of compound subjects.

There are two types of compound subjects and they follow different rules.

1. In the sentence "The server and the phone system are out of date," the subject of the sentence is not the server or the phone system but both of them together, for they are both "out of date." Accordingly, the proper conjugation of the verb *to be* is *are*.

Hint: If you can replace the subject with "they," as in "Dofasco and Inco reported record profits" (which can be recast as "They reported record profits"), the sentence has a compound subject and hence its verb must be conjugated in the plural.

2. Sentences that use *either/or* or *neither/nor* constructions are counterintuitive. At first glance, it seems they should follow the same rule as above; after all, the sentence appears to be dealing with two persons. (e.g., *Either* John *or* Mahmoud will finish the project this weekend.)

However, when using *either/or* or *neither/nor*, the verb of the sentence is conjugated according to the number of the noun closest to the verb.

Thus:

> Either the president or the college's governors are going to have to decide what to do about this problem.

> Either the college's governors or the president is going to have to decide ...

SUBJUNCTIVE MOOD

The subjunctive mood introduces either a wished-for situation or a state of affairs that does not exist and is unlikely to.

If we are to embark on this plan, we might not meet the shareholder's expectations this quarter.

If I were a rich man ... (You are not, but you could be expressing wishful thinking).

If the dog were to jump the fence, it would land in the neighbour's pool.

## Subordinate Conjunctions

Subordinate conjunctions allow two sentences to be linked. When you place a word like "although," "while," or "until" at the beginning of a complete sentence or independent clause (*Until + We discovered that the server was overloaded.*), that sentence becomes a subordinate clause that *depends* (hence the term "dependent clause") on another sentence to keep it from being a sentence fragment.

*Until* we discovered that the server was overloaded, we could not figure out why the e-mails were bouncing back.

(Note the comma that replaced the period after "overloaded." When you begin a sentence with a subordinate conjunction, you have to insert a comma between the dependent clause and the independent clause.)

### Some Subordinate Conjunctions

| | | |
|---|---|---|
| after | before | until |
| although | however | when |
| as long as | if | whenever |
| as soon as | in order to | where |
| as though | since | while |
| because | unless | |

## Verb Tense

The tenses that are of interest to business writers are:

| | |
|---|---|
| Present: | *I work on the project.* |
| Present Progressive: | *I am working on the project.* |
| Simple Past: | *I worked on the project.* |
| Past Progressive: | *I was working on the project before the alarm rang.* |
| Past Perfect: | *I had failed to finish the project.* |
| Future: | *I will work on the project.* |
| Future Anterior: | *I will have worked on the project for two months by then.* |

# WEB REFERENCES

 http://www.ccc.commnet.edu/grammar

This site is maintained by Capital Community College in Hartford, Connecticut, and contains an extremely useful system of tests and lessons for writers with a weak grasp of grammar, punctuation, and sentence sense.

 http://www.english.uiuc.edu/cws/wworkshop/index.htm

This site is maintained by University of Illinois at Urbana-Champaign and contains an online grammar guide.

 http://www.english.uiuc.edu/cws/wworkshop/writer_resources/citation_styles/citation_styles.htm

This site is maintained by University of Illinois at Urbana-Champaign and contains both the Modern Languages Association's and the American Psychological Association's bibliographical guides.

# Grammar and Usage Assignments

## UNDERLINE THE CORRECT WORD.

1. The committee is adverse/averse to the proposal.
2. Management always asks for but never takes our advice/advise.
3. How will the installation of a new server effect/affect our desktop computers?
4. The number/amount of effort that the students have put into their year-end projects surprised the entire staff.
5. What can/may we still do while the computer system is down?
6. The adjudicator was disinterested/uninterested in the evidence we presented to her.
7. We will be able to work on this farther/further at the retreat next week.
8. I'm not sure you are able to imply/infer that from what we heard at the meeting today.
9. Efficiency experts never admit it, but they are always hired to restructure companies so that they end up with fewer/less employees.
10. There/They're is no chance that the board is going to agree to this today.
11. The cable company representative said they would have to run the line through the unused mail tube if we wanted to have Internet access over their/there.
12. The committee jealously guards it's/its prerogatives.
13. Can/may we make the deadline?
14. The business climate has been affected/effected by the government's shaky position.
15. Adverse/averse profit warnings have slowed investment in the oil patch.
16. The last president was so disinterested/uninterested in the administration side of the business that the VP was really running the place.

17. Drive down the road a little further/farther and you will reach the chalet where the retreat is being held.
18. The marketing plan was negatively affected/effected by the fact that following the Boxing Day tsunami, many television stations felt it was inappropriate to run commercials featuring surfers and beach scenes.
19. We will not know the effect/affect of the scandal on the government for about two weeks.
20. There is less/fewer appetite for edgy advertisements now than they're/there was two years ago.

## INSERT COMMAS AS NEEDED IN THE FOLLOWING SENTENCES.

(Every sentence requires at least one comma.)
1. During the recession profits fell 20 percent.
2. After the break-in we ordered new doors windows and alarms.
3. The prime minister the leader of the opposition and the Governor General were all in Alberta to celebrate its 100th birthday.
4. Our accounting software allows us to sort by date type of cheque billing number and city.
5. The company's auditors whom we have been using for the past three years have put two notes on the audited statements.
6. During the first years of this decade Warren Buffett who is the majority shareholder of Berkshire Hathaway investment company kept telling investors to invest in basic products like paint and bricks.
7. Med-Quick which was designed for doctors' offices is now accessed by individuals from their home PCs.
8. After the meeting I went to speak to Bill Rejean Mary and Ali who were extremely upset by what the CEO said about the PR department.
9. Small cable companies cannot afford to provide high-speed Internet voice-over cable and in at least one case even digital service.
10. The greenhouse which is watered by an automated system flooded last night.
11. Rain on Tuesday Wednesday and Thursday prevented filming of the final advertisement.
12. We might be able to finish by next week but to do so we'll have to put in at least 10 hours of overtime.
13. Lower prices for corn and soybeans have caused a credit crunch on the prairies and this has led to more farm bankruptcies than we would have otherwise expected.
14. The problem cannot be solved quickly for it is due to a virus in the main server.
15. We try to meet our clients' demands but we are not always successful.
16. Among our clients are Food-Wise Value Clothes Pets on the Corner and Andrew's Place.

17. Global warming which many in the oil business dismiss as fear mongering is not very well understood by the public.
18. Publishing magazines is a risky business yet it still attracts many.
19. During the Second World War businesses in Canada put their organizational and scientific know-how at the service of the government.
20. Printers which only a few years ago were impressive because of their speed look like Model-Ts next to today's machines that have multiple functions print faster and in color and take up less space.

## FIX THE FOLLOWING MISPLACED MODIFIER ERRORS.

1. The committee almost agreed with the entire proposal.
2. Flat-screen monitors have come down in price; a new one only costs $150.00.
3. Premier Jean Charest nearly spoke to a crowd numbering in the hundreds.
4. Installing alarms, Takis's hand was cut.
5. At the age of five, William's father moved the family to Toronto.

## INSERT PERIODS.

1. Nortel was once Canada's largest company
2. Canada's largest trading partner is the US, but it would like to get special status with the EU
3. The office will open again at 8 am
4. Inflation is running at 25 percent [two point five] a year
5. New federal rules limit exposure to 5 ppm

## INSERT SEMICOLONS.

1. The new website will amaze you it utilizes XTL video technology.
2. Environment Canada has warned that this will be a bad year for the spruce budworm last year the worm destroyed more than 50,000 hectares of forest.
3. Our new internal management team has membership from across the company: Fred Davis, Finance Elsa Singh, Production Norma Rubinowitz, PR and Cornelius Van Valen, VP, Development.
4. In January, we lost 10 days of production because of the ice storm therefore, we were unable to meet the first quarter's production and sales targets.
5. People fear many things perhaps the strangest fear is triskaidekaphobia.

## INSERT COLONS.

1. After winning the 1980 election, Prime Minister Pierre Trudeau began his victory speech "Well, welcome to the 1980s."

2. The new phone system has five functions call display, call waiting, call forwarding, short text messaging, and voice activated dialing.
3. The computer system will be down for maintenance between 2 30 a.m. and 4 30 a.m. on June 3.
4. Since the boss is always quoting from it, before the next meeting we should all read *Sharks and Wolves A Primer for Small Business.*
5. Success in horticulture depends on one thing a willingness to get your hands dirty.
6. Competition in the dry-cleaning business is stiff at least three different local dry cleaners have closed in the past year.
7. Dear Mr Rakis
   Let me begin by thanking you for your letter of May 5, 2005.
8. According to the famous writer Ernest Hemingway, when writing, the proportion of perspiration to inspiration is 90 10.

# APPENDIX II

# BUSINESS WRITING NUTS AND BOLTS

This appendix covers the following "nuts and bolts" of business writing:

- business letter components and conventions;
- business letter appearance;
- memorandum components and conventions;
- report components and conventions;
- e-mail components and conventions;
- facsimile transmission sheet components and conventions;
- use of text density, headings, subparagraphs, fonts, attachments, art boxes, white space, lists, charts, and numbering to help readers read and understand documents;
- acknowledgment of sources of information used in business documents;
- choice of different transmission methods—e-mail, facsimile, internal mail, courier service, Canada Post.

# Business Letters

## COMPONENTS OF THE BUSINESS LETTER

Components are the various elements that are part of a letter, memo, or report—the address, the salutation, complimentary close, notations for distribution of copies, sections, and so forth. Conventions are the rules or practices that govern how the components are used and set out.

The components of a business letter (see Figure A2.2) and the way they are set out are conventions rather than rigid rules and, like any conventions, they change and evolve over time. The business letter of today is less formal and elaborate in style than that of 50 or 100 years ago; for example, we no longer use such complimentary closes as "your obedient servant." Nonetheless, conventions remain to be followed because they are useful—they provide a common approach and allow for easier communication.

## FIGURE A2.1

### ADDRESSING AN ENVELOPE

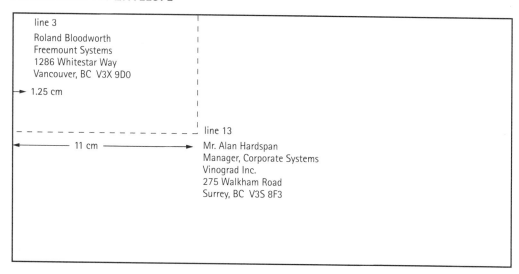

line 3

Roland Bloodworth
Freemount Systems
1286 Whitestar Way
Vancouver, BC  V3X 9D0

1.25 cm

11 cm

line 13

Mr. Alan Hardspan
Manager, Corporate Systems
Vinograd Inc.
275 Walkham Road
Surrey, BC  V3S 8F3

## FIGURE A2.2

### BUSINESS LETTER COMPONENTS

FREEMOUNT SYSTEMS

1286 Whitestar Way, Vancouver, British Columbia V3X 9D0 Canada     Heading.
Tel. (604) 327 3398 Fax. (604) 327 5587     freemount@derva.ca www.freemount.com

February 13, 2007

Mr. Alan Hardspan                                                 Date.
Manager, Corporate Systems
Vinograd Inc.                                                     Inside address:
275 Walkham Road                                                 • Name
Surrey, BC  V3S 8F3                                              • Job title
                                                                • Organization
SUBJECT: Delivery Of 20 FR1700 Series Systems                     name
                                                                • Mailing address
Dear Mr. Hardspan:                                               Salutation

I am writing to confirm that 20 FR1700 Series systems ordered by Vinograd
Inc. will be delivered on March 2, 2007, as scheduled.            Body.

*continued*

This delivery will complete the shipment of the 50 FR1700 Series systems that Vinograd Inc. bought from us in 2006. The system installation, testing, and debugging by our on-site team will take place during the period March 3–18, 2007, as agreed. Your technical staff will be fully involved and, given their experience working with our team over the past few months, should be fully qualified to maintain the systems.

The training program for your other staff members has proved most successful from the evaluation report we commissioned (a copy of the evaluation report is enclosed). The system documentation is being updated in light of some of the suggestions made by the training evaluators and by your staff. We expect that the updated materials will be posted to your intranet by February 20, 2007.

Our president and management group are delighted that the installation of the FR1700 Series system has gone so smoothly. I look forward to a continuing and cooperative relationship with Vinograd Inc.

*Complimentary close.*

Yours sincerely,

Roland Bloodworth
General Manager

*Signature block.*

*Enclosure notation.*

Encl. Evaluation Report

*Distribution notation.*

cc: V. W. J. O'Sullivan

---

## Heading

The heading is the sender's organization's name and mailing address. Usually this will be part of the letterhead (which may include a logo or other design element), although the mailing address may be printed at the bottom of the page; or the letterhead may simply consist of an organization's name and logo. An organization's website address and main e-mail address may be also included in the heading. Where there is no mailing address on the letterhead, include a return mailing address two lines below the heading.

## Date

The date is written at least two lines below the heading. The common alphanumeric form is either May 15, 2007, or 15 May 2007. When the day number follows the month, as in the first example, a comma always follows the number. Thus, we have October 17, 2007, but not 17, October 2007.

In Canada, writing an all-numeric form of the date is traditionally done by placing the day first, followed by the month and year and placing a hyphen between each number; for example, 15-5-2007 or 17-10-2007 (American usage is to place the month first followed by the day, thus 5-15-2007 or 10-17-2007). Computerization has now made it virtually mandatory to add a zero in front of single digits to avoid confusion so that 15-5-2007 becomes 15-05-2007.

Increasingly, the date is being written numerically following the international (ISO 2014) and Canadian (CAN 3-Z234.4-79) standards, using a year, month, day sequence with each separated by a space or hyphen. Thus, 17 October 2007 or October 17, 2007 may be set out as 2007-10-17 or 2007 10 17. Use of the standard is designed to avoid confusion over dating by adopting a common approach.

## Inside Address

The inside address directs the letter to the intended recipient. It will be exactly the same as that on the envelope and will include

1. the recipient's courtesy title (Mr., Ms., Dr., Professor, Senator, etc.), assuming this is known;
2. the recipient's name as he or she writes it;
3. the recipient's job title, if known;
4. the organization's name;
5. the full mailing address.

Courtesy titles can be difficult, particularly in the case of government, judicial, clerical, and diplomatic titles, and it is important to find the correct information if you are unsure of an individual's title and how it is written or abbreviated in correspondence (e.g., Dr. Anne Kearney or Anne Kearney M.D. not Ms. Anne Kearney or Dr. Anne Kearney M.D.). This can be done by consulting a style guide such as *A Canadian Writer's Guide*.

The inside address can be placed either at the top of the letter at least two lines below the heading or at the bottom of the page after the signature block and any notations indicating enclosures (Encl.) and distribution (cc:).

## Box A2.1 THE CANADIAN ADDRESSING GUIDE

Canada Post Corporation publishes the *Canadian Addressing Guide*, which provides how-to instructions and other information, including the use of English and French, for correctly addressing correspondence.

The guide is available at the Canada Post Corporation website:
http://www.canadapost.ca/offerings/address_management/pdf/addressing_guide-e.pdf

### Subject Line

The subject line immediately tells the recipient the subject of the letter and may be used to replace the salutation. It can be placed either two or three lines below the salutation or two or three lines above it and at the left margin or centred. The subject line is underlined and every word is capitalized. A subject line should be concise but nonetheless informative and complete.

### Attention Line

Use an attention line when you want to ensure that a letter reaches an individual whose name you do not know or a certain position or part of an organization; for example:

> ATTENTION:  Sales Manager
>
> ATTENTION:  Sales Department
>
> ATTENTION:  Corporate Services

### Salutation

The salutation is your greeting to the recipient of the letter. It is normally written as Dear ———— followed by a colon and is placed two lines below the subject line or the inside address.

Unless you know the recipient well enough, do not use a first name in the salutation, such as Dear Bob or Dear Jane. While this level of informality is much more widespread than in the past, many people regard the uninvited use of their first name as intrusive, ill-mannered, or simply an ignorant attempt at false intimacy or informality where none should exist. This is particularly the case outside North America.

In those cases when you cannot discern the gender of the recipient from the individual's name (Dale Smith or Leslie Obonsawin), you can either omit the salutation and use a subject line or write the name in full—Dear Dale Smith or Dear Leslie Obonsawin. The latter approach is becoming more common but, to many, appears odd or awkward and again it is an attempt at familiarity where none exists. When you do not know the name of the occupant of a position, you can write Dear Sales Manager or Dear Human Resources Specialist or use an attention line.

Previous usage was to write Dear Sir/Madam, but this is now considered out of date. The salutation can significantly influence the way in which the recipient perceives a letter before reading the content. Using the appropriate salutation is part of knowing your reader.

### Body

Business letters are normally single-spaced. Paragraphs are double-spaced.

### Complimentary Close

When you use a salutation, you should end your letter with a complimentary close such as Yours truly, Yours sincerely, or Sincerely. The first letter of the first word is capitalized. If your letter is informal, you can close with Best wishes, Cheers, Good luck, or similar phrases that reflect your friendly relationship with the reader. The complimentary close is usually two lines below the last line of the letter.

### Signature Block

The signature block is three or four lines below the complimentary close or below the last line of the letter if there is no complimentary close and includes your name and job title if you are writing on behalf of your company or organization. A courtesy title (Mr., Ms., etc.) is not part of the signature block unless the writer wishes to include it; for example, when a name could be either male or female or when a professional or academic title (M.D., Ph.D.) is used.

### Initials

If a letter is prepared by an administrative assistant, traditionally the initials of the writer followed by those of the assistant were placed two lines below the signature block; for example, ASD/df or asd/df. However, many companies no longer use initials and, of course, many more businesspeople now prepare their own letters.

### Enclosures/Attachments

An enclosure or attachment notation is placed two lines below the signature block to signal the recipient that there is an enclosure or attachment being sent with the letter. The notation can be in full (Enclosure or Attachment) or abbreviated (Encl., Att.) and should indicate the number of items (Encl. 3) or a specific enclosure (Encl. Marketing Brochure).

### Distribution

The distribution notation cc: indicates who is going to receive a copy of the letter, and it should be placed two lines below any enclosure notation. If you do not want the recipient of your letter to know that another person is receiving a copy, put bc: (blind copy) on the secondary recipient's copy only.

## Postscript

The postscript is a means of emphasizing or drawing attention to a particular point or statement in a letter. It is placed two lines below any other notation as P.S., followed by the message. The postscript is rarely used in business correspondence except for sales letters where it can help reinforce the arguments being made.

## Pagination

For letters that are longer than one page:

- enter /2 ... at the bottom right-hand side of the first page;
- enter the recipient's name and page 2 at the top left-hand side of the second page; for example, Charles Hampton-page 2, and bold, italicize, or underline the name;
- carry on in the same fashion for subsequent pages.

## APPEARANCE OF THE BUSINESS LETTER

### Letter Forms

The two basic layout forms used for a business letter are block and indented. In the block form, all lines begin flush with the left margin. In the indented form, the sender's address, if not part of the letterhead, is placed at the top right-hand corner, the complimentary close and signature block are aligned at the right with the address, and the first line of each paragraph is indented.

The modified block letter form places the complimentary close and signature block just to the left of the centre of the page.

The simplified block letter form is full block but without salutation and complimentary close. It originated with the Administrative Management Society in the United States and, while it avoids the difficulties that can come with determining an appropriate salutation and close, it may be perceived as discourteous or abrupt.

The personal business letter form, used here by individuals writing their own personal letters on plain notepaper, places the writer's address on the right-hand side and the inside address on the left. The date may be placed either below the writer's address or below the inside address. The complimentary close and signature are aligned with the writer's address. There is, of course, nothing to prevent you from using an indented form for your personal business correspondence if you prefer.

We have set out examples of the block and indented letter forms together with some of the more popular block form variations (see Figure A2.3, Block Letter Form; Figure A2.4, Indented Letter Form; Figure A2.5, Modified Block Letter Form; Figure A2.6, Simplified Block Letter Form; and Figure A2.7, Personal Business Letter Form).

## Block Letter Form

FREEMOUNT SYSTEMS

1286 Whitestar Way, Vancouver, British Columbia V3X 9D0 Canada

Tel. (604) 327 3398 Fax. (604) 327 5587    freemount@derva.ca www.freemount.com

Mr. Alan Hardspan
Manager, Corporate Systems
Vinograd Inc.
275 Walkham Road
Surrey, BC  V3S 8F3                                              Full block.

February 13, 2007                                               Full block.

SUBJECT:   Delivery Of 20 FR1700 Series Systems                Full block.

Dear Mr. Hardspan:

I am writing to confirm that 20 FR1700 Series systems ordered by Vinograd Inc. will    All lines begin at
be delivered on March 2, 2007, as scheduled.                                           the left margin.

This delivery will complete the shipment of the 50 FR1700 Series systems that
Vinograd Inc. bought from us in 2006. The system installation, testing, and debugging
by our on-site team will take place during the period March 3–18, 2007, as agreed.
Your technical staff will be fully involved and, given their experience working with
our team over the past few months, should be fully qualified to maintain the systems.   Full block.

The training program for your other staff members has proved most successful (a copy
of the evaluation report is enclosed). The system documentation is being updated in
light of some of the suggestions made by the training evaluators and by your staff. We
expect that the updated materials will be posted to your intranet by February 20, 2007.   Full block.

Our president and management group are delighted that the installation of the
FR1700 Series system has gone so smoothly. I look forward to a continuing and
cooperative relationship with Vinograd Inc.

Yours sincerely,                                                Full block.

Roland Bloodworth
General Manager

Encl. Evaluation Report                                         Full block.
cc: V. W. J. O'Sullivan

## FIGURE A2.4

### INDENTED LETTER FORM

**FREEMOUNT SYSTEMS**

1286 Whitestar Way, Vancouver, British Columbia V3X 9D0 Canada

Tel. (604) 327 3398 Fax. (604) 327 5587   freemount@derva.ca www.freemount.com

No indent.
February 13, 2007

Mr. Alan Hardspan
Manager, Corporate Systems
No indent.
Vinograd Inc.
275 Walkham Road
Surrey, BC  V3S 8F3

No indent.
SUBJECT:   Delivery Of 20 FR1700 Series Systems

Dear Mr. Hardspan:

No indent.
I am writing to confirm that 20 FR1700 Series systems ordered by Vinograd Inc. will be delivered on March 2, 2007, as scheduled.

Indent.
This delivery will complete the shipment of the 50 FR1700 Series systems that Vinograd Inc. bought from us in 2006. The system installation, testing, and debugging by our on-site team will take place during the period March 3–18, 2007, as agreed. Your technical staff will be fully involved and, given their experience working with our team over the past few months, should be fully qualified to maintain the systems.

Indent.
The training program for your other staff members has proved most successful (a copy of the evaluation report is enclosed). The system documentation is being updated in light of some of the suggestions made by the training evaluators and by your staff. We expect that the updated materials will be posted to your intranet by February 20, 2007.

Indent.
Our president and the management group are delighted that the installation of the FR1700 Series system has gone so smoothly. I look forward to a continuing and cooperative relationship with Vinograd Inc.

Yours sincerely,

Complimentary
close and signature
to the right.

Roland Bloodworth
General Manager

No indent.
Encl. Evaluation Report
cc: V. W. J. O'Sullivan

## Modified Block Letter Form

FREEMOUNT SYSTEMS
1286 Whitestar Way, Vancouver, British Columbia V3X 9D0 Canada
Tel. (604) 327 3398 Fax. (604) 327 5587    freemount@derva.ca www.freemount.com

February 13, 2007                                                                    Full block.

Mr. Alan Hardspan                                                                    Full block.
Manager, Corporate Systems
Vinograd Inc.
275 Walkham Road
Surrey, BC  V3S 8F3

SUBJECT:   Delivery Of 20 FR1700 Series Systems                                       Full block.

Dear Mr. Hardspan:                                                                   Full block.

I am writing to confirm that 20 FR1700 Series systems ordered by Vinograd Inc. will be delivered on       Full block.
March 2, 2007, as scheduled.

This delivery will complete the shipment of the 50 FR1700 Series systems that Vinograd Inc. bought       Full block.
from us in 2006. The system installation, testing, and debugging by our on-site team will take place
during the period March 3–18, 2007, as agreed. Your technical staff will be fully involved and, given
their experience working with our team over the past few months, should be fully qualified to maintain the systems.

The training program for your other staff members has proved most successful (a copy of the evalua-      Full block.
tion report is enclosed). The system documentation is being updated in light of some of the suggestions made by the training evaluators and by your staff. We expect that the updated materials will be
posted to your intranet by February 20, 2007.

Our president and the management group are delighted that the installation of the FR1700 Series           Full block.
system has gone so smoothly. I look forward to a continuing and cooperative relationship with
Vinograd Inc.

                    Yours sincerely,                                                 Complimentary
                                                                                     close and signature
                                                                                     to the left of the
                                                                                     page centre.

                    Roland Bloodworth
                    General Manager

Encl. Evaluation Report                                                              Full block.
cc: V. W. J. O'Sullivan

## SIMPLIFIED BLOCK LETTER FORM

### FREEMOUNT SYSTEMS

1286 Whitestar Way, Vancouver, British Columbia V3X 9D0 Canada

Tel. (604) 327 3398 Fax. (604) 327 5587    freemount@derva.ca www.freemount.com

February 13, 2007

Mr. Alan Hardspan
Manager, Corporate Systems
Vinograd Inc.
275 Walkham Road
Surrey, BC  V3S 8F3

Full block.
No salutation.

I am writing to confirm that 20 FR1700 Series systems ordered by Vinograd Inc. will be delivered on March 2, 2007, as scheduled.

Full block.

This delivery will complete the shipment of the 50 FR1700 Series systems that Vinograd Inc. bought from us in 2006. The system installation, testing, and debugging by our on-site team will take place during the period March 3–18, 2007, as agreed. Your technical staff will be fully involved and, given their experience working with our team over the past few months, should be fully qualified to maintain the systems.

Full block.

The training program for your other staff members has proved most successful (a copy of the evaluation report is enclosed). The system documentation is being updated in light of some of the suggestions made by the training evaluators and by your staff. We expect that the updated materials will be posted to your intranet by February 20, 2007.

Full block.

Our president and management group are delighted that the installation of the FR1700 Series system has gone so smoothly. I look forward to a continuing and cooperative relationship with Vinograd Inc.

Roland Bloodworth

No complimentary
close.

Full block.

General Manager

Full block.

Encl. Evaluation Report
cc: V. W. J. O'Sullivan

## PERSONAL BUSINESS LETTER FORM

411-4, Carpenter Way
London, ON  S3E 4F2                                    Return address.

May 23, 2007                                           Full block.

Ms. Mona Guenette
Sales Director
Renaldo Hair Products
2387 March Street                                      Inside address.
Moncton, NB  E2R 8H1

Dear Ms. Guenette:                                     Salutation.

Thank you for your May 16, 2007, letter offering a further supply of glo gel        Full block.
shampoo. I doubt that I shall want any more since the product has not in
fact helped my hair very much.

I bought a large package of glo gel as a result of your previous mail adver-        Full block.
tisement and began using it some four weeks ago. I wished to give the
product a fair test and so have waited until now to write to you. Your letter
has prodded me into contacting you.

I found that not only does glo gel not make my hair shine with health as it is      Full block.
supposed to do, but I have developed a skin reaction to the product. As a
result, I am returning the remaining supply of glo gel with this letter and
request a refund of the money I sent you.

I look forward to hearing from you.                    Full block.

Yours sincerely,

*Radko Vloski*                                         Complimentary
                                                       close and signature.

Radko Vloski

# Memoranda

Memoranda or memos are essentially business letters used within an organization. Most organizations use printed memo forms, but you can compose and print out your own with or without a letterhead.

The four basic components of the memo are

**TO:**

**FROM:**

**DATE:**

**SUBJECT:**

These words are always in capitals followed by a colon and are usually bolded.

When writing a memo, remember the following points:

1. Do not use a courtesy title (Mr., Ms., etc.) but do use the recipient's job title.
2. Do not use a salutation, complimentary close, or signature block.
3. Do either sign a few lines below the last paragraph or write your initials after your name.
4. Use full block form.
5. Use ragged right, not right justified for all text.
6. Use single spacing for each paragraph and double spacing between paragraphs.
7. Place enclosure or attachment notation (Att., Encl.) flush left and at least two lines below your signature or the last line of the memo.
8. Place distribution notation (cc:) either below the recipient's name or at least two lines below your signature or below any enclosure notation.
9. Paginate in the same way as you would for letters of more than one page.

See Figure A2.8 for an example of a memorandum.

# Report Formats

The layout and structure of business reports depends upon

- whether the report is simply delivering information or presenting an analysis of a situation or issue with conclusions and recommendations;
- whether the report is long and/or complex.

An informal report may be informative or analytical but typically deals with a relatively straightforward issue or situation. The report may be presented in either a letter or memo form depending upon whether it is prepared for an internal or external reader. Formal

MEMORANDUM

IHGT Technologies Ltd.

MEMORANDUM

Heading.

TO:        Istvan Kolics
           Director of Marketing
           cc: Bernard Ribbons, Esther Bumenstock

Recipient.
Job title.
Distribution notation.

FROM:      Monique Carriere
           Trade Shows Coordinator              *hrc*

Sender.

DATE:      October 9, 2006

SUBJECT:   Planning Our Participation At The First InterRama Trade Show,
           21–23 November 2006 Atlanta, Georgia

The InterRama Trade Show is a new show that has taken about three years to plan and launch. We need to determine whether we will take part and, if so, at what level, within the next three weeks to allow for adequate planning time and to ensure that we obtain the space and facilities we require.

The InterRama is produced by IFDS Shows Inc. of New York, one of the world's largest and most well-regarded show organizers. The promotion that has been undertaken by IFDS for InterRama over the past year, through public relations activities in the trade and general business media, advertising, and a direct mail campaign, has created great interest in the industry. Moreover, IFDS is offering special introductory rates for first-time exhibitors, and this will also encourage companies to participate.

I am attaching a copy of the material received from IFDS. You can also obtain the latest information on the show from its website at www.ifds.com/interrama.

If we do participate, we would, given our trade show budget, have to drop one of the shows we currently attend. Based on a comparative analysis of our current show participation (attached), I recommend withdrawing from the Central Exhibition and Show in Minneapolis.

Att: IFDS Brochure; Analysis

Attachment notation.

reports are normally analytical, address a significant issue or problem, and involve considerable research leading to conclusions and recommendations for actions to address the issue or problem.

See Figure A2.9 for an example of an incident report in memo format.

## FIGURE A2.9

Incident Report—Memo Format

*Training Solutions*

Memorandum

TO:        James Sullivan, Director, Computer Training

FROM:      Paul Sarbanes, Computer Trainer

DATE:      October 18, 2006

SUBJECT:   Report Of An Accident That Occurred On October 16, 2006

My right leg was broken on October 16, 2006, in an accident that occurred in training room 231. I was taken to Central Hospital, where my right leg was put in a cast. I will not be able to teach for three weeks but will be able to work in the office.

The accident occurred at approximately 11:45 a.m. while I was teaching PowerPoint presentations. I was standing on the right side of the PowerPoint projector, which was in the middle of the room pointed toward the screen, when a student close to the door asked for my help.

As I walked around the back of the PowerPoint projector, my right leg became entangled in the power cord plugged into the outlet in the front of the class. I lost my balance and fell toward my right, further twisting my right leg. I landed on my right knee.

Immediately after I fell, Mary Thomas, who is a registered practical nurse, came to my aid. I could not put any weight on my foot, which had become swollen. Ms. Thomas took me to Central Hospital.

According to Dr. L. James, the X-rays showed that my ankle had been broken. He found no damage to my knee other than a bruise.

I will be in a full leg cast for the next three weeks. Dr. James said that as long as I do not have to stand for long periods, I may return to work.

# E-Mail

When using e-mail, remember to do the following:

1. Check that the address is correct.
2. Ensure that the subject line is complete, concise, and informative.
3. Include a full electronic signature—at the bottom of an e-mail letter, enter your full name, job title, organization, and telephone and fax numbers; for example:

> Hugh Dalguid
> Marketing Associate
> Harwood Corporation
> Tel (416) 358 3399
> Fax (416) 358 1196

4. Use single space for text and double space between paragraphs.
5. Send any letter, memo, or document over two screens in length as an attachment with an appropriate transmittal message.
6. Tell a recipient where to obtain very lengthy information rather than attaching it as a large file that may take a long time to download and print out (unless, of course, there is no choice or the recipient wants the information).
7. Verify the capacity of a recipient's system before sending large complex files that may tie up or even crash the system.
8. Avoid sending charts or illustrations in the body of an e-mail message since they may not hold their format.
9. Use Standard English and avoid abbreviations, acronyms, "cute" spellings, and "emoticons" or "smileys," such as :-) smile/happiness or :-( frown/unhappiness.

The use of e-mail has become almost universal in business, but it is a medium that encourages fast reactions and a conversational, informal style. This can lead to incoherent or indiscreet messages—it is easy to click on "reply" and send a return message without thinking through what you want to say, especially if you are annoyed or upset by the message you have received. E-mail business writing is, in fact, little different from other business writing and requires the same thought, planning, care, and respect.

# Facsimile (Fax)

As with e-mail, the use of facsimile transmission for sending letters, memos, and other business documents continues to grow.

Faxing a document normally involves preparing a fax cover sheet that includes

1. the organization's name, mailing address, telephone and fax numbers, and e-mail address;

---

**FIGURE A2.10**

Fax Cover Sheet

## IHGT Technologies Ltd.
2397 Fontaine Road, Winnipeg, MB R3T 9R0 Canada
Tel. (204) 286 2974   Fax: (204) 286 8822   ihgt@devra.ca   www.ihgt.ca                  Heading.

FAX MESSAGE

| | | | |
|---|---|---|---|
| TO: | Bernard Ribbons | FAX NO.: (204) 347 2866 | Recipient. Recipient's Fax Number. |
| | Logistics Section | | |

FROM:   Monique Carriere
        Trade Shows Coordinator

DATE:   October 9, 2006

NO. OF PAGES (including cover sheet): 6                    Total pages sent.

SUBJECT:  Planning Our Participation At The First InterRama Trade Show,    Subject line.
          21–23 November 2006 Atlanta, Georgia

Attached is a copy of a memo I have sent today to Istvan Kolics on the above      Message.
subject, together with material on the InterRama show and a comparative
analysis of the shows we currently attend.

I would appreciate receiving your views on whether we should participate in
this new show.

Please call (204) 286 6987 if any pages are not received.                  Contact number.

---

2. the name and fax number of the recipient;
3. the name of the person sending the fax and, as appropriate, his or her job title and department;
4. the date (fax machines print the date and time when a transmission is received);
5. the total number of pages being sent (so that the recipient can be sure that the complete transmission has been received);
6. a contact telephone number in case the recipient does not receive all the pages sent;
7. a subject line indicating what the fax is about;
8. a brief message.

A fax cover sheet may be used on its own to make a request, place an order, or for any other purpose that can be accomplished using just one page. See Figure A2.10 for an example of a fax cover sheet.

Like e-mail, fax is a quick and somewhat informal means of transmitting information and can easily lead to excessive informality or inappropriate messages. Equally, since fax cover sheets can be generated from word processing packages and stored on a hard drive ready for completing and printing, take care to check that the fax number and details are correct before sending.

# Helping the Reader Read and Understand

You want to make any business document you write as easy as possible to read and understand. While much depends upon reader analysis and subject matter, whether you are writing a letter, memo, report, or other document, there are various ways you can hinder or help readers as the following two memoranda show (see Figure A2.11, Non–Reader-Friendly Memorandum and Figure A2.12, Reader-Friendly Memorandum).

## TEXT DENSITY

Avoid dense text. Long paragraphs or documents with a series of long paragraphs may discourage the reader from reading the document at all or encourage the reader to just scan it, therefore missing important details and arguments.

### Paragraphs and Subparagraphs

To the extent possible, use short paragraphs, or use subparagraphs to explain linked ideas.

### Headings and Subheadings

Look at your text to determine where headings can be inserted to mark natural divisions among sections and topics.

NON–READER-FRIENDLY MEMORANDUM

### Acme Medical Supplies Ltd.

TO:       Internal Communications Committee Members

FROM:     Wendy Muir, Director, Corporate Communications

DATE:     21 November 2006

SUBJECT:  Internal Communications Study

As you will recall, it was agreed at the meeting of the Internal Communications Committee on March 13, 2006, that a full study should be undertaken to determine the current situation with regard to both employee morale and communications activities, with a view to identifying and recommending a new internal communications strategy. The committee felt strongly that, while there was no doubt that much effort was being made, the results appeared to be less than what had been expected when senior management instructed it in April 2005 to find approaches to improve communication within the company. Much has taken place in the last year, but I think that the work that was done between April 2005 and March 2006 was valuable and did produce some results, particularly at the plant level. However, the labour difficulties we encountered in the latter part of 2001 made for a difficult situation for undertaking any new internal communications initiatives as well as making it a challenge to keep lines of communication open.

The study was undertaken by Jawal & Associates, a firm of consultants that specializes in internal communications in large organizations. The contract for the study was approved in early April 2006 and work began in early May. Jawal assigned a highly experienced team to the project and developed a research strategy in conjunction with the Corporate Communications Division.

A sample of all employees was interviewed—some 750 people—using a questionnaire sent through the internal mail system. In addition, a series of 10 focus groups with employees were held across the country in our different locations. Focus groups were divided by type and level of employees to ensure that people could speak freely and to ensure proper coverage of the work force. People were encouraged through the company's newsletter and intranet and by managers at their own regular meetings with their staff. Finally, Jawal used a benchmarking approach to determine our situation in relation to other organizations. The company took a confidential "best practices" study it had done of a number of firms of roughly comparable size and compared what it found in our case with these companies' practices to arrive at an evaluation. We are, it turns out, about 75 percent of where we should be to be an excellent organization for internal communications.

*continued*

The study found in particular that we had serious difficulties in terms of employee perceptions of the company's willingness to communicate openly and the commitment of management, especially senior management, to communicate with staff. It also found that the labour troubles of last year were less important than we had expected, that different parts of the company and different locations across Canada showed considerable variations in trust of company information, and that the technical staff were the most skeptical of management and any management-originated communication. There were no significant differences among staff by gender, language, or age. The study made a series of recommendations that we will need to deal with as quickly as possible so that we can report to senior management on the next steps to be taken. In this light, I would ask that each of you in your respective areas please ensure that for the next meeting, you bring details of the initiatives you are taking, those you intend to take, those that have been proposed by your staff or by colleagues, those items that have not worked in the past, and any other ideas.

This study, I believe, has already been and will continue to be an excellent learning opportunity for the more junior members of the committee. They can use it to expand their knowledge of internal communication; understand how to organize and execute an internal communications study; become aware of the type of report that should be expected and its level of expense; and become familiar with the steps necessary to implement the recommendations of such a study. This is a complex matter but it is vital for the organization. The study can be written up and used as a case study for training new managers and for briefing and orienting new members of the committee in future.

*Wendy Muir*

## FIGURE A2.12

### Reader-Friendly Memorandum

### Acme Medical Supplies Ltd.

Informative subject line.

TO:        Internal Communications Committee Members
FROM:    Wendy Muir, Director, Corporate Communications
DATE:    21 November 2006
SUBJECT: Internal Communications Study Final Report

Heading bolded.

**Background**

As you will recall, it was agreed at the meeting of the *Internal Communications Committee* on March 13, 2006, that a full study should be undertaken to:

Clear presentation of study purpose. White space.

- determine the current situation with regard to employee morale and communications activities; and
- recommend a new internal communications strategy.

First paragraph broken into three smaller paragraphs.

The committee felt strongly that, while there was no doubt that much effort was being made, the results appeared to be less than what had been expected when senior management instructed it in April 2005 to find approaches to improve communication within the company.

White space.

Much has taken place in the past year, but I think that the work that was done between April 2005 and March 2006 was valuable and did produce some results, particularly at the plant level. However, the labour difficulties we encountered in the latter part of 2005 made for a difficult situation for undertaking any new internal communications initiatives as well as making it a challenge to keep lines of communication open.

Heading bolded.

**Research Contractor**

The study was undertaken by Jawal & Associates, a firm of consultants that specializes in internal communications in large organizations. The contract for the study was approved in early April 2006 and work began in early May. Jawal assigned a highly experienced team to the project and developed a research strategy in conjunction with the Corporate Communications Division.

*continued*

## Research Process

### Employee Interviews

A sample of all employees was interviewed—some 750 people—using a questionnaire sent through the internal mail system.

### Employee Focus Groups

In addition, a series of 10 focus groups with employees was held across the country in our different locations. Focus groups were divided by type and level of employees to ensure that people could speak freely and to ensure proper coverage of the work force.

### Manager Feedback

People were encouraged through the company's newsletter and intranet and by managers at their own regular meetings with their staff.

### Benchmarking

Finally, Jawal used a benchmarking approach to determine our situation in relation to other organizations. The company took a confidential "best practices" study it had done of a number of firms of roughly comparable size and compared what it found in our case with these companies' practices to arrive at an evaluation.

We are, it turns out, about 75 percent of where we should be to be an excellent organization for internal communications.

## Study Findings

- We had serious difficulties in terms of employee perceptions of the company's willingness to communicate openly and the commitment of management, especially senior management, to communicate with staff.
- The labour troubles of last year were less important than we had expected.
- Different parts of the company and different locations across Canada showed considerable variations in level of trust in company information.
- Technical staff were the most skeptical of management and any management-originated communication.
- There were no significant differences among staff by gender, language, or age.

## Recommendations

The study made a series of recommendations that revolve around developing a new, integrated internal communications strategy. These are laid out in Jawal & Associates' report (attached). We will need to deal with these as quickly as possible so that we can report to senior management on the next steps to be taken.

*continued*

---

Heading bolded.

Subheading italicized.

White space.

Third paragraph broken into smaller paragraphs.

White space.

White space.

Heading bolded.

Use of bullets.

Fourth paragraph broken into smaller paragraphs.

In this light, I would ask that each of you in your respective areas please ensure that for the next meeting you bring details of the initiatives you are taking, those you intend to take, those that have been proposed by your staff or by colleagues, those items that have not worked in the past, and any other ideas.

White space.

### Learning and Development Opportunity

This study, I believe, has already been and will continue to be an excellent learning opportunity for the more junior members of the committee. They can use it to

Use of bullets.

- expand their knowledge of internal communication;
- understand how to organize and execute an internal communications study;
- become aware of the type of report that should be expected;
- understand the level of expense that can be expected;
- become familiar with the steps necessary to implement the recommendations of the study.

Final paragraph broken into two smaller paragraphs.

This is a complex matter but it is vital for the organization. The study can be written up and used as a case study for training new managers and for briefing and orienting new members of the committee in future.

Att: Jawal & Associates' Report

*Wendy Muir*

---

### Numbering

Number sections and subsections to help readers follow them more easily.

### Lists

You can use numbered lists to organize information in an orderly way. A list is easier to read and understand than separate items in lines of text.

### Bullets

Bullets make it easy for readers to see separate items in much the same way as a list. Note, however, that a list normally consists of numbered items. Bullets are a way of signalling and organizing separate pieces of information. Normally, you should not have more than five bulleted items.

### Bold, Italics, Underlining, and Capitalization

Use bold type, italic script, underlining, and capitalization to draw attention to different parts of a document and help the reader to understand the structure and components of the document.

### Fonts

It is better not to use exotic or startling fonts and to avoid mixing different types of fonts in one document. Organizations generally use Times New Roman and Courier fonts for letters, memos, reports, proposals, and so forth.

In the following paragraph, the use of different fonts, bold, and italics does not increase ease of reading, understanding, or impact:

> The Canadian election **will** undoubtedly affect the financial markets. *No matter which party* is ahead in the polls during the campaign, the markets will be skittish. It does **not** matter if the **Liberals** or the **Alliance** (or the **Tories**) are seen to be in the lead. Markets *dislike uncertainty*.

For font size, 12-point is most often used. Anything smaller is difficult for people to read; anything larger takes up too much space.

### Attachments

Attachments or appendixes allow you to provide useful but supporting or complementary information such as statistics, questionnaires, brochures, and corporate profiles, without cluttering or complicating the body of a document.

### White Space

A document needs to use space effectively to contain and surround the text. This allows the eye to rest easily on the page, moves the reader smoothly into the text, and facilitates reading and following the thread of the content.

Make sure that there is plenty of space between paragraphs, subparagraphs, and bullets and items in lists.

### Icons and Clip Art

Icons and clip art can help readers move through a document more easily. However, they should be used sparingly and carefully since, wrongly used, they can be distracting or annoying. Also, some organizations may not allow icons and clip art in documents.

### Boxes

Boxes make information stand out and draw the reader's attention to it.

# Charts and Graphs

Charts are normally not used in letters and rarely in memos. However, they are used in reports to help the reader understand visually the relationship between sets of data; for example, sales volumes over time, revenues and expenditures, production and costs, and so forth. It is generally easier for people to "see" such relationships than to read about them, and using a chart allows you to summarize in a picture what might take paragraphs to describe or explain. As with any other data or information being used in a document, the source of data in charts should be acknowledged.

Word processing and other applications allow for readily constructing and displaying charts and graphs of which the most commonly used are the pie chart, bar chart, and line graph.

## PIE CHARTS

Pie charts (see Figure A2.13) show the relationship of parts within a whole. For maximum clarity, different parts of a pie chart should be assigned different colours or shades. Every section of the pie should be labelled and its percentage indicated.

### Part of a Report Using a Pie Chart

Brice McMann is a business analyst with Terion Business Analysis. Terion has been contracted by the Independent Fuel Sellers Association, which represents independent gas stations across Canada, to prepare a report on the price of gasoline. The purpose of the report is to head-off any attempt by provincial governments to control the price of gasoline at the pump, a policy which, the association believes, would fall more heavily on its members than on filling stations that are owned/franchised by the major oil companies.

Figure A2.13 shows McMann's strategic use of the pie chart entitled "What Makes Up the Price of Gas."

## Report Using a Pie Chart

### What Makes Up the Price of Gas: It's Not a Tale of the Little Guy

The "price of gas at the pump" is different from most other commodities. All commodities begin with the cost of raw materials. The raw material of gasoline is, of course, crude oil. And, as shown on the pie chart below, crude accounts for 28 % of the cost of gasoline.* Another significant part of the cost of gasoline is refining and sales, which include the cost of transportation (of both crude and refined gasoline) and the cost of refining crude. These costs account for some 20 % of the cost of gasoline.

By far, the largest part of the price of gasoline is taxes. Other products, say a package of 20 CDs, are taxed. However, provincial sales taxes and the federal GST are added to the cost of CDs at the cash register. In Ontario, for example, a consumer who picks up a $10.00 package of CDs pays $11.50, but he or she knows that the final $1.50 is made up of the 8 % provincial sales tax and the 7 % GST.

Fifty-five percent (55 %) of the price of a litre of gasoline is made up by taxes. But unlike CDs, Federal Excise Tax, Provincial Sales Tax, and GST are built into the price. Motorists do not fill up by paying $35.00 at the pump and then see taxes added on at the last minute. They may see the breakdown on the fuel pump, but it's doubtful that most busy motorists take the time to process this information. For them, understandably, the "price of gas" is the "price of gas"—and it is always going up.

The smallest part of the price of fuel is "profit." Profit, as shown on the pie chart below, accounts for 2.5 % of the cost of gasoline. "Control the profit in gas and you control the price" may be the rallying cry of certain activist groups that seek to have provincial legislation cap the price of gasoline by limiting "profit." But such rallying cries make poor public policy because such a policy would fall most heavily on independent sellers.

The 2.5 % profit is the only revenue stream available to independent gasoline retailers. Filling stations owned by the oil companies make this profit as well. But they belong to corporations, which make profit through the refining and sales of gasoline as well as through the extraction of crude. In other words, they have four revenue streams.

Legislation to limit the profits that can be made from the selling of gasoline would, therefore, fall most heavily on independent sellers, and, as such, is unfair.

---

*Crude costs include the cost of exploration, extractions, and any royalties charged by countries such as Saudi Arabia.

*continued*

**What makes up the price of gas?**

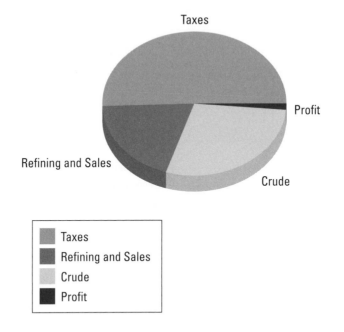

Source: Industry Canada.

## BAR CHARTS

There are several types of bar charts. The most commonly employed in business writing is the single bar chart used to indicate clearly the relationship of various like sums to each other over time, such as produce, meat, and fish costs, or company profits. See Figures A2.14 and A2.15.

### A Memo Using a Horizontal Bar Chart

Charles Grant is a catering supplies manager with a large manufacturing company, DFT Ltd. The company operates canteens at its plants and provides meals for its many thousands of employees. In response to a question, Mr. Grant is notifying his supervisor, Mark Bilik, Vice President, Employee Welfare, of the costs of basic food categories fish, meat, and produce over the past four years.

## Horizontal Bar Chart

DFT LTD.

TO: Mark Bilik, Vice President, Employee Welfare
FROM: Charles Grant, Manager, Catering Supplies
DATE: April 22, 2007

SUBJECT: Food Costs: Fish, Meat, and Produce

As requested, attached is a chart showing overall costs for the above basic food groups for the period 2003–2006.

Relative Costs
Meat costs were highest in each year, followed by produce and fish.

Cost Increases
Costs of meat and produce have increased each year. Fish cost decreased in 2005 from 2004 but returned to 2004 levels in 2006.

However, while produce-cost increases from year to year have more or less kept pace with meat cost increases, they are gaining on meat and in 2006 were almost 80% of meat costs.

Produce, Fish, and Meat Costs

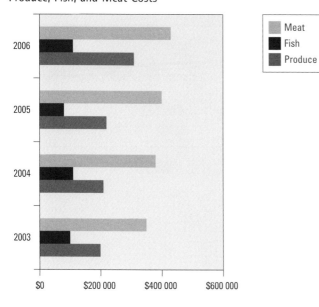

Source: Catering and Statistics Division

*Part of a Business Report Using a Vertical Bar Chart*

Origiana Dwejena is director of finance for Goolibas Cards and Novelties Ltd., a supplier of greeting cards and party novelties. She is drafting a year-end report on the state of the company's finances for her boss, Irma Crump, Vice President, Corporate Administration. To easily show the company's profit trend over the past five years, she uses a vertical bar chart.

## FIGURE A2.15

## REPORT USING A VERTICAL BAR CHART

As can be clearly seen from the attached chart, the trend in profits over the past five years, 2002–2006, has been downward, from $330,000 in 2002 to $205,000 in 2006. In fact, every year has seen a decrease in profit from the previous year.

The overall five-year decline in profits of $125,000 ($330,000–$205,000) represents a five-year *percentage* decrease of 41% or an annual average decease of 8.2% or $25,000. Thus, if the trend shown in the chart continues, we will cease being profitable in a few years.

Company Profits

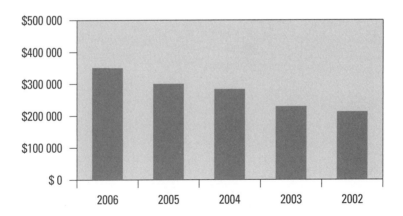

Source: Annual Report, 2006.

*A Memo Using a Bar Chart*

You would use multiple-bar charts to indicate the relationship of similar groups of numbers over time. Note how in Figure A2.16 there are three categories of expenditure of five years.

Erskin Johanson is the accounting manager for Canadian Academic Publishers. She has been asked by the company's CFO to prepare an analysis of CAP's payments to consultants. She chose to use a bar graph because it is particularly useful for showing changes in information over time. She uses subheadings so that the CFO can clearly understand what expense she is discussing.

## FIGURE A2.16

## MEMO USING A BAR CHART

Canadian Academic Publishers

TO:        Ralph Bunch, CFO

FROM:      Erskin Johanson, Accounting Manager

DATE:      May 5, 2007

SUBJECT:   Consultants' Fees 2002–2006.

Attached is a chart detailing CAP's payments to consultants for the years 2002 to 2006 inclusive.

### Legal Fees
In two of the five years, 2002 and 2005, legal expenses significantly exceeded the average of $250,000. Both spikes were due to CAP's acquisitions: in 2002 of Dominion Publishing and in 2005 of Australian School Books.

### Public Relations
In 2002, the public relations' fees were significantly higher than in the other years being considered because of CAP's publication of the *Monster Magic,* the year's bestselling children's book.

### Web Design
Web design fees are absent after 2004 because upkeep and design of CAP's website was brought in-house.

*continued*

Consultants' Fees

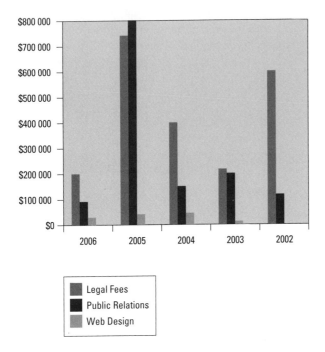

Source: Annual Report, 2007.

### Line Charts and Line Graphs

Line charts and line graphs are particularly useful for showing changes in information over time. They can show one or several series or factors, as in Figure A2.17.

### Part of a Business Report Using a Line Graph

Sandra Eckles is a business analyst for On-Line Canada (O-L-C), a provider of trunk-lines to Internet service providers. She is writing the historical survey part of a report that will be distributed at On-Line Canada's annual general meeting. After reviewing the costs of installing optical fibre and network switches between 2000 and 2005, as well as the cost of labour to install the fibre and switches, she decides to use a line graph to show the costs, because it allows her to use one graph to show three sets of data.

## REPORT USING A LINE GRAPH

In the five years leading up to 2006, the costs of installing operative cable more than doubled. The least expensive component of O-L-C's cost was labour. As can be seen on the chart entitled "The Installation of Fibre Optic Costs," labour costs rose from $250,000 in 2001 to $1 million in 2006. The greatest increase in labour costs occurred between 2001 and 2002, following O-L-C's decision to extend its operations through Eastern Ontario and into the Maritimes. In subsequent years, labour costs remained stable at around $1 million a year.

The purchase and installation of network switches rose from $2.8 million a year in 2001 to $4.6 million in 2006. Over the same period, the number of subscribers served by ISPs that purchased space on O-L-C's trunk-lines increased from 1.2 million to 8.4 million, an almost sevenfold increase. Our contracts with ISPs stipulate that each ISP will have a fixed amount of dedicated space. This space is defined through an equation that takes into account actual space on optical cables and switching capacity.

A portion of each year's expenditure on network switches was dedicated to replacing outdated equipment. It would be a mistake to think that network switch expenditures were cumulative in the sense that at the end of 2005 O-L-C had $22 million worth of switches online. If anything, the development of network switches has been even faster than the development of PCs. Few switches installed in 2001 were still in use in 2005.

The 16 percent rise in costs for network switches between 2005 and 2006 is directly attributable to the changes necessary to comply with new system requirements.

*continued*

Installation of Fibre Optics Costs

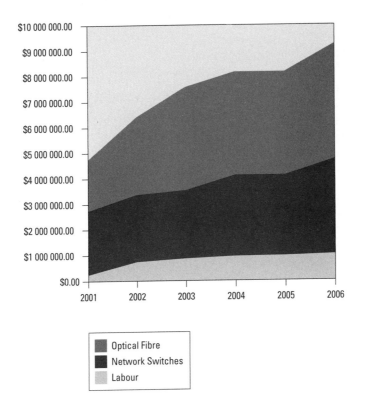

Source: Industry Canada

# Acknowledging Information Sources

## ENDNOTES AND FOOTNOTES

If you have used and referred to information you have gathered in a business document, you must acknowledge the source of the information.

This can be done either by

- listing the source of the information at the end of the document in an endnote; or
- listing the source at the foot of the page in a footnote.

Footnotes are rarely used in business documents, although they may appear in long, formal reports. Endnotes are much more commonly used and are listed at the end of a document usually titled as References or List of References. In each case, superscript numerals within the text indicate that information is being acknowledged.

## Footnotes

The information gathered by researchers[1] over the past two years indicates that our market is in fact disappearing and that we must take steps to realign our strategies.[2] This was underlined recently in a series of articles by Richard Woodhouse in *The Globe and Mail* [3] in which he noted that since the arrival of new technology in the toy industry some 25 years ago, the traditional, handcrafted toys have gradually lost ground.

## Endnotes

The information gathered by researchers[1] over the past two years indicates that our market is in fact disappearing and that we must take steps to realign our strategies.[2] This was underlined recently in a series of articles by Richard Woodhouse in *The Globe and Mail* [3] in which he noted that since the arrival of new technology in the toy industry some 25 years ago the traditional, handcrafted toys have gradually lost ground.

The endnotes will appear in order under the References section of a document.

[1] Desbiens, Marc, Nancy Lorrimer, and George Watson. "Trends in the Canadian Toy Market and Challenges for Canadian Firms." *Business Review.*

[2] Merkovicz, Dianna. "Options for Strategic Realignment." *Strategic Planning Group.*

[3] Woodhouse, Richard. "Canadian Toy Industry in Painful Change." *The Globe and Mail.*

## BIBLIOGRAPHY

A bibliography is a list of books and other materials on a subject arranged in alphabetical order by author. It may include either just the works specifically referred to in the document or all those that were consulted.

There are different conventions for listing entries in a bibliography, but the most common are described below.

## Books

Author's name. Book title (in italics or underlined). Place of publication: publisher's name, publication date.

### One Author
Author. *Book Title*. City: Publisher, date.

Boggs, Arthur W. *Understanding New and Diverse Media*. Toronto: Upshott Press, 1999.

### Same Author—Another Book
———. *How New Media Can Increase Productivity*. Toronto: Upshott Press, 1998.

### More Than One Author
Harnoy, Wanda, Henry Smith, and Marcia Glubb. *Building Better Organizations*. Winnipeg: Harton Ltd., 1999.

### Many Authors and an Editor
Editor, ed. *Book Title*. City: Publisher, date.

Shasklove, Dawn, ed. *Marketing Opportunities in Asian Economies*. Vancouver: University Press, 1997.

### Second or Later Editions of a Book
Greengrass, Nigel. *Investment Strategies for Small Business*. 3rd ed. Montreal: BusinesBooks, 2000.

### Newspaper Article or Story
Author. "Title of Article." Newspaper (in italics or underlined) date: page number.

Erickson, Harry. "Workers in a Competitive Economy." *Ottawa Citizen* 30 June 2000: D2.

### Magazine Articles
Author. "Title of Article." Magazine (in italics or underlined) date: page number.

Tarkson, Henrietta. "Document Management in an Information Rich World." *Records and Documents* July 1999: 34.

### Journal Articles
Author. "Title of Article." Magazine or journal (in italics or underlined) volume, issue number (date): page number.

Tarkson, Henrietta. "Document Management in an Information Rich World." *Records and Documents*, 12.3 (1999): 34.

### Government Publications
Country, province, or municipality. Department or ministry name. Title of publication (in italics or underlined). City: date.

Canada. Industry Canada. *Small Business Growth*. Ottawa: 2000.

### Reports
Author. Title of report (in italics or underlined). Organization issuing report. City: date.

Nelson, Rebecca. *Comparison of Market Entry Strategies by Small Technology Business in Ontario. Robson & Associates*. Toronto: August 12, 2000.

## Online

Author. "Title of article or piece." Source (in italics or underlined). Date. Online indication. Web address.

Diceheart, Andrew. "Using Banner Ads More Effectively." *Ads and Internet.* 18 September 2000. Online. http://www.adsandinternet.com/index.3.

# Using Different Transmission Methods

You can send a letter, memo, or other document by

- e-mail;
- fax;
- internal mail;
- courier service;
- Canada Post.

The means of transmission used is normally a function of the following factors:

- Time pressure. How urgent is the document and how quickly must it reach the recipient?
- Convenience. What is the easiest way of sending the document, other things being equal?
- Cost. What is the cheapest method of transmission, given urgency and other factors?
- Legal status of the document and need for a hard copy. Although electronic signatures are becoming legal in developed countries, organizations and individuals usually prefer to have tangible, properly signed documents of a legal nature such as contracts, employment notices, and so forth.
- Stage of preparation. It may be both convenient and acceptable, and certainly more efficient to e-mail or fax someone a draft version of a document for comment, but the final version may need to be sent in hard copy.
- Length of the document and its complexity. A very long document, with various sections and appendixes, is not normally suitable for sending by fax—the recipient's machine is occupied for long periods of time and may run out of paper, and pages may not be transmitted. E-mail may not be suitable either since the recipient's system may not have the capacity to process the document, and the recipient must in any event print it out.
- Copies required. How many copies are needed? Does every recipient require a signed or high-quality hard copy?
- Image. How important is it that the document have a good appearance? Is there a need for use of good quality paper with a letterhead, properly laid out with an original signature? Is the recipient of superior status in the organization?

# INDEX

# D

Damage to equipment, 85
Date, 404–405
Demonstrative pronoun, 392
Descriptive summary, 41–47
Diener, Seymour, "User
    Beware: E-mail Not as
    Private as You Think," 69
Directions. *See* Instructional
    memo
*disinterested, uninterested*, 382
Disraeli, Benjamin, 49
Distribution notation (cc:), 407
"Do Not Wear a Tongue Ring
    to Your Job Interview"
    (Manley), 282
Dubay, William H., 13

# E

"E-books Perfect for Manuals,
    Textbooks, Niche Authors"
    (Tapscott), 43
E-filing, 328–330
E-mail, 24
    attachments, 26
    naming conventions,
        220–221
    readability, 25–26
    résumé, 305
    style, 221, 249–250
    white space, 25
    writing tips, 417
E-mail address, 220
E-mail attachments, 26
E-mail résumé, 305
Editorial Eye Index, 30
Editorial writing, 202–204,
    205–206
*effect, affect*, 382
*either/or* constructions, 396
Electronic mail. *See* E-mail

Electronic résumé, 337–339
Ellipsis (...), 387
Emoticons, 24, 417
Emotional persuasion, 262
Employee training. *See*
    Convention/training reports
Endnotes, 434–435
Envelope, 403
Ethics and persuasion, 265
Ethos, 262
Evaluative summary, 48–51
Exclamation mark, 388
External writing. *See also*
    individual subject headings
    bad news and sales letters,
        248–279
    cover letters and résumés,
        280–317
    grant applications,
        348–377
    routine and good news
        business letters,
        218–247
    writing for the Web,
        318–346

# F

Facsimile (fax), 417–419
*farther, further*, 382
Fax cover sheet, 418
Feature article, 196–199
Feelings, 144
*fewer, less*, 383
Fienberg, Howard, "Psst.
    GMOs Are Scary. Pass It
    On," 67
Focus questions (FQs), 6
    accident/incident reports,
        81, 82–83
    bad news letter, 258
    convention/training
        reports, 128–129

cover letter, 291–292
feature article, 196–197
good news letter, 230
grant applications,
    362–368
instructional memo,
    102–103
opinion writing, 203
persuasive claim letter,
    268–269
progress reports, 173–174
sales letter, 265–266
suggestion memo/short
    proposal, 147
Web documents, 335–336
Focused writing, 3
Font, 303
Footnotes, 434–435
Formal tone, 17
Format, 18
Foundation support. *See* Grant
    applications
FQs. *See* Focus questions
    (FQs)
French language, 204, 381–382
Functional résumé, 301–303
Funding proposals. *See* Grant
    applications
Future perfect tense, 171
Future tense, 171

# G

Gender bias, 220
Geographical names, 380–381
"Getting the Message"
    (MacLean), 201
"Gimli Glider, The" (Nelson),
    96
*Globe and Mail Style Book, The*,
    204
Good news letter. *See also*
    Business letter

cultural context, 229
focus questions, 230
purpose questions, 226
purpose statement, 230
reader, 226–230. *See also*
Audience analysis
sample letter, 223,
237–239
structure, 231–232
Got Marketing, 216
Grammar, 383–398
abbreviations, 383
acronym, 384
adjective, 384
adverb, 384
cliché, 385
comparative, 387
coordinate conjunctions,
387
ellipsis (...), 387
misplaced modifiers, 388
parentheses, 389
passive voice, 388–389
possessive, 389
prepositional phrases, 390
pronoun, 390–392
punctuation. *See*
Punctuation
restrictive/nonrestrictive
clause, 393
run-on sentence, 393
sentence, 394–395
sentence fragment, 395
split infinitive, 395
subject–verb agreement,
395
subjunctive mood,
396–397
subordinate conjunction,
397
superlative, 387
verb tense, 397. *See also*
Verb tense

websites. *See* Web
references
Grammar-checking program,
13, 378–379
Grant applications, 348–377
administrative aspects, 355
editing practice, 357–360,
370–375
focus questions for
eligibility, 362–363
focus questions for project
description, 363
hard data, 349
purpose questions for
eligibility, 361
purpose questions for
project description,
363–368
purpose statement, 365
sample application,
366–369
sample preprinted form,
352–354
soft data, 350
steps in process, 355
substantive aspects, 355
teamwork/dedicated staff
member, 355–356
writing tips, 356–357
Grantwriters.com, 377
Graphs. *See* Charts and graphs
Green, Heather, "Picking Up
Where Search Leaves Off,"
320
"Gretzky in Eighty-Four"
(Richler), 11

# H

Habitual action, 170
Hacking, 330
Hard data, 349
Historic past tense, 170

Hof, Robert D., "Picking Up
Where Search Leaves Off,"
320
Horizontal bar chart, 429
House style, 204
Hypertext links, 330

# I

Identity theft, 330
*imply, infer,* 382–383
Incident reports. *See*
Accident/incident reports
Indefinite pronoun, 391
Indented letter form, 410
Informal tone, 18
Informative writing, 26
accident/incident reports,
72–93
convention/training
reports, 120–137
instructional memos,
94–118
newsletters, 190–216
websites, 318–346
Inside address, 405
Instructional memo, 94–118
audience analysis, 97
coherence, 101, 106
contact, 101
focus questions, 102–103
introduction, 101
introductory paragraphs,
103
list form memo, 104–105
paragraph form memo,
105–107
purpose questions, 101–102
purpose statement, 103
sample memos, 98, 104,
106–107
steps, 101
structure, 101